Spirited Women

Spirited Women

Gender, Religion, and Cultural Identity in the Nepal Himalaya

Joanne C. Watkins

Columbia University Press

NEW YORK

Columbia University Press
New York   Chichester, West Sussex

Library of Congress Cataloging-in-Publication Data

Watkins, Joanne C.
Spirited women : gender, religion, and cultural identity in the
Nepal Himalaya / Joanne C. Watkins.
p.   cm.
Includes bibliographical references and index.
ISBN 0–231–10214–3 (cloth : alk. paper). — ISBN 0–231–10215–1
(pbk. : alk. paper)
1. Nyishangba (Nepalese people)—Social conditions.   2. Women,
Nyishangba.   3. Sex role—Nepal.   4. Nepal—Social conditions.
5. Buddhism—Nepal—Customs and practices.   I. Title.
DS493.9.N94W37   1996
305.3'095496—dc20   95–37003
CIP

Printed in the United States of America

c 10 9 8 7 6 5 4 3 2 1
p 10 9 8 7 6 5 4 3 2 1

CONTENTS

Maps

1. Location of research sites and major Nyeshangte settlements in Nepal
2. Nyeshangte trade destinations in South Asia
3. Nyeshangte trade networks extend from northeast India to Southeast Asia

Photographs

1. Gathered for the consecration of a shrine, village women visit with friends
2. Religious shrines delineate the sacred boundaries of the village
3. Adolescent girls return to the village with heavy loads of firewood
4. A middle-aged woman takes care of her granddaughter
5. A Nyeshangte home in Kathmandu
6. Every morning before dawn, Nyeshangte women converge on Swayambhu
7. A Tibetan nomad sews fur lining onto woolen clothing
8. All along the Annapurna Circuit, women run lodges and small shops
9. A Nyeshangte family

ACKNOWLEDGMENTS

FOR THE PEOPLE of Nyeshang Tsesum—orche, orche. I thank you for sharing your stories, your history, and your lives with me. Without your interest, encouragement, and patience, this book would never have been possible. Many individuals and families—in Kathmandu, Pokhara, Nyeshang, Bangkok, and elsewhere—opened their homes to a stranger and extended their trust. I hope I have not let you down.

I am deeply grateful to the Venerable Sherab Gyaltsen Rinpoche, who gave me his blessings for the project and suggested the manuscript be called *The Nyesyangpa Book*. I must demur—instead I offer this flawed account with my sincere apologies. *The Nyesyangpa Book* will be written, but not by me.

I thank Lama K. for his unfailing cheerfulness, his wonderful tales, and his ability to make me laugh when I most needed to. Nima and Chungta graciously shared their chocolate bars and patiently explained what they had been up to during their three-year retreat at the monastery. Soner offered me a home, a place by the fire, and good company. Tukten, Michung, Tashi, Pema, Tripple, Bami, Kunsang, Sunita, Sonam, Karma, Dorje, Kema, Salima, Amina, and several other friends in Nyeshang Tsesum, Kathmandu, Pokhara, and Bangkok provided invaluable help. I am indebted to Tsering for her friendship. Without her family's enthusiasm and support I would never have started, much less continued, this project.

Many other people in Nepal offered their advice and assistance. I would like to thank Navin Rai, Om Gurung, Bishnu Bhandari, Ratnaman Pradhan, Dilli Ram Dahal, and also the staff at the U.S. Education Foundation, Tribhuvan University, and the Centre for Nepal and Asian Studies for providing the necessary visas, research permits, and the much appreciated affiliation.

I would like to acknowledge the assistance and support of my doctoral committee at the University of Wisconsin-Madison: Maria Lepowsky (chair), Mark Kenoyer, Kirin Narayan, Joe Elder, and Katherine Bowie. They provided insightful comments on earlier incarnations of this manuscript, and their encouragement and good advice helped it on its way to becoming a book.

Several other people assisted with the writing of this book. I would like to thank Joanne Rappaport, and the two reviewers for Columbia University Press for their careful reading of a later draft. Their generous commentary and thoughtful suggestions guided me through the final revisions. Many students and friends shared their views about ethnographies and served as a continual reminder of my intent to make this work accessible to a general audience. I would also like to thank John Michel and the editorial staff at Columbia University Press for their help.

This present study was made possible by the combined support of several institutions. I am pleased to acknowledge their assistance, and wish to thank them for sponsoring my doctoral research. A National Resource Fellowship (Foreign Language Area Study [FLAS] grant) in 1985 and 1986 provided my initial language training in Nepali and Hindi at the University of Wisconsin. Fieldwork in Nepal (1988–1989) was supported by a U.S. Department of Education Fulbright-Hays Doctoral Dissertation Award. In 1990 a National Resource Fellowship (FLAS grant) enabled me to attend the Southeast Asia Summer Institute at Cornell University where I could study Thai and do some library research before tackling additional fieldwork in Southeast Asia. Various stays in Thailand and Hong Kong between 1990 and 1992 were supported by the Institute for Intercultural Studies, the Woodrow Wilson National Fellowship Foundation (Women's Studies Grant), and the University of Madison Graduate School (Vilas Travel Award).

Finally, I want to express my appreciation to my family who shared in the making of this book. My husband, John Greenside, and my son Jesse Watkins-Gibbs, accompanied me to Nyeshang Tsesum during my initial visit in 1988 and helped me in countless ways. Their support and commitment through the years made it possible for me to finish an impossible project.

As a researcher I feel that my primary obligation is to protect the privacy of my informants and the standing of the host community; to that effect the names of all Nyeshangte individuals in the text have been changed. Pseudonyms (indicated by an asterisk [*] the first time they appear in the text) have been used for villages in the homeland and for certain locales in Kathmandu. Although I make extensive use of case histories and anecdotes throughout the text, in several instances I have taken the liberty of altering particular details or circumstances in order to disguise the identities of individuals and families.

There has been some speculation about the extent and nature of Nyeshangte involvement in illegal trade activities. As most stereotypes go, this one is somewhat unwarranted. In this book I am concerned with trade only as it relates to my central focus on gender relations, representations, and cultural identity. References to black market trade are based on secondary sources: Nepali newspapers, periodicals, and other published ethnographic accounts.

NYESHANG IS AN unwritten language with close affinities to Tibetan and Gurung. Sounds in the Nyeshang language have been transcribed as closely as possible to the orthographic conventions used for Tibetan. Some initial consonant clusters in Nyeshang are characteristic of Gurung but are not found in modern spoken Tibetan. These include, for example, *phy, my, thy, pr, mr, kr, ml, pw, mw, kw*. In addition, Nyeshang has four contrastive tones, which for simplicity's sake are not marked in this text. I have attempted to provide the classical Tibetan spelling for corresponding Nyeshang words wherever possible, so, for example, *gompa* (temple) appears as *dgon pa* throughout the text.

Words in Nepali, Tibetan, and the Nyeshang dialect are italicized only the first time they appear in the text. Key words are listed in their romanized forms in the glossary at the end of the book. Nepali words are transcribed according to Turner (1931). I transcribe Tibetan words according to the orthographic conventions used by Wylie (1959), with the exception of *lama* (Buddhist priest), which has current usage in the English language and is transcribed phonetically instead of in the classical Tibetan spelling "bla ma." Also, note that Tibetan syllables are indicated only by a space ("bla ma"), rather than with a hyphen ("bla-ma"). Nepali, Tibetan, and Nyeshang proper names appear in the text without diacritics or any special indication.

Spirited Women

PART ONE

Kaleidoscope

CHAPTER ONE

Kathmandu Connections

IN THE CROWDED and noisy dressing room of the Kathmandu Sports Club a clear voice rang out, "I am Nyeshangte." It was Maya, a 15-year-old girl—one of the regulars in the aerobics class—who was hurriedly changing out of her yellow- and blue-striped leotard into her street clothes: stone-washed denim jeans, Madonna T-shirt, and black ski parka. Jumping up from the bench, she glanced in the mirror and ran her fingers through her short-cropped hair. Maya stuffed her workout clothes into a backpack and then glanced at me with an open friendly look. "Come to my house tomorrow. My uncle's here. He's a big lama from Nyeshang. Just ask for Sonam Orkhe's house. Everyone knows us in the neighborhood."

With a hasty "see you," Maya slipped through the curtained door and stepped outside the club. Stopping for a moment to put on her running shoes, she turned and said good-bye to a group of sārī-clad women who were chatting on the verandah. The women, an assortment of affluent Marwari, Chhetri, and Newar in their twenties and early thirties, were all waiting for husbands, brothers, or hired "drivers" to pick them up after class.[1] Maya waved once more in my direction, shouted *"ciao"* in a final farewell, and sprinted away on her mountain bike.

And with that casual encounter my fieldwork began. For a few weeks I had been trying to locate members of the Nyeshangte community in

Kathmandu. Roaming the narrow alleys of Asan Tole and Thamel, popping in and out of clothing and curio shops, I eventually mustered up enough courage to make some inquiries.[2] But I had no luck; the shop owners I spoke with were not from Nyeshang.

I knew where their residential neighborhoods were. I had spent a few afternoons wandering the streets, staring at the massive three-story houses that were painted orange and yellow, their rooftops strung with tall white prayer flags that proclaimed their Tibetan Buddhist heritage. But the houses were set back from the lanes, enclosed by high walls and iron-wrought gates; they remained off-limits. I could only peer through the iron bars and wonder if I would ever have the chance to meet the families who lived there.

And so one evening I confided to my friend Kunchong, a young Tibetan woman who taught aerobic dance at the club, that I was having trouble making contacts with villagers from Nyeshang. "Oh there is someone here, I think, who can help you," and she pointed to the teenage girl in the locker room.

This ethnography examines the nature of gender relations among Nyeshangte (pronounced "Knee-shong-tay"), an ethnic Tibetan Buddhist group from north central Nepal. Broadly defined, the study of gender relations encompasses the general interaction between women and men in various domains, the difference in power relations between the sexes, and how gendered individuals compare in their effects on others. It includes the relative social position of women and men, and how this social status varies in different contexts over the course of life.

In this book I am particularly concerned with the interplay between changing trade patterns, gender meanings, and cultural identity in Nyeshang society. It is a society whose gender system is characterized primarily by relations of equivalence rather than overt dominance or subordination.

The study takes a historical perspective: I begin with the idea that gender relations are constituted by a complex array of factors (social arrangements, ideologies, division of labor), which are formed in historically and culturally specific instances. Gender systems, on the one hand, are linked with preexisting social formations, as reflected in specific traditions of descent, marriage, residence, and cultural values peculiar to Nyeshangte. But on the other hand, gender relations are also influenced by new forms of economic production and by the larger forces of social change, including urbanization, migration to Kathmandu, greater incorporation into the

Nepalese mainstream, and increased exposure to foreign ideologies—Hindu values as well as western or capitalist values stemming from global trade and market economies. This dual perspective on change and continuity, external forces and local traditions, is woven throughout the book in an attempt to show how these social and cultural transformations are experienced, mediated, and interpreted through individual lives.

Many studies on the effects of capital penetration, the expansion of the world market system, and the incorporation of minority groups into centralized states often find that these political and economic changes lead to the subordination of women through their loss of customary property, marriage, and legal rights, or through a general devaluation of their work, their social status, and their loss of autonomy. However, as the Nyeshangte case will demonstrate, this overall subordination does not always occur: Nyeshangte women in their roles as economic, social, and moral agents have maintained their cultural centrality and their customary authority in society. Adult women see themselves and are perceived by other members of the community as central agents in the reproduction of the Nyeshang order.

Constructing Nyeshangte Identities: Trade, Religion, and Gender

In addition to looking at how gender roles and gender relations are constituted, reinterpreted, or negotiated as a result of recent economic changes, I will also consider the ideological dimension as it is reflected in society's prestige structures: in this case, international trade and Buddhism. The pairing of trade and religion may seem odd to readers unfamiliar with the larger Tibetan cultural realm, but it allows me to penetrate to the heart, so to speak, of Nyeshangte society. For Nyeshangte, as is true of many ethnic Tibetan groups,[3] trade and religion are the central institutions that define their highest goals and provide avenues of social power for individuals. Individuals may exchange some of their trade profits for prestige and religious merit by making donations to the monastic community, building Buddhist monuments, or sponsoring village celebrations and religious performances. International trade and adherence to Buddhist values and rituals are also ethnic markers of Nyeshangte identity within the overall predominantly Hindu, Nepalese society.

The links between a society's gender system and its core structures are quite evident: sex role patterns and gender ideologies are closely tied to wider systems of power and prestige, and these, in turn, are found within the society's "central institutions."[4] Furthermore, gender constructs are gen-

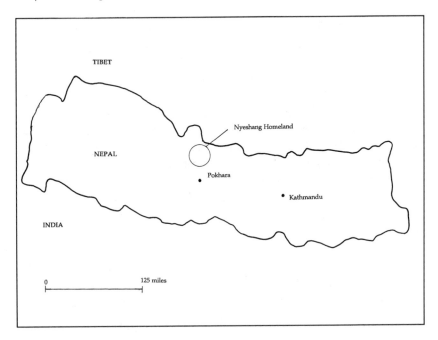

MAP I. Location of research sites and major Nyeshangte settlements in Nepal.

erally bound up with indigenous concepts of self and often serve as markers of group identity (cf. Devereaux 1987; Sanday 1990a). In the Nyeshangte case, individual and group identities are framed within a somewhat contradictory idiom that emphasizes their spirituality as devout Buddhists, their cleverness as traders, and their aggressiveness when provoked or challenged. Nyeshangte are frequently described *by outsiders* as possessing "bigheartedness," the impudent, gutsy outlook that is the hallmark of this prosperous Himalayan trading community.

Another theme I explore is how the emerging conflict between current economic practices and religious goals has shaped gender identities *within the community*. This tension has heightened in recent decades as the moral contradictions and dangers surrounding the very profitable (but sometimes illegal) trade in consumer goods has become an issue of concern, especially among the elders of the community. The paradoxes, conflicts, and ambivalence surrounding this apparent contradiction between enduring religious values and current trade practices, between those who aspire toward indigenous (Buddhist) notions of "good persons" and those whose imaginings lean toward the glamour of "life in the fast lane," have been cast into a largely genderized framework that centers on the metaphors of "spirited" women and "big-hearted" men.[5]

The development of this genderized discourse is paralleled by a renewed emphasis on particular oral histories and ritual observances that links women with the founding of Buddhism in the homeland (the Nyeshang valley) and, conversely, links men to a martial past: a warrior tradition that is highlighted during the week-long Paten festival with its themes of human sacrifice, heroic feats, and allegiance to a shaman king.[6] The elaboration of these folk models and indigenous frameworks reflects a collective concern with changing gender roles and ideologies, with new attitudes about appropriate kinds of work, and with a pervasive longing for the homeland (*yul*) and for the "simple, good life" of the past.

Envisioning the Past: The Homeland and Nyeshangte Identity

The role of imagined pasts, reconstructed landscapes, and homelands, and their significance as vehicles that in some sense fashion, as well as represent, collective identities, have been discussed in a number of recent works.[7] Nostalgia and a concern with collective historical memories often figure prominently among diasporic or deterritorialized populations; this is particularly true of the Nyeshangte community where many individuals and families are dispersed in trade centers across the Asian continent: in Hong Kong, Bangkok, Singapore, in northern India, as well as urban locales like Pokhara and Kathmandu in Nepal—places that are culturally, economically, and socially distant from the Nyeshang valley and from its subsistence-oriented (farming and herding) way of life.

However, I should point out that views toward the past and the homeland vary among Nyeshangte and are not necessarily monolithic. The desire to return to the homeland, with its widely perceived customary way of life, is generally strongest among the elderly; they have been known to go on hunger strikes—refusing to eat or talk—if their adult children, in an attempt to keep aging parents and grandparents in Kathmandu, refuse to make arrangements for their return trip home. On the other hand, although many of the middle-aged long-term residents of Kathmandu expressed a sincere desire to return to the Nyeshang valley (either for a visit or for retirement), they often failed to do so—frequently citing an illness, business commitments, or claiming that the journey was too difficult on foot. And a few adults (mostly males) in their late twenties and thirties stated outright that they prefer the "developed" life of Pokhara or Kathmandu with its various "facilities." I also encountered a handful of city residents—again, mostly men—who announced, quite frankly, that they have absolutely no intention of returning to a way of life they view as harsh, difficult, and backward (*jangali*).[8] However, these negative perceptions of the homeland seem to be relatively rare, and most Nyeshangte, even those who have never been to the valley, tend to be more enamored of the homeland and of the mystique that surrounds this sacred place.

In recent years the native models and genderized frameworks associated with the oral traditions and everyday practices of the homeland have taken on added significance as Nyeshangte, individually and collectively, struggle to make sense of the changes sweeping through their community and through a world being rapidly transformed by translocal forces: global capitalism, western representations, and the politics of nation-building in Nepal. In this changing landscape, emergent nationalism(s) may often be expressed as an invigorated sort of regionalism, where claims of ethnic and cultural identity and concerns with revitalizing or reinventing indigenous customs are enacted or embodied through a localized practice—one often labeled "authentic" and one primarily associated with the ancestral homeland.[9] However, today, more than ever, these concerns and claims are also being played out in the public arena for a larger, more cosmopolitan audience. This audience includes not only government officials (who control trade policies and tariffs), but also anthropologists, tourists, and development workers, in addition to the usual local audience—the variety of Hindu caste and ethnic groups found in Kathmandu and other urban areas where Nyeshangte have settled in recent years.

Scrambled Visions, Fragmented Knowledge

I turn now to a brief discussion of Nyeshangte subjectivity and historical awareness, so that the reader may get a better grasp of how this community is positioned or, perhaps more accurately, is moving across the contemporary "ethnoscape" (Appadurai 1991) of modern-day Nepal. The question, to what extent are Nyeshangte rather singular and unlike other communities in Nepal, will be sidestepped for the time being. I suspect, however, that as our knowledge increases of historical processes in the Himalaya, and what have been perceived as "marginal, out-of the-way"[10] sorts of places, other cases like the Nyeshangte will continue to surface.[11]

Working with Nyeshangte, I quickly realized that as individuals and groups become more conscious of the politics of difference and more aware of how they are situated within shifting spheres of power, these new understandings often lead them to an "objectification of" or a "distancing from" their own culture. At first I had assumed that it was merely chance or coincidence when I kept bumping into people who seemed unusually reflective about their lives. Then, perhaps more cynically, I suspected that some of my acquaintances were acting as "community reps," who were ordered to keep an eye on me, hoping perhaps that their volunteered insights would hasten my study, and therefore my departure from the area. Although some of my suspicions were not totally unfounded, the truth lay elsewhere: many of the women and men I met did in fact have an unusual sensibility or awareness of their own history, their own cultural identity, and their own place within the larger scheme of things.

Here, permit me to digress briefly and to share a couple of anecdotes that perhaps will illustrate why I was so frequently discomfited by my encounters with Nyeshangte and their visions of the world. Sometimes the parallels drawn by Nyeshangte speakers, the identifications made, left me astonished and at a complete loss for words. During my first trip into "the field," I stayed a few days in one of the villages in the lower Marsyandi valley where some of the poorer Nyeshangte households migrated during the winter. There, one afternoon as I sat idly in the sun and watched a few Nyeshangte boys practice shooting arrows at a target, a young man strutted toward me, waved a fist full of arrows in my face, and shouted in English, "See, we are just like the Indians in the West that all you white people killed."

Who was this irascible fellow? And where had he picked up this sardonic view of American history and this affinity with dispossessed "Indians"? Could he be one of the few high school or college graduates in Nepal who had elected to return to the village after living in Kathmandu and now felt frustrated and bitter with his decision and his life circumstances? But this was unlikely, since until fairly recently most Nyeshangte rarely had the opportunity (or desire) to attend Nepalese schools. Even today few youngsters in the community receive their school-leaving certificates (SLC),[12] and most Nyeshangte adults over the age of 30 are illiterate, unless they had been taught to read Tibetan scriptures by the village lama. But those religious texts certainly had little to say about arrows and American Indians.

I learned, though, that for many Nyeshangte, this knowledge of history and this self-awareness about their own culture had not been acquired through the usual academic channels. Maya once told me that "world history" (the endless litany of people, places, and events that many of us were subjected to in high school) was not offered in the Nepalese curriculum, but was learned instead through the popular mass media: through western (primarily American) films, videos, and paperback novels.

The actual existence of this partial or scrambled knowledge was especially hard for me to fathom at first, since many of my young Nyeshangte friends in Kathmandu seemed at times so worldly, so sophisticated (yet paradoxically so Americanized) in language, dress, and mannerisms. They also seemed generally more self-possessed and more widely informed than many of the youths I had known in California, friends of my own teenage son. But I came to realize that this fragmented knowledge was quite pervasive and that it occupied a central place in the imaginations of Nyeshangte youths.[13] My growing awareness of just how widespread these scrambled visions were occurred following a series of breaks or disjunctures, which needled me throughout my fieldwork and on occasion still manage to confound me when I receive letters, faxes, and those middle-of-the-night phone calls from some of my more cosmopolitan Nyeshangte friends in Nepal, Thailand, or Hong Kong. One more story illustrates the nature of this fragmented knowledge among Nyeshangte youth.

After inviting Maya to see Oliver Stone's *Platoon* at the American "rec center" in Kathmandu, I was concerned about her reaction to the violence in the film. When the film ended, after showing how the U.S. forces were overrun by North Vietnamese soldiers and Charlie Sheen was nearly murdered by his own sergeant, Maya was unusually quiet. I asked her if she liked the film, and she replied in a puzzled manner, "Yes. But I thought the Americans had won the Vietnam War. Is this [movie] a true story? How can that be? All the others I've seen showed the Americans winning."

That, for most Nyeshangte youths, actual experience eventually takes precedence over media representations in the construction of self and group identities is no doubt reassuring to their elders (and to anthropologists), who have reason to worry that a steady diet of popcorn, Stallone clones, and glorified "action-adventure" films might lead to a particularly skewed view of the West, and of the world in general. I turn now to Nyeshangte constructions of identity and of difference based on "lived" experience and what might generally be referred to as the group's "social memory" (cf. Connerton 1992).

Foot-Loose: Identities on the Move

Nyeshangte women and men have made their way in the world, capitalizing, as it were, on cultural differences. Since the turn of the century, on the

Indian plains (of the South Asian variety), they sold medicinal herbs, yak tails, musk, and other exotic items. There, they traded not only in Himalayan goods, but also trafficked in the Himalayan mystique: of possessing special medical skills, knowledge, and ritual power simply because they were high-mountain dwellers from the snowy peaks of this sacred range.

Subsequently, their business acumen and their flair for merging into local ethnoscapes enabled them to find suitable niches throughout mainland Southeast Asia. In Burma—one of their favorite stomping grounds between the 1930s and 1950s—Nyeshangte who took part in the Thai border trade were generally believed to be members of one of the dissident minority groups from Upper Burma; this mistaken assumption was held by some of their Chinese competitors and the British military authorities. Occupying a similar niche, as black market profiteers in Vietnam and Laos during the 1960s and 1970s, Nyeshangte traders told me that in their dealings with American GIs in Saigon and Vientiane, they had passed as generic "Indo-Chinese" or "indigenes."

In the late 1960s and 1970s, amid the growing international tourist consumption of "Hill Tribes Culture," Nyeshangte entrepreneurs set up shop in northern Thailand, selling tribal crafts and posing for pictures on the outskirts of Chiang Mai, where they were frequently mistaken for authentic Thai "natives" by western tourists who arrived in air-conditioned minivans to "do the village." A few Nyeshangte families owned and operated souvenir shops in Chiang Mai, and several individuals hawked jewelry, embroidered wall hangings, teak carvings, and other items from Burma at the ubiquitous night markets that were held daily on the streets and sidewalks in town. When asked by westerners where they were from, they were just as likely to reply Burma or China or the Thai hill region, whatever suited their mood or the occasion at hand.

In the course of their excursions out and about on the Asian continent, Nyeshangte encountered (and learned to deal with) not only Chinese warlords, British colonial officers, western tourists, and American GIs, but also on occasion came face to face with their favorite western icons. One of my acquaintances in Kathmandu proudly showed me a photograph in his office that was taken in Chiang Mai: he and his younger brother were dwarfed by a smiling Sylvester Stallone, who stood between them with his arms draped around their shoulders. Apparently, while filming on location in northern Thailand, Stallone had visited the family's souvenir shop and posed for the photo with the two Nyeshangte brothers.

Amid all these cultural mixings, as western representations and expectations collide and mingle with the contemporary realities of Asian life, the one thing that stands out is that Nyeshangte individuals have proven themselves, over and over again, to be quite capable of staging and defining this encounter largely (though not entirely) on their own terms. The point I wish to emphasize here is that Nyeshangte are not simply at the receiving end of western cultural flows, nor is their self-awareness necessarily a very recent phenomenon brought about in the last few years by "democratization" or "modernization" in Nepal. What might appear as a collage of bizarre incidents or stories reflects a pattern of agency and subjectivity that all too often has been overlooked in many ethnographic studies of Nepal, where accounts of the past are frozen until 1951,[14] and people, like the proverbial billiard balls, are pushed around by an unseen hand, and history is something that happens from the outside.

One of the unintended consequences and ironies that ensued from their chameleonlike existence and their consummate performance of "identity" is that Nyeshangte have occasionally been mistaken for Americans by other westerners; stranger still, they have been mistaken for westerners by other Nepalese. Two incidents, both involving Nyeshangte youths, illustrate how ethnic categories sometimes get turned upside down amid the chaotic swirl of Kathmandu's modernity, where Nepalese hierarchies and western consumerism, Nyeshangte identities and anthropological expectations, come together in unexpected ways.

One morning while waiting for the bus—for the first leg of the long trek back to Nyeshang—I was struck by the image of my research assistant, Spike, a 19-year-old Nyeshangte male who had volunteered to join me only a few days earlier. Decked out in hot-pink "jams" (surfer shorts), a neon-yellow T-shirt, top-of-the-line Reebok shoes, and a Sony Walkman dangling around his neck, Spike managed to look (and sound) more Californian than the motley crew of tourists milling about, including the anthropologist. Although he had been to the Nyeshang valley once before, I later found out that he had never actually walked the trail.

Three days into the trip, the track climbed continuously, and there was little shade to soften the intense heat of the afternoon sun. Halfway up the rise we passed a westerner resting on the trail alongside his Sherpa guide, and we stopped to greet them. After watching our group's rapid progress up the steep switch backs, they suggested we slow down a bit. Palsang, my Sherpa guide-assistant laughed and, pointing at me, said, "No problem. She is walking like us, very quickly." "Maybe so," replied Claude, who turned out to be a French medical doctor, "but her friend, the *other American* who went by, did not look so well." Worried about the "other American," we hurried ahead and ten minutes later caught up with Spike, who we found sprawled beneath the shade of a banyan tree. His face was ashen: he was dehydrated and overcome by the heat.

The Sherpas teased him about being a city boy, and Spike sheepishly grinned: "I am the son of a 'big person.' I don't usually carry a pack. When I travel with my family we fly, and then our relatives meet us with horses. We don't ever *walk* to Nyeshang." Claude was astonished to find out that Spike, who spoke English with a healthy command of four-letter words and was dressed right out of a California Macy's ad—minus the skateboard— was not, after all, an American trekker, but a Nepalese teenager. And I, with growing amazement, gradually realized that Spike (just like my husband a few months before) was suffering from a severe case of culture shock, as I listened to him complain about the food, the accommodations, and the general discomforts of life on the trail, which seemed to increase steadily as we continued to climb toward the mountains.

The second example of mixed-up identities took place in Kathmandu and involved individuals who were Nepalese. During one of my shorter stays in Kathmandu, when I was recovering from the rigors and illness of a previous trip to Nyeshang, I had made arrangements for Kema, a 17-year-old Nyeshangte woman who attended boarding school in Darjeeling, to join me at the American rec center. There, on the expansive grounds of the compound, we could always find a quiet spot to "work" without being interrupted by the assortment of younger nieces, nephews, and cousins who invaded her home during the school holidays.

Not sure exactly when she would arrive, I had entered her name on the "guest" list and left instructions with the Nepalese guard at the front gate so she would be cleared through security without any hassles. Kema arrived at the rec center with a puzzled look on her face. She told me that the Nepalese guard had mistaken her for an American "dependent" and (in English) had asked to see her membership ID. When she responded in Nepali to his questions, he did not seem to understand her. In frustration, Kema tried again to explain in Nepali that her name was listed on the *guest list* (using the English word this time) and pointed to the register in the checkpost. Finally the guard understood: he thought the young "American" was a Peace Corp volunteer, and explained to her that Peace Corp volunteers did not need special permission to use the facilities there.

This incident was very disturbing to Kema; she kept bringing it up, pondering the implications of mistaken identities. Kema later confided to me that on two occasions Nyeshangte, meeting her for the first time, had actually asked her if she were a Newar (another ethnic group in Nepal); but never before had she been mistaken for a westerner or foreigner. Similar incidents occurred when she came to visit me at the office after hours: the Nepalese "watchmen" (*chaukīdār*) often assumed she was an American. Eventually, after considering the irony of being mistaken for a "foreigner" in her own country, Kema found these incidents amusing.

As these anecdotes demonstrate, ethnicity, cultural identity, and the construction of cultural differences were topics that were of interest to many Nepalese I met during the course of my fieldwork. Although new social formations may be emerging in urbanized areas of Nepal, the process of class formation is by and large incomplete, and class did not seem to be the dominant category for affiliation (or a category that evoked much commentary). Instead, caste, ethnic, and religious differences were still the medium through which many people constructed their identities. In numerous conversations with friends and acquaintances, both in the city and in rural areas in north central Nepal, the boundaries of common identity shifted to include and at times exclude various groups, based on perceived cultural practices, especially those pertaining to gender roles, household arrangements, and religious and marriage customs.[15] In general, though, both women and men consistently used a common vocabulary that highlighted locally understood differences between Hindu caste practices and those commonly associated with "Tibetans"—including Sherpa, Nyeshangte, and Tibetan Muslims.[16] These contrasts were often couched in a gendered framework that focused on the customary rights, agency, and authority of Tibetan women in different communities throughout Nepal.

Gender Problems Revisited

I turn now to the subject of gender relations and consider how some of these gender issues are framed within the specific context of Nyeshang society. A few points need to be stressed here. First, gender relations are shaped by a multitude of factors, not by one key determinant or variable. Nyeshangte women as a category have a solid power base grounded in economic realities—for example, land ownership and control of money within the household, among other things.[17] But their agency and moral authority also result from their symbolic alignment with the sacred domain and from their roles as culture bearers and "knowledge holders."[18] Adult women are seen as the foundation and preservers of the homeland and of the group's cultural identity. Second, because gender systems are shaped by a series of intricately linked factors, shifts in one area are likely to have repercussions in other areas, including the way gender meanings are constituted, understood, and manipulated. Finally, although many of the necessary conditions that foster nonhierarchical gender arrangements may be found in Nyeshang society, individual Nyeshangte women must still secure their overall position in everyday life. This is especially true today as the internal equality that was characteristic of Nyeshang before the 1960s is gradually being eroded by the pressures of external political and economic forces.

However, despite the profound economic and demographic changes of the past three decades, my overall impression is that Nyeshang society may still be characterized as having fairly balanced or complementary gender relations, with neither sex dominating the other. I will discuss the particular features or conditions that support these gender arrangements in a moment, but first I will address the issue of definitions: what is implied by the labels "dominance," "subordination," or "gender equality," and what problems are inherent in our analytical frameworks and our analyses of nonwestern gender systems.

A number of recent works (for example, di Leonardo 1991; Strathern 1987b, 1988) point out that the concept of inequality is a western historical construct. Judgment about what categories of people are equal or not equal generally reflect western ideas about where authority, influence, and social power are found, and about what constitutes valued and effective action. These works suggest that discussions of dominance and subordination should be framed instead in terms of culturally defined goals and valued activities—categories that reflect local contexts and local meanings. The notion of subordination, equality, or dominance must also be tied to indigenous notions of personhood, of what it means to be a man or a woman and what it means to be a wife, mother, or daughter in a particular society (see, for example, Errington and Gewertz 1987).

Local expectations and indigenous meanings of gendered behavior are often quite different than gender constructs in our own society. However, since our interpretations of these nonwestern gender systems may be derived in part from our own (largely unexamined) assumptions about male-female relations in the West, this particular bias may lead us to see subordination (or false consciousness) where perhaps none exists. For example, one anthropologist who worked in an Andean village, described the initial resentment she felt (and her subsequent rethinking) about an incident that took place when the mistress of the household was away. Her male host/landlord had prepared their evening meal, but subsequently asked the anthropologist to serve the food that he had so ably cooked. Allen (1988, 78) explains:

> Of women's tasks, the one most unsuitable for men is ladling food from cooking pot to plate. At first this struck me as a manifestation of male dominance, but with time I realized that serving is a woman's prerogative, for it emphasizes her proprietorship of the food as well as the man's obligation to her. Men seldom fail to thank their wives for cooked food, even in the most casual setting.

According to one fairly common definition (used by many feminist writers), subordination or dominance occurs when individuals are barred from domains, activities, or roles considered prestigious in a particular society. Subordination refers to conditions that prevent categories of individuals from attaining culturally defined positions of worth or from prominent roles (Errington and Gewertz 1987). My findings suggest that in the Nyeshang case neither men nor women are barred or prevented from participating in their society's two central institutions: international trade and Buddhist ritual practice.

I should point out, however, that Nyeshang is not a completely egalitarian society, that inequities do exist, and in recent years some trends such as rural/urban differences and incipient class distinctions seem to be increasing. This development is tied to the reorganization of trade in the mid-1960s that led to the emergence of an urban-based class of full-time international traders whose cash income enables them to establish permanent homes in Kathmandu. The small-scale traders, on the other hand, are still dependent on the village-based economy, and their family members continue to engage in agricultural and pastoral pursuits in the homeland. In Nyeshang, there are (and always have been) some differences in wealth, in access to land, in opportunities for education or trade, as well as differences in the constraints individuals must face, but these tend to fall along an axis based on age, generation, or rank within a household. Gender is not usually an overriding factor. Women and men within the same stage of life tend to have equivalent social statuses and similar responsibilities, opportunities, and restrictions.[19]

Despite the recent evidence of increasing stratification within the community, general consensus in the community suggests that only 10 percent of all Nyeshangte households fall into the very rich category, the vast majority (or 80 percent) are in the median "neither rich, nor poor" category, and 10 percent are poor (dependent on their relatives, community assistance, or both). I should also point out that overall levels of household wealth, even in the median bracket, far surpass the average income for Nepalese households.[20] Given the highly redistributive nature of Nyeshangte social life, the continued emphasis on generosity and reciprocal exchange, and their insistence that "all Nyeshangte are one, the same," one might reasonably assume that the egalitarian ethos and social relations of earlier times (pre-1960) are still fairly intact. Most Nyeshangte women and men, of various ages, usually downplay the apparent social and economic differences between the rural and urban populations, overlook the emerging class distinctions, and generally regard one another with mutual respect.

The conditions or local factors that helped create a relatively egalitarian social order reflect the coalescence of particular political, economic, cultural, and social features that are, for the most part, unique to the Nyeshang valley. Although Nyeshang cultural traditions and social organization have been influenced by the larger Tibetan Buddhist civilization (Nyeshangte trace their origins to Tibet, and their ancestors migrated to the valley more than six hundred years ago), these localized factors set it somewhat apart from other ethnic Tibetan communities. Briefly, these factors include significant autonomy from state structures both Tibetan and Nepalese;[21] a small-scale society[22] with low population density (the second lowest in Nepal); communally held resources that include pasture land, forest, and water rights; minimal political ranking or ascribed positions; localized rule based on consensus of individual household representatives; yearly rotation of council and village posts; an emphasis on reciprocal exchange; an intensely collective life that features work parties, labor exchange, and mutual aid; and a general respect for individual autonomy.

In addition, numerous cultural and social features also contribute to the balanced gender relations found in Nyeshang. These include features such as bilateral kinship and cross-cousin marriage,[23] which presuppose the equality of intermarrying groups; weak corporate clan structure; religious and social ideologies that do not denigrate women or portray them as polluting; little concern with regulating or controlling female sexuality or limiting women's physical mobility; a division of labor that is largely overlapping and loosely defined, where both male and female activities are considered important and "hard workers" of either sex are perceived as virtuous and widely respected in the community; authority is based largely on age seniority in the household and community; similar traits are valued in men and women; husband and wife are seen as a complementary unit; women inherit land and movable wealth and have user rights to fallow land; and women can initiate divorce and have considerable say in who they will accept as a marriage partner.

Although I use the terms *gender egalitarian* and *relations of equivalence,* this does not imply that men and women have identical roles, responsibilities, or privileges. Nor does it imply sameness in activities or behavior. Rather, I use these terms to highlight the overall symmetry, balance, and complementary relationship between the sexes. Neither men nor women as categories prevent others from engaging in culturally defined prestigious activities. The degree of prominence or control manifested in particular circumstances by individual men or women may vary, but for the most part, social and gender relations in this society are not hierarchical.

Throughout the book I maintain a dual perspective: first, I am concerned with identifying the conditions, arrangements, and cultural values that promote gender equality. So, for example—with the exception of part 1, which serves as a general introduction—each of the three major sections of the book focuses on the structural organization of Nyeshang society: part 2 looks at the economy; part 3, social institutions and kinship; and part 4, religion. Throughout I examine the patterns or features that most of my Nyeshangte acquaintances would describe as customary or typical Nyeshangte ways of doing things: I look at the organization of labor, households, and trade (chapters 2 and 3); marriage, property rights, and kinship (chapter 5); and, finally, the gender ideologies, worldview, and organization of local Buddhist sects (chapter 7). Although the focus in these chapters is on structural features that support a nonhierarchical gender system, these features or patterns are examined in a historical context so that the processes of social reproduction and transformation are revealed.

Then, in the chapters immediately following—for example, in chapters 4, 6, and 8—the perspective shifts to how individual men and women both perceive and experience these transformations; that is, how they variously embrace, tolerate, oppose, or ignore emergent trends that are linked to changing trade and residence patterns, to increasing differences in wealth among households, and to new gender ideologies. In short, my goal is to show how the wider forces of change are manifested at the local level through individual lives. The focus in these chapters is on agency, on subjectivity, on reactions to changes taking place within the community. For example, in chapter 6, I look at how women's support of customary practices—or what are locally defined as "traditional" institutions—stems from their aversion to the alien values and extrinsic forces associated with the world market. Their support of "tradition" mirrors their dissatisfaction with the increasing commoditization of labor and sociality, of emotion and selves. In chapter 8, I explore the significance of women's agency in the religious domain and examine how the currents of modernity that are sweeping through the community have led to an elaboration of cultural archetypes—gender metaphors that portray adult women as possessing the necessary virtue, responsibility, and moral authority to uphold (and redefine) the Nyeshang social order.

The deliberate emphasis throughout this book on women's agency, their activities, or particular aspects of their lives is not to suggest or imply that Nyeshangte women as a class of individuals "dominate" men of their own group; rather, this emphasis serves as an antidote or correction to the common assumption that women are universally subordinated or that women inevitably lose their customary rights whenever minority groups and small-scale societies are incorporated into national polities and global market economies. Second, this emphasis on (individual) women is tied to the problematics of ethnographic representation: specifically, the range and varied circumstances of women's lives in Nyeshang society have simply not been addressed in previous studies of the community (Cooke 1985a; Gurung 1977a). Finally, I have tried to present a detailed, vivid portrait of Nyeshang society in order to avoid burying the voices and varied experiences of individual women (and men) under essentializing categories. This has meant retaining some of the messiness, contradictions, and ambiguities that ultimately convey the complexities of daily life—both as expressed by my informants and as observed by me as a field-worker—in an attempt to portray how external forces or global processes are manifested in local contexts and experienced, engaged, or reworked by local communities.

While various facets of women's lives are highlighted—as positioned individuals and social agents, as international traders and Buddhist practitioners—these glimpses must be understood in the overall context of social relations; that is, in the context of men and women living together, or apart, as the case may be. Although recent shifts in migration and trade patterns have led to an increase in female-headed households, most Nyeshangte women do not spend their entire lives alone—they still have fathers, brothers, husbands, and sons. Therefore, the question of women's opportunities or constraints, the degree of autonomy, and the extent to which they are in charge of their own (and other people's) lives must be understood relative to that of men's—in particular, the men of their own class and age group.

I have tried to maintain a balanced perspective, one that is both descriptive yet analytical, moving from the lives of individual women and men to general statements about the range of experiences and conditions shared by various groups in the Nyeshangte community. The cast of characters is quite diverse: it includes members of the Devil's Gang, youths (mostly teenage boys) who frequent the discos of five-star luxury hotels and hang out at popular "fast food" joints in Kathmandu; the Pink Ladies, a clique of privileged young women who attend elite boarding schools in Darjeeling; the hard-working village girls who labor in the fields together, and at night sing, dance, and feast in their group's "tsha house";[24] and the young nuns who emerged after three years of seclusion and were honored by the community in a week-long celebration. There are also self-assured widows, who manage lodges and shops: their clients include trekkers searching for provisions—chocolate bars, yak cheese, and sweet red apples in preparation for the arduous hike over the Thorung Pass—as well as Tibetan herdsmen, Gurung soldiers, and farmers from neighboring districts, who need lodging for one night, or perhaps just a snack of roasted potatoes, a pitcher of beer (*chang*), and an hour of gossip and rest to break up their long journey. There are rugged, middle-aged men who traversed the hilly jungles of Assam, Burma, and Thailand and roamed as far as Vientiane and Saigon—where, during the Vietnam War, they peddled fake gems to American soldiers. Some of the village men, crowned with streaming, long black hair, clad in Tibetan robes (*chuba*) and knee-high boots, still ride sturdy mountain ponies across the high mountain passes; others, sporting Hawaiian shirts and Levi jeans, fly to Bangkok, Singapore, and Hong Kong.

The Nyeshangte community is rapidly changing; I have tried to capture the essence of that change and show how it affects the lives of its members. Although differences in wealth are becoming more apparent—especially among the urban residents—strong family ties have prevented the split between villagers and city dwellers. This study treats the rural and urban Nyeshangte as members of one community, as they insist they are. It is, after all, the way they see themselves.

Reimagining "Community"

Although the notion of "community" seemed self-evident to most of my Nyeshangte friends, for me both the concept and reality of "Nyeshangte community"—as something that could first be defined and then studied—seemed fraught with problems. How do you go about doing a multisite ethnography in a community that is dispersed, not just in two or three locations in Nepal, but in two or three countries? How do you carry out research with a group whose members it seems are always on the move. But rather than agonize over the preliminary stuff—the defining, the mapping, the planning (in short, figuring out the actual logistics of doing an impossible project)—I skipped all that and just started moving—on foot or horseback, by bus or plane—guided by a simple belief that if it made "sense" to them, then it would eventually make sense to me.

It was during the course of my commutes to and from Kathmandu every few months—when I periodically retraced my steps along the Nyeshang trail—that the networks and the "confederation of households"[25] that marked the contours of the Nyeshangte community became apparent. And during subsequent stints of fieldwork, as I shuttled back and forth between Chiang Mai, Bangkok, Hong Kong, and other Southeast Asian cities where Nyeshangte "settled," the international dimensions of this community gradually became clearer. It was these *journeys*, then—between the homeland, Kathmandu, and various Nyeshangte settlements—in the company of traders, nuns, professional kick boxers, and assorted others that enabled me to understand their lives, as individuals caught between the exigencies of city and village life. It is only now, after working with Nyeshangte over a period of three years, that I have come to realize that *travel*, the haphazard time spent "on the road" *between field sites*, probably yielded greater understanding and insight into Nyeshangte lives than the more methodically planned research carried out once I "arrived."

The Nyeshangte community may be widely scattered (geographically speaking), but it is still, nonetheless, a very tightly knit group: news, gifts, money, letters, all circulate or flow between the various "outposts" with amazing efficiency. I too became part of this network, delivering letters and medicines from Kathmandu, carrying gifts of food—powdered milk, sugar, tea—to lamas and nuns in the valley, and returning to the city with watches that needed repairs, sometimes traveling with elderly villagers who needed assistance on the long trek back to the city. Even long-term migrants, who may not return home—either to Kathmandu or to Nyeshang—for years at a time, still belong to the community by virtue of having been born into it, by speaking the Nyeshangte dialect, and by continuing to meet their labor and financial obligations to the community through the auspices of resident household members. Although the community appears to be acephalous and composed of diverse elements—businessmen in Delhi, street hawkers in Singapore, schoolchildren in Darjeeling, lamas in Hong Kong—there is a strong nerve center that monitors the collective body: significant events and their repercussions are felt rather swiftly throughout the community. Nyeshangte may be a heterogeneous lot, but in the face of outside threats they are capable of regrouping instantaneously, and always seem to present a common unified front. It is these various dimensions of "community"—in both their urban and rural aspects—that I wish to highlight in the final part of this chapter.

City Visions: "Community" in Kathmandu

One of the nuns (*jomo*) I had met at a dgon pa located a few miles north of Kathmandu told me that Nyeshangte began to settle permanently in Kathmandu during the mid- to late 1970s. Soner's family, as it turned out, was closely aligned with (my research assistant) Spike's family; the 27-year-old nun explained that the two families, who were among the first to leave the valley, had migrated together to the city. "Our fathers are very close friends, they're like brothers. We lived together in one house when we first moved to Kathmandu in 1974. We were not so rich then, so the parents together bought a small house, then a few years later we sold that and we all built our [separate] houses."

After relocating permanently in Kathmandu, the families had prospered and had invested their savings in real estate. Each family owned two multistoried houses in *Tengal, an affluent neighborhood at the edge of Kathmandu, where many Sherpas, Tibetans, and Nyeshangte reside today. The flats or lower levels of these houses are often leased for additional income, and tenants may include fellow Buddhists—other Nyeshangte or Tibetans—or Hindu merchants from India.

Soner's parents also own additional land outside of town, near the sacred Buddhist site of Swayambhu, where they have built a "small" house that will serve as a religious retreat for their approaching retirement. Many Nyeshangte from the homeland spend the winter near this pilgrimage site; others, like Soner's parents, expect to live there in semiretirement all year round. At Swayambhu, the Nyeshangte community has constructed several dgon pa (temple complexes); these facilities also contain housing units for elderly, widowed, or less affluent Nyeshangte who wish to spend the remaining years of their lives doing *mani* (religious works) near the sacred *stūpa* (shrine).[26]

The dgon pa compounds, with their community hall and spacious grounds, are also the site of many Nyeshangte gatherings in the city:

archery competitions, harvest dances, and other celebrations that are still observed annually in the homeland are replicated in Kathmandu by permanent city residents. A few of the communitywide festivals are recent innovations that seem instrumental in constructing the group's identity in the city; these celebrations are attended by all the Nyeshangte migrants, regardless of their village or origin, and have no parallel in the homeland where the majority of annual rituals and festivals are staged separately in each village. (Nyeshangte men are fined if they do not attend the annual observances either in the homeland or in the city.) Other events, like the archery competition (*mitha prenba*) and harvest dances that continue to be observed independently in each of the Nyeshang villages, are also celebrated individually in Kathmandu, where they are attended exclusively by the former residents of particular villages.[27]

A more localized, village-based identity is also evident in the residential patterns of urban migrants: although most Nyeshangte generally live near other Buddhist families (Tibetans and Sherpa), they also exhibit a strong preference for "village clustering" in specific Kathmandu neighborhoods— a pattern that also reflects differences in wealth. Households from the same or from adjacent villages in Nyeshang are linked by kinship and marriage bonds, by reciprocal exchanges of labor and goods, and by other social ties that are partially reproduced in the city through these "village neighborhoods."

The neighborhood clustering of Buddhists is typical not only of residential areas and religious centers but is also seen in some of the commercial districts of Kathmandu. Many small businesses in Thamel District that cater to the burgeoning tourist market are owned and managed by Nyeshangte, Sherpa, and other ethnic Tibetans. Nyeshangte generally specialize in souvenir and jewelry stores that feature items imported from Burma, Thailand, India, and Hong Kong, whereas Sherpa and Tibetans specialize in trekking and mountaineering equipment or run restaurants offering a wide variety of inexpensive meals. Shop owners can frequently be seen sitting on the steps chatting with their neighbors, and they often keep an eye on the premises if their associates have to run an errand. Clients are generally referred to neighboring shops, and favors are routinely exchanged. These business networks provide urban migrants and small-scale merchants with support and assistance in a highly sociable and friendly atmosphere.

Although the Nyeshangte have a reputation for being a "closed" group, most of the urban residents I interviewed have extensive social ties with other ethnic groups. Maya and her family, for example, regularly attend weddings of Sherpa and Tibetan friends, sometimes traveling as far as Darjeeling to take part in the festivities sponsored by the bride or groom's families (who may live outside Nepal). The children of Sherpa, Nyeshangte, and Tibetan business associates (and neighbors) also socialize at birthday parties and New Year celebrations, and often enroll in the same private schools in Kathmandu or Darjeeling where they form strong friendships.

I turn now to a description of the rural community: the links between the two worlds are the result of dispersed family networks that channel people and goods between Kathmandu and their homeland, the Nyeshang valley in north central Nepal.

The Nyeshang Homeland

Nyeshang, a beautiful high alpine valley, is forested with scattered stands of pine, fir, and juniper on its lower slopes, and is encircled by majestic white peaks that reach upward to heights of eight thousand meters. Extending about twenty-five kilometers from east to west, the broad, relatively level valley is situated at the upper reaches of the Marsyandi River, which flows along the northern flanks of Annapurna and forms the watershed between the Annapurna and Manuslu Himal.

One of my strongest impressions of the homeland was the striking absence of men in many of the villages, particularly during the early weeks of spring. Elsewhere in Nepal, it seemed that men were part of the landscape: as solitary figures working in distant fields stooped behind plows, or in a succession of barefooted porters shuffling along narrow trails. Men were everywhere: they could be seen squatting on their haunches idly smoking cigarettes, framed in doorways basking in the sun's warmth, or clustered in crowded tea shops. Along the congested boulevards of Kathmandu, in the open-air markets, and in crowded city buses, their presence was certainly conspicuous; in the narrow alleys of Thamel their presence was even a bit intimidating: walking by, you could sometimes feel the challenging, defiant stares of the blue denim clones, the young gang members who loitered on shop steps and sidewalks, enmeshed in the hustle of Kathmandu's street life.

But in Nyeshang the men were, well, they were just not there. And many of those who eventually did surface in subsequent months seemed somehow diminished or pale, like shadowy figures that faded before the bright manner and ebullient voices of village girls; they appeared inconspicuous against the backdrop of women who bustled about the village carrying baskets filled with compost, hoes, and rakes to their fields, or the women visible on the flat rooftops who shouted greetings to neighbors on adjacent terraces and extended invitations to friends passing in the narrow lanes below.

During my initial visit to the area, in early March 1989, several of the village women told me they had spent the winter alone, caring for their cattle and goats, which were kept in the sheltered courtyards, while their husbands, children, and in some cases parents and siblings spent the winter in Kathmandu. The first day as we wandered through the village of *Churi, an elderly woman hailed us from her roof and deftly scampered down two levels to open the heavy wooden doors from the lower courtyard. We followed her inside and climbed a narrow notched log that served as a steep ladder linking the floors of the three-story house, which consisted of open terraces and rooms arranged around a central courtyard. Michung, dressed in the customary gray *bakhu* (Tibetan dress), brightly colored blouse, and turquoise and coral necklace, spread a yak wool carpet in a sunny quarter of the terrace and invited us to sit down. She disappeared inside again and brought a glass of sweet milk tea for me, then returned with two more for my husband and 12-year-old son.

Michung showed us pictures of her family: she had several grandchildren, two married sons whose families were permanently settled in Kathmandu, and one 38-year-old married daughter, who would soon be arriving from the city to help her manage the household and farm work. Michung was in her late fifties, widowed, and living in a house that her husband had inherited from his parents at the time of the couple's marriage. The house, fields, and livestock now belonged to her. Her daughter, who was directly involved in maintaining the property and looking after her elderly mother, would inherit most of the estate. It seemed that her two brothers, who earned their living exclusively from urban trade, had no interest in returning to the rural homeland, nor in claiming their portion of the estate.

Another woman waved as we left Michung's house and made our way through the lower tiers of the village, and she too beckoned us inside. Tsering was 25 years old, unmarried, and had passed the winter alone. Her parents and brothers were also in Kathmandu, but she preferred to stay in the village and take advantage of the winter solitude to spend her time in religious practice. Her chores were quite minimal, since the family did not keep any livestock, and she pointed to the *lha khang* (literally, "god room" or chapel) where she usually stayed in "retreat." The room was quite small but well appointed with low, cushioned benches along two walls that were flanked by a narrow table on which lay many ritual implements—various drums, bells, and loose sheaves inscribed with Tibetan prayers. The altar was furnished with small bowls of water, a tray with grain offerings, butter lamps, and images of Padmasambhava, a legendary (male) rNying ma teacher, and another of a bKa rgyud lama. Both images were draped with *kha btags* (white ceremonial scarves) and represented the two religious traditions of the valley, which are largely supported by laywomen.

In other villages in the Nyeshang valley, similar scenes unfolded and similar tales were heard. In *Kangri and *Tumje, where many of the narrow winding alleys were filled with several feet of compacted snow, sullied at winter's end with a grimy layer of ash, mud, and straw, the most numerous inhabitants seemed to be young goats that peered over the terrace ledges and scampered about in the streets. In addition to the resident caretakers, who were predominantly women, we also caught glimpses of a few maroon-robed lamas sitting in sheltered recesses of the open terraces where the light was bright enough to read. Occasionally, we detected a whiff of juniper fragrance mixed with burning incense and heard the pleasing refrains of chanting as we passed by the dgon pa. In each of the villages a few monks had remained during the long winter to offer ritual services for the year-round residents.

My first impressions of the homeland, then, were of a community made up primarily of women of all ages, with a sprinkling of a few very young boys, a few very old men, and a handful of lamas or monks. The preponderance of female-headed households in the valley today is the end result of changing trade practices that began to emerge in the 1960s. These changes led to the frequent and prolonged absence of most adult males from the district and coincided with an increase in the permanent and seasonal migration of many households to Kathmandu. Of the households that remain in the homeland, the majority are headed by adult women who live with their unmarried daughters.

Perched on steep hillsides and built in ascending tiers of tightly clustered stone houses, the villages range in elevation from 3,350 to 4,200 meters, and vary in size from sixty to three hundred houses. Ecological conditions and natural resources also vary locally, so that the amount and quality of agricultural land, pasture, and water available for irrigation differ in each community. In turn, the relative importance placed on farming, raising livestock, and long-distance trade tends to vary from village to village.

Each village has its own communal pasture, which begins high above the valley sides and the terraced fields, where herds of yak, sheep, and goat are driven during the spring and summer seasons. Near the high pastures

1. Gathered for the consecration of a shrine, village women visit with friends.

(*kharka*) are clusters of low shelters made of rough-hewn stone with bare dirt floors and simple hearths made from a circle of stones. The shelters in most of the kharka are in various states of collapse, rarely used anymore except by a few Drokpa, impoverished Tibetan nomads hired by Nyeshangte to tend the village herds. The huts with tumble-down roofs have long since been abandoned by their Nyeshangte owners who no longer follow the ancient rhythms of other Himalayan communities, where entire families move from the main village and fields to the high-altitude settlements and pastures during the summer months.

High above the villages, often at an hour or more walk, are the forest areas (*jangal*) where villagers can cut firewood, gather wild plants, mushrooms, medicinal herbs, and collect juniper branches which are burned daily as incense to purify the home. Like many other regions in Nepal the valley has suffered from extensive deforestation, and the young women, upon whom this burden falls the heaviest, lament their long climb to the upper forested slopes to collect fuel for cooking. The cutting of timber is regulated by the local village council: individuals must pay for firewood, and fines are imposed for illegal cutting. With assistance from the central government and foreign aid conservation programs, Nyeshangte and other Nepalese are attempting to reforest portions of the valley. But since the region was first opened to foreigners in 1977, the demand for fuel wood has continually increased: every year thousands of western trekkers hike the Annapurna Circuit and order meals, boiled water, and hot showers in village inns where wood stoves are commonly used. In 1984, when the central government installed power lines to all the Nyeshang villages, the Nyeshangte enjoyed the benefits of electricity in their homes for a total of four months—until the turbine was damaged by an avalanche, and subsequently never repaired—a casualty of districtwide politics and bureaucratic priorities.

Although Nyeshangte have a strong sense of group identity, which is readily asserted within the broader sphere of Nepalese society, at the local level, villages tend to have their own character and style. To a great extent this is maintained by a general preference for village endogamy, and is reinforced by the numerous festivals and religious ceremonies that are celebrated (at slightly different times) in each village. Minor variations are also apparent in village political organization, clan membership, and in the local Nyeshang dialect (Cooke 1985a). A subtle division also exists within the valley between the settlements located at the head of the valley and those at the eastern end. Largely because of their proximity to one another, villages in each of these two clusters tend to have stronger social ties with their immediate neighbors. These social ties include frequent labor exchanges for agricultural work, livestock supervision, and general community projects, as well as for occasional intermarriages, funeral services, or joint sponsorship of consecration rites (*rab gnas*).

The landscape throughout the valley is dotted with Buddhist temples and shrines: including *mchod rten*, which bear a slight resemblance to pagodas in Southeast Asia; *kani*, the arched gateways that mark village boundaries; and *mantang*, the banks of prayer wheels and white-washed walls covered with stone slabs that are inscribed with Tibetan prayers and images of Buddhist deities. High above the valley, built in secluded areas, are the meditation retreats. Nestled against rocky crags, these small, gray stone huts are often invisible against the backdrop of silver-brown scrub brush: their only telltale presence are the tall, white fluttering prayer flags that reach upward toward the mountain summits.

On the opposite side of the river is a track that climbs steeply through loose scree and dwarfed juniper shrubs, as it winds its way upward to the grassy meadows of the high plateau. Beyond this shelf, which is marked by an occasional herder's hut and is cloaked in a verdant expanse of alpine grasses and tiny clusters of brightly colored wildflowers, lies the forbidding zone of rock and icefall. There a glacier, a living mass that grumbles, sends tons of snow and rock crashing and roaring down to the valley floor every few hours. Looking out from the shelf, the entire valley is visible below revealing a landscape that is continuously transforming itself, depending on the play of light, the movement of clouds, and the change of seasons. It is at once harsh and severe: the Nyeshang valley is scarred by many huge gashes and mounds of stony rubble, the occasional buildup of moraine deposits from glaciers, but more frequently the result of landslides and avalanches that exact a heavy toll on livestock each year.

From November, when the harvest is gathered in the valley, the landscape turns monochromatic—to shades of gray brown—highlighted by glistening ice caps framed against a clear, cobalt-blue sky. The villages are emptied of people, and in December and January the snow piles up in the narrow cobbled lanes. The valley is buffeted by wild gusts of wind, making the already freezing temperatures more glacial. Inside the dark smoky stone houses, the few caretakers who remain behind—often old women and men—huddle around the hearth, spinning wool, sloshing down innumerable cups of salty Tibetan tea, and resting, after performing their winter chores: shoveling the flat rooftops that would collapse under the weight of snow; dragging bundles of fodder to the courtyard, where the family's livestock—fed on scanty rations—tenuously cling to life until spring.

By March the worst of winter has passed, but the clear sunny skies of early mornings give way to uniform gray, as the valley darkens by mid-day, and the villagers hurry inside to escape the snow flurries and bitter winds that come punctually every afternoon. It is difficult to imagine anything growing in this setting, but by April, when the villagers trickle back home from Kathmandu, the fields are ready for planting, and soon after, sprouts of green appear. The skies are bright blue, the stars visible at night, the winds have eased, and the young girls who awaken at dawn every morning to fetch water no longer find ice in the fountain troughs.

May is a delightful month, temperate, warm, and sunny. The valley is fully awakened. Flocks of birds, resembling crows, circle overhead; high above, solitary griffons and lammergeiers maintain their lonely vigilance. Green terraced fields of potato plants, millet, and *sāg* (a spinachlike plant) fill the landscape; flowers appear even on the ubiquitous thorny scrub bushes that choke the hillsides, cover stone walls, and form prickly barriers between the planted fields.

In the hazy light of pre-monsoon June, the greenness deepens; the peaks become shrouded, swallowed by swirling, fat white clouds; and light misty

2. Religious shrines delineate the sacred boundaries of the village.

rain gives way to an occasional tumultuous downpour. Splatters of mud and water drip inside the small rooms, as the earthen roofs withstand the summer rains, which are generally subdued and gentle in the rain shadow area beneath the Annapurna range.

By September and October the red ripening fields of buckwheat and the tall stands of wheat and millet are slashed and bundled into sheaves: some neatly lined up in rows are left to dry in the fields; others are gathered into piles that lean against the stone houses. Overnight, it seems, the valley has changed; the only splashes of bright color are the flowers, grown in window boxes and rusty tin pots clustered on the terraces, and the deep blue sky, which brings out the sharp relief of craggy peaks, stony ridges, and strangely eroded pillars of yellow-brown sandstone. During the frosty autumn nights the stars illuminate the valley, which glimmers under a full moon and in the silvery light reflected off the mountain peaks. On rooftops village men and women dance all night, slowly swaying in circles, singing a melodious refrain accompanied by the echoes of drums. After these harvest festivals and before the onslaught of winter, the villages begin to empty and the Nyeshangte make their way to warmer climates: to Kathmandu, to Pokhara, to India, and some to cities throughout Southeast Asia.

PART TWO

Transformations at Work

CHAPTER TWO

A Place of Many Works

When I was young, I would go to the fields with my friend to do the work of farming. Not only the planting and weeding, but we would also gather wood and fertilizer together. We did everything together, all kinds of work except plowing, because the villagers have an idea that to plow the fields is man's work and women can't do that. In those days, we did labor exchange (nang tse) and we grew a lot of grain, more than people are growing today.

At that time, I had two other girlfriends—they were twins—and we also exchanged work with them. After planting, we would all go to the temple for singing and dancing. When I was young I liked to sing and dance. At that time, since I was just 16, I did not want to get married, though my parents wished it.

During that time before I got married, my girlfriends and I traveled together. We went to many places on pilgrimage—Lumbini, Bodhgaya, Saranath, Banaras—and there we slept outside under trees. We also did some business in Narayanghat and Patna and all around. We didn't have any record of expenditure for where we traveled, for rail tickets, or what we bought. We distributed everything equally, whether it was food or money, everything we shared. Some things we brought from here: herbs, birch paper, yak tails, and things we made with wool. Some things we bought in India like cloth and dye. Sometimes we had misunderstandings and disagreements among our group, but we did not break up. Instead of splitting up, we tied up the friendship with a ritual bond (chetu), and then we celebrated with liquor.

In my youthful days, we lived a simple life: we ate plain food and wore old clothes. I only had one set of clothes and never changed them. No one had ever taught me to keep clean or to cook good food. But I didn't have to worry about my life. People were honest then and lived simply. In those days, we used only coins of fifty paisa or twenty-five paisa [a few cents]. No one was arrogant like some of the people today who have the high living: who eat many different kinds of foods and can change their clothes every day. These people are greedy and not so honest.

*After I turned 20, my parents arranged my marriage and it was agreeable to me then. Many people were invited; and they came and drank whiskey and beer. After a few years I had a child, and my husband went to do business between Tibet and Nyeshang. Later, after my son was grown, the boy went to Calcutta and did business there. But he never came back to *Nyangkhu, and I began to worry. So I went to Calcutta and found him. I stayed there with my son for several months, and then he came back with me to Nyangkhu. And I told him, "Now that you are staying here, you should build a temple."*

*Before that time, for three days every month we used to do a meditation retreat in the forest. Without eating, without speaking, we would sit and pray at that place. So when my son came back, I told him that he should build a temple there near *Tumje. Then my son built the temple and now the people are all going there. Other people helped, but my son was the main sponsor.*

I had a friend who lived in Tumje, she was my senior by one year. And we both had children. My friend was able to visit her children in Kathmandu, but because of my blindness I could not go with her. My friend's family was very rich, richer than mine, though we are quite rich. I have a big family—sons, daughters, and many grandchildren—all of them are rich. But I don't care for my family; I prefer to stay in the monastery, the forest, or the cave. I prefer to do religious works rather than earn money. My son wants me to live with him in Kathmandu. But I don't want to spend the rest of my life in town living a luxury life. My son is rich and all he thinks about is business. But I prefer the hard life. I have left the sinful life, and now I just want to die peacefully.

—Dolma Sangmo, an 88-year-old woman

Written from a historical perspective, this chapter focuses on the organization of work in Nyeshang. Particular emphasis is placed on the division of labor, the various idioms or indigenous meanings of "work," and the cultural logic that shapes gender-based work practices. For this discussion I draw on a number of sources: life history materials that were collected from women and men who ranged in age from their mid-twenties to late eighties, as well as conversations with city and village residents who spoke about their parents' and grandparents' lives. These historical data are supplemented by my observations of several "intact" households: nuclear families whose primary residences in 1988 were still in Nyeshang, and whose livelihoods depended mainly on farming, herding, and small-scale trade or tourism.[1] In addition, I comment on the attitudes and behavior of returning or visiting males in both rural and urban households so that we can get a better grasp of the changes, the continuities, and the range of variation in contemporary gender practices. Together, these sources provide a broad sweep of Nyeshangte work patterns and family life, both in the valley and outside the homeland, from the turn of this century through 1988 when my initial fieldwork was carried out in Nepal.

At the outset I would like to make a few qualifications. First of all, when I refer to earlier noncapitalist patterns of work as customary, I am not suggesting that Nyeshang society was static or frozen in some sort of pristine past until the mid-1970s, when Nyeshangte first began to settle permanently in Kathmandu. Local oral traditions indicate that the valley's economic base underwent several transformations: early residents relied to different degrees on a combination of strategies: pastoralism, swidden cropping, hunting wild game, and collecting forest produce.[2] This diversified economic base remained important for later populations as well, but subsequently, more emphasis was placed on irrigation agriculture, pastoralism, and various forms of long-distance trade. These shifts in subsistence strategies were linked to an increase in population and a decline in regional warfare, which permitted offshoot members of the founding clans to leave the cramped (but easily defended) settlements in the rocky defiles and cliffs above Nyangkhu in order to build larger permanent villages near the fertile valley floor.[3]

Second, I should point out that many of the traditional patterns and idioms of work still exist today in rural (and some urban) households, though these cultural forms may appear in somewhat modified forms alongside newer labor and gender arrangements. As we shall see, both types of work patterns have enabled Nyeshangte women to exercise a high level of control over household decisions and resources and over their own lives relative to Nyeshangte men of similar age.

The Overlapping Sexual Division of Labor

Like many highland communities, both in the Himalaya and the Andes, Nyeshang's agro-pastoral economy was shaped by several ecological constraints—extreme cold, low rainfall, short growing seasons, poor soil, and rugged terrain—which often resulted in food deficits that had to be offset with seasonal migratory trade. Orlove (1985), in his comparative study of the two regions, observed that this typical "montane production strategy" was characterized not only by the careful orchestration of agricultural and pastoral activities in fields and pastures at different altitudes, but also by a fairly minimal sexual division of labor.

In the Himalayan context, studies undertaken in Nepal, India, and Tibet suggest that a household's economic success or basic survival depended largely on the ability of its members to take on a wide variety of tasks.[4] Food processing, storage of crops and animal products, herding, trade, planting, and harvesting several crops that often required sequential timing and resulted in a wide range of activities undertaken in different altitudinal zones at different times of the year (Panter-Brick 1986; Orlove 1985). This requirement for a flexible labor pool could be met most easily in societies where few restrictions barred women or men from taking on particular kinds of work.

Aziz, for example, in her study of a Tibetan community in northern Nepal, commented that "no task is ever so exclusive that others cannot learn it, or that roles cannot change. That the sexes can interchange so readily in various economic roles is a key to the economic success of the Dingri household" (1978:108). Although some activities such as herding may be assumed primarily by adolescent males or adult men, Aziz noted that "if there are insufficient men in the unit, then women assume responsibility for the herd." Similarly Goldstein (1975a), reporting on the agro-pastoralists of Limi in northwest Nepal, and Panter-Brick (1986), writing about the Tamang (a Tibeto-Burman highland group) in central Nepal, observed that both male and female adults might be found working in the agricultural and pastoral sectors, and both sexes were often engaged in craft production and petty trade.

Nyeshang's noncapitalist economy was organized along similar lines to these other highland communities, where the household was the basic unit of production, consumption, and exchange. However, unlike the Tibetan societies described by Goldstein and Aziz, Nyeshangte did not practice polyandrous marriages; in contrast to the joint, extended, or polyandrous households found in other Himalayan societies, the typical Nyeshangte nuclear family household seldom included other "resident" adults to take up the slack if the husband or wife was away or ill. Individual households in Nyeshang often suffered chronic labor shortages.[5] Similar constraints also seemed to have affected many of the nuclear family households of the

Sherpas in Solu-Khumbu, another area where polyandry was not the norm (see Ortner 1989:33–36).

Faced with the need of allocating limited labor resources to a broad range of pursuits, with few exceptions most tasks in Nyeshang were performed by either women or men. No cultural proscriptions limited women's physical mobility or restricted their productive activities to the immediate village area and nearby fields;[6] certainly none confined them to seclusion in their own houses or courtyards to carry out household chores in what is sometimes referred to as the private sphere or the domestic domain.[7]

The Work of Farming

Before the development of large-scale trade in the 1970s, Nyeshangte women and men lived and worked together nearly year-round. Parents and older children labored side by side, and young children and infants were often brought to the fields where they played (or slept) under the gaze of adults who were working nearby. In the spring, everyone carried heavy loads of compost to the wheat, barley, and buckwheat fields that were scattered around the village and nearby hills.

After the fields were prepared and sown, they were watered and weeded at regular intervals. Usually this time-consuming task was left to young unmarried women, since females were thought to be more patient and more adept at separating grasses from the new shoots of wheat and barley. The young women often worked with a group of girlfriends, who exchanged labor (*nang tse*) and weeded each member's fields in succession.[8]

Sometimes during the busy months of April and May, work parties (nang tse) were organized to handle the initial irrigation of the newly sown fields. These groups, comprised of one adult male or female from each participating household, would alter the water course to irrigate a cluster of adjoining fields. Fields were owned jointly by husband and wife, and water allotments were awarded to the household as a unit.[9] Households that wished to have their fields irrigated by the work group but whose own members were busy with other chores could provide the group with meals—large quantities of beer and roasted potatoes—instead of the usual labor.

During harvest, an intensely busy period that lasted from late August to early October, everyone within the household, including children and the "retired" elderly, helped with the cutting, threshing, and drying of the grain crop. Villagers also relied on casual assistance (roo la tse) from friends, neighbors, and relatives.[10]

Roo la tse, which literally means "doing friendship," differs from nang tse since this type of help is offered freely without any expectation of immediate return (Cooke 1985a:54). Besides voluntary labor, roo la tse includes the small gifts of cash, grain, salt, and other staples that are donated to poorer households. Friends who spend the day together, collecting firewood, mushrooms, and herbs in the forest, would also be considered roo la tse. Nang tse arrangements are more organized and formal in that members who join agree to work in one another's fields for a specific number of days. Members are expected to meet this obligation and, if necessary, will send another family member as a substitute. The composition of nang tse groups was also more stable than that of roo la tse, typically lasting the entire year. In some groups a basic core of young adults might remain for several years—dropping out after they got married, or a few years later when children were born.

Recent Changes in Agricultural Production

Although the basic features of agricultural production remain the same, households today increasingly rely on servants (usually unmarried males) to offset the labor shortage caused by the recent out-migration of Nyeshangte men. Nyeshangte, however, do not and will not work for wages: the servants are all *outsiders*. Most unmarried male servants and day laborers come from poorer families in the middle hills district of Lamjung, though some also come from neighboring areas including Nar and Lo. Male servants, ranging in age from 12 to 40 years, do household chores, tend domestic livestock, chop and collect firewood, and help in the fields. In general, live-in servants, as opposed to temporary day laborers, are treated as household members. They often work alongside and share meals with the resident women, who address them by kin terms (younger or older brother). Relations between servants and family members are casual and friendly and often involve the usual joking, teasing, and sexual bantering that are commonly heard between unrelated men and women.

During harvest, many households hire additional male and female day laborers from surrounding districts, as well as from more distant regions like Dolpo and Nupri. In 1988–89 these seasonal laborers were paid thirty rupees a day (u.s.$1.20) plus meals. Nyeshangte women take pride in their hospitality and boast that laborers who come to the valley "get fat" because they are so well fed.[11]

3. Adolescent girls return to the village with heavy loads of firewood.

Although wage labor has become such a prominent feature of the village economy, communal work parties and reciprocal labor exchange still exist in Nyeshang. Since the agricultural cycle of each village varies by a few weeks (owing to differences in altitude and exposure), families whose fields have already been cut will frequently send a child to a neighboring village to help out. A group of neighbors, relatives, or friends may also pitch in to build a house or to help "needy" villagers with their farm work. Some households may have no resident males to do the plowing; they may be troubled by labor shortages or illness; or they may not have enough cash to hire servants. The woman I lived with, a wealthy middle-aged widow, would occasionally send one of her servants (or her teenage daughter) to stay with a family that needed assistance.

In 1984, when an exceptionally large group of Nyeshangte settled permanently in Kathmandu, the number of nang tse groups in the valley declined dramatically. Today, most of the formal labor exchange groups are smaller and include mostly adolescent girls and young adult women. These groups seem to share many of the characteristics of traditional nang tse groups, differing only in size and gender composition. During my stay in Nyeshang, communal work parties were used to rebuild a bridge that had been destroyed in the winter, to widen the main trail in the valley, and to repair some of the irrigation channels. These groups were mobilized by a town crier who wandered through the village, reminding the residents of their obligations to send a volunteer. In these instances, either an adult male or female could be sent, since the value placed on female and male labor is the same.

The Work of Herding

In the past herding played a major role in the Nyeshangte economy, although the relative importance of pastoral production tended to vary somewhat among villages and individual households. Some of the retired men in *Tungtar and *Lhakpa told me that during the early decades of this century, their parents and grandparents had owned many yak, "two times too many," as they often put it.[12] At that time (roughly between 1900 and 1940), the domestic economies of many Nyeshangte households had centered mainly on farming and raising livestock—goats, yak, horses, and cattle—and these families had relied less on long-distance trade.[13]

In general, pastoral production, like agriculture, was highly cooperative in Nyeshang, and most herding arrangements were organized at the village level. Each year a village committee hired shepherds, settled salaries, negotiated pasture rights with neighboring villages, and determined how much grain to collect from each family who participated in these collective arrangements.[14] Households that owned few livestock sometimes chose to work alone, or they pooled their animals into a joint herd with another family.

Ownership of livestock, like farmland, was invested in the conjugal or spousal pair and was not controlled by lineage or corporate clan groups. Decisions to sell or divide household property, including herds and fields, were made jointly by husbands and wives. Within the household, young children (often boys) were responsible for taking the family's milk cows to the outskirts of the village each morning and returning with them in the late afternoon. During the summer, household members divided their time between agricultural chores near the village and work at the herding settlement where most families owned a house and sometimes a few fields as well. Women, men, and older children regularly helped with the milking of cows and goats, the processing of dairy products, and the overall care of household animals.

Although some women and men thought that the job of "village" shepherd was most suitable for young unmarried males, others indicated that, in principle at least, either sex could do this sort of work, though in fact "boys" were usually hired. Two middle-aged women explained that a lot depended on an individual's temperament, whether "a boy or a girl" minded being alone or was easily frightened. And one fellow in his mid-thirties, who previously had earned a living importing clothing from Bangkok, added that the shelters near some of the high pastures were "not so nice." Pema pointed out that most villagers would find "the simple life [of herding] difficult," especially the young men and women who had experienced "the high living" of the city. Although Pema and his wife lived in the valley for about eight months of the year, they too had hired a couple from Nar to look after their livestock, and the couple's teenage children also had been hired as live-in servants: to collect firewood, haul compost to the fields, and perform other chores that Pema and his wife found difficult or disagreeable.

This ambivalent attitude toward some aspects of village work reflects the divergent generational experiences of Nyeshangte youths and elders, as well as the divergent class and gender-based expectations of rural and urban individuals. Several of the younger men in Kathmandu and a few of the middle-aged men also seemed self-conscious about being labeled *jaṅgali* (uncivilized). The life of a herder or farmer simply was not congruent with their aspirations of being sophisticated and worldly. This ideology of work also coincides with other shifts in the Nyeshang economy—rising trade incomes, increasing urban migration, and a decline in the size and number of yak herds, as surplus wealth is channeled into Kathmandu real estate.[15] Several merchant families in Kathmandu sold their livestock when they realized it was easier to manage city property in absentia than to manage a herd of yak or horses. However, other city residents who return to the valley each summer still own animals, but not nearly as many as the year-round residents of Nyeshang.

Today, the paid yak herders are mostly outsiders, Tibetan men who are recruited from pastoral communities in Nar, Dolpo, and southwestern Tibet. These experienced herders are generally regarded more highly by Nyeshangte than the seasonal laborers who perform unskilled work, and are rarely entrusted with livestock, a household's most valuable investment. Nyeshangte also have a strong affinity with herders from neighboring areas, since all of them are ethnic Tibetans and Buddhists.

Gender Equality: Habits of the Past

Although gender studies have moved away from the "categorical thinking" (Errington 1990:7) that characterized the field during the 1970s—with questions concerning cross-cultural variations in "women's status," "women's subordination," and so forth—at times I find this perspective useful as a starting point, a heuristic device for subsequent discussion about the ways indigenous models of gender differ from western analytical categories.[16] I use these earlier theories to make a few points about the organization of work in Nyeshang: what implications can be drawn regarding the question of egalitarian gender relations, the construction of gender identities, and the reproduction of these structures.

I start by considering some general points about the division of labor and women's economic autonomy, then shift gears in an attempt to explain why certain features of the Nyeshangte gender system seem to persist despite the economic transformations that have taken place during the past two decades. Although our notions of culture have become increasingly historicized, and the invented nature of tradition has become a commonplace observance, Dirks et al. (1994:2) point out that now and then we may run into a few cases where cultural patterns seem remarkably enduring. The reproduction of these configurations, whether it involves the cultural schemas that structure Sherpa history (Ortner 1989), the deliberate adherence to custom or tradition in New Guinea (Lepowsky 1993), or the rituals and statecraft associated with precolonial Bali (Geertz 1980), raises important issues concerning the "durability" of structures and cultural systems and the role of human agents in maintaining them. As Dirks et al. (1994:2) note, "We now realize that this [durability] is a peculiar state of affairs, requiring very sharp questioning and investigation."

Returning to the Nyeshangte case, the dimensions of these cultural forms will become clearer as we consider specific examples of contemporary gender practices, and look at indigenous meanings of "work." Here I situate Nyeshangte notions of work within a Buddhist framework, and consider how the concept of "gender hegemonies" (Ortner 1990a) might be used to explain the apparent resiliency of these gender configurations.

Women, Work, and Wealth

Many writers concerned with cross-cultural variations in gender relations have noted that the way a society organizes its labor force and structures its production and exchange systems will have a direct impact on women's economic power. Sanday (1974), for example, observed that women's economic control and social prestige was usually greater in societies where men and women contributed equally to subsistence work. In Nyeshang, wives operated as "equal partners" alongside their husbands; they took part in major household decisions and maintained significant control over the rural subsistence economy. In addition, women customarily inherited livestock and some farmland from their parents, and many women told me they had entered their marriages with considerable amounts of personal property.

"Ama," the 56-year-old widow I lived with, inherited most of her parent's property after both of her brothers and two of her five sisters died. This includes three houses in Nyangkhu and twenty average-sized fields. When she married, her husband moved into her natal household as an adopted bridegroom (*magpa*). Her "middle" sister (now 52), was given three fields by her parents when she married Ama's husband's younger brother. The youngest sister (aged 38) never married and lives alone in a large house that Ama owns.

Researchers have noted that women's ability to own and inherit property, to control basic resources, and to make important decisions on the use and exchange of subsistence and surplus products are important indicators of their economic and social status.[17] The economic factors discussed so far also suggest that if Nyeshang was not a thoroughly egalitarian society, it was at least an "equal opportunity" society where women wielded considerable power and authority in their own households and had effective control over their own lives.[18]

The characteristic flexible division of labor in Nyeshang may also have contributed to this state of affairs. Anthropologists, who work in societies where men's and women's tasks overlap, where women and men often work together in mixed groups, and where male and female labor and skills are similarly valued, have remarked that these factors are "predictors" of gender equality, and in turn help reinforce more symmetrical gender relations.[19] Based on his observations of an egalitarian society in insular Southeast Asia, Bacdayan (1977:286–87) suggested that an overlap of roles or "mechanistic cooperation" led to an easy rapport between men and women, a sense of closeness and familiarity that in turn encouraged an ethic of cooperation, trust, and mutual support. Bacdayan noted that among western Bontoc, husbands and wives tended to depend on each other and frequently sought each other's advice.

The issues of "housework," reproduction, and the gender-based division of labor have also figured prominently in the analysis of women's subordination.[20] Anthropologists have found that in communities where men share in the daily round of domestic tasks, power relations within the household may be more balanced, and women (as wives) are less likely to be subordinated (see, for example, Rosaldo 1974; Sanday 1981). Instead, as

Bacdayan (1977:287) observed, "a genuine appreciation of the interdependence of the two as equal partners is most likely to develop."

Although this type of labor arrangement may contribute to more equitable relations between the sexes, as a causal factor it may not be sufficient in and of itself. Gender relations, after all, are a composite of many different factors. I would argue that, in the Nyeshangte case, the egalitarian relations I observed during my first field stay in 1988–89 were more likely the result of underlying ideologies or "egalitarian hegemonies" (Ortner 1990a) than the result of a particular type of labor division, since the latter had already begun to change as a result of various capitalist transformations in the trade sector.

Ortner's notion of "gender hegemonies" is particularly useful because it highlights both the discursive aspects of ideologies (the symbolic constructs and representations of gender) and the "embeddedness" of these power relations in the institutions and activities of everyday life. "It is in the recognition of the wholeness of the process that the concept of 'hegemony' goes beyond 'ideology.' What is decisive is not only the conscious system of ideas and beliefs, but the whole lived social process as practically organized by specific and dominant meanings and values" (Williams 1977:108–9; quoted in Ortner 1990a:44). Based on Williams's interpretation of hegemony, Ortner's concept on the one hand hints at the totalizing effect of power—in defining reality and shaping practices—but on the other acknowledges that alternative, contradictory gender discourses and practices exist alongside the dominant or prevailing versions. As Ortner reminds us, "No society or culture is totally consistent" (45).

Keeping in mind both the pervasive qualities of hegemonic discourses, and the realization that inconsistencies always exist, I turn now to look at gender hegemonies in Nyeshang, leaving the question of contradictory ideologies until later.[21] Egalitarian hegemonies in Nyeshang stem from local Buddhist perspectives about the nature of "work," morality, and personhood, and are embedded in the beliefs, outlooks, and everyday activities of Nyeshangte individuals. At this point we need to take a short detour to consider a few points about Buddhist moral perspectives and how these inform indigenous notions of work.

Moral Perspectives

As Buddhists, Nyeshangte (depending on their individual level of understanding or commitment) share a common view about the nature of reality as intransigent and empty[22] and more or less follow a set of basic precepts similar to that outlined in the Middle Path, the doctrine expounded by Buddha that explains how to escape the cycle of endless rebirths and suffering in this world.[23] For the most part this involves two major tasks: avoiding sinful behavior (*pāp*; *sdig pa*) and bringing the mind under control. First, let us deal with the more obvious injunction: Abstention from sinful behavior includes serious transgressions (lying, stealing, and killing) as well as some cardinal vices (greed and laziness). Greed (*senti laba*), selfishness, or stinginess are especially singled out by Nyeshangte as negative qualities that undermine not only their community's ethos, but also run counter to the fundamental Buddhist goals—of negating "self-interest" and attachments to the false notion of an enduring Self. Preoccupation with one's self leads to material attachments and desires that in turn generate more suffering—given the Buddhist tenet that all things, conditions, and states are impermanent.[24] (Impermanence, or rather the inability to accept this universal condition, is one of the major causes of human suffering and unhappiness).

Laziness is also a serious flaw. Lazy people, Nyeshangte say, are those (in Kathmandu, for example) who sleep too late to join the throng of athletic devotees doing their spiritual gymnastics around the Swayambhu stūpa at five every morning. In contrast a virtuous person devotes much of her time to merit-making activities; reciting mantras and spinning prayer wheels, circumambulating stūpas and lighting butter lamps. In the Buddhist scheme of things, industriousness is needed to ensure a sufficient store of merit (*dge ba*), as merit is continually being depleted by the conditions of daily life that makes some sins unavoidable (Lichter and Epstein 1983:232).[25] Essentially, Buddhists avoid bad deeds (*a sebba laba*) by shunning as much as possible the tasks that involve the taking of life (butchering or plowing) or tasks that are inherently polluting (blacksmithing), and by being aware not only of the consequences of their actions (*las*) but also the consequences of their thoughts (*bsam pa*).

Controlling the mind (*sems*), then, is the second factor that needs to be considered, one that is essential to the Buddhist enterprise of avoiding grasping or clinging to sensory or material objects. A mind that is out of control is a state Nyeshangte often describe as a "whirring and spinning" of endless images, sensations, and thoughts. Although this in itself may be relatively harmless, sort of like revving the engine while it's in neutral, it doesn't get you anywhere—and sticking to the Buddhist path involves not only right action but also right intent and right mindfulness. As Lichter and

Epstein point out, "The karmic values of an act depends upon the actor's intention (bsam pa)." In other circumstances, however, the consequences of an out-of-control mind may be more serious. Nyeshangte explain that this lack of mindfulness or self-control, if coupled with greediness, may lead some people to inadvertently become witches (*mang*): men and women through their uncontrollable envy may cause illness or misfortune to strike their victims.[26] Lack of mindfulness, clarity, or self-awareness may also be brought about by states of pollution that vary in their intensity or duration. Anger, fighting, and violence, as well as excessive drinking or eating, may bring on temporary dullness, while individuals who are *lāṭa* (retarded, deaf, or mute) are afflicted with a more serious and permanent state of pollution (*sgrib*). In contrast to these less desirable qualities, Nyeshangte say, a good person is one who develops compassion and wisdom in equal measure, one who is generous, kind, selfless, or "good-hearted" (*sems sebba*).

As Buddhists, some knowledgeable Nyeshangte may strive for the ultimate goal of enlightenment (Nirvana or Bodhisattvahood), whereas others less sophisticated in their understanding of liturgical doctrines may set their sights somewhat lower: striving for rebirth in one of the heavens or merely for a better human rebirth, perhaps as a religious specialist or lama; still others simply hope to avoid rebirth as an animal or, worse yet, a denizen in one of the Buddhist hells. Like their Buddhist counterparts elsewhere, Nyeshangte, then, are naturally concerned with karma (*las*), merit (*dge ba*), and sin (*digs pa*), which determine one's fate in the next lifetime.

Good Works, Bad Works

I attended several merit-making marathons (three-day retreats known as *Smyung nas*) and noticed that women greatly outnumbered men at all these events, an observation that was confirmed by the head lama. He pointed out that at Nyeshang Kurti dgon pa, about a hundred people were in attendance and seventy to eighty of them were women. Curious what the reason might be, I asked the lama: Do women need to earn more merit than men? Do they attend these retreats to attain a higher rebirth as a male? Similar explanations have been used to explain Thai women's greater preoccupation with merit-making (see, for example, Kirsch 1983), and perhaps some Nyeshangte shared the same Buddhist outlook about the natural state or karmic condition of women (as being "low born").

Lama Yeshe responded, "No, there are always more women at the dgon pa because men are too involved in business, always thinking of money.

Women, if they lead good lives, can reach enlightenment, no different than men. Either man or woman can get a good birth *or* a bad one."

According to the local rationale, women are identified with life-giving and religious works (mani), whereas men, during their early and middle adult years, are associated with life-taking in their customary roles as hunters and "warrior-traders."[27] The link between femaleness and spirituality has been reinforced in recent years, as men have come to specialize in full-time trade. Lama Yeshe's comment also reflects the ambivalence many elderly Nyeshangte men and women feel toward current trade practices and black-market activities, where to be a successful "big" trader, one must often break a few (Buddhist) rules. For this reason, many men at the age of retirement dedicate their remaining years to religious works, hoping to gain enough merit to cancel the sins of a lifetime of "bad works" (*a sebba laba*).

Another elderly man, who spent more than three years at a retreat dgon pa for laypeople explained:

> Women do farm work and sometimes that brings small sins because the insects and worms are killed. So women work for two or three days, then go to the dgon pa and pray. They do like that and wipe away sins. But farming is the good life, not so bad. The boys [men] they do business, they lie and steal. Stealing is worse, more sinful than farming.

This man retired from commerce and left his wife and adult children in Kathmandu in order to study with a local lama in the valley. His views were shared by many informants of both sexes, since men and women as Buddhists face similar problems; karma (las) in this case is gender blind.

Here, a few comments about the notions of "works" (*las ka*), good or bad, may be relevant. My insight into these indigenous perceptions about the gender-based work identities came about in a rather indirect fashion. When I asked, "What type of work (*kām*) do most women dislike or prefer not to do?" the question brought uniform, but totally unexpected responses. For many Nyeshangte, the meaning of "work" had little reference to our own notions of chores or livelihood, but rather included all sorts of activities that could have a karmic impact, as Namgyal's explanation reveals:

> What is it that women are not liking to do? What [kind of] works? Is that it? [OK]. First of all, I tell you about eating [*khāncha*] habits.[28] In Nyeshang, mostly women do not smoke and do not drink alcohol. Some, a few, not many, but some of them do smoke and drink. Such

women are seen to be very bad, even by the [individual] women themselves.

Many male and female informants pointed out that Nyeshangte women's innate "goodness" and their avoidance of "bad works" like smoking and drinking distinguish them from women of other ethnic groups from the middle hills who smoke openly in public, as well as from their own men who drink quite heavily. However, modesty and a reluctance to judge the karmic status of others may lead some women to discuss only the "bad deeds" or demerits inherent in their own work—farming, for example—and refrain from elaborating the sins involved in doing business or in drinking.

The Buddhist moral perspective outlined above has hegemonic status in Nyeshang, and has consequences not only for valuations of work but also for valuations of people. As such, it has direct bearing on issues of power and agency (topics I examine in later chapters), and on gender relations. In fact, I would argue that this Buddhist hegemony is largely responsible for the egalitarian gender configurations that are present in Nyeshang (and in Kathmandu). The resiliency of Nyeshangte gender practices and their link to this prevailing Buddhist ideology or hegemony will become clearer when we consider a few specific examples.

Contemporary Gender Practices

I turn now to my observations of Nyeshangte households and draw freely on case studies and interviews with rural and urban women and men. I should point out that although in recent years the organization of work has become more sharply divided along gender lines, there still seems to be an underlying cultural disposition that favors a loosely defined division of labor. The attitudes of my rural informants—male and female, young and old—toward work are rather pragmatic: if something needs to be done, men or women seem equally capable and willing to do it.

In *Tsuri, a small Nyeshangte village located in the lower Marsyandi valley, I watched Kalu, a man in his late thirties, taking care of his month-old daughter. When the baby awoke, Kalu picked her up from her bed—a medium-sized cardboard box packed with cloth remnants and crumpled towels—and held the naked baby aloft, waiting patiently for her to eliminate before wiping her bottom and placing her back in her bed. Though she was his fourth-born child (and third daughter), Kalu seemed quite taken with the baby, rocking her gently and talking softly while she lay across his lap. Kalu also prepared dinner for his family and took some food to his wife, who was in bed. Chongdu had fallen sick after the baby's birth and had not yet recovered.

It is not considered inappropriate for men to do these domestic chores if women are otherwise occupied, ill, or absent, though this attitude may be changing among some of the younger generation of city-bred boys for whom "housework" has become synonymous with *ketīko kām*, or "girls' work."[29] However, this outlook is fairly circumscribed and was not characteristic of most Nyeshangte individuals in their mid- or late adulthood. I also found it interesting that two of the city boys who talked about "housework" as "girls' work" offered to cook, tend the fire, and haul water when they stayed in the village.

Plowing, slaughtering, and hunting animals, however, are three activities that all women and all male religious specialists (lamas) are forbidden to perform. In fact, these days, most Nyeshangte men also avoid slaughtering domestic animals and prefer to employ untouchable service castes to do this work. I should point out, however, that until the late 1970s, when animal products—deer musk and bear organs—were still important trade items, Nyeshangte males routinely hunted game in the homeland and in the Assam hills of Northeast India. In contrast, women and young girls did not hunt; they collected wild plants, bark, and various herbs that were used as trade items.[30]

Plowing is considered a sinful activity because it "brings pain" to draught animals and, many informants add, because it kills insects and worms in the soil. I was told by my Sherpa assistant, Palsang, that there was even a law barring women (Hindu or Buddhist) from this task. Of course, this restriction also effectively curtails the autonomy of single or widowed women who would have to rely on the good-will of male relatives or hire male laborers to plow. I know of only two cases where women disregarded cultural conventions and broke the law, risking fines and possible imprisonment. Palsang, who is from Solu, told me about a young widow from his village who used to dress in men's clothing whenever she plowed her fields. The Sherpa villagers disregarded her behavior, but a visiting government worker reported the woman to district officials, and she was subsequently fined. The other case was brought to my attention while Palsang and I were conducting a household survey in one of the smaller Nyeshang villages. The village headman, a genial fellow in his early fifties, painstakingly enumerated a wealth of details about each and every household in the village. During this lengthy recital, the headman mentioned an unmarried 35-year-old woman who lived alone in her parents' house and worked her family's land. The rest of the family had settled permanently in Kathmandu and had more or less abandoned the rural property. When I asked how this woman could manage alone, the headman chuckled and said, "Well, she just puts on boy's clothes, then she plows."

Although there may be strong cultural restrictions against particular kinds of activities, there seems to be a great tolerance in Nyeshang toward wayward behavior and individual eccentricities, as well as a sense that people should not interfere unnecessarily in the lives of others. This live-and-let-live attitude is justified in two ways: in a Buddhist social order, some comfort may be derived from the knowledge that an individual's actions will in due course bring their own just rewards or punishment; second, someone who meddles unnecessarily in the personal affairs of another, or complains about some petty transgression, may be harshly criticized for being disagreeable and for disturbing village social relations.

Work roles and daily tasks are determined in large measure by individual preferences and aptitudes, rather than by cultural prescriptions, and are balanced with the "communal needs" of the household.[31] As the case described below demonstrates, personality rather than gender may determine whether an individual engages in itinerant trade in foreign countries or adopts a more settled life as a farmer in the valley.

In a household with no males to take on the role of a professional year-round trader, the job inevitably falls to Mindu, the eldest of five daughters, who seems to have many of the qualities necessary to be a successful trader: she is outgoing, confident, assertive, willing to take risks, and enjoys "adventures." The 24-year-old trader shuttles back and forth between Kathmandu and Bangkok importing the usual variety of consumer goods, and gives about half her income to her family. She is unmarried and always jokes that her husband is dead when asked about her marital status. She has no intention of marrying and enjoys her itinerant life, occasionally returning to the village to visit family and friends. For whatever reason, her 46-year-old father prefers to remain year-round in the village with his wife and look after the fields and livestock.

Mingku, 18, the second-born daughter, can often be found at the high pasture and herding settlement three hours from Tumje, tending the family's large herd of goats and sheep. She explained that she doesn't mind the solitude that comes with her job, and welcomes the escape from the monotonous routine of farm work. The two youngest daughters, aged 7 and 9, attended school for two years, then dropped out because their labor was needed in the fields. The middle daughter, Tsering, who is 15, wished to become a nun and just completed a three-year training course at a monastery in the valley.

This example also demonstrates that to some extent the varying choices, opportunities, and constraints that an individual faces may be influenced by birth order among the sibling group rather than by gender.

Buddhist Values, Sociality, and Personhood

Nyeshangte may be extremely tolerant of personality quirks or idiosyncrasies, but this is balanced by an emphasis on social responsibility. Adults between the ages of 20 and 50 are expected to take an active role in village social life, and obligations (for men) include political service. For both sexes, duties include sponsorship of village rituals and donating labor and food for various village projects and to the dgon pa.

Both male and female children are raised in a social environment that values cooperation, nurturing, and kindness, qualities that are best exemplified by parental love. Frequently, men (and women) are seen comforting, holding, and playing with infants and small children unrelated to them. At Maya's house in Kathmandu I watched a middle-aged man play with her sister's 14-month-old toddler. I later asked who the relative was and where he lived, and Maya expressed surprise, "But he is no relative. He has come to ask Uncle (the lama) for help. You see his father has died in the city, and Uncle will delay his trip [to India] now for this funeral."

Attitudes such as sharing and cooperation are instilled at a very young age and are reflected in numerous circumstances of everyday life. Young children save candy to share with playmates, and city youths often spend their trade profits entertaining friends in restaurants.[32] In many rural homes I have seen young men (and women) who were *not* household members help with various chores without being asked. Village boys who stopped by to visit my landlady's daughter joined the women who were busy with food preparation, helping to chop meat and peel potatoes. My research assistants, youths from Kathmandu, also helped serve meals when paying guests were staying at the lodge. (This was done out of compassion, since Ama was not accustomed to cooking for many people, her teenage daughter was totally inept in the kitchen, and trekkers often had to wait a few hours for a meal.)

Although children are indulged by most adults and raised rather permissively, at the same time they are expected to show respect and defer to elders.[33] As individual men and women move through various stages in the life cycle, their social status, measured in terms of authority and esteem, generally increases. Married householders who are middle-aged and active in village affairs have the most power to make decisions that affect others. However, when they reach their late fifties or early sixties, men and women are expected to devote their energies to religious pursuits. Although they are not as active in community affairs, retired individuals are still held in high regard and often sought after for advice.

Whether in the realm of work or other social interactions, Nyeshangte men and women generally treat one another with consideration. This prevailing ethic in Nyeshang, which values similar qualities in men and women and accords individuals freedom to pursue their own ends, is characteristic of other small-scale societies that researchers have described as possessing relatively egalitarian gender relations.[34]

CHAPTER THREE

Foot-Loose and Duty-Free

Many years back Nyangkhu had a bad harvest. Nothing had grown and there was a famine. So the people of Nyangkhu village started a business, selling jaṅgal medicines from Nepal to India and Burma. At that time they didn't have passports, so they would cross the borders illegally at night. But after some time, the government of Nepal came to know that Nyeshang was a very dry, barren place. So they granted our appeals [for trade and travel rights] and issued passports to every Nyeshangte who requested one. Since then, most of us have acquired a passport, and for a long time now, we have been traveling all around.

—Dolma Sangmo

NYESHANGTE CULTURAL IDENTITY is inextricably tied to their history as itinerant traders, which in turn leads us back to questions of power and privilege, and their peculiar relations with the Nepalese state. In many ways Nyeshangte identity was defined, fabricated if you will, against this backdrop of trade—and here it would seem that the motor of history, the unseen hand, clearly derives from an external source. But this history is also one of negotiation, of mutual construction. The residents of the Nyeshang valley also played a role in delineating, and then maintaining, their social boundaries—in an effort to exclude others and safeguard their trading rights, and in an attempt to imagine a "community" where none previously existed. But that is the subject of another story.

In this chapter I touch only briefly on a few aspects of this link between ethnicity and state policies. My aim, rather, is to situate the Nyeshangte community in a wider ethnographic context by discussing their mercantile networks in northern India and Southeast Asia. The history and development of Nyeshangte itinerant trade are presented in some detail, so that the extent of women's involvement will be revealed—a topic that has been neglected in the existing literature on Nyeshang.[1] As in the previous chapter I rely on a variety of sources: trade histories collected from elderly villagers, conversations with middle-aged women and men about their parents' and grandparents' lives, as well as descriptive travel accounts written by mountaineers and researchers who visited the district in the 1950s and early 1960s. In addition, Nepalese government documents concerning Nyeshangte trade privileges and tax obligations helped me frame the overall chronology and provided me with supplementary information about local economic conditions in the Nyeshang valley.[2]

Nyeshangte Trade and the Nepalese State

Before turning to a survey of women's trade networks during the 1900s, a few comments about Nyeshang and the role of the state may be in order. Two main factors set Nyeshangte apart from other Himalayan trading communities: geography and a long history of special trading dispensations from the central Nepalese government.

With regard to geography, the Nyeshang valley is not strategically situated along a major river valley or trade route that connects the Tibetan Plateau with the middle hills of Nepal. As a result Nyeshangte played a minor role in the trans-Himalayan salt-wool-grain trade.[3] Most of this commerce passed along the Kali Gandaki valley to the west of Nyeshang, where it was controlled by local Thakali communities. A secondary route, which lay along the Dudh River south of Nyeshang, was controlled by Gurung factions.

Although geographical factors may have limited Nyeshangte participation in the salt-grain trade, government control was the ultimate deciding factor. The central Nepalese government rigidly controlled trade routes and privileges throughout most of the country. The state parceled out trade zones to specific minority groups as a way of gaining their allegiance and curtailing their power. There were many restrictions governing access to particular sections of a trade route, as well as limits on the quantity and type of goods that could be exchanged. This government control effectively divided (or actually created) various communities (and "ethnicities") within the region and, subsequently, minimized the threat that these Tibetan Buddhist border populations had once posed for the central Hindu state.[4]

Although Nyeshangte enjoyed relative autonomy from the central government, documents dating to the late eighteenth century indicate that valley residents regularly paid a nominal tributary tax. In exchange for their allegiance to the Hindu state, Nyeshangte were granted duty-free privileges and passports that enabled them to travel to India and, subsequently, to Southeast Asia. The practice of granting trade concessions, land rights, and special rights to particular groups was a strategic way for the central government to exert political influence in peripheral areas where the state had only nominal control. In this respect Nyeshang was not unique: other groups benefited from government grants. However, until recently, Nyeshangte were the only group in Nepal to be granted international trading rights.

The earliest documentary evidence dates to the 1780s, when the Gorkha king, Rana Bahadur Shah, granted Nyeshang residents an exemption from customs duties and gave them permission to trade in Nepal and India. These royal grants were known as *lāl mohar* in reference to the red seals affixed on official documents. In later *lāl* mohar, the precedent for renewing Nyeshangte trade rights was justified on the basis of "tradition"—that is, on the already established "tradition of their forefathers" to engage in duty-free trade. There is also some evidence that the Gorkha king, Rana Bahadur Shah, acknowledged these "customary rights" because they had been granted by an earlier king of Lamjung (cf. Gurung 1977a:233). (The Lamjung king was subsequently defeated by Gorkha forces in the late eighteenth century.)

Two oral traditions suggest that Nyeshangte may have obtained trade rights from kings who reigned before the Gorkha conquest. One account explains that Nyeshangte received these dispensations from the Lamjung king after they had done an exceptional job building a fortress for him at Gaon Shahar (Gurung 1980:226). Although this explanation was widely accepted in Gaon Shahar, in Nyeshang it was given little credence. In contrast, I was told by several Nyeshangte elders that their ancestors originally had been granted these rights because a lama from their group had saved a king from an epidemic that had decimated the Kathmandu valley. According to this account, the lama prevented the king's death by retrieving one of his "escaped" souls. In order to restore the king's life force and find his lost soul, his shaman priests were indiscriminately cutting down "life trees," and presumably causing many other deaths in the Kathmandu valley.[5] But the lama from Nyeshang found the missing soul, restored the king to well-being, and stopped the epidemic as well. The king subsequently granted the lama and his people "many things"—including the right to cross Nepal's borders and to import and export goods without paying any tariffs—concessions that were continually offered by successive kings.

A remarkably similar legend from Helambu (an area north of Kathmandu) tells of a lama from Kyirong (Tibet) who was called by the Newar king in Kathmandu to end an epidemic in the Kathmandu valley. As a reward for his efforts, the lama was given land to build a hermitage (Clarke 1980:17). Clarke also suggests that this particular epidemic may have taken place in 1717, when nearly twenty thousand people reportedly died of disease in the Kathmandu valley (18).[6]

Historical facts aside, the Nyeshangte version of this account is interesting because of the emphasis it places on the healing and psychic powers of the lama. In contrast to the Lamjung version, which highlights the martial experience, skills, and knowledge that enabled Nyeshangte to build a top-notch fortress, the Nyeshangte account reflects the political astuteness of the narrators. It plays up the community's alliance with a powerful Kathmandu dynasty, rather than an inconsequential local king who was ultimately overthrown. Whether the Lamjung king or the Newar king of Kathmandu actually awarded Nyeshangte their original trading concessions, it seems they had been involved in regional trade for quite some time—specializing in medicinal plants and a variety of animal organs that were used for pharmaceutical purposes. They also had a widespread reputation as healers throughout central Nepal, and they sold their jangal medicines to tribal groups as far away as Assam (northeast India) and Bengal.

In later government documents, justification for renewing Nyeshangte privileges is made not only on the basis of tradition, but also on the grounds that the inclement conditions in the "land of snow" prevented valley residents from earning their living from agriculture—hence their reliance on trade and their need for tariff exemptions. However, several researchers have pointed out that the agricultural conditions in Nyeshang were really no different than in other Himalayan valleys (cf. Cooke 1985a:312–17; Gurung 1980:227). But the Nyeshangte were quite skilled in bargaining and their strategies usually involved pleading a case of extreme hardship and abject poverty. When they were faced with an increase in tariffs and local taxes in 1964, Nyeshangte submitted a document to the authorities in Kathmandu stating:

> We the inhabitants of seven villages in the Himalayan (Bhot) region, including Manang, have no lands, and depend on foreign trade for our livelihood.... Since we do not have any agricultural incomes, but depend on trade for our livelihood, we are unable to make the *sirto* (land tax) payment at 100 percent of the existing rate. Until, therefore, our lands are surveyed, and taxes assessed, we pray that we be allowed to pay the ... levies, and supply the prescribed goods as usual ..., and that the usual amount of expenses for our journey be paid to us. (Cooke 1985a:309–10)

Cooke explains that the taxes levied for Nyeshang and Nar (together) at 1962 exchange rates were only U.S.$236 per year, a total that was substantially lower than the amounts collected in other unproductive mountain districts. In addition to the annual tax payment, the Nyeshang community had to bring two pairs of *docha* (Tibetan-style boots), one musk deer, one musk pod, and two blue sheep skins to Kathmandu each year. This token tribute was clearly not a significant amount (1985a:310). The outcome of this particular exchange resulted in the government honoring the Nyeshangte petition. And, as far as I know, a land survey or tax assessment has never yet been carried out in the valley.

It seems fairly clear that government authority in Nyeshang was negligible. Cooke (1985a:313) points out that the unusually low taxes suggests that the government's interest in this payment consisted in the fact that it implied Nyeshang's recognition of Kathmandu as a sovereign power and not in its value as a revenue source. The unusual custom of reimbursing the Nyeshang leader for expenses he incurred in traveling in order to present payment to the government, as well as the more common practice of granting tax remissions to localities afflicted by hardship and of granting selective tax exemptions, support this interpretation (cf. Regmi 1978:63).

Indeed, a review of the documents dating back to the late eighteenth century indicates that Nyeshangte remained autonomous and were quite successful in having their demands met by the central government. A royal grant issued in 1824–25 by King Rajendra acknowledged Nyeshang's right to self-governance except in the case of major crimes. In later grants (1845, 1883, and 1905), their right to move freely throughout Nepal and across the Indian border without having to pay import or export taxes was also reaffirmed.[7]

The favorable relationship with the government continued relatively unchanged through much of the 1960s. Nepalese passports were issued to Nyeshangte in 1962, and they were among the first Nepalese citizens to receive them. In 1967 residents of Nyeshang were eligible to apply for an import license at the district center in Chame, which would permit individuals to bring in up to thirty thousand rupees worth of goods duty free each year, in addition to personal baggage allowances.[8] Cooke (1985a:79), in discussing the implications of this special privilege, writes:

> This distinguished Nyishang traders from other categories of Nepalese citizens such as government officials, students studying abroad, and the Gurkha soldiers with foreign posting who were able to obtain passports for international travel but fell under strict limitations of personal baggage allowances upon their return to Nepal. Goods in excess of the personal baggage allowance for these individuals were subject to confiscation.

However, the unique privileges that Nyeshangte had enjoyed for so long were gradually taken away. In 1973 King Birendra allowed *all residents* of Manang District (this includes Gyasumdo, Nyeshang, and Nar) to apply for import licenses that permitted individuals to bring in ten thousand rupees worth of goods. However, these items were no longer exempt from customs duties. Residents from Gyasumdo who claimed that they were now entitled to passports and import licenses, as a result of this new royal decree, were challenged by Nyeshangte, who saw these changes as encroachments on their customary rights. After 1975 all Nepalese citizens were able to apply for passports, but the majority were restricted to individual baggage allowances of up to a thousand rupees worth of goods annually.[9] Naturally, resentment against Nyeshangte increased because they were still entitled to bring in ten thousand rupees of duty-free merchandise. After 1977 the government did not renew their licenses and the privileges lapsed. Since then, Nyeshangte ostensibly operate under the same rules as other Nepalese passport-holders.

The curtailment of these special trade rights in 1977 also marked a change in the traditional relationship between Nyeshangte and the central government. Several events also took place during the late 1960s and mid-1970s that altered Nyeshang's long-standing independence. First, the central government was threatened by the political unrest that followed China's seizure of Tibet in 1959. The skirmishes in Tibet led to an influx of Khampa guerrillas along the border. Eventually, the Nepalese government was forced to intervene in order to regain control of Lo, Dolpo, Nyeshang, and

Nar. By 1975 the Khampa factions had been removed and the central government's authority into these peripheral areas was more firmly established. In Nyeshang the traditional clan-based village council was replaced by a national system of government.

Another incident that occurred during this period suggests that the state's concerns about the loyalty of its border populations were not unfounded. Apparently, Nyeshang residents came to possess a rather large arsenal of modern weapons: "more than a hundred automatic and semi-automatic rifles and about two hundred pistols" (Cooke 1985a:134). The state's excessively benign policy toward the Nyeshangte, in terms of generally leaving them alone, might have been based on fear (a fairly reasonable response given the group's predilection for collecting guns)—fear of a rather powerful minority group whose economic ties in Southeast Asia possibly included connections to "underworld" societies that operated in Hong Kong, Thailand, and Burma, groups that profited from smuggling rice, guns, and other contraband across international borders.

Following their voluntary cooperation with Kathmandu officials, Nyeshangte were gradually drawn in to the political and social life of Nepal. The valley was opened up to tourism for the first time in 1977, but apparently not without some mishaps. My Sherpa assistant's elder brother had the misfortune of accompanying one of the first organized treks into the area, and recalls sitting in his tent, surrounded by angry villagers waving rifles. The tourists had felt the natural curiosity of the "natives" to be overwhelming, and had withdrawn to the privacy of their tents, hiding behind zippered flaps to avoid the stares and giggles of the villagers. Offended and angry, some of the younger men rushed off to get whatever rifles had been "overlooked" during the government roundup and proceeded to evict the foreigners from their valley. The incident was resolved more or less peacefully, but many Sherpa guides have confessed to feeling a bit uneasy in Nyeshang, even today. Besides the incursion of tourists, government aid workers also entered the valley, and a few of their development projects—trail improvements and the building of schools—were quite appreciated.

Although Nyeshangte no longer possess a monopoly on trading rights, their history of nearly two hundred years of government-supported trade has given them enough of an edge to retain their preeminent position today as international traders in Nepal.

The following section presents an outline of Nyeshangte trading activities, with a particular focus on women's roles in trade. This information serves as a background for understanding how the reorganization of trade in the late 1960s, and the economic and social changes that followed, affected Nyeshangte gender relations.

Despite the bewildering profusion of trade goods, trade routes, and strategies, the pre-1960 phase can be summed up with a few generalizations. Initially, most Nyeshangte households migrated to the southern regions of Nepal and to towns near the Ganges River in northern India during the winter months from November to March. Family units, comprised of husbands, wives, and unmarried children, earned a living as itinerant hawkers selling medicinal herbs and animal and woolen commodities that had been collected or processed in Nyeshang; others set up small shops and stalls near bazaars or displayed their goods by the side of the road.

Although the details of trade—destinations, networks, and products— varied through the decades, the basic organizational features remained the same: male and female traders operated in small kin-based groups. Capital resources and trade goods were often pooled and the profits evenly divided among partners. Young Nyeshangte who needed a starting fund usually received small amounts of cash from parents and close relatives. Sometimes several small groups—comprised of relatives, members of nuclear families, or close friends—banded together for safety and companionship, especially if they were traveling to distant markets. But the larger, corporate trade groups, which characterize Nyeshangte trade today, were uncommon before the 1960s.

Female Migrants

Although the division of labor was overlapping during this earlier period, not all households remained together for the entire winter. Among the households that migrated during the winter, a variety of patterns may be discerned. Women migrants often established semipermanent residences near small towns and led more settled lives than their male counterparts (cf. Schuler 1977). In many instances women regularly returned to their winter quarters in the southern regions of Nepal and in northeastern India year after year. From these bases, adult women engaged in petty trade in nearby bazaars or earned their living selling alcohol to Indian and Tibetan travelers, merchants, Gurkha soldiers, and local Hindu residents. Other women ran small shops while their husbands left for markets in the Himachal Pradesh, Bihar, and Assam regions of northern India. Male absences varied from a few days to several months, as some men ventured even further afield, to towns and villages scattered across Burma and Malaysia.

Some women, after settling their families into temporary winter quarters, left their young children under the care of a Nyeshangte neighbor—usually an elderly relative—and formed trading groups with other female friends and relatives. These small groups made several trips to bazaars in the Nepal Terai, where they purchased household staples. Other women ventured across the border, caught the train at Raxaul or Nautanwa, and headed for small towns scattered over the Ganges Plain where they also purchased cloth and oil. Some of these goods were resold in the middle hills of Nepal; the remainder were kept for personal use and carried to Nyeshang. Over the course of the winter, some women made three or four trips carrying domestic supplies and trade goods from the lowlands to Nyeshang. These women often shared living costs, traveling expenses, and child care responsibilities with their female companions.

Household members generally would return together to Nyeshang for the start of the agricultural season in April. Although in some instances, male traders who traveled farther abroad would return separately at a later date. However, most villagers were forced to return before the start of the monsoon in June or else wait until the river levels subsided and bridges were repaired in September, since the trail to Nyeshang was generally impassable during the summer months.[10]

In sum, patterns of seasonal migration varied substantially among Nyeshangte households during this sixty-year period. Specific migration patterns also varied slightly from village to village depending on traders' previous experiences in particular regions. Stories of success or losses would circulate among relatives and close friends who usually lived in the same village. Strategies for the following season were discussed by the entire family, and elders shared their knowledge with adolescent boys and girls, who often took up trading at age 12 or 13 (with one or both parents). New opportunities and new markets were discovered by individual entrepreneurs, who worked alone and were willing to undertake great risks. In this manner Nyeshangte trading networks gradually extended to Burma, Thailand, and, for a brief period (during the Vietnam War), to Laos, Cambodia, and Vietnam.

Women's involvement in trade at this time is evident from oral histories and from brief references found in travelers' accounts. Some of these narratives comment on Nyeshangte's apparent worldliness and their surprising fluency in Hindi, a north Indian language.[11] Even today, when Nepalese institutions and media have penetrated the Nyeshang valley, and much of the population spends several months each year in Kathmandu, some of the village women have minimal fluency in Nepali—a fact that reflects women's limited involvement in business transactions and their reduced roles in the market economies of contemporary Nepalese urban centers. Yet many of these women's mothers and grandmothers, who in the past regularly traveled to India on trading expeditions, were competent Hindi speakers. Their linguistic talents no doubt developed as a result of these repeated excursions into northern India, where many of them earned a living as merchants, selling goods at urban markets, at religious fairs (*melā*), and at Gurkha army posts.[12]

One particularly amusing (but rather unflattering) account of Nyeshangte women and their foreign language skills was written by Tilman (1952), a British mountain climber who led an expedition through Nyeshang in May 1950. He remarked as follows:

> In the remote Himalaya it is rare to find a man who speaks this lingua franca of the plains, rarer still a woman, who, if she stays at home and works hard as hill women must, has neither the time nor opportunity for language. In fact one would suspect a woman who did speak Hindustani of have made a business of entertaining travelers, and of being for business purposes not a very sturdy moralist. However, the people of this Pisang suburb [a Nyeshang village] seemed so dirty and ignorant that the women might once be acquitted of either improvement or impropriety. (136–37)

Tilman, who apparently had a wretched time in the valley, complained that Nyeshangte refused to sell his party any food, nor were they willing to work as porters for his expedition.[13] He speculated that their India trade must have satisfied all their cash needs, since Nyeshangte (unlike other Nepalese peasants) were not interested in selling their labor or their food.

Having presented a general overview of Nyeshangte migration and trade patterns, I now turn to a more detailed discussion of the type of goods, networks, and the specific developments that occurred during various phases of this international trade.

Trade in the Early 1900s to 1920s

In general, most of the western accounts that contain specific references to Nyeshangte trade were written after the 1950s, when Nepal (re)opened its borders to foreign visitors. As a result these sources do not shed much light on the early stages of Nyeshangte trade in India. Overall, there was little documentation of the Nepal-India trade until 1875, when British officials began to keep records of the trade passing through Bihar and Bengal into Nepal; however, British documents and Nepalese sources do reveal that Jang Bahadur Shah, the Nepalese ruler, imposed severe customs and travel restrictions on his citizens, which essentially prevented most Nepalese traders from crossing into India (Adhikari 1975).[14] Consequently, Nyeshangte trade during this early period probably centered on domestic markets, and involved the barter exchange of local items and subsistence goods that were produced in neighboring districts (Nar, Lo, Lamjung), as well as commodities from different ecozones—southern Tibet and the Terai region of Nepal. However, it seems that by 1884 some Nepalese merchants, including Nyeshangte, were granted special tax exemptions and were permitted to travel freely across the border to India (Cooke 1985b:74).

Major trade routes during this period passed through the Nepalese customs post at Thori, and from there Nyeshangte traveled on foot to various markets and towns in north central India. The expansion of the British rail system in northern India during the early 1900s made travel easier, and by the 1920s some Nyeshangte traders had visited Delhi, and a few had even traveled to Kashmir and Himachal Pradesh (van Spengen 1987:177). Most of the case studies suggest, however, that Nyeshangte women and men peddled their goods in Bihar and in towns north of the Ganges River.

The trade items during this early period included cottage industry goods such as woolen blankets and scarves, plants used for medicine and incense, and animal products like musk, goat skins, and yak tails. These items were sold for cash or bartered for rice, oil, and other household essentials. In addition, traders purchased a large variety of Indian manufactured wares, as well as cloth and jewelry, for resale to Nepalese customers and shopkeepers in the Terai and middle hills. During the early 1900s, as Nepal gradually shifted from a subsistence to a cash-based economy, the demand for manufactured products in Nepal continually increased, and Nyeshangte found their trade levels and profits rising. Wholesale traders also sold supplies to Newar merchants, who opened many small retail shops in the expanding market towns of central Nepal.[15]

Several women have given me detailed accounts of their travels to India. One of the villagers, who at nearly 90 years of age was the oldest member of the community, told me she married at age 20, so these trips must have occurred in around 1915 to 1920. (A brief and edited version of her life history was presented in chapter 2.) In the early stages of trade development, profits were small, and much of the trade involved barter exchanges for food grains like rice and corn. Other transactions generally involved small amounts of cash, and usually not much capital was left over for reinvestment. Some women and children earned additional cash by transporting various goods from the Nepal border to shopkeepers in the middle hills.[16] But by the 1950s, all but the poorest Nyeshangte seemed reluctant to sell their labor.

As itinerant peddlers, Nyeshangte avoided most of the overhead costs of lodging and rent for small shops. In order to minimize expenses, many women and men slept outdoors and moved from town to town, selling their "mountain" products to pilgrims at religious fairs.[17] Indian customers were captivated by the mystique and reputed healing skills of these Himalayan dwellers and were drawn to their exotic wares: blue sheep and leopard skins, tiger claws, fragrant herbs, deer musk, and rock salt from the Tibetan plateau.

Mary Helms (1993), in an insightful look at the symbolism and ideology that surrounds long-distance trade and goods from faraway places, brings up several points that are relevant here. Helms explains that in many non-western cosmologies, concepts like "geographical distance" are not neutral, but tend to be evaluated in moral terms—as more powerful, more dangerous, or less desirable, less worthy—comparatively speaking, to the homeland (3). Similarly, Helms explains that items brought from distant places are often imbued with the characteristics or qualities inherent in that land. Since these properties are inalienable from the material goods, the exchange or transfer of these items, in effect, brings the particular qualities, power, or mystique from that distant place to the home society (96). The imagery of the Himalaya and Tibet has always been "symbolically charged with meaning," to borrow one of Helms's own phrases, and some of this mystique attached itself to Nyeshangte traders and to their merchandise, wherever they traveled.

Trade in the 1930s and 1940s

Subsequently, in the late 1920s, many Nyeshangte began to shift their business ventures to northeast India. During this period the hill stations and tea plantations near Darjeeling, Kalimpong, and Shillong were expanding, and the large influx of Nepalese migrant laborers into the eastern hill regions provided the traders with many clients (Caplan 1970).[18] Traders walked the trail along the Marsyandi River and reached the Indian border in two weeks. Some women and men first traveled to pilgrimage sites at Saranath

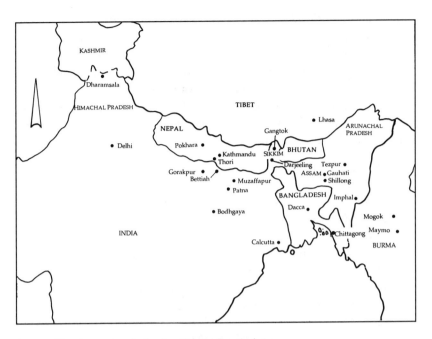

Map 2. Nyeshangte trade destinations in South Asia.

and Bodhgaya, combining itinerant trade with merit-making activities, and then headed for Calcutta and Assam.[19] Others, after crossing the Nepalese border at Thori, traveled by train to Calcutta, later making their way north to Assam. In Calcutta, valerian, gentian, musk, and animal skins were sold, and the earnings were used to purchase turquoise and coral beads, *nakalī* (imitation) gem stones, and inexpensive rings.[20] This inventory of jewelry, along with a variety of manufactured commodities, were subsequently sold to Nepalese migrants, Gurkha soldiers, and indigenous "tribals" in Assam, Arunachal Pradesh (northeast India), and Sikkim. Some traders also brought knives (*khukurī*) and articles of clothing from Nepal to sell to other Nepalese migrants in India.

In Assam, many Nyeshangte women and men also sold homemade items—blankets, rope, clothing made from yak and goat wool, boots—and the usual stock of "forest" products that were collected in Nyeshang including wild garlic, bear bile, birch paper, as well as yak tails and live mastiff puppies.[21] Handicrafts from the Naga hills, like arrows and Assamese homespun cloth, were also purchased by Nyeshangte and later sold in Calcutta and Nepal (van Spengen 1987:183). On the return leg, most traders purchased cotton cloth and clothing in Calcutta and then returned to Nepal, where they used some of their earnings to purchase rice for their families.

Profits from the Assam-Calcutta trade steadily increased and several families took up long-term residence in Shillong in the late 1930s and 1940s. One of my informants, a successful businessman who built a "middle-sized" house in Kathmandu (in the early 1980s) for 1.5 million rupees (about u.s.$60,000) and owns additional property in Nyeshang, told me about his family's experiences in Assam:

> Mother used to live in Shillong, India. At that time [about 1941] I was just 6 years old. There were many families staying in Shillong, some just for the winter, but some like us staying for many years. We stayed in a rented house and my parents did a small business in Shillong and Calcutta. Mother sometimes went to Calcutta, but mostly Father did. He brought back used clothes, some rings and fake stones, cloth and sewing things: needles, thread, buttons, and dyes. We sold them in our small shop, and Father did business in other places too—in Tezpur, Cooch Behar in Imphal and Gauhati, and sometimes in Bhutan. Nyeshangte people also made medicine and some became OK [well-off] from this work. Mother too sold medicine, some from plants carried from Nyeshang, and others that we found [locally].
>
> After some time, Father was not liking this work, so he went to Nyeshang to see how things were. After staying with Mother for four years, I did not like that place [Shillong], so I went back to Nyeshang too. In Nyeshang, we had lots of land and lots of yak.
>
> When I was 12 years of age, my parents sent me to Burma together with other friends. We did not have passports, so we entered Burma illegally, crossing the jungles of India. When they reached Burma, it was a few years after the Japan-Burma War [1947–48]. We reached Monywa and from there took a train to Mandalay; from there we went to a large Buddhist temple, which was similar to Bodhnath [in Kathmandu], but this temple was in Rangoon. We had been told by other Nyeshangte that once you go to the temple and are staying there, the police cannot arrest you. So we hid there. There were four other Nepalese there too. We inquired from other Nyeshangte there how to get a passport in Burma. The older men went to the concerned authorities and said that they had come to Burma from India to fight in the Japanese war. But after their army unit was defeated, they had fled to the jungles and stayed there many years. So they do not have passports because they stayed so long there. So they now are applying

for passports. But inquiries were made and many questions were asked. Only those who could give correct replies got passports. Only 20 percent in that group got the passports.

Trading in Burma during the 1930s and 1940s was considered a risky enterprise. The overland route through the mountainous jungles was not an easy one, and Nyeshangte men also had to contend with soldiers at the border check posts. After Rangoon fell in 1942 to invading Japanese forces, many Nyeshangte, as well as other Nepalese and Indians, lost their fortunes, and a few lost their lives on the hasty retreat back to India. Later, after the war was over, Nyeshangte returned to pursue the ruby and sapphire trade in northern Burma, but encountered groups of insurgents and rebel forces. During this two-decade interlude in Burma, several Nyeshangte were killed by armed robbers, and a few were shot as spies by the Burmese military. But despite the personal risks involved, the opportunities for making large profits attracted many Nyeshangte men.

They earned a living trading in gems, pearls, ivory, and silver, as well as selling staples like rice, dried fish, and basic household necessities. These domestic items were purchased in Rangoon and later sold in small towns and villages in central Burma, where a significant Nepalese immigrant population provided the traders with a stable market. Most of the men worked as itinerant peddlers, but a few ran shops that stocked food supplies, clothing, and other domestic wares. Remittances from several months of itinerant trade, ranging from two thousand to three thousand rupees (U.S.$80–$120) were sent back to Nepal. Several men told me they had earned larger profits from selling black market rice. Some Nyeshangte merchants also operated as moneylenders and their clients included Nepalese, Indian, and Burmese nationals.[22] And a few men were also involved in smuggling gems across the Thai border. Gems acquired in Burma were later sold in urban markets in India, Malaysia, and Singapore, whereas coral and jade were sold primarily to Tibetans and Gurung in Nepal.

Because travel in Burma during the 1930s and 1940s was so difficult, very few Nyeshangte women ventured there. However, one man told me about the journey he had taken with his wife. The young, childless couple had made their way through Burma into Thailand and down the peninsula to Singapore, where they caught a steamer and eventually returned to Nepal via Calcutta.

Their trip, which lasted nearly three years, started in Calcutta, where they sold their customary supplies of musk, valerian, gentian, and incense, and purchased a wide variety of inexpensive jewelry and trinkets. From there they proceeded to Dacca, and subsequently made their way to Chittagong, where they crossed the Burmese border without travel papers. Once in Burma they made their way to Maymo, where a "cousin-brother" operated a dry goods store that sold a variety of provisions as well as handicrafts, clothing, and knives imported from Nepal.

During the year they spent in Burma, they traveled widely, visiting Buddhist shrines in the Rangoon area where they supported themselves by hawking glass bangles, imitation gem stones, and religious commodities like prayer wheels and rosary beads. Leaving Rangoon, after they had purchased a variety of domestic goods, they returned to their "base" at Maymo and made several trips to neighboring villages to peddle their merchandise, which also included black market rice from Thailand.[23] Before leaving Burma, they traveled north to Mogok to purchase rubies, and then crossed the Thai border near Chiang Mai where they sold some of their gems. From there they headed south to Bangkok and then made their way to Singapore, stopping in numerous towns along the Malay Peninsula where other Nepalese lived. Their Nepalese clients purchased batik cloth, watches, clothing, and "heirlooms" of dubious antiquity—including religious figurines and amulets—that the couple had picked up in Bangkok.

In Singapore, they purchased cameras, silk cloth, gold jewelry and watches, then returned to Calcutta and eventually to Nyeshang. During the course of this three-year trip, they not only had made a profit but had also managed to "buy" Burmese and Indian passports. These documents allowed them to move about freely in Southeast Asia and permitted them to return "legally" by ship, instead of by foot "overland."

Their success was typical of many Nyeshangte, who were able to take advantage of the community's far-flung networks of friends, relatives, and clients that also included Nepalese migrants and soldiers. These trading networks, which often center around the homes or stores of a few long-term migrants, provide Nyeshangte individuals who are new to a particular area with valuable information—about merchandise and prices and ways to obtain travel documents and circumvent bureaucratic restrictions—a place to stay, and a "safety net" in case of trouble.

Although few women had ventured to Burma during the 1930s and 1940s, this began to change during the following decade, when increasing numbers of women, and sometimes entire families, began to travel by ship to Rangoon and to other ports in Southeast Asia.

1950s to Early 1960s: Calcutta to Southeast Asia

During the 1950s trade practices became increasingly varied. Growing numbers of Nyeshangte women and men took up winter residence in Calcutta, where they established a niche for themselves at the local markets and bazaars. Several families would first travel to Assam in order to sell their inventory of medicinal herbs and animal products and to acquire enough cash to buy supplies. This merchandise was sold in Kathmandu and other towns in Nepal where there was a growing demand for modern consumer goods.

Other traders expanded their customary inventory of Nepalese, Burmese, and Assamese handicrafts and jewelry to include Tibetan artifacts. The political disturbances in Tibet had caused an exodus of Tibetan refugees who sold or traded family heirlooms in bazaars in Kalimpong, Dharamsala, and Gangtok. Several Nyeshangte women and men focused exclusively on this trade, initially selling Tibetan items in Calcutta; subsequently, with the expansion of the tourist and GI market during the 1960s, these "relics" were also sold to large numbers of westerners in Kathmandu, Bangkok, and Chiang Mai.

Some households still retained their semipermanent winter base in Shillong, and a few of their family members made periodic trips to Calcutta. Several women told me they accompanied their parents or husbands on these trade ventures. Other women, traveling with friends and relatives, went directly from Nepal to Calcutta where they purchased household goods like axes, gas lanterns, clothing and shoes, as well as coral and jade. They returned to Nepal where they sold these items in Pokhara and Terai markets and, with the cash earned, purchased oil, rice, tea, and sugar for domestic use.

Overall, though, the importance of Shillong as a major Nyeshangte trade center had declined by the mid-1950s, for a number of reasons: first, the sale of used clothing and homemade herbal remedies decreased somewhat since hill tribals and other residents in Assam preferred to buy commercially produced "western" medicines and new clothing; second, movement through areas of Assam and Arunachal Pradesh became more difficult after the Indian government imposed travel restrictions in the tribal areas. More important, perhaps, new opportunities abounded in Calcutta and many Nyeshangte were quick to take advantage of these developments.

In Calcutta, Nyeshangte were able to "purchase" Indian passports that enabled them to travel by boat to other ports in Southeast Asia, including Rangoon, Penang, and Singapore. With travel papers and cash reserves, many traders could afford to purchase tickets on steamships to Burma, and the hardships of overland travel were avoided. Burma, Thailand, and Malaysia became important centers for Nyeshangte activities, and many Nyeshangte traders continued to sell Burmese gems as itinerant hawkers in Bangkok, Singapore, and the Malay Peninsula. In fact Burma retained its importance as a major source of gems until the mid-1960s, when the new military socialist government of General Ne Win took control of foreign trade and forced all traders (except Burmese nationals) to leave the country. Apparently, a few Nyeshangte men managed to stay on since they had Burmese passports. I was told that one of these men married a Burmese woman and never returned to Nyeshang, though the other men eventually did.

In the mid-1950s several Nyeshangte men began to visit Chiang Mai where they were involved in the illicit Thai-Burma border trade centering on opium, guns, and rubies (cf. van Spengen 1987). As this border trade continued to expand through the 1960s, it drew increasing numbers of Nyeshangte. Some individuals (mostly males) were involved in black market sales, whereas others opened up retail shops that sold "fancy" goods: clothing, cosmetics, perfumes, and small appliances. Many women and men made regular visits to hill tribes living in the vicinity, where they sold a variety of basic goods including cheap clothing, shoes, cotton cloth, and plastic housewares. Some families established long-term residences in Chiang Mai, and at least two that I know owned shops specializing in "tourist" merchandise—handicrafts, jewelry, and T-shirts—until just a few years ago when the shops were sold. A few Nyeshangte women and men acquired Thai citizenship, which enabled them to purchase property. Nyeshangte holdings included at least three shops in Chiang Mai, a hotel in Bangkok, and private homes in both these locations.

With the decline of Assam as a major winter settlement, increasing numbers of Nyeshangte men, women, and children migrated to Singapore and the Malay Peninsula for the three- to four-month-long winter trading season. Musk, rhinoceros horns, bear bile, ivory, and jade were profitable items of trade and were sold largely to Chinese merchants. In addition, itinerant peddlers visited the numerous Gurkha cantonments and sold clothing, spices, dried fish, and kitchen supplies in villages and small towns throughout the peninsula. In Penang and Singapore, some traders set up sidewalk displays where they sold rings, bangles, and handicrafts brought from Nepal, India, and Burma. Cash earnings were reinvested in cameras, watches, and radios that were available at cheap prices in Singapore markets. These were sold primarily in India until 1958, when the Indian government began to impose restrictions on foreign imports (cf. Gurung

1977a). Western-style clothing, cotton and silk cloth, porcelain cups, large thermoses, and other housewares were resold in Calcutta, in Kathmandu, and in towns along the India-Nepal border, and many traders began to bring some of these luxury items to Nyeshang for personal use.

Sometimes entire families stayed abroad for a few years at a time. This became more common during the 1960s when, according to one informant, ten Nyeshangte families were living in Singapore and a few others had settled in villages throughout the peninsula. Among these long-term migrants, a familiar pattern emerged similar to what had occurred in Assam. Women, in general, tended to lead more stationary lives. They ran small shops that sold household supplies and clothing to Nepalese, Malay, and Chinese clients. In contrast, male family members traveled around the countryside by bus and train and making periodic excursions to cities like Penang, Singapore, or Bangkok to purchase additional merchandise.

In general, however, trade remained a seasonal activity that supplemented the rural economy in the Nyeshang valley, where most households maintained their primary residences. What distinguishes the organization of work during this "noncapitalist" period from the contemporary pattern that began to emerge during the 1970s is that the sexual division of labor was balanced. Both men and women were similarly involved in daily subsistence activities and the cottage industry production of trade goods. Long-distance trade in India and Southeast Asia was typically a family affair, where capital resources were pooled and profits divided among individual households or between small groups of friends and relatives.

The proliferation of formally organized corporate trading groups and the trends toward permanent urban migration and male specialization in year-round trade are changes associated with the reorganization of trade. But before turning to these recent developments, I would like to consider the significance of women's involvement in trade.

Women in Trade: Autonomy and Social Power

The results of women's economic agency, in the past as well as today, seem to be the same: women's commercial activities enhanced their overall position in the household and community. After all, the economic circumstances of female itinerant traders in the Ganges region did not differ greatly from those of their more sedentary counterparts who operated shops in Assam, nor for that matter from the circumstances of today's women who run lodges in Nyeshang or souvenir shops in Kathmandu.

Researchers have noted that women who earn a cash income, whether

4. A middle-aged woman takes care of her granddaughter.

they work for wages or sell homemade commodities and surplus produce, usually have more control over household decisions and strategic resources than women who work only in the subsistence sector, performing unpaid domestic or agricultural labor (cf. Acharya and Bennett 1983). The generation of cash income, rather than the overall contribution to the household subsistence economy, seems to be a decisive factor.

Through small-scale production—the making of liquor and trade items and the collection of forest produce—a certain degree of economic independence was within reach of most Nyeshangte women. The sale of cottage industry goods permitted some women to support themselves and their dependent children during the winter migratory period when their husbands traveled to distant markets. In general, Nyeshangte women were able to participate in trade and entrepreneurial activities on an equal basis with men, since the start-up capital was available to most women. They required only small amounts of grain to produce liquor, or wool to make blankets, and anyone could take the initiative to collect herbs in the forest. Other young women borrowed funds from relatives or pooled resources with trading friends; still others, depending on skill, luck, and initiative, amassed sufficient capital to invest in consumer or luxury goods that yielded higher profits.

Unmarried girls living with parents were also encouraged to engage in small-scale commerce. Although a portion of trade earnings might occasionally be turned over to parents, generally a young woman retained control of her own earnings.[24] Involvement in market activities also prompted some young women to delay their marriages until their mid- to late twenties, until they had established a more secure economic base. Women's ability to earn a living independently of family-owned land or herds also provided them with a sense of security, and an alternative if they wished to separate from their husbands or remain single and live apart from their natal families (cf. Molnar 1980). It fostered a "sense of individual identity" apart from the usual kin-based roles of daughter, wife, or mother (cf. Barnes 1990).

Owning personal property and having access to personal income also improved the social status and standing of young women (and men) in the community. Individuals who were successful in trade were admired and respected by other men and women for being industrious, clever, and resourceful. In addition, women who were hard-working and enterprising were sought as marriage partners.[25] Their ability to contribute to the household's income and labor force generally assured them a welcome from parents and siblings, if their marriages ended and they elected to return home.

Nyeshangte women who lived or traveled with other female traders, relatives, and friends forged ties that extended beyond their own households. These personal networks and alliances provided migrant women with loans, advice, shelter, and child care. Female solidarity among migrants and traders created an independent power base that was largely separate from conjugal ties of male networks. Women also established widespread networks of clients and partners—relationships that were often strengthened by ritual bonds of friendship.

In general, adult and adolescent women enjoyed a significant amount of autonomy. Physical mobility and the ability to establish "extra-domestic ties" (social and trading alliances outside the kin-based unit) are frequently cited as cross-cultural indicators of women's "high status" relative to men of similar age and circumstance.[26]

While the income of some traders was used to offset seasonal food deficits, in other instances women's cash earnings were channeled into prestige goods. Like the Muria Gond "tribals" of India that Alfred Gell writes about, Nyeshangte households who experienced a rising income and standard of living often bought prestige goods, not for personal use or private luxury, but for collective use or group display—what Gell calls "public consumption" (1986:128). In the Nyeshangte case, these status commodities included rice, which was served or distributed (uncooked) on ceremonial occasions, as well as porcelain cups, brass serving dishes, and fine carpets that were brought out "to honor" guests or used during communal feasts "to honor" the village.

Women's earnings also enabled households to take an active role in village ritual life, another arena of public consumption where cash is needed for payments to ritual specialists, for temple donations, and for offerings at funerals, births, and marriages. As profits from trade steadily increased, religious institutions flourished in the Nyeshang valley, and more households began to vie for ritual and social status through "merit-making." Women, in their roles as mothers or wives, were in a position to use this wealth to accrue merit and to advance their families' social standing by lavish displays of hospitality and generosity.[27]

The notion of "social power" in its various manifestations is particularly useful in summing up the "categorical position" of adult Nyeshangte women, given the material presented so far.[28] A discussion of social power, in terms of both culture and political economy, also highlights a central concern of this book: the tangled, complicated, and ambiguous connections between women, trade, and religion—a concern that is woven throughout the remaining chapters.

But, here, let me just say that the evidence presented in chapters 2 and 3 suggests that some middle-aged women wielded "social power" in a political or economic sense in that they were able to control the lives of others outside the household, by directing their labor or by "appropriating the products" of their labor.[29] From a cultural perspective, they possessed social power of a different sort—one that went beyond questions of autonomy, authority, or control of resources. Social power in this sense has more to do with "the ability to define social reality, to impose visions of the world" and "the ability to make others accept and enact one's representation of the world" (Gal 1991:177, 197). Finally, "social power" can be defined from an indigenous, rather than a western perspective. Shelly Errington (1990) observes that the concept of "power" in the West, with its images of action, coercion, order-giving, and aggressiveness, may not be recognized in areas of island Southeast Asia. Errington explains that in many cases, "to exert force, to make explicit commands, or to engage in direct activity—in other words, to exert 'power' in a western sense—reveals a lack of spiritual power and effective potency, and consequently diminishes prestige" (5). Although Nyeshangte notions of power as "spiritual potency" come close to what Errington describes, the construction of gender differences in these cases varies. A common observation about Southeast Asian societies is that women may control economic resources, but because they are enmeshed in worldly or practical concerns, they are less likely to be associated with spiritual power—consequently their prestige is rather low (cf. Errington 1990:6–7; Kirsch 1983). In this case, gender differences and efficacy—spiritual or material—seem to be fixed, whereas in Nyeshang access to spiritual power or prestige is less circumscribed. Furthermore, in the Nyeshangte gender system, adult women seem to occupy positions as mediators or agents capable of transforming wealth into power or "spiritual capital" (cf. Ong 1989:298).

The convergence of these types of social power may be illustrated by one brief example: the ability of one elderly mother to channel not only her middle-aged son's trade wealth into the religious arena for "public consumption," but to motivate other villagers to help finance and build a village temple that would benefit and "do honor to" the entire community.[30] That adult Nyeshangte women can take part in prestigious activities, and translate their economic influence into social power by soliciting contributions for temple construction and other merit-generating acts, suggests they occupy a relatively high social position in what appears to be a gender egalitarian society.[31]

Although their customary authority and power are rooted in a "moral" economic base, women have always had to secure their position and have done so in different ways with varying degrees of success. Young and old, single and married, rural and urban, Nyeshangte women have responded differently to the upheavals of the past two decades. The nature and causes of these transformations and their effects on women's lives are the subject of the following chapter.

CHAPTER FOUR

Of Money, Musk, and Men

WITH A COMFORTABLE NICHE established in several areas of mainland Southeast Asia, Nyeshangte were able to widen their trade networks and find a new market for one of their regular commodities. Musk, derived from Himalayan deer, was a high profit, concentrated substance that was easy to transport. It was sold to Chinese pharmacies in Singapore, Bangkok, and Hong Kong, where in the 1960s and 1970s it brought up to u.s.$300–$450 an ounce for its reputed aphrodisiac and medicinal values (Cooke 1985b). Profits from the sale of musk (*lau phinyi*) in these urban centers greatly exceeded what Nyeshangte peddlers had earned in the bazaars and villages of northern India and Assam. Chinese merchants and pharmacists were willing to pay considerably higher prices for musk pods and other animal "organs" in order to meet the demand created by the large overseas Chinese communities. The expansion of the musk trade was also facilitated by newly established airline services that linked Dacca, Calcutta, and subsequently Kathmandu with cities in Southeast Asia.

Capital accumulation from musk sales enabled Nyeshangte entrepreneurs to invest in large quantities of consumer luxury goods and high-profit commodities like gold which were sold to Indian and Nepalese clients. Since success in commerce depends on having adequate funds for reinvestment, this accumulation of wealth, combined with the usual Nyeshangte

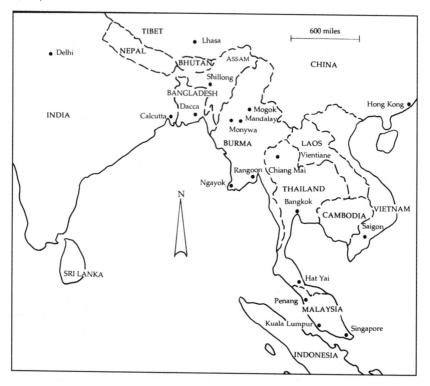

Map 3. Nyeshangte trade networks extend from northeast India to Southeast

practice of pooling financial resources, served as a major catalyst for subsequent trade growth. Many Nyeshangte men began to specialize in "high-value merchandise" that yielded better profit margins than the customary sales of second-hand clothing, housewares, or herbal medicines. Rising household income, increased urban migration, and the significant changes in social organization that followed may be directly attributed to the newly expanded musk trade.

Improvements in transportation and rising income further encouraged the development of Nyeshangte ventures. Direct flights into Kathmandu allowed some merchants who could afford the higher airfares to transport goods without risking Indian customs, where substantial "fines" were levied and goods were often confiscated. In 1968 the initiation of direct flights between Kathmandu and Bangkok prompted many Nyeshangte to sell their inventory of Nepalese and Tibetan "souvenirs"—prayer wheels, religious scrolls (*thang ka*), daggers, and jewelry—to a rapidly growing international tourist and GI market. This included a large number of American military personnel who were stationed in Thailand, U.S. soldiers of temporary leave (R&R) from Vietnam, and other (civilian) westerners visiting Bangkok and the beach resort at Pattaya (cf. Cooke 1985a, 1985c). The Vietnam War also enable the traders to gain a foothold in Indochina, where they thrived in the "gray-black market" conditions as middlemen. In Vietnam, Laos, and Cambodia, they handled a variety of commodities like rice, weapons, and American PX goods that were lucrative in a war zone (cf. van Spengen 1987).

In Nepal, increasing monetization and rising consumer demands also boosted the growth of Nyeshangte trade. By the mid-1960s, as domestic transportation improved and Kathmandu became an important center for domestic commerce, Nyeshangte men began to rent flats and establish permanent bases in the capital city, returning less frequently to the homeland. Soon afterward, as profits from trade continued to increase, more families relocated to Kathmandu, where they built large homes to accommodate the influx of relatives and friends who left the mountains each winter to escape the severe cold. With the advent of newly built "all-weather roads" and bus service between the central hill region and the capital, families who customarily migrated to the Terai or India also began to spend the winter in Kathmandu. By the 1980s, Kathmandu became the major destination of most seasonal and permanent migrants—nearly 80 percent of all Nyeshangte traveled there every winter.

Continuities with the Past: Small Traders

The economic transformations stemming from the musk trade did not sweep through the community all at once: continuities with earlier trade practices were still evident a few years later. Dobremez and Jest, two French researchers who were traveling along the Marsyandi Trail in November 1970, met a band of Nyeshangte—adult men, women, and children—who were heading for India. Loaded down with baskets, the group carried a variety of traditional trade goods: goat and deer skins, live dogs, valerian, rhubarb, yak tails, and woven cloth, in addition to one stuffed yak head destined for a museum in Calcutta (1972:41–42). Gurung (1977:40–43) encountered thirteen Nyeshangte families living in the towns of Gauhati and Shillong (Assam) in 1975. During the winter these families operated dry goods stores, and in some shops herbal potions were still being prepared for Nepalese clients and indigenous "tribals." Most of these storefront shops were operated by women whose husbands were away for sev-

5. A Nyeshangte home in Kathmandu.

eral months—in other regions of northern India or in Thailand and Malaysia.

On one of my trips to Nyeshang, I stayed in Bhote Odar, where I met a few families whose itinerant lifestyles and seasonal trade practices also showed some affinity with the past.[1] Until the 1960s many Nyeshangte families passed the entire winter here, where they supported themselves by bartering alpine products for local produce—rice, corn, and millet. Although most households shifted their winter quarters to Pokhara or Kathmandu as soon as their economic circumstances improved, some elected to buy property in Bhote Odar and were transformed overnight from indigent squatters sleeping in the fields to landlords. Chongdu Lhamo and her husband Onger rented the lower floor of their house to a Newar couple who also managed their small store-front shop. In addition, they owned two fields nearby, which they leased to a low-caste Kami family who split the harvest of paddy in half with them.

Onger explained to me why they stayed in Bhote Odar when most Nyeshangte families spent the winter in Kathmandu: "Here we live the slower life, one that is not so risky. In Kathmandu, everything is happening quickly. People can make money quickly, but lose it too. Here we are not rich, not poor. But we don't have to worry so much." This sentiment was also expressed by two other Nyeshangte men who chose to live the life of a "small trader" in the quiet rural setting of Pokhara, rather than compete for higher stakes in Kathmandu.

The upper stories of Chongdu's house were crowded with friends and relatives from Nyeshang, who were waiting a few more days before heading back up the trail. Outside in the warm sunshine four young men played card and dice games, and sitting on faded strips of carpet two elderly women and an old grizzly fellow mumbled prayers and spun their handheld prayer wheels. Inside the house adult women were busy preparing corn porridge for lunch and churning gallons of salty Tibetan tea for the lingering house guests. After a fortnight the house would be vacant. Chongdu and Onger, who were waiting for their eldest daughter to return from Bangkok, would return together to Nyeshang to cultivate their fields.

Continuities with the past are also seen in the group's "bootstrap" philosophy, a view commonly expressed by males in their mid- to late adulthood. In numerous life stories I was presented with the image of a "barefoot" itinerant trader who begins his modest career selling wares on the sidewalks of Penang, Chiang Mai, or Pattaya, hoping to amass enough capital to purchase manufactured goods in Singapore or Bangkok for resale in Kathmandu. Short of cash, these young male traders usually operate on shoe-string levels: traveling between market towns by bus or train, staying in cheap inns, or taking advantage of the free lodging offered at Buddhist temples. Many of these itinerant vendors eventually join the ranks of "big traders" who regularly fly between Kathmandu and Hong Kong and Bangkok, purchasing large inventories of consumer goods that are freighted back to Nepal.

Individual initiative and entrepreneurial skills are highly valued in the community, and many Nyeshangte feel that anyone (male or female) may become a successful trader—it takes some luck and a lot of hard work. The case of Sonam, a 36-year-old man who currently operates a lodge in Nyeshang with his wife, is fairly typical of Nyeshangte enterprise and mobility. It also illustrates a common behavioral sequence of Nyeshangte males: a prolonged adolescence characterized by spending sprees and excessive drinking; settling down and assuming a more serious approach to earning money; then, later in mid-life, becoming more concerned with Buddhist practice and merit-making.

I first met Sonam in early March 1989 when he was returning to Nyeshang to open his tourist lodge for the upcoming trekking season. He had spent three months traveling to Buddhist shrines in India with his wife, who planned to rejoin him a few weeks later when the weather improved in the valley. We happened to be staying overnight at the same family-run lodge in *Traklung, and over the course of the evening he recounted much of his life story. Later, in June, I spent two weeks with Sonam and Tsering at their lodge and understood a bit better the ambivalence some valley residents feel toward the growth of tourism in the valley.

Sonam left his natal village of Lhakpa in 1965 when he was 13 years old. Traveling "barefoot" to India, he eventually made his way to Calcutta where he earned enough money to purchase an airline ticket to Bangkok. His foremost desire was to learn Thai kick boxing. Sonam was apparently quite skilled at this sort of thing, for he managed to earn a living boxing in Bangkok for several years—until the age of 22 when he was forced to retire after receiving an assortment of broken bones. Despite his fighting success, Sonam often found himself broke—especially after several nights of "partying" in Bangkok's nightclubs with other Nyeshangte youths. So he and his friends would head north to Chiang Mai, where they could earn some cash by picking grapes for a few weeks.

From his mid-twenties on, Sonam returned periodically to Thailand and became quite a successful merchant. Although he enjoyed living overseas (he is very proud of the fact that he speaks fluent Thai), he eventually tired of "doing [black market] business." So he invested about 180,000 rupees (u.s.$7,500) in building and furnishing a multiroom lodge in Nyeshang, which yields a yearly profit of 80,000 rupees (u.s.$3,400). In addition to this cash income, Sonam and his wife own a few yak, horses, and cows, and produce enough food from their fields to be fairly self-sufficient.

When I visited him a few months later in June, I found that Sonam was quite tired of running the lodge and wanted to lease it to a tenant. He was weary of arguing and fighting with tourists who complained about the food and often left without paying. A few tourists had even stolen canned goods from his store. Several times he pointed to the shot gun in the kitchen corner and said, "I won't kill animals, but I do tell tourists [that] if they cheat me and start trouble, those kind of people I will shoot." Sonam, without a pause, switched subjects and told me of his plans for next year's pilgrimage. Our conversation was interrupted when two American male trekkers poked their heads through the kitchen doorway and inquired about lodging. "No, no rooms here today," Sonam abruptly told them. The place was empty, but after the trekkers left Sonam explained, "I don't want my wife to have to cook tonight."

Sonam confided that in the future he would like to travel more with his wife and also start a postcard business. He has an extensive collection of camera equipment and hopes to shoot many photographs in Nyeshang. Sonam already produced a video that featured the masked dance dramas and exorcisms that take place during the harvest celebrations. He plans to take the slides to Bangkok for printing, and then hopes to sell the postcards to booksellers and souvenir shops in Kathmandu. "Now that kind of business," he assures me, referring to the photography and the postcard selling, "is a *good* business. No lying. No cheating. And no tourists."

This pride in self-advancement was a common theme woven through many of the life histories of the Nyeshangte I met. In these narratives some of the wealthiest traders in the community—men in their late thirties and forties—reminisced like Sonam about their "barefoot" days: when they slept outdoors and learned the business literally from the ground up. Most of them, when interviewed in their well-appointed Kathmandu homes, would proudly point out: "Look, we had nothing before. Now we have good clothes. Our children go to school. If they get sick, there are doctors here. Our city houses are warm. We have water inside and electricity." When I asked them and their wives what I should write about, what they were most proud of, they spoke of similar things: about being hard-working people who were willing to help one another; about being unschooled mountain people who taught themselves how to "do business" in many countries; about how they were illiterate but learned to speak many foreign languages; about becoming modern "Nepalese" citizens loyal to a (Hindu) king but also proud of their ancestral ways, their Buddhist traditions, and their rapid rise in the world. "From having nothing, to all this," one 35-year-old fellow explained, as he gestured around the room, which was filled with new furniture and carpets, a large screen TV and VCR. Then he indicated his own clothing, "Before we wore old clothes, not so nice. Now this," pointing to his brown-leather flight jacket, Levi blue jeans, and hi-top athletic shoes.

Reflected in these narratives is an underlying assumption that Nyeshang is a basic equal-opportunity society—anyone can get started in trade and make a comfortable living, even a fortune. Although most Nyeshangte can turn to relatives or friends for starting funds and work their way up—those with close connections to "big-traders" begin their careers with a head start. They have access to large loans, established trade networks, and "mentors" to teach them the intricacies of the high-risk trade in gold and luxury goods. The "big people" who have "made it" (mostly male traders and a few women) tend to be idealistic about the opportunities and assistance extended to newcomers. Although there is a strong ethic that relatives should advance interest-free loans to those who need capital, the reality from the other side, those doing the asking, is somewhat different. A number of young women and men, both in the village and city, said that it was increasingly difficult to get advances from trade groups now that these associations were no longer strictly family-based and were organized along corporate lines.

In the following section I describe some of these changes and discuss how they threatened to undermine the egalitarian principles and social relations that characterized Nyeshang society before the 1970s.

The Roots of Inequality: Big Traders and Corporate Trading Groups

In some ways today's corporate groups (*tsong roo*) share certain continuities with the informal kin-based groups described in chapter 3. These associations are based on similar principles: resources are pooled, and all profits, losses, and expenses are equally shared. In both groups members are usually linked by kinship ties or ritual friendship (*chetu*). However, during the past two decades certain differences have become apparent in the corporate groups: the notable absence of Nyeshangte women and the inclusion of men from other ethnic groups. These "outside" men are often connected to elite circles in Kathmandu society, and generally have access to the large sums of money that are needed to finance Nyeshangte businesses.

Nyeshangte who hope to join the ranks of an established trading group generally approach an older male relative who agrees to act as a mentor and provides the novice with a small advance. In the meantime, while the apprentice learns the business, he generally performs menial housekeeping chores, runs errands, and undertakes some of the riskier tasks for the group (cf. Cooke 1985a:102–3). If the newcomer is successful and earns a large-enough profit for the group, he may be invited to join as a regular member.

However, to avoid the power and control of senior men, some novices prefer to strike out on their own and form new partnerships with other young traders. Although Nyeshangte youths find the egalitarian ethics and camaraderie of these coalitions appealing, the newer associations rarely have enough capital to compete in the high-profit gold trade (cf. Cooke 1985b). Lacking funds for initial investment and an established connection to external credit sources, these traders cannot afford to move their families to the city, nor can they overcome their dependence on the village-based economy (76). This widening gap between households and between urban and village residents is thus perpetuated by the new structures of trade—the monetization of social relations and the capital accumulation of the big traders.

As far as membership in these wealthy, powerful groups is concerned, younger male and female traders are equally disadvantaged, since neither are likely to be accepted as members—only as subordinate apprentices or "carriers" (*leba*). Only the sons of successful big traders can be assured of getting a partnership in these elite business circles. In general, most women and many of the male "small traders" prefer to operate in an environment governed by friendship and kin-based values rather than work as subordinates for older, more affluent men.

Dissonance in the Community: Urban and Rural Residents

Although differences between city and village residents, small and big traders, are allayed somewhat by kinship and other cross-cutting ties, these categorical divisions may widen in the future. Several men in the city have relinquished their social obligations in the village, and these traders would rather pay the fines levied by village councils than return to the homeland to attend the mandatory celebrations. Kathmandu-based men frequently avoid serving as ritual sponsors or committee members who oversee the communal aspects of daily village life—duties and posts that customarily rotate each year among Nyeshangte households.

Many middle-aged male and female residents in the Nyeshang valley lament the decline of rural life—saddened that the yearly archery contests are attended only by a handful of elderly men and young boys; bitter that there is no money to replace the satin costumes and painted masks for the harvest celebrations. In recent years a large proportion of surplus wealth and community funds has been channeled into expanding the Nyeshangte temple complex near Kathmandu. In the village, on the other hand, religious sponsorship is undertaken by individuals or individual households.

Feelings between urban and rural Nyeshangte are sometimes strained. Some villagers complain that their affluent city relatives do not always live up to the group's customary expectations of generosity, and urban residents sometimes resent the burden of supporting numerous relatives for four months each winter. Yet the high value placed on hospitality requires that hosts hide their sentiments or risk a serious breach among relatives. Other urban dwellers feel beleaguered by requests for financial assistance: to pay for a village child's boarding school fees, to provide loans for new business ventures, or to give spending money to an errant nephew who leads an idle existence in town.

These requests are difficult to turn down, for the community's values stress cooperation, sharing, and a fierce egalitarianism. "We are all one people; if someone needs help or money, he or she can always get [it] from friends or relatives," a refrain frequently heard in conversations with well-established city residents. In a society where bilateral kin ties are very important and an individual's circle of relatives is quite large, this could lead to an unending chain of demands from poorer friends and relatives. In contrast, some of the elderly women and men complain about the pervasive greed and stinginess of many city residents. Clearly, perceptions about Nyeshangte social relations vary significantly along lines of residence (city or rural) and between generations. Regardless of one's perspectives—the one giving or the one asking—idealistic expectations about Nyeshangte social relations make it certain that some people will not be able or willing to conform to the community's standards of generosity. Others are bound to be disappointed, and a few will give up trying.

For many urban families, village bonds that once determined marriage choices and business partnerships have been replaced by class considerations. Social status, education, and wealth now form the basis of newly established ties, which also include many individuals from "outside" ethnic groups. Marriage partners are no longer sought from one's natal village but rather from urban Nyeshangte families of equal wealth. Although these changes are significant, they remain for the most part slight cracks underlying the surface of the community's tight-knit image. Whether these differences become more pronounced and lead to major rifts between the city and rural Nyeshangte, between newly "emerging" classes, is difficult to predict. Other forces are at work to present a unified front in an alien cultural environment: their zealous devotion to Buddhist ritual, their lavish patronage of Buddhist institutions in and around Kathmandu, and their regular celebration of "village festivals" and "traditions" in the city all help to reinforce the group's self- and public image as a "closed" unified community.

Whether this image can be maintained will depend on the next generation of Nyeshangte. For the trade reorganization that brought prosperity to their parents has also transformed the lives of the children born in Kathmandu, many of whom have never visited their rural homeland. Born in an urban setting where the social order has been shaped by the concerns and values of the dominant Hindu caste groups, and influenced by a pervasive western tourist culture, their lives are quite different from their village relatives. Differences in educational levels, in socialization with children from upper levels of Nepalese, Indian, and Tibetan society at expensive boarding schools, and in extensive travel experience outside Nepal will contribute to a widening gap between city and village youth. Some of these disparities become evident when we look at changes in gender roles and attitudes toward women in trade.

Women's Involvement in Trade Decreases After the 1960s

Several factors led to the apparent decline in women's trading activities during the past three decades. Some causes reflect changing gender ideologies associated with the city environment; others hinge on the logistical concerns of allocating household labor in the rural district. Even wealthy families who have permanent homes in Kathmandu find the cost of airfare prohibitive: the expense alone discourages most families from traveling to Southeast Asia during the winter months. In addition to the higher travel costs, the pursuit of full-time, year-round trade by one or two male household members often results in additional labor costs for the rural-based household. Village households facing labor shortages frequently engage servants on a yearly or seasonal basis; these fixed costs put a further strain on household budgets that depend on unreliable trade income—where large profits and significant losses are equally common. Few families can afford the luxury of sending additional members abroad to accompany the traders. Instead, cash resources are used to hire household labor and to improve the family's living standards: by purchasing consumer items, clothing, and medical care and sending some children to more prestigious boarding schools in Kathmandu, Pokhara, or Darjeeling.

In addition to rising labor and transportation costs, certain bureaucratic regulations also contributed to the changing gender-based pattern of Nyeshang trade. Although the Nepalese government's lenient trade policies, with its generous dispensation of passports and customs exemptions, spurred the community's overall economic growth during the 1960s, it also had a negative effect on women's participation in international trade. By 1976 Nyeshangte traders were required to apply directly to the Finance Ministry for their annual import licenses and customs exemptions. Under these Nepalese regulations, adult Nyeshangte men were entitled to import between fifteen thousand and thirty thousand rupees (u.s.$600–$1,200) worth of goods, whereas adolescent males and women were restricted to significantly lesser amounts (Cooke 1985a:130). In addition, a government-imposed ban on the collection and export of medicinal herbs and animal products in 1970 also undercut Nyeshangte women's customary inventory of trade goods and their supplementary income as healers (cf. van Spengen

1987:228).[2] Since there was little demand for these homemade items and jaṅgal products in Kathmandu, women who migrated to the city during winter months led relatively idle lives, staying in small rented rooms with their children while their husbands traveled abroad and brought back their duty-free quota of consumer goods.

Some Nyeshangte, willing to risk imprisonment and hefty fines, continued to smuggle musk and herbs for sale in foreign markets. But the community generally disapproved of subjecting women to similar dangers. Cooke (1985a:76–77) reports that male elders instituted a formal ban on female trading activities during this period. Some women defied the ban and were fined ten thousand rupees (u.s.$400). The prohibition of female trading was subsequently repealed by community consensus in the early 1970s, but many Nyeshangte men and women still feel that the risks involved in smuggling—including imprisonment—make this type of work unsuitable for women.[3]

Today, the appeal of this "risky" business seems to attract many male youths who embrace a collective "urban warrior" mentality. These ventures are seen as a rite of passage, a "manly" thing to do. I had my first glimpse of this "boys' business" (*ketāko kām*) when I inadvertently walked in on a "gang" meeting and saw my friend Paljor, an 18 year old who had introduced me to several families in Kathmandu.[4] Although the proprietor of the restaurant panicked as I walked in and rushed over to tell me they were "closed," Paljor simply greeted me and asked the Newar owner to bring some coffee out to us on the terrace as we caught up on some news. Paljor, the youngest of three sons, was able to remain in school through the tenth grade, passed his slc exams, and had started college when I first met him. I had not seen him for some time and asked what he had been up to. He explained that his classes at the university had been canceled (because of the pro-democracy protests), so he had decided to go abroad to do some "business." In an unspoken agreement we let that topic drop, and our conversation shifted to the festivals planned for the following week at the Nyeshangte dgon pa.

On an earlier occasion, Paljor had mentioned that although he had no need to work—his two older brothers were quite successful in managing the family's commercial affairs—he had felt some peer pressure when he was 15 to try his luck in the Hong Kong market.[5] Although the exact nature of this business was not discussed (as a rule I never ask), Paljor confided that he had been a bit scared (which told me more than I needed to know). On his first trip he had made nearly sixty thousand rupees (u.s.$2,400), and then spent the entire amount in less than four months. Considering that the average yearly income for Nepali households was not much higher than u.s.$180 at the time, this was an extraordinary feat. My curiosity finally triumphed; I just had to ask how he had spent the money. Paljor explained that he had purchased American-brand clothes in Bangkok for himself and his two sisters; subsequently, when he returned to Kathmandu, the money was literally "eaten." He splurged and bought meat every day for his family, and the rest of the money was spent in Thamel restaurants, playing "snookers" or pool, and entertaining his friends and fellow gang members.

In recent years a few Nyeshangte males have spent time in Kathmandu jails for engaging in various black market schemes. Generally, their prison terms are shortened when relatives or trade partners pay "fines" or direct other funds to appropriate officials. Life in prison is not considered particularly difficult, as Nyeshangte prisoners are paid wages by their trade bosses and inmates in Nepalese jails are not forced to labor. Further, regular supplies of food or money are sent by relatives to augment the standard prison fare of coarse rice. However, prison conditions are rather grim, and most women and men feel that the inevitable hardships of jail would be totally inappropriate for women of their own community.

In addition, since Nyeshangte have moved into the mainstream of Nepalese life, community elders are somewhat concerned about their group's image. Stereotypes of "Manangi" youth, "Manangi" gangs, and "Manangi" business practices are sometimes a source of embarrassment to Nyeshangte women and men. The term *Manangi* has become a catch-all category for drug and gold smugglers who are intercepted regularly at the Kathmandu airport—events that appear in the *Rising Nepal,* a government-sponsored daily newspaper published in English. Most of these individuals are not Nyeshangte but belong to a variety of other ethnic-caste groups in Nepal who happen to share similar clan or last names. Likewise, the gangs in Kathmandu that prompt foreign embassies to issue circulars from time to time warning tourists of the threat of muggings or assaults are often assumed to be "Manangi." Yet the members of these groups are predominantly Newar boys from middle-class urban families or are members of other ethnic groups who recently migrated from the middle hills. Nyeshangte youths are rarely (if ever) involved in petty street crime.[6] Nevertheless, the negative images still prevail, and Nyeshangte who have made remarkable gains in their overall living standards are now trying to establish a more respectable presence in Kathmandu by purchasing legitimate businesses—hotels, grocery shops, jewelry and souvenir stores, and factories—and by downplaying the group's involvement in the "import-export" business. These concerns with propriety also explain why many Nyeshangte individuals are reluctant to discuss women's (and men's) current involvement in trade.

Of course not all forms of trade were illicit. Some Nyeshangte who preferred to engage in legal, low-risk ventures, continued to hawk jewelry in urban street markets in Southeast Asia, investing the profits in consumer goods for resale in Nepal. The legality of this trade depended largely on current trade regulations, which varied over the years. In other words, whether a trader "broke the law" depended on the "duty-free limits" set by the government. Some traders resigned themselves to paying import taxes; others smuggled goods through customs, paying bribes or occasionally fines for exceeding the set limit. In 1976, when the government established uniform trade regulations for all citizens, Nyeshangte began to organize legal shopping tours to take advantage of the new rules that permitted each citizen to import a thousand rupees (u.s.$40) of duty-free goods once a year. This became the domain of "small traders," the men and women who specialized in buying inexpensive clothing and electronic goods in Bangkok and Singapore. In contrast, the "big traders" operated out of Hong Kong and dealt primarily in gold.

To some extent, the apparent decline in female traders during the past three decades hinges on this distinction between "big business" and the more modest enterprises that center on wholesale and retail sales of clothing and other consumer goods. Many of the activities pursued by female entrepreneurs are simply not classified as "business," which is the domain of corporate trading groups (tsong roo). Tsangmo, an 18-year-old woman who helped her parents run a lodge in Nyeshang, is a "small trader." The eldest of six siblings, Tsangmo makes two trips a year to Bangkok and Chiang Mai with a girlfriend. They sell Nepalese jewelry and Tibetan souvenirs at the night markets and, for the return trip, Tsangmo buys items like opium pipes, embroidered Burmese wall hangings, Levi blue jeans, and denim jackets to sell in Kathmandu.

When Tsangmo first began trading, she worked as a carrier and was paid five hundred rupees (u.s.$20) plus airfare and a small supplement to cover her living expenses in Bangkok. As part of the deal, she cleared customs wearing her allotment of duty-free clothing, and carrying other items—watches, calculators, postcards, and spices—that were turned over to the trade boss who organized the trip.[7] After a few trips as a carrier, Tsangmo had enough experience to work on her own, and her parents and a couple of relatives gave her enough cash to buy an airline ticket and some merchandise. After two years she repaid her relatives, and now she makes a small profit, which she splits in half with her parents.[8] Tsangmo also works at the lodge during the busy trekking season, as well as helping to take care of her five younger siblings.

In contrast, "doing business" the tsong roo way typically involves investments of several thousand dollars: capital is raised through large investments from outside the community and through a rotating fund where each member contributes a fixed amount. The working capital is loaned to individual members for a set period of time, then the losses and profits are shared among the entire group. Although tsong roo groups are not strictly closed to women, none of the women I met were members. Most women worked independently with a friend or cousin or, if married, with their husband. Chongdu, a married woman who operated a lodge along the Nyeshang Trail north of Bhote Odar, told me that she used to accompany her husband to Bangkok and Hong Kong until the birth of her second daughter five years earlier. Since then she had a son and was now expecting her fourth child, and she rarely ventured from home. Some of the married women in Kathmandu resume their business travels after their children reach school age, but most of the village women, like Chongdu, lead more sedentary lives.

Gender Roles and Ideologies: Attitudes Toward Trade

Attitudes toward married urban female traders vary. The men and women I spoke with gave a variety of responses, from "they are just helping their families" to "they are bored at home and enjoy traveling." A few explained that some women "have minds like a boy; they are more business-minded and clever at this work."[9] Only two individuals (a teenage girl and a middle-aged man) suggested that female traders in affluent households who continue to work do so out of greed. Many male and female informants echoed the comments made by another middle-aged man who responded: "All kinds of women do business, single ones, young ones, old, married, widows, all kinds, but mostly the poorer ones. There is no other kind of work they can do there [in Kathmandu]."

Although trade has become more closely associated with "men's work" during the past three decades, it is not exclusively so—there is still overlap between male and female roles; that is, although many Nyeshangte women and men say that today mostly "men do business," this statement is based on the simple facts that only 10 to 15 percent of Nyeshangte traders are women and that "small trade" and "big business" are perceived differently. In short, even though some tasks are associated more strongly with one sex than the other, individuals in Nyeshang society are seldom barred from specific occupational domains. Women who cross gender boundaries do so because of personality characteristics—"they have minds like a boy's"—but this does not detract from their identity as women. Whether women pursue the nomadic lifestyle of an itinerant trader depends largely on initiative and personality. Some village women and adolescent girls from poorer households (those with no trade income) gave innumerable reasons why they as women could not become traders. These reasons centered on their inability to read or write, their lack of experience and worldliness, and their reluctance to leave their village homes to travel to distant cities. Yet many young women in similar circumstances seemed to thrive on adventure and conducted their business affairs with skill despite their illiteracy. Other women perceived the life of a trader as one of particular hardship and danger, and clearly preferred to work in familiar surroundings with friends and relatives.[10] This preference for leading a more settled life within a circle of kin was also apparent from the accounts of many female migrants and entrepreneurs who had established temporary winter quarters in southern Nepal or Assam and conducted small-scale business from these bases.

City Lives: Women at Work, Women at Home

The overall decline in women's trade activities might lead us to expect that their social power and authority in the household would also diminish, but this has not occurred. Although most middle-aged women in the city are not engaged in (what economists call) "productive labor," they do manage the household budget and receive remittances and trade goods from husbands and unmarried sons who may be away for months at a time.[11] Younger wives also are expected to manage their husbands' earnings, to oversee household expenses, and to make decisions on everyday domestic matters. Furthermore, marriage relationships are not hierarchical and are not predicated on patriarchal lines: the spousal pair is perceived to be a complementary, balanced unit—two equal halves designed to work in tandem to achieve social prestige, wealth, and well-being.[12] When husbands return to their homes in Kathmandu or the Nyeshang valley, especially after long absences, their roles are not unlike those of guests, and the day-to-day control of the household still remains with the wives.

6. Every morning before dawn, Nyeshangte women converge on Swayambhu.

Among coresident spouses decision making is usually a joint affair, but women are still considered more frugal, less impulsive, and better suited for handling money. Several men and women told me that men tend to take greater risks in business, are inclined to gamble, and will waste money on alcohol or meat to lavishly entertain friends. As a rule, married women in their roles as senior females in nuclear households are expected to manage the family's grain supplies and cash reserves until the women choose to retire and withdraw from daily household affairs.

Some urban women do work outside the home: they run family-owned jewelry and clothing shops or supervise non-Nyeshangte employees hired to manage the stores. Other women assist their husbands by picking up merchandise at the Kathmandu airport or by inviting potential buyers—neighbors, friends, and other business associates—to their homes to view the latest shipment of goods. In general, because many urban Nyeshangte wives are directly involved in their husbands' social and business affairs, there is no reversal of authority when husbands return home. Wives are not displaced from their position as mistress of the household—quite the contrary. Usually the intensity of social and ritual life picks up, and the wife oversees the hospitality arrangements for the endless stream of visitors who drop by.

Although most middle-aged urban women do not work outside the home, they are not socially isolated. Every morning they gather at Swayambhu stūpa to circumambulate the sacred hill, light candles at the shrines, and prostrate before the Buddha images near the main gate. Then the women return home, stopping to visit with friends along the way. However, young mothers who have small children and whose husbands are away have less time to socialize. Unless they have servants or relatives living with them to help ease the burden of household chores and child care, these young women rarely have time to meet "village" friends in the mornings at Swayambhu stūpa. Their isolation is lessened somewhat by the residential clustering of Nyeshangte, Tibetan, and Sherpa households in Kathmandu, and young women do rely on their neighbors for companionship and assistance. Although the circumstances of individual women's lives in Kathmandu are quite varied, in most cases gender relations within the household have not shifted dramatically. Adult women have maintained their customary authority in household matters, their prominent roles in the urban community's social networks, and their autonomy to go about as they please. There is one notable exception. The activities and mobility of adolescent girls are more curtailed in the city. In general, they have less autonomy than their male peers in the city or their female cohorts in the valley. It is perhaps this group of young urban women who are most affected by the return of their trader fathers and older brothers. Several teenage girls complained about the restrictions imposed on them by returning male relatives. In contrast, their mothers and older sisters usually let them (and their younger brothers) do as they please: they could accompany friends to movies, dinners, or parties in the evenings. Young teenage boys also feel oppressed by their fathers, but they usually have no qualms about defying parental rules and staying away from home if things become too unpleasant.

Parents, especially fathers who travel widely in India and mainland Southeast Asia, are quite aware of the dangers and problems of modern city life. In Hong Kong, Singapore, Bangkok, and Delhi, Nyeshangte traders generally stay in cheap accommodations in the low rent, "red-light" districts which also house nightclubs and bars that draw large crowds of tourists and locals, along with the usual assortment of drug dealers, junkies, and prostitutes. In Kathmandu these problems exist on a much smaller scale, but nevertheless they are present. The number of heroin addicts continues to increase in the city, and several Nyeshangte youths (only males, as far as I know) are addicts or serving prison terms for drug trafficking. Furthermore, with the imminent threat of AIDS, it would seem that before long the community may have to face this problem as well. Although the number of reported AIDS cases in Nepal is low, the magnitude of the problem in India and Thailand would suggest otherwise.

Parents, however, are not responding to this somewhat abstract threat, but rather to the immediate dangers that city life poses for their children, especially their daughters, who they fear might be pushed into an unsuitable marriage outside the Nyeshangte community. Premarital sexual relations were not an issue in the valley, where most partners were likely to be members of the community and therefore suitable as spouses. In Kathmandu the situation is quite different; Nyeshangte youths attend school and socialize with individuals from outside the community. Parents do not want their daughters or sons to marry non-Nyeshangte. Furthermore, parents are concerned for the safety of their daughters in Kathmandu, where young women—Nepalese and western—are subject to frequent sexual harassment on the streets and buses.

Some Nyeshangte elders are also concerned with their children's obsession with western youth culture—dress, gangs, drug use, music, and so on—and the "imagined" or "possible" lives these cultural symbols represent.[13] If parents seem especially intent on protecting and controlling their adolescent children, particularly their daughters, it is in response to the threat the city poses to their customary way of life.

I turn now to the homeland and consider how the restructuring of trade has affected village life. I begin with a discussion of migration, since this is a key factor behind many of the changes that have occurred in the rural community.

Migration Patterns: Impact on Village Society

Decisions to migrate are usually made jointly by the adult members of a household. In Nyeshang, four types of migrants may be distinguished.[14] When entire households are absent year-round from the valley and have settled in Kathmandu or Pokhara, they are permanent urban migrants. Households may send one or two (usually male) members to Kathmandu, where they maintain rented quarters and engage in full-time, year-round trade. These individuals are long-term urban migrants. Villagers with primary residences in the valley who spend the winter in urban areas but are generally not active traders themselves are seasonal migrants. They often share rented quarters with other household members or stay with relatives who own homes in town. Small traders who migrate to commercial centers during the winter but are still dependent on the village economy are seasonal traders. Generally, these are village farmers who make an occasional trip each year to purchase provisions and manufactured items for domestic use and to earn some cash from surplus sales.

Trying to document migratory patterns in Nyeshang is somewhat problematic. Distrust of government representatives and most outsiders makes it difficult to administer demographic surveys. Furthermore, the entire population is quite mobile, shifting residences according to labor demands, seasonal factors, and personal whims. In addition, migratory rates vary among the seven Nyeshangte villages. This differential rate, as I indicated in chapter 2, is based on varying subsistence strategies: villages with the most substantial investment in pastoralism have the greatest number of year-round residents.

However, migration rates not only reflect choices but also constraints. Although the villages at the higher elevations were better suited for pastoralism, they were disadvantaged with regard to agriculture: compared to other settlements in the valley, the average land holdings were smaller and the fields less productive. It seems that Nyeshangte from these villages were less able to convert their livestock and dairy "surplus" into cash, since trading histories indicate that few households could amass sufficient amounts of working capital to undertake regular long-distance trips beyond the Nepalese and Indian borders. In fact, most of the "small" traders who engaged in seasonal itinerant trade in northern India, Assam, and areas of the Nepal Terai into the 1970s and 1980s came from these smaller, high-altitude pastoral settlements.

In contrast, the villages that have larger quantities of fertile, arable land seemed to have a greater commitment to long-distance trade, the highest level of out-migration, and the greatest involvement in the profitable "big business" markets of Bangkok, Hong Kong, and Singapore. Households from these larger villages were most likely to have surplus commodities to exchange or sell, and trading parties from these agriculturally based villages had more capital to invest in early trade ventures.

The difficult task of sorting out demographic patterns in the community is compounded not only by intravillage differences in migration, but also by the limited amount of census data available.[15] However, with the aid of material collected by earlier travelers and scholars, whose visits to the valley span a time frame of twenty-five years (1960–85), along with the preliminary surveys I conducted in five villages in 1989, we can get an overall picture of the permanent and seasonal migratory patterns. At best, the figures presented in this section are rough estimates, but nonetheless they helped sharpen my impressions of village life and helped clarify my understanding of village social processes. A brief look at these demographic processes—long-term male absences, female-headed households, the influx of non-Nyeshangte residents, and the abandonment of village homes and fields—will help the reader see how much the community has been affected by changing trade patterns and urbanization. It is against this background of rapid and pervasive change that we can better understand the significance of women's agency in refashioning and upholding the social order.

Looking at various census figures for an estimate of absentee households and the migration rates from various villages, several trends become clear. There has been a dramatic population decline in Nyeshang—about 29 percent between 1971 and 1988—that is the result of permanent out-migration.[16] Approximately two hundred families now have their primary residences in Kathmandu. Another thirty families have settled in Pokhara. The survey I undertook also revealed which households were still dependent on village-based revenues and how many of these households were year-round residents.[17] For the most part, year-round residents included families with significant involvement in herding; elderly retired couples or individuals who live at the meditation or retreat centers (ser khyim); families with young children who do not have the cash or labor resources to take part in the urban commercial economy; and widows and unmarried young women who remain in the valley to look after family property or to farm their own land. Several of these women told me that they prefer living alone or "independently" in Nyeshang, rather than in Kathmandu where they found it difficult to make ends meet.

The expanding tourist market has also encouraged year-round residence, as some lodge owners stay through the winter to receive the small groups of trekkers who attempt to cross the Thorung Pass.[18] This continual expansion of the tourist industry may partially offset the rate of permanent out-migration from the valley, and a few Nyeshangte families are planning to build new lodges and restaurants in the valley. Development in the outlying rural areas may also attract former residents. Some men and women in Kathmandu told me that they would return to the valley if basic amenities like schooling and medical care could be improved. They also hoped that the government would eventually extend the Dumre Road north to Nyeshang, as the proposed road would reduce the cost of food and household supplies and would make it easier for city residents (especially the middle-aged and elderly) to return home more often.[19] Whether these projects would actually stem the flow of migrants and restore vitality to village life is difficult to predict; Nyeshangte elders remain optimistic though nothing has been done so far.

Nyeshang: A Summer Resort?

Although many city residents feel ambivalent about the abandonment of village homes and the perceived decline of traditional village life, others manage to find a balance between their longing for the homeland and their appreciation of modern urban amenities. They return to the valley every year to inspect the condition of their fields and houses, and to visit friends. A number of women and children go to the mountains during the monsoon season to avoid the heat and illness that pervade Kathmandu. Some city residents like to visit the valley to take part in the round of summer and harvest celebrations; others, especially youths, enjoy volunteering for communal activities—helping to repair a trail or build a new bridge. Some also come up to collect their share of rent during harvest, and others to work in their own fields.

On one of my trips to Nyeshang I met a "big trader" who was returning to the homeland to join his wife and eldest daughter who had left a few weeks earlier with a group of female friends. Namgyal, a slender, animated fellow who looked younger than his 50 years, was going "up" to help with the wheat and barley sowing. His only son was enrolled in a boarding school and seldom came home. Namgyal also had a 14-year-old daughter who was studying to become a nun and had been in seclusion during a three-year meditation retreat in Nyeshang. The nuns were nearing the end of their retreat, and Namgyal and his wife Soner were planning to sponsor a community celebration, or *tamāshā* as he called it, to honor the occasion. Namgyal and Soner were well liked and respected in both the urban and rural community. Namgyal had been extremely successful as a trader. When he was young he traded in north India and Burma with his father, and now he worked primarily in Singapore and Hong Kong. Despite the family's wealth—they owned two large houses in Kathmandu—he and his wife elected to live modestly and returned to their village home for six months each year to farm their land (with the help of a servant), and to manage their yak and sheep herds, though the income from trade far surpassed the revenues from their property in Nyeshang.[20] The couple were generous supporters of the monastic community—providing food, beer, and cash donations—and volunteered their labor whenever it was requested.

While some summer visitors work their land with the help of live-in servants, others choose not to farm and the fields are left fallow. Villagers are saddened by the outright abandonment of homes and fields, and prefer to see resident caretakers managing the property so that roofs and walls do not collapse from neglect, casting an air of decay over the village. Several houses are now occupied by resident caretakers who were originally from surrounding districts: Lo, Dolpo, Nar, or Larkya. Many immigrants are Tibetan refugees who were forced to flee to Nepal during the political upheavals of recent decades. Although many of the immigrant caretakers were impoverished and viewed as "low-status" individuals (because they were "outsiders" without any clan affiliations), quite a few have since been accepted as permanent residents.[21] Some of their children have been adopted by childless Nyeshangte couples.[22] Other Tibetan immigrants are incorporated into Nyeshang households as live-in servants (cf. Gurung 1977a:18).

Female-Headed Households

During this period of trade reorganization we can also see a gradual increase in the number and length of adult male absences from the valley. Before 1962 there were not many permanent migrants, and most traders returned to the homeland after a few months' absence (Gurung 1976:51). However, by the late 1960s, business interests kept many adult males away for most of the year. Harka Gurung, a Nepalese researcher who visited Nyeshang during October 1973, reported that in one of the larger villages 230 males were away on trading expeditions; in another village, 70 men were absent; and in each of the smaller settlements, at least 40 men were gone (1980:228). Male absences from the *entire valley* increased from 21 percent in 1973 to 77 percent in 1989.[23] At the village level, some of the rates of out-migration were even higher. By looking at the total number of adult males who were listed in the 1988 district census as having their primary residence in Nyeshang, and comparing this figure with the data from household surveys that I conducted in April and May of 1989, I found that the rate of migration for males between the ages of 16 and 65 ranged between 85 percent and 90 percent in four of the five villages surveyed.[24] (In village "E" the rate was only 38 percent, and I have no data for two other villages in the valley.)

7. A Tibetan nomad sews fur lining onto woolen clothing.

As trade became increasingly "professionalized" as a full-time, year-round male activity, this gender-based division of labor led to the rather lopsided sex ratio that exists in the valley today. The ratio of men and women is most imbalanced among "working adults"—that is, individuals between the ages of 16 and 50. Around the age of 55 the sex imbalance is somewhat redressed, since many men and women "retire" to the valley where some remain active farming and others spend most of their time at the monastery. The overall result of these demographic processes is a fairly high number of female-headed households in the valley, roughly about 45 percent.[25]

Included in this category are women who are widowed, single mothers, and single women over 30 years of age who are not likely to marry. These percentages are based on the number of year-round resident households and the total number of households present during the spring months. However, if this category were broadened to include all *married women* whose husbands' were outside the district for trade, the percentages would be significantly higher. In general, I did not include the female seasonal migrants who spend the winter in Kathmandu with their husbands or male kin, and then return to the valley for the remainder of the year with their children. However, these women often serve as household heads; their husbands rarely spend any time in the valley and the family property is left entirely in the hands of the women.

Male Absence and Female Authority

Several researchers have noted that male absence may be a key variable in fostering conditions that enhance women's control over basic resources and over their own lives.[26] Male migration and long-term absences are quite common in the middle hills of Nepal, and a few anthropologists have commented on the connection between male out-migration and women's central roles in the economic and social domains. McDougal (1969:33), for example, found that male migration for wage labor or trade in a community where he worked in the western region of Nepal resulted in female control of agricultural and domestic matters. Jones and Jones, who specifically studied women's roles among the Limbu, an ethnic group of eastern Nepal, noted that long-term male absences led to "more independent-minded females" and "new patterns of female authority" that were associated with an increase in female-headed households, which in the Limbu community reached about 20 percent (1976:47). They also observed that women's authority and decision making were not just limited to household affairs but extended outward into the community. During the winter season, when many men were absent for trade, Limbu women directed the village's religious life.[27] They "oversee the maintenance of symbols which have dominated village life" (47). Limbu women also maintained labor exchange networks and supervised the redistribution of labor and material goods within their community.

A similar conclusion was reached by Sanday (1974), whose historical study of Iroquois gender organization found that female control of agricultural production was strengthened by the long-term absence of male traders. As a result of male specialization in the fur trade, women's overall contributions to subsistence increased, as did their power as they effectively organized cooperative work groups and controlled the supply of provisions that were needed by traders (202). Agricultural production as a separate domain controlled by women provided them with a separate source of autonomy and prestige and an independent base for wielding influence in the household and the community. From a more recent period, we may consider Gewertz's (1983) restudy of the Chambri (Tchambuli) of New Guinea. The absence of adult males because of wage and plantation labor in the 1930s enabled adult women to live as autonomous and independent beings who effectively managed the "homeland."[28]

These findings contrast with some of the literature concerned with women's economic status in other agrarian societies. For example, in some Nepalese and Indian communities, women may be the primary agricultural workers in the subsistence sector, but as Sanday (1981) points out, these women are virtually indentured servants for they have no control over the end product. Some writers, drawing conclusions from studies of West Africa and India, have suggested that the position of women who are primarily engaged in subsistence farming will generally be subordinate to adult household males who are involved in market economies and sell their products or labor for cash.[29] These women, they suggest, wield less power and have less authority to make decisions or control resources. Other researchers have noted that women who contribute cash earnings to the household have a greater voice in domestic affairs than women involved solely in subsistence agriculture.[30]

Nyeshang women, however, do not seem to have suffered a loss of social or economic status as a result of their agricultural specialization and their decreasing involvement in trade (cash-generating) activities. A number of factors account for this. In Nyeshang, gender relations seem to resemble the patterns described in the Limbu and the Iroquois cases, where male absence enabled women to secure their authority and their rights to land and other resources. As sole managers of family estates and primary decision-makers, many adult women have become self-reliant and "independent-minded" in a manner similar to the Limbu (Jones and Jones 1976:46). Furthermore, in many rural-based households women's economic roles have taken on added importance since small traders are generally dependent on female labor and subsistence production.

Although rising income levels and steady rates of permanent migration to Kathmandu suggest that growing numbers of families are joining the ranks of urban elite, the majority of Nyeshangte households still rely on their land and livestock production to meet their basic subsistence needs. This is particularly true for households of median income, which constitute approximately 75–80 percent of the Nyeshang community. Income from small traders is generally not sufficient to support the family in the city environment where other family members are unable to earn wage income. Uneducated Nyeshangte with inadequate Nepalese language skills are seldom able to find employment and cannot successfully compete with the better-educated ethnic groups and high castes who have long-standing connections with Nepalese bureaucratic institutions. Without supplementary income from wage labor or subsistence farming, the profit margins earned by small traders from the resale of imported consumer items are generally insufficient to support the entire household year-round in an urban setting where living expenses are high.

The difficulty of finding wage work in Kathmandu is widely recognized by village women. Although Kathmandu's tourist industry provides many Nepalese with jobs in hotels, restaurants, and trekking companies, it is mostly young men with English-language skills who are employed in this sector. Lack of employment options is one reason why village women, who stay with husbands or relatives in Kathmandu during the winter, prefer their lives in the village where they are proud of their agricultural work, their support of traditional village life, and their ability to manage the family estate: "We have no work here, how will we eat? We are happy to return to the village, it is too hot here during the summer; the air and water is bad and people get sick. We have friends in the village, and we all work together; here everybody is sitting home alone."

In the village setting, women make valuable contributions to the household economy, and small traders generally acknowledge their dependence on women's subsistence production. Lacking large capital reserves, losses from theft, fines, or confiscation by customs officials can be quite disastrous for most small traders who usually exist on the margin. Profits from trade tend to fluctuate widely each year, so that women's subsistence production often provides the household with much of its daily food requirements and takes on added importance as a cushion against economic disaster.

In addition, domestic labor requirements in these median-level households also make it necessary for at least one adult to manage the family's village herds and properties. Although labor shortages and the burden of household management are eased by live-in servants and seasonal laborers, women's residence in the village enables them to guard family interests and supervise the work of hired help. In households of average wealth, female labor is essential and most daughters and wives cannot be spared from the round of village work. It seems that in the Nyeshang case, complementarity of male-female roles, with each sex specializing in different areas, is also conducive to egalitarian relations.[31]

New Opportunities for Women

Despite the number of hired caretakers and tenant farmers, a large proportion of farm land remains fallow, though the rates vary significantly among villages.[32] As in the past, Nyeshangte kinsmen and poorer households always have priority to unused fields and generally do not pay any rent. Furthermore, since most Nyeshangte will not sell property to "outsiders," many city residents end up giving their property to relatives in the valley. The result is that categories of individuals (single, divorced, or widowed women, or younger sons), often considered marginal in other societies because of their nonlanded status, are seldom disenfranchised in Nyeshang. Schuler (1987) who worked in Baragaon, an area adjacent to Nyeshang, found that polyandrous marriage patterns resulted in a "surplus" of unmarried females who occupy a peripheral or low rank in what is described as a stratified society. These women, Schuler argued, were marginalized and dependent on kin for their livelihood. In this context, Schuler saw nonentitled single women as permanent low-status dependents who provided their landed kin with a cheap source of labor. One problem with her analysis is that she did not look at single (landless) men to see if they were similarly exploited. The material from Nyeshang suggests that neither single men nor single women are low-status dependents. They produce sufficient food to get by at subsistence levels, and many women and men supplement this living with small-scale trade.

In fact, household surveys taken in four villages reveal that several unmarried women (and men) have established independent households. Some act as caretakers of village houses; others, with their own homes

8. All along the Annapurna Circuit, women run lodges and small shops.

nearby, cultivate these surplus fields in addition to their own. Some, by default (after older male siblings relinquished their claims to family property), have inherited their parents' homes and fields. The point is that sufficient land is available for women who choose not to marry or who prefer to remain in the village and earn a living farming.[33]

Since the opening of the Annapurna Circuit in 1977—a popular three-week trekking route that extends from Dumre to Nyeshang and ends in Pokhara—many Nyeshangte women have earned supplementary cash through a variety of tourist-related enterprises. Some knit gloves, scarves, and hats and sell them to trekkers who need winter gear for crossing the high pass. Several women offer trekkers lodging and simple meals in their own homes. Other women own small shops that cater to villagers as well as passing tourists—they sell canned and dried food, household commodities, toiletry items, and postcards.

Some of these family enterprises are run jointly by married couples who have seized the opportunity that increasing tourism has presented to remain together in the homeland. During my first visit to Traklung I stayed at a lodge run by a Nyeshangte couple whose economic circumstances had greatly improved as a result of tourism. Kanda and Tigri moved their family to Traklung in 1978 after they had suffered some major setbacks, including the loss of their yak and *dzo* (crossbreeds), and a failed trading venture. They were originally from a small hamlet near Nyangkhu and had owned very little land. At first, the lodge consisted of a single room that had been added on to their main dwelling. By 1987 they had enough capital to construct a separate hotel that had an additional six rooms and twenty beds on the upper floor. The following year Kanda built another kitchen and common room for the trekkers so that his family would no longer have to share their kitchen and living quarters with paying guests.

Another lodge in the village of Lhakpa is currently managed by three unmarried women in their early twenties. The parents of each "hostess" contributed some cash for a starting fund, and other relatives and friends pitched in to refurbish an empty house that belonged to one of the girl's uncles. The young women work in shifts—cooking for guests and attending to their regular farm chores—and share the profits from the inn. In addition, the three women have a reputation for making excellent beer and wine, which they sell to local men who stop by every evening to visit. Profits from alcohol sales are good, ranging from fourteen rupees (U.S.$ .56) a bottle to two hundred rupees (U.S.$8.00) per batch. The business gives the young women financial independence and personal autonomy.

The demographic trends discussed in this chapter—urban migration, male absence, increase in female-headed households—have been instrumental in reinforcing Nyeshang women's central roles in village society. These women are respected as hardworking productive members of their community whose actions and livelihoods help preserve the homeland as a sanctuary against the exigencies of modern life.[34]

In the city many of the Nyeshangte men I interviewed also spoke of their wives with admiration and respect. These men acknowledge that their wives have worked hard for many years and state that now the women deserve to rest—"*basne ra khāne*" (literally, to sit and eat); some men add, " . . . and watch videos all day." Female labor supported the village-based economy while men tried to secure a commercial foothold in Kathmandu. Many women supplemented household cash income by portering goods from Terai markets to the middle hills during the slack agricultural season. Others wove wool rugs and earned wages at the Tibetan carpet factories outside Kathmandu during the 1970s, when many Nyeshangte began to establish permanent residences in the capital. Regardless of where they worked, in the city or in the rural district, Nyeshang women's economic support made the transition to urban life possible for many households. In a sense, senior women are living on accumulated prestige from many years of hard work in the villages, in addition to their contributions during the early period of urban settlement.

PART THREE

Social Realms

CHAPTER FIVE

Familiar Circles

ALTHOUGH NEW FORMS of economic production have had a far reaching effect on Nyeshang society—both in the village and urban context—certain social arrangements reflected in kinship, marriage, and inheritance practices remain relatively constant. These social formations, which are indelibly meshed to Nyeshangte ethnic identity and cultural history, play a significant role in structuring gender relations and in preserving the overall egalitarian quality of Nyeshang life. The selective reproduction of these "customary" features reflects a deliberate and collective effort by the Nyeshangte to distinguish themselves from neighboring Buddhist societies of similar ethnic background, as well as from the culturally distinct and politically dominant Hindu majority.[1]

This chapter identifies the basic characteristics of Nyeshang social organization and examines the range of alternatives and roles available to individual women. I pay particular attention to the rights, obligations, and privileges associated with bilateral kinship, marital status, and residence patterns that govern women's access to property. Attention to case studies will reveal both the structural principles that shape Nyeshangte social life and the way individuals are both enabled and constrained by these structures. Before turning to the Nyeshang material, I would like to bring up a few other points that frame this discussion of gender and social organization.

In recent years, the relevance of western analytical categories for under-standing the lives of men and women in other parts of the world, has come under increasing scrutiny. Native exegeses often reveal that individuals are positioned in their societies in rather unique ways, and this social reality may be misunderstood when we rely exclusively on dichotomous models.[2] Others have noted that women's roles and circumstances may differ greatly within a single society—within various domains and within the kinship system (Sacks 1979; Bennett 1983; Raheja 1994c). In addition, the way women perceive their situations, the extent to which they accept, under-stand, or ignore prevailing ideologies, will also vary.[3] These differences become clearer if we avoid characterizing "women" as a monolithic unit, and focus instead on local process and individual circumstances as well as issues of power, agency, or practice.[4]

A similar critique has been directed at the study of social organization, where the utility of our kinship models and theoretical frameworks in delineating the various principles governing alliance, descent, and marriage patterns in nonwestern societies have also been questioned.[5] Some anthro-pologists have found that these kinship models may be distorted by Eurocentric notions of family or biased by our implicit notions concerning the natural division between "domestic" and "public" domains. This divi-sion, they argue, is derived largely from an American folk model of kin-ship.[6] Other writers have challenged traditional approaches that focus on normative aspects or customary law and largely "ignore the female point of view" (Lamphere 1974; Aziz 1978; Molnar 1980). The importance of indi-vidual choice and individual action is frequently overlooked when highly abstracted views of society are presented. Too often these views are derived from idealized social models that assume a homogeneous and unchanging social order, one frequently described and informed by primarily male per-spectives and concerns.[7]

Nyeshang Social Organization: A Comparative View

Social facts in Nyeshang have a way of eluding neat categorization. This poor fit reflects the shortcomings inherent in the models we use, as well as the limitations of many conventional ethnographies that emphasize closure and orderliness. Another problem is that there seems to be a latent inertia in our descriptions of social organization: our readings of "X society" are built on the impressions of earlier accounts; as a result, certain features are reinforced and others overlooked or misconstrued in successive renderings.

This issue was addressed by Robert Borofsky (1987:1–6) in an attempt to understand why earlier western reports, written by missionaries, government officials, and anthropologists, had overlooked a prominent feature of social organization on the Polynesian atoll where he worked. In trying to explain the existence of these divergent accounts, Borofsky identifies two "fault lines" that run through many ethnographic texts, and points out that these problems do not result from particular accounts being more or less accurate than others:

> What is at issue is something of broader significance: How different people construct different versions of the atoll's past. In unraveling the problem, we perceive the dynamic nature of Pukapukan knowledge regarding the past, how Pukapukans, in the process of learning and validating their traditions, continually change them. And we see how anthropologists, in the process of writing about these traditions for western audiences, overstructure them, how they emphasize uniformity at the expense of diversity, stasis at the expense of change. (1987:2)

I was confronted with a similar problem when I tried to reconcile earlier reports of Nyeshang social organization with my own impressions. Although a few anthropologists have described communities like Nyeshang as strictly patrilineal with virilocal residence (e.g., Cooke 1985a; Gurung 1977a), the situation is more complex than these two studies would suggest. Other researchers (Aziz 1978; March 1979), who carried out in-depth studies of household and social organization in similar societies (Tibetan, Sherpa, Tamang), have noted that bilateral affiliation, parallel descent, and bilocal or neolocal residence may be a more accurate description than the patrilineal/virilocal categories found in much of the earlier literature. Regarding this apparent conundrum over descent classification, I turn again to Borofsky, whose own work in Polynesia seems particularly relevant here. Borofsky notes that an important difference exists between describing a social group as having a "patrilineal bias" and saying that the community is comprised of patrilineages. He explains that a "patrilineal bias in social grouping does not necessitate formal patrilineages or clans. In fact, a patrilineal bias can coexist with cognatic descent groups and bilateral patterns of affiliation" (1987:19).

In this section my aim is first to identify some of the conceptual difficulties in classifying Nyeshang society and, second, to compare Nyeshang with other ethnic Tibetan communities to get an idea of where Nyeshang fits in the overall scheme of things. Some of the problems are caused by slippage in the way researchers define and use various analytical terms to describe marriage, inheritance, and residence rules. In relation to this problem of translation and comparison, Tambiah points out:

> There are the difficulties of adequately grasping the details of a local custom, practice, or institution and then giving it a label in the English language. This is a problem of translating, labeling, and assimilating the "alien" phenomenon to our anthropological categories of understanding. On the other hand, there is the problem of taking the analytic adequacy of an anthropological concept for granted and then finding that it does not fit and grasp meaningfully the empirical details on the ground.[8] (1989:414)

Second, in an attempt to present a formal model of society, some researchers overlook the existence of variant social rules and flexible social practices; some rules are discarded, others are given paramount status. The elevation of one ideal pattern above the others as the basis for labeling a particular social formation leads to a distorted view of social reality that can be corrected by considering the entire repertoire of rules (and practices) that exist, and noting the limited contexts in which they are applied.

For example, in Nyeshang, residence rules and actual practices differ from one stage of marriage to another. Again, attention to this sort of variation makes it difficult to label Nyeshang according to conventional frameworks, but this strategy also provides a more accurate reflection of my informants' explanations and *their* social reality. My notes and taped interviews are filled with statements of the sort, "We always do like this . . . ," followed immediately by, "but we also do like that . . ." Rules exist in variant forms, and sometimes neither version has precedence over the others. They simply exist as alternatives. This complexity should really come as no surprise, given the existence of cultural values that foster an ethic of respect for individuals and a high tolerance of anomalous conduct. The existence of "flexible" social arrangements helps to create a society where opportunities for men and women are commensurate and balanced, though not necessarily always identical.[9]

Again, much of this confusion stems from the limitations of our dichotomous models and the inherent problems of classification. In actuality, the patrilineal descent rules that do exist in Nyeshang have limited application: they determine clan affiliation, but variant rules for clan affiliation do exist. For example, a *magpa* (adopted bridegroom) becomes a member of his wife's clan and lives in her natal household. Residence rules also vary. After the final marriage ceremony takes place, the ideal pattern in Nyeshang is neolocal residence. However, during the initial marriage (betrothal) phase, the ideal pattern is to reside with the wife's parents. During the intermediate stages, one to four years after the betrothal phase, the couple may reside with the groom's parents until a house is built or given to them, and each spouse receives his or her share of the parental estate. Marriage in Nyeshang is processual and the sequence of stages may take place rapidly within a year or two or may be spread over a period of five years or longer, depending on economic circumstances, the couple's compatibility, and the type of marriage—elopement or "kidnapping," arranged or "love" marriages.

Again, a certain fuzziness exists about the meaning of marriage and divorce in Nyeshang. Some couples may be married without celebrating the final rites, though their marriage may have been arranged with a formal betrothal. Several women and men use the same phrasing, "We just started to live together and the babies came." For whatever reason, perhaps a death in the family or some other inconvenience, the families were prevented from holding the customary celebration. But if the relationship is stable and the couple resides together, their social and legal status as a couple is recognized. Although a number of marriages never proceed beyond the first stage, when the groom lives with or visits his bride in her natal home, most Nyeshangte claim that divorce is rare in their community. Breakups during this initial stage or trial marriage are not considered divorces. Generally no children are involved, and property transfers are minimal. Often, inheritance from the parents' estates is delayed until the marriage appears to be stable. Again, it is important to note how different rules and different meanings are invested in the notion of marriage (and divorce) in Nyeshang, and how these meanings vary from our own western concepts of these same institutions.

In addition to problems of meaning and slippage, social analysis is also complicated by the existence of rules that come into play only in limited circumstances. Aziz, for example, found that patrilineal descent was of minor importance in "Dingri," a Tibetan community in north-central Nepal, and it operated in a limited context: among a minority of lineages belonging to *miser* (outcaste) families and *sgnags pa* (shaman-sorcerer) lines where the "essence" or spiritual ability (or in the case of the outcaste, the tainted substance) was passed on from father to son (1978:118). Among the commoners who comprised 90 percent of the population, Aziz found that household identity took precedence over patrilineal reckoning. A household's overall social standing was dependent not only on the coresident males, but also on their *namsa* (wife's) status and her affiliation to her natal home (123).[10]

In many Tibetan communities like Dingri, residence is also bilocal during the early stages of marriage. Subsequently, brides move to their husbands' home or to a neolocal residence. Residence may also be uxorilocal if the bride's parents have no sons. In that event the husband becomes an adopted son and lives at his bride's natal home. Patrilineal reckoning did not seem to be a factor in inheritance practices either, as a number of researchers report that most Tibetans seemed unconcerned whether the estate passed through sons or through daughters (Miller 1980:162; Aziz 1974). Again, this seems to point to a bilateral descent pattern. Furthermore, Miller writes, in Tibet, "the disposition of all property, both real and movable, may be stipulated by written will to include or exclude various potential heirs, regardless of sex" (162).

Although Nyeshangte traditions indicate that sons generally receive a larger share of land and daughters receive most of the movable property, the majority of my male and female informants also stressed that the actual division of the family estate depended ultimately on the parents' personal inclinations. Some would say, "Mother and Father give as they wish." Others added that usually fathers and mothers gave daughters money, animals, jewelry, and one or two pieces of land, and the remaining land was divided equally among the sons.[11] One man commented, "But [parents], they don't have to give anything to [this] boy or to [that] girl if they don't like. People will feel badly if the land is not divided well [fairly], but it is for mother and father to decide." It seems that the patrilineal "bias" governing inheritance rules in Nyeshang is weakened by a corresponding emphasis placed on individual choice.

Although March (1979:158) describes both Sherpa and Tamang societies as patrilineal (because an individual takes on the father's clan affiliation), she notes that these societies have, in effect, parallel inheritance: daughters receive property from their mothers, sons inherit from their fathers, a system that "creates conceptual family subgroups of a mother and her children (especially daughters) on the one hand and a father and his children (especially sons) on the other." This "effective system of parallel inheritance" and the subgroups that result are given recognition in Tamang society by the terms *mheme* and *phepe*, and by the fact that in both Tamang and Sherpa societies, women who are widowed, divorced, or remarried are entitled to keep their daughters with them, despite the formal rules associated with patrilineal clan organization (158–59).

9. A Nyeshangte family.

Bilateral Kinship in Nyeshang

In Nyeshang there is also a system of parallel inheritance, and the important of bilateral kinship is recognized in the social groups referred to as *mame* (relatives on the mother's side) and *phabe* (paternal clan relatives). Individuals maintain close relationships with both their matrilateral and patrilateral relatives, who can be called upon to provide money for trading ventures, hospitality when visiting in the village or city, and overall support during times of personal crisis. Children of divorced parents generally reside with their mothers until age 15, at which time they may choose to live with their patrilateral kin. Regardless of residence, these children are entitled to inherit from their father's and mother's estate.

In many ways Nyeshangte society occupies an intermediate position between the patrilineal Tibetan Bhotia populations of northern Nepal and the truly bilateral societies of central Tibet.[12] Patrilineal descent groups or lineages play a negligible role in Nyeshang life; they do not own land or control resources.[13] Instead, patrilineal ascription is used only to define eligible marriage partners: one must marry outside his or her natal clan.[14]

In Nyeshang, given the preference for bilateral cross-cousin marriage (either matrilateral or patrilateral cross-cousins) and village endogamy, a woman's affines are likely to be relatives and her in-laws are often aunts and uncles.[15] Relations between affines and daughters-in-law (or sons-in-law) are generally more familiar and easy-going than the strained relations that have been reported in some extended patrilineal Hindu families.[16] This system of preferred marriage presupposes the equality of clans and places certain importance on sibling ties, as brothers' and sisters' children may be potential marriage partners.[17]

Sibling Ties: Real and Classificatory

Affective ties are especially strong among peers and same-sex siblings who are close in age. These bonds reflect the marked generational emphasis in Nyeshangte society and are expressed by the terms *cousin-brothers* and *cousin-sisters*. These classificatory siblings may be parallel or cross-cousins or more distantly related "clan brothers and sisters." In fact, Nyeshangte youths use the reference term *cousin-brother* or *cousin-sister* for their peers, as a way to separate them from "outsiders." This ethic of brother- or sisterhood, which normally includes fellow clan members, is thus extended outward to include all Nyeshangte in an expression of group solidarity that is particularly strong in the Kathmandu community.

When Maya, a teenage girl in Kathmandu, told me that she had been harassed by a group of young men in Thamel (the tourist district in Kathmandu), I asked her what had happened and whether the boys in question were from her community. "No, of course not," she replied, "Nyeshangte boys are my cousin-brothers, they do not say things like that to us [girls]. Nyeshangte boys do not treat us like that. We are sisters to them, and if we need [assistance], they will help."

Although bonds among age-mates (including real and classificatory siblings) are usually very close, ties between older and younger siblings are characterized by more reserve, and are often expressed in a parental idiom of protection.

Tashi, for example, an 18-year-old boy, felt responsible for his 14-year-old sister's welfare, and was especially protective of her in Kathmandu. He worried that she might be harassed on the streets or that she might be "kidnapped" or would elope with an unsuitable Nyeshangte male. Tashi explained how these kidnappings take place:

Usually if a boy likes a girl, he will ask his parents to help with the marriage arrangements. But if they [the girl's family] are not our relatives, then our parents cannot arrange [a marriage]. So if I like that

10. A young woman from Kathmandu offers to help village girls prepare food.

girl, I will speak to my sister or other girlfriend who will help. She will go to the girl and bring her outside. Then we will stay away for a few days, until our parents have had a chance to arrange a betrothal. Then we return and are engaged, and will later be married.

When I asked what happened if the girl objected, Tashi looked very surprised. "The girl, she always is married after that." But after further questioning, he added, "The girl could return home and marry someone else. If she is kidnapped and the girl does not want to stay, her parents will have to pay a fine to the boy's family."[18] Tashi then told me about his sister:

My older sister was kidnapped here. My parents were really upset because they didn't like the boy or his family. But my sister was in love with him and a friend of hers helped arrange it. After a few days, my parents came to accept it, but I don't want the same thing to happen to my younger sister. We Nyeshangte do marriages only during the winter months in Kathmandu, so I keep an eye on my sister and which boys are talking to her, especially in the winter time. If I don't like them, I tell them to stay away.

When I pointed out that his sister was only 14 years old and not likely to marry for at least another five or six years, Tashi replied, "I feel responsible for her. I love her very much and worry about her. I don't want her to get hurt. Didn't Sangden [a mutual friend of ours] tell you about the kidnappings in Kathmandu?" He laughed and explained, "That is why I don't want my sister to go out."[19]

Social Traditions as Markers of Ethnic Identity

In the same way that Nyeshangte youths use an idiom of kinship to distinguish themselves from all outsiders, Nyeshangte social traditions are also invoked and held up as markers of their separate ethnic identity. For example, differences in marriage practices among Nyeshangte and neighboring Buddhist and Hindu communities were often mentioned by my male and female acquaintances. Nyeshangte are well aware that variant practices exist in other groups and are quick to assert that "here we do things differently." On the subject of polyandry, all my informants insisted that Nyeshangte never married polyandrously, nor did men ever take two wives. "We always do like this: one to one, one to one," an 80-year-old woman explained as she held up two fingers. "In Mustang, they do like this (holding up three fingers), and sometimes even this," she said laughing, as she held up four fingers. My informants never derided these types of polyandrous marriages and could not give me a reason why Nyeshangte only married monogamously, saying only, "We've always done it like this, since a long time before."[20]

Many of my male and female informants also made a point of distinguishing customary Nyeshang practices from those of Hindu groups. For example, in Nyeshang, affines are not hierarchically differentiated—the bride's and groom's families are considered equals.[21] Namgyal explained, "I know Hindu people do like this: the father and mother of the bride must show respect and sit lower than the husband's family, but not here. Here, both are the same, both are equal, and boys and girls must show respect to both [sets of] parents equally. There is no question of who is bigger or who is higher."[22]

In the past, in some (high-caste) Hindu communities, prepubescent girls were married as early as at the age of 8 or 9, often transferred to their husband's home at the onset of menarche or even before.[23] Some marriages were heavily invested and large dowries often accompanied the "gift of the virgin" to the affine's home.[24] Virginity was highly valued and most families did not wish to risk the "dangers" of having an unmarried daughter at home who could bring shame and cast an inauspicious mark on the family.[25] In contrast to these values, which are characteristic of the Brahmanical ideological pattern found in some Hindu communities in northern India and Nepal, women in Nyeshang are not believed to be ritually dangerous nor is their sexuality particularly threatening. There is no cultural elaboration of pollution rules in general, and thus no concern about the polluting aspects of bodily fluids during menstruation, child birth, or sexual relations. Sexual relations often occur during the engagement phase and resulting children are welcomed.[26] In general, since marriages in Tibetan Buddhist societies are viewed as purely secular concerns, these events are not sanctioned or governed by religious precepts and occur largely outside the ritual domain of lamas and monks.

As a result of these cultural ideals and practices, marriages in Nyeshang take place at a relatively late age (mid- to late twenties). Since the labor of unmarried children is always welcome in the natal household, Nyeshangte parents usually wait until their children indicate that they wish to get married before making arrangements with the parents of a prospective spouse. And, as an elderly man pointed out, "If a girl doesn't like the boy [chosen by her parents], she won't go [with him]. She will look for another boy."

Marriage is not a traumatic process for Nyeshangte women and does not involve a severing of ties with childhood and village friends, nor with natal families. Most marriages are contracted between families within the same village. The second most common pattern is to marry someone from an adjacent village, usually no more than half an hour away. In sum, the strong preference for village endogamy, the relatively late age of marriage, the lack of concern with controlling female sexuality, and the processual nature of marriage, which requires consent from both parties to succeed, and conversely the ease of divorce, contribute to Nyeshang women's ability to effectively control their own lives.

Nyeshangte pride in their group's identity and distinctive traditions is also paralleled (not surprisingly) by a strong belief in their group's innate superiority. As evidence, male and female informants mention the unusually large size of most Nyeshangte babies, who often weigh nine pounds at birth. While knowledge of exact birth weights is a recent development, informants are quite aware that most Nepalese babies are considerably smaller and, from their point of view, "weaker." Many elderly women and men also cite longevity as proof of their group's superior constitutions. In several of the oral accounts I collected, Nyeshangte women mentioned ancestors who lived long, healthy lives (some to 100 years of age) "without

11. A widow in her late fifties.

[western] medicines." In addition to birth size, stature, physical strength, and longevity, the Nyeshangte pride themselves in a few rather elusive qualities as well. Maya, for example, tried to explain (in English) what sets Nyeshangte apart from other people: "We have a saying here in Kathmandu. We Nyeshangte do not smell . . . [pause] What do you call this? [reply: arm pit] Yes, we say, Nyeshangte people do not stink under the arm pit."

Nyeshangte beliefs about their group's innate superiority are also paralleled by a strong preference for group endogamy. If an illegitimate child is born from a "mixed" union with an "outsider," the child is known as *yulu*. Yulu children, however, are accepted by the community, and in the words of one 30-year-old male, "Yulu, if strong, with nice strong faces, they too can get a Nyeshangte husband or wife." Again, the emphasis here is on strength and vigor.

Indeed, these qualities seem to be prominent in many of my Nyeshangte acquaintances—both male and female. Watching a middle-aged Nyeshangte matron stride purposefully through the Kathmandu streets, dressed in an ankle-length woolen bakhu and running shoes, one gets the impression of a battleship in full sail sweeping down on the crowds. There is nothing timid, retiring, or shy about Nyeshangte women, and likewise, Nyeshangte men are known to be arrogant, blustery, and quick to fight. Neither men nor women adopt a deferential, submissive attitude before high-caste Hindus (a posture often seen among lower-status Nepalese).

In fact, one of my first glimpses of this "martial spirit" occurred when Maya showed me photographs of her parents during my early fieldwork in Kathmandu. In one photo, her father, a handsome man in his late twenties with long black hair streaming in the wind, was sitting astride a white horse. He was accompanied by five other men similarly dressed in chuba (robes) and knee-high boots. They had just crossed a high pass on their mountain ponies and were returning home after a trading expedition to Lo. Posed in a semicircle on their horses, with a rugged jaunty air about them, they looked like warriors.

The photo of Maya's mother, also in traditional garments, shows a large handsome woman with a composed regal air. She was several years older than her husband and appeared to be his equal in stature and size. I had the impression that this woman could hold her own (physically and mentally) in any setting: whether buying gold in the Hong Kong jewelry marts, haggling with Thai vendors in Bangkok's night markets, or terrorizing the clerks at the Kathmandu airport.

Although a few Nyeshangte women marry outsiders (usually Tibetans), it is primarily Nyeshangte male traders who contract the fairly limited number of unions with outsiders. These may be women from other Nepalese groups or women from another country, usually Thailand or Burma.[27] However, the qualities inherent in Nyeshangte blood are generally thought to be dominant over outside blood. Thus a male trader in his thirties, who initially voiced his concern over the dispersal of the Nyeshangte community outside the homeland, ended the conversation on a somewhat different note: "Even if Nyeshangte are living in so many places, and a few are taking philing [western] wives, it just means we Nyeshangte are becoming more [in number]. One boy, he took a German girl and they have a child, but that child will be Nyeshangte. [Laughing] We will have Nyeshangte everywhere—in Europe, in Australia, everywhere."

Despite these few references to outside marriages, group endogamy is still quite prevalent among the Kathmandu-born generation. In fact, one evening when I was visiting one of the local neighborhood gangs whose members were mostly Nyeshangte, Tibetans, and a few Sherpas, one of the Tibetan boys chided my Nyeshangte friend. These comments were made in a friendly, half-joking manner, but the resentment was clear: "You Nyeshangte think you are better than everyone. We are your friends, since a long time before, but you think we are not good enough. You Nyeshangte marry only Nyeshangte, no one else."[28] My informant said nothing as this chorus was picked up by some of the other young men. He looked somewhat sheepish after this unexpected outburst, and when he resumed the conversation, it was on another subject.

Although marriage traditions and group endogamy reaffirm Nyeshangte identity as being distinct from other Tibetan Buddhist groups, usually this discourse is used to highlight the differences between Nyeshangte (and Tibetans) and various Hindu groups. The customary independence and authority of Nyeshangte (and other Tibetan) women are topics that are often brought up by both male and female informants for contrastive purposes. This discourse is quite effective, as in a number of conversations with Newar and Hindu men, the prevailing image of Nyeshangte women that emerged was one of mythic proportions on a par with the legendary Amazons. One Newar fellow, a wealthy merchant who also happened to be my landlord during my initial stay in Kathmandu, knew a lot about Nyeshangte business practices. "Yes," he assured me, "Nyeshangte women do business. They control everything. You should see them at the airport and on the planes. The airline people are afraid of them. And one of them is a big boss, running everything. She yells at the police and the customs clerks. She protects her people [carriers], no one stops her. They are afraid to argue with her."

The customary authority of the Nyeshangte wife was also revealed in conversations with Nyeshangte men. Again, the contrasts were drawn with Hindu female roles.[29] One Nyeshangte man in his fifties talked about these differences while we sat in his Kathmandu jewelry store:

> We have our own customs, and they are different. Brahmin-Chhetri women have to respect their husbands. If the husband doesn't come home and the women are hungry, they can't eat. In Nyeshang, if he doesn't come home and she is hungry, she can eat. Men, women, they are equal. Women do farm work like men. They are equal to men because of Buddhist [*dharma*] teachings, and because they can help their husbands. Brahmin-Chhetri [wives] can't help [their] husbands; if problem at office comes, [their wives] can't help. But women here [in the Nyeshang community], they can do work like we do.

These differences were highlighted in yet another context. In a conversation with a teenage Nyeshangte girl and two young Tibetan Muslim women in Kathmandu, the topic of domestic violence came up spontaneously. All of them commiserated with women from Hindu families and certain ethnic groups (like Tamang) who had no options if their husbands beat them. Their perceptions were based on the personal histories of their Tamang domestic servants, and I too had heard a similar story from a Tamang woman who helped me with housework and laundry chores for a few months. Jameela, a 24 year old who was engaged, commented,

> These [Hindu and Tamang] women have nowhere to go. They live at the husband's house and cannot go home. No man would dare beat a Tibetan wife (referring to both Nyeshangte and the Tibetan Muslim community). A Tibetan wife, she can work, she can go home to mother and father, she would just leave. We do not have to stay. That is why no man [in our community] can take another wife [a second one]. We don't allow that, we would break the marriage and go home or live alone. Isn't that so? I think it is the same with you Nyeshangte too.

One final example, somewhat more gruesome, illustrates the inconceivable distance between Nyeshangte perspectives on family life and the nightmarish reality of domestic relations in some Hindu communities. One day Maya dropped by my rooftop apartment. I had been away for six weeks, and she had a lot of news to share. Sitting on the roof terrace, Maya pointed to a distant house, which was also visible from her own home nearby, and said,

Chimmi [a 17-year-old Nyeshangte girl] is not well. A few days before, she saw a girl on that balcony who was burned. I think she was a servant to that (Hindu) Newar family, but no one knows. Chimmi is still sick and will not leave her room. She heard the girl screaming and saw she was on fire. They [various neighbors] called the police and police came, but it was too late. The girl died the next day in the hospital. The family said it was an accident, but Chimmi, she says that the girl's hands were tied. "How do you burn yourself cooking if your hands are tied?" we asked the police. They do nothing. And even the papers, they say it was an accident, just like that.

Sure enough, when I looked through that week's stack of the *Rising Nepal*, I saw several references to deaths due to accidental burning and poisoning. It seemed that only young Hindu women had a predilection for ingesting rat poison or catching on fire while cooking dinner. Although the murder (and suicides)[30] of young women (wives) are not as common in Kathmandu as the well-publicized dowry deaths (and suicides) in India, no doubt similar motives and constraints were in operation. Chimmi had still not recovered from her shock when I went to see her: she was nervous, restless, and unable to sleep or eat. Maya too was disturbed and quite worried about her best friend. The family called in several lamas who performed a *lha bsang* rite to drive away evil forces and appease the household spirits with offerings of incense. In time the vivid memories faded, and Chimmi no longer heard the screams. We never talked about the incident in her presence.

These examples illustrate some of the ways that Nyeshangte men and women use a genderized framework—notions about gender roles and women's authority—to emphasize the distance and the differences between themselves and Hindu caste groups. In many ways, Nyeshangte and other ethnic Tibetans share similar attitudes about gender relations and the roles of women and men: an egalitarian ethos pervades many aspects of social life; men and women mix freely at social gatherings; they often labor side by side in mixed work parties in the fields or at the dgon pa, where they prepare food and offerings for community celebrations. Social relations between men and women are characterized by a casual, easy-going attitude. These characteristics contrast sharply with gender relations in some Hindu communities—the Nyeshangte are aware of that, and most outsiders are aware of it also.

In essence, the maintenance of "traditional" Nyeshang social patterns reflects an overriding concern with preserving Nyeshangte identity in the homeland and Kathmandu; at the same time, these social features also promote egalitarian gender relations within the community. On the one hand, this rhetoric emphasizes the innate superiority of Nyeshangte relative to outsiders; on the other, it proclaims the basic equality of all members within the group.

This image of a closed, unified group of people who are proud of their own cultural traditions, who have a reputation for being somewhat aloof, somewhat dangerous, and always quick to anger—and for having fierce and independent-minded women—also ensures a general "hands-off" attitude from the rest of the Nepalese community. Whether at the airport or in the streets of Kathmandu, most outsiders are not willing to tangle with individual Nyeshangte and risk a confrontation with the entire group. Although young Nepalese women (and western women) are subject to frequent sexual harassment on the streets and buses of Kathmandu, most Nyeshangte women are left alone. Whether it is their dress, their stature, or their self-confident demeanor that marks their identity, Nyeshangte women go about their daily business for the most part unhampered.

In the first section of this chapter, I presented a comparative overview of Nyeshang social organization in order to place it in a wider frame of reference, both theoretically and ethnographically. I also examined how Nyeshang discourses about their traditional social practices are used to reinforce their ethnic identity. I would like to shift levels now and move from a general comparative framework to a more detailed level: here, I will use a number of case studies to consider how residence patterns, marital practices, and inheritance rules variously affect the circumstances of individual women and, in turn, show how these women variously manipulate, negotiate, or accept the social structures that constitute their lives. Residence, marriage, and inheritance patterns are also keys to understanding the influence and authority of middle-aged Nyeshang women in the household and community.

Inheritance Practices in Nyeshang

Dowry, variously called *nurkhal, palee keeba,* and *payar thapa*—to distinguish kinds of property given at different stages of the marriage process— is defined here as the "process whereby parental property is distributed to a daughter at her marriage" rather than at the holder's death (Goody 1976:6).[31] In Nyeshang this property belongs to the wife and remains under her control even after divorce (*phreba*). Her husband also brings property to the marriage.

Parents generally divide the estate at the time of their eldest son's marriage, and each son is entitled to an equal share of the fields.[32] However, the parents usually retain control over their unmarried sons' shares and effectively manage the entire property until their sons formally separate and establish their own households.[33] Daughters generally receive less land than sons but are given more mobile property—livestock, money, housewares, and jewelry—at the time of their marriage. (A turquoise and coral necklace alone may be worth a thousand to twenty-five thousand rupees [u.s.$400–$1,000]. In some instances a portion of this personal property is passed on from mother to daughter, reflecting the existence of parallel lines of inheritance. One woman commented, "My parents gave me some money, and grain, also clothes and a few goats at the time of my marriage, but from my mother I received two fields and jewelry." If a woman has no daughters, she may will this personal property to her sisters' daughters or pass it on to her sons. The decision is hers.

Regardless of which line of inheritance it follows, a daughter may receive either a portion (or her entire share) during the initial engagement phase, depending on her age, household resources, and the likely stability of the marriage. Sometimes the bulk of the female inheritance is offered only after the final rites have been celebrated.[34] Since Nyeshangte marriages are processual (much like marriages among Sherpa and other Tibetan groups), property division and transfers may be delayed for several years. This delayed transfer also affects sons, since many do not receive their full inheritance until they too move out of their parents' home.

Female property may not be alienated from a woman by her male siblings nor by her husband, though most married women put these resources to joint or communal use within their own households. Unmarried daughters and nuns are also entitled to an equal share of mobile and immobile property, and they too reserve the sole authority to dispose of it.[35] If an unmarried daughter wishes to live apart from her natal family, parents generally make an effort to provide her with a house, and sufficient land to support herself.

Although Cooke (1985a) states that Nyeshangte resemble other Tibetan patrilineal societies in that the youngest son (and his wife) generally live with the parents and provide for them in their old age (cf. Goldstein 1973), I found little evidence of this pattern in Nyeshang or in Kathmandu.[36] Household surveys and interviews with many middle-aged women reveal that parents are more likely to choose a *favorite* child or grandchild to act as their caretaker, rather than automatically delegating this responsibility to their youngest son. Similar practices are apparently found in many ethnic

Tibetan communities outside Nepal, where questions of compatibility take precedence over formal rules of succession.[37] In fact, most women indicated that parents frequently chose daughters over sons, simply because of the inherent difficulties involved in living with daughters-in-law, especially unrelated ones. They point out that incoming husbands pose less of a problem, since males are not expected to manage the daily affairs of the household, and most of them are absent for the greater part of the year.

In order to illustrate the variations in residence and inheritance patterns in Nyeshang, I include a sample of households where parents chose an unmarried adult daughter to remain with them as caretaker.

Unmarried Daughters as Caretakers

Household 1.   Jalen Gurung, a 74-year-old man, lives in Tungtar year-round with his 35-year-old unmarried daughter and her one-year-old child. Both adults farm and raise livestock. Five other family members reside in Kathmandu.

Household 2.   Rinje Ghale, a 70-year-old man whose wife died thirty-three years ago, lives all year in Tipli with his unmarried adult daughter who is mute. Rinje has one son in Kathmandu and another married daughter in nearby Kangri village. Rinje and his daughter work together in the fields and look after their herd of ninety yak.

Household 3.   Dolma Lhamo, a 60-year-old widow, lives in Lhakpa all year with her 20-year-old unmarried daughter. Dolma has three sons in Kathmandu, aged 37, 35, and 25, who occasionally visit and help with the farming.

Household 4.   Samden Gurung, a 50-year-old widow, lives in Churi all year with her 30-year-old daughter who "will not marry." Samden has one married son in Kathmandu who sends her money from his trade earnings. Samden farms with her daughter and also rents some of her land to tenants.

Household 5.   Orke Ghale, a 75-year-old widow, lives in Tumje all year with her unmarried 42-year-old daughter who is mute. The daughter farms. Orke also has one son in Kathmandu who does "business" and sends her money.

In recent years, with so many Nyeshangte men living outside the district, this caretaking task is sometimes performed by unrelated individuals. In Tumje, an impoverished Drokpa couple (Tibetan nomads) were initially hired as laborers by an elderly Nyeshangte couple who had no children. The refugees were paid wages to work in the fields and to care for the couple's goat herd. The Drokpa husband spent many months living in rough shelters, tending the goats in the high pastures at some distance from the village. In the winter he rejoined his wife, who had a small room on the ground floor of the couple's home, an area often reserved for livestock and grain storage. When the Nyeshangte couple became ill and more incapacitated with their advancing age, the Drokpa wife took on additional household chores and looked after their needs. The bond between the two couples grew and, in gratitude for the Drokpa's service, the Nyeshangte couple made them their sole legal heirs. They eventually inherited the entire estate.

Although not that common in the past, a number of childless couples have chosen non-Nyeshangte or unrelated villagers to be their heirs in recent years. No doubt this trend has increased after the exodus of many villagers to Kathmandu.[38] Some of the elderly, who actually have children or grandchildren, refuse to stay with their children in Kathmandu. And many urban Nyeshangte (men) are reluctant to leave their comfortable urban homes to care for aging relatives in the valley, preferring instead to send gifts of money. Sometimes Nyeshangte neighbors will take on the responsibility of looking after an older villager, and they too may inherit some of the property. Generally, elderly individuals will find other relatives to remain with them, as the rest of the examples below indicate.

Other Relatives as Heirs and Caretakers

Household 1.   Kanda Ghale, a 70-year-old widow, spends most of her time at the *ser kyim* (retreat for laypersons) near the village of Churi. She occasionally returns to her home in Kangri, where an unmarried mother from Nar and two of her children work as servants. Kanda also hires a male laborer to plow the fields and help with the harvest. Her seven children are dead; most of them died from childhood diseases at a very early age. However, one son died only five years ago from "drink." Her husband passed away thirty years before. Soon after, Kanda began to spend more time at the retreat center and arranged for a house to be built there. The woman from Nar has been designated her adopted heir.

Household 2.   Menchoma Gurung, a 75-year-old widow, lives year-round in Nyangkhu and shares her home with a grandson and his wife who help with the farming. Menchoma has a second grandson in Chame and another in Kathmandu, who both send her money. Her only daughter died twenty-five years ago. Her husband died thirty years ago. She also rents some of her land to tenants.

Household 3.   Lakpalma Ghale and her two granddaughters are year-round residents in Tumje, where they earn a living from farming. Her son, Tashi, lives in Kathmandu and never married, though he had two daughters. No mention was made of what happened to the girls' mother, but the girls were sent to Tumje at an early age to be raised by their grandmother.

Household 4.   Mennilta Gurung, 69 years old, lives with her granddaughter in Churi where they farm. They both spend the winter in Kathmandu with Punzo, Mennilta's widowed son.

Household 5.   Sonam Gurung, a 65-year-old woman, lives with her unmarried 40-year-old son in Tumje and farms. Her husband had died only a few days before. She has no other children.

Widows without any children are entitled to use half the husband's family property during their lifetime.[39] They may adopt an heir to pass on this share. The other half is split between her husband's closest kinsmen, her own brothers, and their sons and grandsons. However, widows with children retain control of the entire estate: they will act as regents until their sons reach maturity or marry and the property is divided among them. These women continue to be acknowledged as household heads until they die, though they may choose a son or male relative to represent them at village political meetings. A young widow (or widower) with no children can remarry, move back to her natal home, or establish a separate residence apart from her parents and unmarried siblings. However, Nyeshangte men and women who have been married for several years or who have children will rarely remarry if their spouses die.[40]

Another Type of Female Inheritance

In families without sons, the eldest (or favorite) daughter will be designated the legal heir and will be asked to remain in the natal house. When this daughter marries, her husband moves into her household as an adopted son (*magpa*) and takes on his wife's clan (phabe) affiliation. The married resident daughter and her children will inherit the bulk of the estate, and another portion is divided among her sisters. This type of marriage is fairly common, though it often involves men from poorer households or from families with a large number of male offspring. In general, the men I spoke with (whether they were adopted sons or not) did not feel that this type of marriage was less prestigious or less desirable than other marriages that involved neolocal or virilocal residence.

The following case further demonstrates the rather pragmatic approach most Nyeshangte take toward arranged marriages. Pema Ghale, a 59-year-old man originally from Churi village, now runs a small curio shop in the heart of Thamel District. His 40-year-old wife, Sonam from Kangri, helps him manage the shop and takes over whenever Pema leaves for Thailand and India to purchase tribal handicrafts on his annual winter trading trips. During the rest of the year, Sonam lives in Kangri and farms her land. Her sister, Tigri, married Pema's older brother, and the couple still resides in Kangri. Sonam's and Tigri's parents had no other surviving children, so when the young women were of marriageable age, the parents arranged for their husbands to become magpa and to live in Kangri. A separate house was built for Sonam and her husband adjacent to the parents' home. Tigri remained in her childhood home, and her parents moved to their retreat house at the ser kyim. The fields and livestock were divided equally among the two daughters, both of whom looked after the aging parents.

Pema explained that he and his brother were landless, so the arrangement worked out well. Apparently, at one time his family had been prosperous, but a series of misfortunes changed all that. "At the time of my grandfather, the hill fell down on our house and destroyed our land [irrigated fields]. They had been very rich, but they didn't rebuild the house. My father died when I was young, and I can't remember what he looked like. Mother died when I was eight years old. My wife had land, a house, and money, so I marry [her] and go to live in her village."

The discussion of customary inheritance practices reveals that Nyeshangte women had several recourses for getting access to productive property and retaining control over their share of the family estate. And in recent years, whether through informal user-rights or outright inheritance, women's access to land has actually increased. With the permanent out-migration of more than a quarter of the population, sufficient land is available for women who prefer to remain in the village and earn a living farming. In addition, recent modifications in the Nepalese national law entitles unmarried women over the age of 35 to claim an equal share of the parental estate. This, in a sense, does not change local Nyeshangte practices (as unmarried daughters and nuns were already entitled to equal shares), but it does act as a reinforcement. As a result of these various changes, it appears that more Nyeshangte women are electing to remain single, particularly in the homeland.

Changing Marriage Practices

In addition to the inheritance factors cited above, this may be directly linked to male migration patterns and long-term male absence. Many arranged marriages never proceed beyond the initial engagement stage that ends when the bride (and her children) leave her natal home to set up a neolocal residence with the groom. Usually, this final step in the processual marriage is celebrated by the end of the first or second year; in the past, it often happened within a few months. One woman, the wealthy owner of a large and very successful tourist lodge in Nyangkhu, told me that she was concerned about this trend: her own adult daughter had a five-year-old child and was still living at home. Apparently the daughter's fiancée was always away on business, and the couple had not yet established their own household. However, despite the lengthy delay, the mother thought the couple would eventually marry.

These days, many engagements are broken. Young women lose interest in partners who are never around; they are less likely to conceive and give birth to the one (or more) children that usually prompt the couple to move into their own home. Although community ideals dictate that married men should reside with their wives in the village while their children are young, this is seldom the case. Most husbands are absent a good part of the year, and until they are ready to retire at age 50 or 55, the majority of men rarely return to the village except for short visits.

Today, young men are simply not following the expected life course (marked by a series of stages: childhood, adolescence, bachelorhood, householder, retiree) in the customary timely fashion. In a sense, many males seemed trapped in a perpetual state of adolescence. Although they do drop out of school to begin their trade apprenticeships at the customary age of 12 or 13, the rest of the pattern has changed. Until a few decades ago, most young men would have amassed enough capital and gained enough experience to separate from their natal families when they reached their early to mid-twenties. Usually, by their late twenties, their marriages would be secure and they would have set up independent households with their wives and young children.

Although young traders today do earn substantial amounts of money, they also tend to go on wild spending sprees and are caught up in western-style consumerism in the city: spending money on motorbikes and, in some cases, expensive cars with four-wheel drive. Some of these successful traders are also reluctant to settle down: many are delaying marriage until their late thirties or early forties. Others have "mistresses" or wives in foreign cities.[41]

Young women who are reluctant to marry may also be concerned about sharing their lives with unreliable, immature males. In addition, those who do marry sometimes worry that their husbands will be jailed or killed in the course of doing business overseas. Several married men in their mid-thirties told me that they would encourage their young daughters to continue their education through high school and to pursue a career that would enable them to support themselves if their husbands "disappeared." Many urban women also felt that girls should receive more education in order to fend for themselves in Kathmandu. Rural women seemed more secure knowing they could get by with farming, livestock raising, and petty trade in the valley. Some of these village women were reluctant to abandon their rural homes, as they knew they had no chance of finding work in Kathmandu. Without education or job skills, these women cannot live in the city year-round without becoming dependent on relatives or, worse, without having to rely on irresponsible young husbands.[42]

The increasing rate of nonmarriage may also be linked to changing marital practices: the costs of weddings and the financial transactions that take place have escalated. One old woman in Nyangkhu, who was 71, complained about this trend:

> We do marriages much the same as before, but now it's very expensive. In Nyeshang some are rich, some are poor. Poor ones find it difficult to get married. Both [sets of] parents have to pay. In the past, a son discusses his wish [to marry] with his parents, then his father goes asking respectfully to the girl's house with a bottle of chang and a ceremonial scarf [kha btags]. He gives maybe fifty paisa or *tin mohar* [a few cents]; now five hundred rupees [u.s.$20] he must give.
>
> Out of a hundred [arranged marriages] in the past, perhaps ninety would be OK and maybe ten would end up in divorce. What happens is that a boy will stay for over six months or one year at the girl's house. If, for whatever reason, the girl does not like him anymore, her parents will not allow the boy into the house. Then the girl's parents will go to the boy's house and offer their apologies, and bring a kha btags and often some money. In the case of love marriages, where there was no exchange of kha btags and chang from the boy's side to the girl's, then both parents will meet and decide what to do.
>
> For a divorce, it used to cost four hundred rupees (u.s.$16), and the one who wanted to leave would have to pay. But now some girls have to give five thousand to ten thousand rupees to the boy's parents (u.s.$200–$400). If a boy doesn't like the girl, then his parents must

pay. Sometimes the parents meet and no one asks for money; they just decide to dissolve it. Other times the negotiation is very tough. Some parents become angry and may ask for forty thousand rupees (U.S.$1,600). Then they negotiate.

If a girl gives birth to a child, by then she usually has moved to the boy's house, which at that point may be separate from his parents' house. If the husband decides he no longer wants to live with her, he stays away, and the house becomes hers. Once the marriage ceremony is performed, the new couple stays separated from both sets of parents.

If marriage occurred by elopement, without parental consent, then there is generally no compensation, and the couple just separates. Most divorces occur in the early stages of the relationship, usually before any children are born. There may be a public declaration of separation, after which either party may remarry. There is no loss or ritual or social status involved, no concern about virginity, and most men and women remarry successfully the second time, generally choosing their own partners, since their parents seldom wish to try their luck again arranging another marriage.

In a few instances when marriages have broken up, the women involved left their infants with their husbands or husbands' families and remarried. In two cases the husbands were alcohol or drug abusers and serving jail sentences for smuggling gold. Both young wives were fed up with their husbands' behavior and simply left the house, the kids, everything behind, and started their lives again in another town and married other Nyeshangte men. Although having a child does not necessarily prevent an individual from remarrying, most divorced men and women who keep their children with them seldom remarry. Some divorced or widowed individuals may have lovers, but these relationships are not discussed openly.[43] In my village surveys, I came across only two households of unmarried men with children; it is more common for the children to remain with their mothers.

If either party breaks off the engagement or refuses to go through the final stage of marriage (*payar thapa*), the parents of the "guilty" party must pay a fine to the other family. These fines now amount to several hundred dollars and may run higher depending on the status and wealth of the families involved. One young woman, Chongdu, broke off her prearranged engagement to a cousin in order to marry a man she "loved." Chongdu had grown up with her cousin in the village and felt that she could not marry him because he was "too close, like a brother." She told me that her lover's parents paid a U.S.$3,000 fine (*jaro*) to her cousin's family in order to release her from the marriage obligation. When I joked with her and said, "You were certainly expensive," she smiled. "We wanted each other very much, and I am worth it." Both families belong to the wealthiest tier of the urban community, and the Chongdu's elder sister had already married (by arrangement) her husband's older brother, so the families were strongly allied.

Arranged marriages are still fairly common: about half of all my married informants told me that their parents had "given them." In this respect, both young men and women are subject to their parents' will. One man surprised me when he told me about his first marriage. After returning from Thailand, Tsong's parents arranged his marriage. As he tells it, "The girl chose me, but after four or five years I don't want her. That girl chose me, so my father gave me, and I went to live at her house." Since the couple had no children the marriage was annulled, but Tsong's parents had to pay the girl's family a thirteen-thousand-rupee fine (U.S.$1,850).[44]

Tsong is quite content with his second "love" marriage, though the couple have no children. I stayed with them several times and noticed that even after ten years of marriage they were still quite affectionate. In the early evenings, Tsong and Chhimi could often be found sitting side by side on the doorstep, holding hands, watching the sunset over the Annapurna ridge.

In recent years the amount of money and property being transferred during the marriage celebrations has also increased. Parents and close relatives of the bride and groom may each offer the new couple as much as U.S.$2,000 during the two- or three-day celebration, which is held at the groom's house. This is in addition to the money (about U.S.$200) that the bride's relatives traditionally offer her on the eve of the wedding. Marriages used to take place during the summer months in Nyeshang when most traders had returned to the homeland and were reunited with their families. Now, all wedding festivities are held in the winter in Kathmandu—it is the only time when most of the community are together. Considerable expenses are incurred by both families: musicians are hired, and in addition to the actual wedding celebration, both families must house, feed, and entertain numerous guests. Among the more affluent households, the pressure to display their wealth often results in extravagant spending.

Some couples avoid these complications by eloping. Since these "love marriages" are not arranged, parents are under no obligations to give money or goods (though most do). In the city, Nyeshangte youth have also revived the tradition of kidnapping brides (usually with the woman's consent and assistance), forcing both families to more or less accept the situation when enough time has elapsed and tempers have settled. This recourse is used when there are no social ties between the families or when the economic differences are such that parents could not conceivably negotiate with the other family about a prospective match between their children.

Many young men from poorer urban and village families told me that they could not "afford" to get married and would wait until they had amassed enough wealth from trade. Women, on the other hand, seem to have more personal reasons for not getting married—money (or lack of it) did not seem to be the deciding issue. Some married women openly expressed regrets that they had married and borne children. Marriage, women say, brings entanglements, worry, and *dukha* (suffering or pain). Some of these sentiments are reflected in the case histories described below.

Sange Karma, a 40-year-old woman who runs a tea house in her home in Tumje, was married to a 26-year-old Gurung man originally from Kathmandu. She was born in Tungtar and had two older sisters and one older brother who were living in nearby villages. Both her parents were dead; her mother had died in childbirth. Sange married at age 30, and her first child was born six years later. She had two boys, a 5 year old and a 3 year old, and one 4-month-old daughter. She had met her non-Nyeshangte husband where he was employed as a servant at one of the tea houses near the Thorung pass; they decided to elope and have a "love marriage." They now manage that lodge with the help of another servant, in addition to farming rented land in Tumje where they keep half the crop. Sange, when asked about improving her lot or changing her life, replied, "If I can stay in Kathmandu, life is better there. In the village it is very cold and there is too much snow." Then, reflecting a bit more, she added, "I would like to stay without marriage. If women marry, they become with children, then [life is] no good. I would prefer to not be married; I would stay alone at the hotel above [near the pass]. That would make me happy, to live alone up there."

One day at *Khare, the jaṅgal area above Nyangkhu, I encountered a group of women resting after they had collected firewood. An old Nyeshangte woman was butchering and skinning a goat nearby. She and her Tibetan husband tended the village flock and lived in a stone shelter near the high pasture. Her sharp crackling voice periodically punctuated the conversation, which had turned to the subject of marriage or, in this case, nonmarriage, and the pain of childbirth. The other women were from Nyangkhu. One, named Orke, was 36 years old but looked 50: Orke's clothes were dirty, ragged, her hair was unkempt, her skin etched with deep lines. But she laughed a lot, and her face was pleasant, graced by a warm smile. She had brought her 8-year-old daughter and her 2-year-old twins. Her 29-year-old unmarried friend, Samden, sat next to her.

Samden, dressed in the customary bakhu (dress), with red- and white-striped kneesocks and worn-out canvas "tennies," looked athletic and strong—a pragmatic, no-nonsense sort of person. Samden explained why she chose not to marry, "Bacchā pāuncha, dukha āuncha" (Conceive a baby, then suffering will come). She laughed and gestured the outline of a swollen belly, then added, "I know about these things. I saw my friend [pointing to Orke], that one really cried and screamed." Samden demonstrated by rolling on her back, thrashing about, and moaning pitifully.

Everyone laughed, and Orke admitted a bit sheepishly, "Yes, the twins were very painful." Her 8-year-old daughter leaped up and shouted, "Bacchā āuncha, puti dukhyo" (Baby comes, then vagina hurts). For a moment everyone was silent and looked shocked, then they all laughed hysterically.

A lovely young woman of 17 who had been quietly brushing the little girl's hair also spoke, "I too will not marry; it brings too much pain." But her friends disagreed with her, both insisting, "Yes, that one will marry; she will have a love marriage and live in Kathmandu." Orke jokingly added, "She already has two children," pointing to the twins who affectionately huddled against the teenager. The teenager was quite beautiful; she looked like a portrait of a Japanese "geisha"—shiny black hair smoothed neatly in a bun, an ivory complexion, and small pearly teeth. Although she had been working alongside the others, she was not disheveled, nor was she wearing the dull-colored brown or gray bakhu. Instead she was wrapped in a brightly colored flower-print skirt, wearing a pink blouse, with an emerald green shawl draped elegantly about her shoulders. Apparently, her extraordinary beauty left no doubt (in everyone's mind) that she would be able to choose her own mate from among the well-to-do families in Kathmandu.

In general most Nyeshangte men and women are expected to marry, and informants state that perhaps only "5 or 6 percent" elect to remain single.[45] There are, however, a number of customary reasons for not marrying. One is being afflicted with a physical deformity or being otherwise disabled. Some villages have a high percentage of people who are mentally retarded, deaf, or mute (possibly the result of iodine deficiency). These individuals usually live with parents or siblings. One middle-aged woman said, "Some girls do not marry because they are not good, not speaking nicely."[46] She singled out a 28-year-old woman, the eldest of four daughters (in a family with no sons), who earned her living primarily in trade. The young woman had a reputation for being disrespectful to her parents, and even of "beating up" her father. Several women told me, though, that "most Nyeshangte marry unless they are too ugly." The example given was a young girl born with a club foot. Deformities and personalities aside, the only other acceptable reason for remaining single was to follow a religious vocation. Village women and men say that they are "saddened" when a boy or girl does not marry, unless it is to become a monk or a nun. In recent years, a significant number of young women have taken this path, and as a result the valley's monastic tradition has enjoyed renewed vitality despite the high levels of out-migration.

Residence Patterns for Unmarried Individuals

Household composition fluctuates tremendously in Nyeshang as members migrate between city and village residences, and as changing circumstances and personal preferences lead some individuals to move in with different relatives or to live alone. A survey of nonconjugal households revealed a variety of types that could be classified in various ways.[47] Unmarried and single adults in the households surveyed all owned land, with the exception of two unmarried women with illegitimate children who rented land from other families. Both of these women were from Lhakpa, a village where many lineages in the past were believed to be tainted by witches, an inherited condition thought to be passed on from mother to daughter. This stigma usually results in high rates of illegitimate children, as few men are willing to marry these women.[48]

Below I include several brief cases to illustrate the variety of nonconjugal households found in Nyeshang.

Siblings Living Together

Household 1.   Twenty-nine-year-old Shatar Ghale and her 31-year-old sister, Pau, live all year in Churi with their elder brother who is also single. They farm and care for livestock. Their father is in Kathmandu. (Their mother's whereabouts are unknown.)

Household 2.   Tarke Buddhi, an unmarried 67-year-old woman, lives in Nyangkhu with her 50-year-old unmarried brother who is mute. They both farm.

Household 3.   Tashi Ghale, 35 years old and unmarried, lives all year in Lhakpa with his 30-year-old sister who is also single. They help care for their father, an 80-year-old widower. Both siblings are lāta (mute, deaf, and/or retarded).[49]

Household 4.   Sange Gurung, age 37, lives in Tungtar all year with her 26-year-old sister who is also unmarried. They help their 63-year-old widowed father with the farming. They have one brother living in Kathmandu who is a trader.

Household 5.   Kanda Choma, a 49-year-old widow, lives in Nyangkhu with her 25-year-old sister who is married. Each has her own home in the village, but the younger sister prefers to stay with Kanda since her husband is based in Kathmandu and rarely visits the valley. Kanda has one 14-year-old daughter living with her. She has two other daughters in Kathmandu, one of whom is married and does business. Kanda also has two sons living in the city—a 10 year old and an 18 year old. She visits Kathmandu during the winter and spends four months "in meditation" at the Nyeshangte dgon pa.

Household 6.   Buddhi Soner, 80 years old, was widowed twenty years ago and lives with her 70-year-old brother who lost his wife five years ago. They stay year-round in Tipli and have a live-in servant who helps with the farm work, while they spend many days at the ser khyim.

Single Parents and Children

Household 1.   Kanca Lama, a 30-year-old unmarried man, lives in Nyangkhu and farms with his young son. His parents live in Kathmandu, along with three other family members.

Household 2.   Dendolma Buddhi, a 35-year-old unmarried woman, lives in Kangri with her 3-year-old daughter and 2-month-old son. She has no land or house and so has always lived with other families, working as a servant. (This is the only such case documented in Nyeshang, as most villagers never work for wages.)

Household 3.   Tarke Lama, an unmarried 40-year-old woman with a 3-year-old son, lives in Lhakpa in a house that belongs to a Kathmandu family. She acts as caretaker of their property and farms their land rent-free.

Household 4.   Leche Soner, a 70-year-old unmarried woman with one son, lives in a house that belongs to a Kathmandu family. Her unmarried adult son rents additional fields. His father lives in nearby Churi but offers no support or help. The illegitimate son is not entitled to any inheritance from his father.

Household 5. Mindo Gurung, a 50-year-old unmarried woman in Lhakpa is described by other villagers as "mute but clever." She has user rights to her cousin's fields and farms on her own. She has a married daughter who lives in Tipli, but the daughter often stays with her and helps her farm. Mindo has no land of her own. Her parents sold the few parcels they owned; they were quite poor, and the father had a drinking problem. He died in Nagaland (India) while on a trading trip. Mindo's lover was from her village, but he offers no help of any kind.

Individuals Living Alone

Household 1. Dorje Mindu, 45 years old, lives in Churi year-round and has a small farm. His wife died twenty years ago. One married daughter in Kathmandu is a trader and sends him money. The other lives with an aunt in Pokhara and attends school. According to the village headman, Dorje is "crazy, his mind is cracked," but he still manages to take care of himself.

Household 2. Komi Srimendzo, 66 years old, stays in the valley all year and farms with hired help. His wife is dead. He has one married daughter in Kathmandu; four sons are in business and two are lamas, also living in Kathmandu.

Household 3. Lheji Ghale, a 40-year-old unmarried woman, lives alone in Tumje all year and farms with a hired servant. Her brother, who lives in Kathmandu, gave her all his village property.

Household 4. Dolkar Gurung, a 69-year-old unmarried woman, lives in Lhakpa alone. Though she is blind, "she takes cares of herself." Another family has lent her a house; she does not pay rent. She has one daughter, a trader in Kathmandu, who sends her money. The father (now dead) was a local man from Tipli. He never helped his daughter or Dolkar.

Household 5. Klenjong Tarke, 45, never married; she lives in Kangri all year and farms. She inherited land and rents several fields to villagers from Nar. She has no brothers or sisters.

Household 6. Pema Sanga, a 35-year-old female, is "crazy." She lives alone. Her parents, who live in Kathmandu, send money to a neighbor who looks after her. They tried several times to bring her to Kathmandu, but she refused to move. Not willing, literally, to drag her on a plane or tie her on a horse, her family decided to let her stay in the village.

Household 7.   Tigri Lama, a 30-year-old unmarried woman, lives alone in Nyangku and farms. Her father died last year, and at that time her mother moved to Kathmandu to live with one of her sons. Tigri has another brother and sister in Kathmandu who are both married.

Household 8.   Palsang Lama, 67 years old, never married and lives in Tipli all year and farms. She inherited land and also rents some fields to tenants. She has one brother in Kathmandu.

Although the survey showed a variety of household units, the most common type of nonconjugal household in the valley centers around female links and is often matricentric: mothers and their children (mostly daughters). Married sisters (and other female relatives) also exchange labor and stay at each other's home for extended periods when husbands are away. Indeed, these networks are the mainstay of the community: the valley's social, ritual, and economic well-being revolve around this "circle of female kin."[50]

The data from Nyeshang contrast sharply with Schuler's (1987) findings in neighboring Baragaon. There are few households or individuals living alone in Nyeshang who are marginalized or landless. Overall, surveys and interviews with countless numbers of Nyeshangte suggest that most households and the majority of individuals have an adequate standard of living.[51] In this regard, single women were not necessarily more disadvantaged than single men, and in most instances, unmarried women who remained in the valley, or women whose husbands were absent, could rely on extensive social and kin networks for support and assistance. Although establishing one's own household in Nyeshang involves a formal and material separation from parents and siblings, there is generally a great deal of cooperation and contact among family members and this relationship tends to be reciprocal rather than exploitative (cf. Schuler 1987).

What becomes clear after reviewing the data from household surveys is that Nyeshangte live in a society that offers individual men and women a wide range of choices. These idiosyncratic patterns are tempered by factors that vary with an individual's age, seniority, and household resources—variables that are often more important than gender per se in shaping individual lives.

The range of choices has increased in recent years as women (and men) take advantage of new developments—tourism, surplus farm land, and remittances from relatives in Kathmandu. The number of women choosing not to marry in part reflects these increased economic opportunities, as well as the fact that nonmarriage, in conjunction with a religious vocation, has always been a prestigious option for Nyeshangte men and women. When asked if they could change just one thing about their lives, several married women and men in their middle adulthood (thirties to fifties) said they regret their marriages and regret having had children. If they could do it all over again, they would remain single in order to avoid family responsibilities which detract from religious pursuits. With rising levels of wealth in the community, more households can now afford to hire year-round servants to free those members who wish to do "religious work."

The increase in nonmarriage among rural women may also be linked to western-influenced expectations of a marriage founded in romance and love. Whereas previously a village woman might be desired as a wife because she was a hard worker and a "good person," spouses now may be selected because they are beautiful, fashionable, or "modern." Two decades ago, when differences in wealth were not so apparent, many urban families would find village wives for their sons. But now urban families generally arrange marriages with other urban households of similar wealth, whose children have also been educated in Kathmandu. In one case, the parents were furious when their middle son eloped with a Nyeshangte woman from a poor urban household. Although, in the past, she would have been considered a good match, since her family was from the same village as the boy's family, they were now considered "small people," not part of the urban elite. In addition, the boy had been studying to become a monk at a monastery near Kathmandu and broke his vows to get married. However, after the initial disappointment, the boy's family accepted the girl as their son's wife, especially since she already had given birth to their granddaughter.

Although these factors may seem to imply that village women are remaining single, not out of free choice but as a result of constraints or external forces that impinge on them, this is not altogether true. For comparative purposes, we might consider the evidence from Nar, a valley adjacent to Nyeshang where the people still earn their living through pastoralism and agriculture and domestic petty trade. The headman of Nar village told me that many women there did not want to marry. At least sixteen women (between the ages of 25 and 45), out of a total village population of 370, chose to remain single. He explained, "Some live with parents and if the parents have a large house they will divide it. Some stay with brothers, but often they quarrel with the brother's wife. Some rent other people's homes. If some families own more than one house, then the daughters get it; otherwise the brothers get it. Parents, they have to build a house for her [the unmarried daughter] and give her some land, though less than brothers."

Although he gave no explanations as to why these women made these choices,[52] interviews with Nyeshangte women and with women from other Tibetan communities in nearby Muktinath indicate personal reasons: emotional bonds to their mothers and reluctance to become dependent on unreliable young males. Another young woman from Nyangkhu told me that she too did not want to marry and leave her mother: "Before, some time ago, some Nyeshangte men were always drinking and throwing pots and dishes around. Some say a few maybe hit their wives, but I'm not sure, maybe they did or not, who can say. Now, this drinking and throwing pots really doesn't happen often, but still, I want to stay with Mother."

Although domestic violence seems rare (I never witnessed any incident nor heard anyone, man or woman, mention specific cases of battery, except for the daughter who supposedly beat her father), it must occur occasionally. But what the statement above reveals are the close ties daughters have with their mothers and with other siblings. With so many men absent from the villages, these "daughter–mother units" effectively manage the household's daily affairs and have grown accustomed to working and living together. It is not surprising really that young women are unwilling to give up the security of their natal homes for the uncertainty of city life with a husband they may not know well.

In the past two decades, changing migratory and trade patterns mean that young boys from the age of 12 or so leave the homeland and move to Kathmandu to work for a relative and learn about trade practices. Some young boys may have left the village even earlier to attend boarding schools in town. The tight-knit age groups and labor exchange parties of adolescent village boys and girls, which enabled Nyeshangte youths to work and socialize with potential future spouses, no longer exist. When it comes time to arrange marriages now, prospective spouses may be virtual strangers and no longer have the assurance that comes with having grown up together. This union between "strangers" might also explain why the initial betrothal stage or courting stage, where the young woman receives visits from her fiancée in her parents' home has been stretched out—sometimes lasting five years before the couple establish their own home together.

However, this ability to delay the marriage process indicates that women retain important rights as individuals: they can safeguard their interests by not rushing into a potentially disastrous marriage or they can remain single. Women essentially are free to enter and sever marriage bonds. They are able to inherit real property, fields and houses, in addition to movable wealth—money, jewelry, and livestock. The marked bilateral emphasis in Nyeshang society contributes to Nyeshangte women's autonomy, which is underwritten by strong lasting support from her natal family and clan relatives.

Even in the city, where one might expect to see a patterning of family relations and household structure to resemble those of the dominant society, there has been no perceptible shift toward Parbatiya high-caste values, Hindu marriage practices, or an overall "patriarchal" ideology. Concerns with group endogamy have become more preeminent given the heterogeneous environment of the capital, but this is not a question of adhering to a Brahmanical code about female sexual purity or virginity before marriage. Nyeshangte parents simply do not want their daughters (or their sons) to marry outsiders and have yulu offspring.

In this chapter I have suggested that Nyeshangte men and women are concerned with redefining their group's boundaries and reasserting their group's distinctive cultural identity, an identity that is also inextricably tied to the Nyeshang homeland. Nyeshangte identity hinges around their prominent and visible roles as traders and devout Buddhists, as well as their characteristic social traditions that separate them from other Tibetan groups and from all Hindu groups. This notion of self, of community, of "Nyeshangness," is not a primordial, unchanging kind of ethnicity. Rather, "Nyeshangness," or what it means to be Nyeshangte, is continually evolving in a dialogic relation with various categories of outsiders.[53] In recent years, this discourse about group identity has been cast into a largely genderized framework: notions about sex roles, about marriage practices, about egalitarian relations between the sexes, affines and spouses, and about women's traditional authority are part of the cultural logic that enables Nyeshangte to proclaim the ongoing vitality and continuity of their customary patterns or way of life, despite the massive dislocations and changes taking place within the community.

Some anthropologists have suggested that if egalitarian gender relations and the authority of women form an integral part of a group's ethnic identity, then perhaps these social patterns are likely to endure (Friedl 1975; Sanday 1990a). The use of these gender representations and native folk models to proclaim Nyeshangte superiority and an "enduring" identity reflects the convergence of community interests with women's own gendered interests. However, although these cultural attitudes and social features promote gender equality, women as individuals must still secure their base of authority and power. The next chapter examines in more detail women's roles in upholding and reproducing the Nyeshang social order.

CHAPTER SIX

Tangled Relations

IN THIS CHAPTER I look more closely at women's agency in reproducing the Nyeshang social order through their support of various community institutions. I suggest that women's social ties and extensive networks throughout the community play an important part in maintaining the egalitarian model on which Nyeshangte social relations are based.

However, these practices must also be examined in the context of changing social realities. The power of centralizing states, the forces of development, capitalism, and, in the past, colonialism often led to major social transformations, which had adverse effects on indigenous women's lives.[1] Sexual norms, the division of labor, and control over household decisions and resources may shift, and new forms of gender hierarchies may arise. For example, in Nepal and India, research on tribal, ethnic minorities, or low-caste occupational groups showed that urbanization, migration, or increased wealth often led to status emulation of high-caste groups with its associated restrictions on women's mobility and participation in the labor force.[2] In areas of central and northwestern Nepal, where Gurung and ethnic Tibetan groups have coexisted with dominant Hindu groups for many years, "local" social and cultural practices are often realigned with Hindu ideological formulations.[3]

Although an understanding of these political and economic forces is important in trying to assess their overall impact on women's lives, one should not neglect the corresponding perspective: that is, how individual women as "subject-agents" perceive these forces and how they alternatively contest, accept, or ignore the various currents that impinge on their lives. Recent studies have shown that in some societies women have been able to secure their authority in the face of these changes by taking advantage of new opportunities and actively resisting the adoption of foreign ideologies and social patterns (e.g., Sanday 1990a; Povinelli 1991, 1994; Lepowsky 1993). This dual perspective on change and continuity, on external forces and local traditions, is woven throughout the remaining chapters of the book, as I consider women's roles in maintaining and refashioning the Nyeshang social order.

In the Society of Women

Women's networks play a central role in the ordering of daily Nyeshang life. Reliance on these social ties has increased during the past three decades with so many men absent from the community. Women's support networks are varied: some are informal, based on friendship or neighborly ties; others are derived from clan or kinship bonds. Some obligations and expectations are defined by more formal associations established through ritual ceremonies, by membership in age sets as well as participation in village institutions and community groups. Often these various categories overlap so that individual women are situated in the center of numerous social circles that radiate throughout the village, the entire valley, and even beyond: to include non-Nyeshangte in neighboring districts as well as community members scattered in urban areas like Kathmandu and Pokhara.

The importance and extent of women's social networks were revealed to me in two distinct settings and under two very different circumstances: in the village arena my understanding of these ties gradually deepened as I came to know my host family, a middle-aged widow, Ama, and her teenage daughter, Yangdzom, and as I took part in the ordinary round of village activities; but it was on the trail, while traveling with Nyeshangte women, that these perceptions were crystallized into a series of vivid images that remained sharp long after the bewilderment over an unpleasant scene had vanished.

An attack by a trusted assistant left me paralyzed with fear and inadvertently propelled me right into the midst of these female networks. On one of my return trips to Nyeshang in early June 1989, Palsang, my Sherpa guide, simply blew up: an outburst of hatred and resentment surfaced:

snatches of conversation or brief incidents from the past two months came out in a torrent of emotional waste. (His moodiness, occasional bad temper, and annoying habit of continuously muttering to himself: "Palsang is no good; I am no good," had me wondering periodically about his mental state, but I had been reluctant to fire him outright, as his disgruntled outlook on life was probably not far removed from mine at times, just more transparent.) Fortunately, we were quite near Traklung when he turned violent. Palsang started shouting, and I realized quickly that this was not one of his usual grumbling sessions. He tried to knock me down and grabbed my day pack, which contained my field notebooks, camera, and sleeping bag. Since we were roughly the same size, I managed to hold him off until a Nyeshangte couple pulled him away. Unhurt, except for some minor bruises and scratches, I was escorted to a lodge by two women who were horrified by the Sherpa's outrageous behavior.

The event marked a turning point in my relations with Nyeshangte villagers. Alone, without an assistant for the remainder of my fieldwork, I was absorbed into the social world of women. After the incident two Nyeshang women, whom I had never met before, insisted that I travel the rest of the way with them. Pema and her 17-year-old daughter, Soner, both residents of Kathmandu, were going to Churi to check on their village property. They shared my worries that the Sherpa might be waiting further up the trail but joked that with three women he would have his hands full.

In their company some of the shock faded, as their combined cheerfulness and solicitous gestures enabled me to continue the journey. Traveling with them, stopping frequently to visit friends and relatives along the way, I saw how strongly "connected" women were: in part, these bonds between urban and village Nyeshang women breached the gap between the past and the future, the old and the young, between the homeland and the ways of the city. I realized too, having watched many city teenagers (even the brash, wild ones like Spike) turn into more or less civilized creatures in the company of older women from the valley, that Nyeshangte women played a major role in upholding the moral order, in transmitting their values and their notions of what constitutes a "good person."

This transmission of traditional values was evident in the daughter Soner, who switched easily from an independent, educated woman accustomed to the responsibilities and benefits that come with working and living in the city to a respectful young person in the company of her village elders. On the trail, for example, when we encountered three aged women who were sitting by the low stone wall of a *cautāro* (a platform rest area), we stopped to greet them; Soner, in keeping with Nyeshang hospitality, politely offered each of the women some roasted wheat kernels and a drink of water before sitting down to rest and exchange news.

Unlike some teenage boys who have trouble adjusting to village life (they complain of boredom, the cold, and lack of "facilities"), many of the city girls like Soner seemed to adapt quite readily, moving easily in and out of rural society. This tendency, I suspect, is the result of two factors: cultural expectations of gendered behavior and the early socialization of Nyeshang girls as "proper human beings." In the city, even young girls who attend school or work in retail shops are enveloped in the world of Nyeshang women—with its attendant rounds of informal visiting and casual but warm hospitality. Young males, on the other hand, often remain "outside society," enveloped by the values of the street; they are given some leeway for being brash, prone to fighting, and generally less "civilized" during their youth.[4]

Hospitality and Food as a Medium of Exchange

During the course of our trip to Nyeshang, I watched as Soner and her mother took part in a series of exchanges with various female friends and relatives in other Nyeshang villages. When we left Traklung the following morning, Pema had received a cloth bundle filled with *sāg* (a spinachlike green) from the lodge owner, who was a childhood friend formerly from Churi. Later that day, when we stopped at a lodge in Tipli, and as we sat around the hearth waiting for the midday meal to be ready, I watched Pema, over the hostess's repeated protests, continue to throw several handfuls of roasted *tsampa* (barley flour) from her own bag into the large cooking pot. When we were ready to leave, the hostess refused to accept payment for the food and tea, so Pema thanked her profusely and left her a small bag of powdered milk (and I surreptitiously left some rupees under my bowl).

This continual exchange of foodstuffs and token gifts characterized the remainder of the journey through the valley. In Kangri, less than an hour's walk from Tipli, we stopped again to visit another of Pema's friends: an unmarried woman in her early fifties who presented an elegant portrait; she was dignified in demeanor but slightly impoverished, dressed in clothes that were well cut but worn and frayed around the hem. Her living quarters consisted of a single room with a dirt floor that was sparsely furnished but kept in a very tidy manner, reflecting the ascetic lifestyle of the owner who devoted much of her time to religious practice. Pema greeted her friend warmly, and then introduced her daughter and me. After a lengthy visit and innumerable refills of tea, Pema pulled out her heavy sack of tsampa and insisted that the woman keep the entire bag.

These small gifts of food are used to reaffirm friendships, and the informal exchanges do much to strengthen social ties and smooth out relations among more distant kin and acquaintances who are seen infrequently. No expectation of immediate or exact reciprocity is apparent, but there is a general sense that in the long run hospitality and gifts are balanced. Under certain conditions, however, the flow of goods is more one-sided: relatives and villagers who are well-off are expected to help support individuals of more modest means—the elderly, widowed, or religious specialists without trade income. Pema, in providing her unmarried friend (a distant cousin or clan sister) in Kangri with a large supply of tsampa, a staple food, was following the norms of Nyeshang social practice. Likewise, my landlady, an elderly (but affluent) widow herself, provided her unmarried mentally retarded sister with regular supplies of salt, tea, cooking oil, and sugar, commodities that must be purchased with cash, which is in short supply in many non-trading households. However, the recipient always makes some effort to offer visitors tea, and they may help the donor household during harvest or ritual celebrations when occasionally an extra hand is needed. The donor, on the other hand, enhances her social standing in the community through these acts of generosity. Nyeshangte are expected not only to assist their poorer relatives through regular donations of food, clothing, or volunteer labor, as in the cases described above, but also any other Nyeshangte villagers who may be indigent. Women, because they are more in tune with the village grapevine and aware of the fluctuating circumstances of individual households, usually take the initiative to distribute donated supplies.

On a day-to-day basis, however, women often maintain regular relationships with neighbors and work group members who come from households of comparable wealth. The intensive but casual pattern of interhousehold visiting, whether to borrow a cup of salt or to organize a labor exchange, tends to follow economic lines linking households with similar resources. Providing meals for members of one's work group is easier when each hostess can reciprocate the quality or quantity of food offered by others (cf. Molnar 1980), and most Nyeshangte women would feel ashamed if they could not perform the role of hostess adequately. However, since the majority of households (about 80–90 percent) in Nyeshang are self-sufficient in staple foods like grains and potatoes, most households manage to meet expected levels of hospitality without too much difficulty.

On the other hand, women visitors who drop by frequently are treated usually as informal guests, resulting in less fuss and expense than, say, the more formal etiquette required by the visit of a male elder or a village lama. In this sense women are freer to visit throughout the village and maintain social ties with women in poorer households, especially where childhood friendships or close kin relations are involved. In these cases, familiarity and affection will override any strain or embarrassment surrounding unequal exchange.

Women's Voices: Gossip and Intervillage Networks

Women's networks are not only channels for the redistribution and circulation of material and labor resources but for important social information as well. Gossip, news—any information that serves as a current social barometer—all this is digested and passed on through these alliances. This ability to evaluate information, people, and current affairs provides women with an important means of control. Men are kept abreast of village events: new births, deaths, marital disputes, property division, and intended marriages largely through their female kin. As a result of their prolonged absences from the valley, men have also become more dependent on women's perceptions of village affairs. It is also largely through female relatives who migrate seasonally between village and urban locales that permanent Kathmandu residents retain their connections to village society.

Although women traditionally did not hold formal positions of authority on village councils,[5] their voices were heard quite effectively through these informal channels. Women's authority in the household was also expressed through their husbands or other male kin who were chosen by them to act as household representatives at village meetings. Senior women thus managed to have a great deal of influence on men's political decisions, as the position a man espoused was generally reached in consensus with his wife or, in the case of a younger man, reflected the opinion of his mother or female relative who acted as household head. However, women (as well as other men who were not current office-holders or household delegates) were permitted to attend these meetings and address the village council whenever they wished. Most of the women I spoke with had little interest in the proceedings of these council meetings, which usually focused on intervillage or wider Nyeshang affairs. In contrast, adult women as property owners concerned themselves with the decisions of the livestock committee and irrigation committee, and frequently attended these meetings to voice their complaints, their requests, and their opinions on matters they felt were important.

Women also had the power to influence decisions and shape social opinion through their regular exchange of information.[6] The efficacy of these verbal exchanges and the efficiency of intervillage communication were revealed to me in the aftermath of what became known as the "Sherpa incident." By the time our small group (myself, Pema, and her daughter) had left Tipli, one of the villages located near the entrance of the Nyeshang valley, the story of the "Sherpa and the phiphing" had spread quickly throughout the valley and actually reached Nyangkhu village before I did.

However, not only were the details of the incident known but, more significant, community consensus had already been reached and village leaders had decided on a course of action with astonishing rapidity. This agreement became evident as we entered each of the villages in the lower Nyeshang valley; various men would approach and assure me that if Palsang attempted to enter the valley from the southern route via Tipli or from the north over the Thorung pass that Nyeshangte "would take care of him." Some indicated that he would be handcuffed and taken to police headquarters at the district office in Chame; others simply stated that he would be beaten and chased from the valley. Although their promise was a relief— I did not have to worry about running into Palsang on an isolated trail between villages and could move about alone to conduct interviews—what was most reassuring was that I had the community's support. Public reaction could easily have swung the other way, toward general indifference and reluctance to meddle in the problems of outsiders; or people might have become hostile and uncooperative if Palsang had reached Nyangkhu before me and had been able to garner support among his Sherpa and Nyeshangte male acquaintances in that village. In either case, if Palsang had remained in the valley, my work would have been jeopardized and my mobility severely curtailed.

Women's Agency: Politics and Social Power

Pema's actions on my behalf, and her success in rallying the villagers to come to my aid, reveal much about the dynamics of political process and power in Nyeshang. A closer look at the series of events that took place in Traklung and the discussions that ensued among various villagers further demonstrates how Nyeshangte women use their social ties to request assistance and mobilize political support and how women's informal power can

12. Village youths.

influence an individual's social standing and behavior. Sufficient background information is included in the following case so that readers can understand why a perceived breach of friendship and hospitality on the part of a former Nyangkhu villager, Karma of the "Dorje Hotel," led some rival Churi villagers to denounce him (and all Nyangkhu villagers) for not acting as responsible Nyeshangte hosts. The incident also demonstrates how Nyeshangte women can manipulate latent rivalries among factions to further their own personal agendas.

My initial reaction after the assault was to seek refuge at the Dorje Hotel in Traklung, since I knew the lodge owners, Karma and his wife Sonam, fairly well and felt they would help me. My husband and son had stayed there twice, and the family had been grateful when we successfully treated their two youngest children for boils.

The medical favor was returned during another visit, when I arrived at their lodge exhausted, limping from blisters and a knee injury and suffering from bronchitis and general edema, the aftereffects of a fascinating but incredibly stupid foray into a neighboring valley—over an eighteen-thousand-foot pass, with minimal food supplies or camping gear—followed by an exhausting sixteen-hour march back to Traklung. It took a few days to recuperate; Karma and Sonam treated me with special teas and poultices made from Tibetan salt and provided basins of warm salty water in which to soak my swollen arms. (Salt from the Tibetan plateau is used for a variety of illnesses including high-altitude edema.)

Palsang usually accompanied me on these excursions, and he was known throughout Nyeshang as my assistant. He had stayed several times in Traklung and was generally regarded as a friend rather than a servant. He played with the children, often helping me distribute small gifts and treats for them, and was always pleasant and helpful around our hosts.

Karma, perhaps thinking the quarrel was not so serious and would be settled the next day, allowed Palsang to spend the night at the lodge. Almost instantly, an elderly woman staying in the room next to mine warned me that "the Sherpa" had arrived and was in the room next to hers. She suggested I stay at the Star Hotel instead (which was run by Churi rather than Nyangkhu people) and watched from the balcony as I hurried across the lane to my new lodgings.

Although Karma told us the next morning that Palsang had left earlier for Nyeshang and was somewhere on the trail ahead of us, we later passed three old women at the rest area above Traklung who insisted otherwise. The woman, who had initially warned me, and her two female companions, who were returning to their village (Tipli), had slept in the room next door to Palsang. When they heard him leave in the middle of the night, they had followed him outside to see which way he would go, and then watched in the bright moonlight as he disappeared down the trail headed *away* from Nyeshang.

I'm not sure why Karma deliberately lied to me about Palsang's destination; perhaps he simply wasn't sure or didn't want to get involved with police officials. His wife, Sonam, who was ill in bed during this interval, was too weak to intervene or to talk at length with me. Although Karma's behavior puzzled me, I assumed he was trying to be fair to both of us by staying neutral and uncommitted. Perhaps, though, as a male, he tended to be more sympathetic to Palsang and gave him a chance to get away. In the same manner, the uniform responses of various women toward the incident—Pema, her friends, and the old women—suggested they were acting collectively, as a defense against perceived male aggression.[7]

Pema harshly denounced Karma since he had not taken proper action against "the Sherpa" and had failed to protect me, a family friend and a "guest of Nyangkhu village." Her views were shared by other Nyeshangte patrons at the Star Hotel—mostly women and a few men from Traklung as well as other Nyeshangte travelers who were allied with the owners from

Churi village. The consensus around the hearth that night indicated a rather low opinion of Karma (and his wife) and Nyangkhu villagers in general. In their view, Karma had a double obligation to "protect" me since I sought shelter in his home. Furthermore, they added, as former Nyangkhu residents, the couple had an additional responsibility to assist me because I had spent most of my time in "their village" among "their people."

Pema's opinion of Karma certainly did not improve the next day, when he refused to turn over a parcel that belonged to my landlady, Ama, containing jewelry and watches that had been repaired in Kathmandu. Palsang had kept the box in his pack. At the Star Hotel, I mentioned this to the group sitting around the hearth, knowing that this news would spread quickly in Traklung and that Palsang would not dare leave the village with Ama's jewelry and risk having Nyeshangte track him down in Kathmandu. Palsang later handed the box over to Karma; the next day, Karma claimed that his eldest daughter would deliver it to Ama later in the week. Pema, doubtful he would do any such thing at all, made a point of mentioning this incident to everyone she met on the trail, in a way ensuring that Karma would have to keep his promise or completely lose his social standing, even risk a feud between my landlady's relatives and his family.

However, Pema later dropped this particular issue when one of the three elderly women we encountered on the trail told her not to worry. "That Dorje Hotel man may be no good, but his wife is related to the old woman [Ama] in Nyangkhu. She will get her jewelry soon." Pema deferred to the older woman, respecting her opinion and her greater knowledge of kin networks in the valley. Pema, now reassured that even the "disreputable" Karma would not sink to stealing from a relative, redirected her energies to solving the "Sherpa problem."

Pema used two arguments—one appealing to pan-Nyeshangte values, the other playing on old rivalries between Nyangkhu and Churi villagers to make her point. Her rhetoric was at times plaintive: "What can we women do? We are not so big, not so strong. Oh, what can I do, I am an old woman"—then indignant: "How could this thing happen in our community? Those outsiders, those porters and Sherpas do things like that now in our land! What will the government people think of us, that we let this happen to westerners here? How is it now people are no good, it is not safe to walk about any more. There is too much greed these days."

These comments were addressed primarily to a female audience during the course of our journey—sometimes Pema stopped along a village lane to greet someone she knew, at other times she spoke in a friend's kitchen—but her words were overheard by curious males who were drawn into the discussion and subsequently obliged to act. Pema's women friends in Tipli and Kangri also commiserated with her about their lack of strength, their need for protection, deploring the general decline of values. These words were accompanied by many sighs, hands thrown up in the air, soft mutterings about "evil people," and a spirit of dejection that was all quite dramatic and effective.

Through these theatrical devices as well as indirect channels, Pema got her message across, but still stayed within the norms of social interaction: most Nyeshangte women exert social pressure through gossip, avoiding direct confrontation or the appearance of giving direct orders unless they feel the situation warrants such action. Instead, women's agency and social power comes largely from their ability to manipulate or shape public opinion. Often, Nyeshangte women (and many Nyeshangte men) prefer to solicit public support through tactful requests that play on their helplessness as individuals or appeal to the group's pride and to the community's sense of honor or spirited independence.

Speech, Power, and Authority: Male and Female Leaders Compared

This style of female speech and the tactic of garnering support by gradually drawing the audience to one's position resembles the dynamics of formal council meetings and is not so different from strategies employed by individual male speakers at village meetings:

> It is not unusual in the early stages of the discussion for more than half the participants to be talking at once. They tend to address themselves not to immediate neighbors but towards the opposite side of the circle where people may or may not be listening. The general cacophony is heightened by energetic gesturing. . . . Yet the disorder is more apparent than real. Those who find themselves without an audience trail off into silence. . . . Eventually, one speaker holds the floor and, whether by the essential soundness of his proposal or by the simple dynamics of the group, his views become the material on which consensus is built. (Cooke 1985a:157)

As Cooke subsequently points out, male leadership or the "ability to be listened to" is intricately tied to a man's social standing. Individuals with the skills of persuasion and the ability to influence decision making emerge as natural leaders only if they have already attained a certain measure of respect in the community (1985a). In particular, respect is shown to individuals who have a reputation of being sincere and speaking truthfully in a Buddhist sense, as opposed to just speaking "from the mouth [but] not from the heart" (158). Although Nyeshangte political processes—at council meetings or informal social gatherings—place considerable emphasis on group accord and individual equality (anyone, male or female, is free to speak), this concern with sincerity and Buddhist precepts of "right speech" and "right action" tends to muffle the competing voices of villagers who lead less than exemplary lives. Although Cooke's statements refer specifically to his own observations of male leaders and their roles at village council meetings, I found these dynamics of leadership and social interaction to be relevant in a variety of casual settings as well, where they apply to both men and women in their roles as social actors or agents.

These same principles of leadership also apply to women who hold informal positions of authority and who wield power through intravillage social networks. Pema succeeded in influencing other villagers in part because of her status—a middle-aged woman from a moderately successful urban household who was still "well connected" with the rural community in the sense that she participated regularly in village ritual life and maintained her friendships in the homeland. By raising her concerns at a variety of gatherings, she was able to feel out her audience and sense what turn public opinion would take. These conversations about an absent "third party" allow Nyeshangte women (and men) to express harsh criticisms and to listen to varying claims without directly confronting or insulting the "culprit," which could lead to an irreparable breach in social relations. Eventually, the concerned parties settle on a more moderate position that reflects group opinion, avoiding extreme views and unjust accusations. Even Pema, for example, desisted in her attack against Karma (in the matter of the jewelry) when the old Tipli woman disagreed with her and pointed out why she was wrong.

Although harmony and group accord are widely prized by Nyeshangte, the incident at Traklung also reveals a number of things about the way female networks operate. Although these alliances serve to bind women from different villages, sometimes clan and village loyalties may take precedence over casual friendships and may be divisive forces. In this particular case, the cleavages followed village lines: the Star Hotel, which was run by Churi villagers and patronized by Pema and her daughter, came to my assistance; as a result, public opinion (which included Nyeshangte from Tipli, Kangri, and Traklung) turned against the Dorje Hotel owners and, by implication, Nyangkhu villagers as well. Through their ties throughout the valley, these women expressed their indignation and distress over the Sherpa's outrageous behavior and Karma's (or Nyangkhu's) severe case of bad manners. Their harangue—delivered at times with outrage, at times with a shrug of helplessness—had a wondrous effect in part because it exploited the tradition of rivalry and feuding between two of the larger villages in the valley, Nyangkhu and Churi, and also manipulated Nyeshangte values concerning social relations: the stronger should protect the weaker.[8] These values play on male-female relations, as well as on relations of power between Nyangkhu (a larger, wealthier, more urban-oriented village) and all the other smaller, more conservative Nyeshang villages that occasionally unite in their resentment against Nyangkhu's preeminent status and paternalistic role in community affairs (see, for example, Cooke 1985a:115–75).

Although women's political action may seem disruptive or divisive (at least from the victim's point of view—in this case, Karma's or that of Nyangkhu village), at other times women's collective action has served as a mediating force that transcended intervillage feuds and brought peace to the valley.[9] In one case, a minor dispute between two men over pasture use turned into a major conflagration that involved another village, and then spread throughout the valley and lasted three years (see also Gurung 1977a:156). Because of the seriousness of the conflict (several villagers were killed) and the failure of Nyeshangte leaders to reestablish peace, representatives of warring groups sought outside intervention and presented the case to His Majesty's Government (Nepal) for resolution. Gurung describes the role women played as mediators:

> The group members (male members) who were blamed for killing the son of the other group leader could not visit Kathmandu. So this group sent their wives, sisters and daughters to Kathmandu to represent them. His Majesty's government made [a] last attempt to settle their fight. At the same time, women of both groups internally held a meeting in order to normalize the conflict. Women of the two groups united and proposed peace in the villages to the . . . leaders of both groups. . . . Thus through the help of the members of the Gurung subba [leaders from the adjacent district], His Majesty's Government and women of both groups, their conflict was settled in 1953. . . . Since then normal life resumed in Nyeshang valley until 1966. (1977a:157)

Several other disputes—some internal to Nyangkhu, others involving multiple villages—occurred in the following decades (see, for example,

Gurung 1977a:157–60, and Cooke 1985a:159–75), leading some Nyeshangte males to jokingly refer to their history of violent feuding as "our civil wars" (Cooke 1985a). Again, in these situations women play important roles in conflict resolution. They may assist their own relatives by providing them a safe shelter or bringing food and supplies to their forest hideouts, but these acts do not impair their neutral status as mediators. During times of village conflicts and valleywide feuding, only women are free to move around openly without risk of attack by opposing groups. The alliances that women maintain throughout the valley and their traditional neutral status allow them to play a major role in Nyeshang's political and social affairs.

Disputes Between Women

Although peaceful coexistence seems to be especially valued in this community (given the history of feuds and the male predilection for being violent and quick to anger), women here also "fight." However, although women may get involved in the disputes of their menfolk or stage quarrels of their own, these female quarrels tend to remain more localized within the village, among neighbors or relatives, and are resolved fairly quickly. Women's style of interaction and the end result of their disputes differ significantly from the arguments that arise between males. Women do not resort to physical violence. (I never heard of women killing or seriously injuring another person.) Women's disputes rarely turn into long-term feuds, and women are seen as mediators, not instigators, of serious conflicts. As I indicated earlier, individual women (and some men) may air their grievance before a third uninvolved party, to see if public opinion is behind them. Social pressure is usually strong enough to force an agreement and settle the problem without disrupting the equilibrium with direct accusations, shouting, and "loss of face."

However, when the individuals involved are of different status (in terms of age and generation), the confrontation may be quite direct, immediate, and public. The senior elder woman (or man) can expect with reasonable certainty that the younger women (or men) will usually back down and not tangle with her over the issue. If they did, public opinion would probably turn against them for not deferring to their elders and for spreading "bad feelings" throughout the village, especially if the conflict revolved around a relatively minor dispute as the following example demonstrates.

One day Orke, a prominent woman in her mid- to late fifties who occupied a central role in many of the dgon pa rituals and village festivals, walked past the water tap near the village center and began to scold several younger women (including me) for washing our clothes and our hair there. Though the village council (comprised mostly of men) had posted signs in English and Nepali "NO WASHING, NO BATHING" at every water tap in the village, many women (and a few men) routinely disregarded the notices. It was inconvenient to go to the river below to do laundry or to bathe, and it was hard work to haul several canisters of water up two or more notched ladders to roof terraces so that dishes, clothes, and bodies could be washed at home.

Most women who wished to bathe or wash dishes waited until mid-morning or mid-afternoon when traffic at the tap and adjacent water troughs was slow. Early mornings were always busy times at the tap: livestock were watered and young girls were often lined up at the four spigots waiting to fill large plastic jugs that they lugged back to their houses.

However, as it was late spring when this incident occurred, most of the livestock had already been driven up to the high pastures, and plenty of water was available from the snow melt-off so there was no risk of the water source drying up (as it occasionally did in the late autumn or in the winter when the streams froze). There was really no reason to forbid anyone from doing their wash there.

As Orke began to warm up, her voice carried throughout the neighborhood, drawing everyone to peer out their windows or look down from their roof terraces. As I gathered my bucket and laundry and tried to slip away (embarrassed to be embroiled in such a public scene), two of my older female cohorts, married women in their late thirties and early forties, shouted back angrily, telling the old woman to "do her own work" (mind her own business) and leave them alone. They were the only ones who dared speak back to her. The teenage girls did not respond at all, but two of them looked at me and shrugged; another smiled in sympathy, knowing how uncomfortable I felt. The two 30-year-old men from Kathmandu stood by sheepishly clasping their toothbrushes and soap but did not say a word. Finally, my landlady and her next-door neighbor, a man in his fifties (also a village council member) climbed down from their roof terraces and tried to soothe Orke, who was quite indignant by then, because the two "guilty" women had stood up to her and argued back. I suspect that if I had not been present, the chastised group would have been sent off, reinforced by Orke, the village councilman, and my landlady, who *always* washed her dishes, her laundry, and her hair at home. But since I was literally in the middle, Ama and her neighbor tried to reason with Orke, saying we did no harm, as it was mid-day and the water was running continuously in the stream above. A few weeks later when I happened to be walking through another section of the village, I saw Orke, the "enforcer," scolding several children and two adolescent girls who were bathing at the tap. Although a few adult women poked their heads out to see what the fuss was about, no one intervened on their behalf and the youngsters scampered off without a word.

Another incident involving a dispute between women of widely disparate ages also shows how generation and rank often take precedence in arguments. One day in Lhakpa, some local village men and (Nepalese) government workers came to the Yak Hotel, a lodge run by three young women in their twenties. The women had just finished brewing a large batch of *raksī* (distilled alcohol made from wheat), and word had spread that the brew was very good. One grizzled old fellow kept coming back for refills, and by early afternoon he was quite drunk, barely able to climb the ladder to reach the lodge terrace. A few minutes after he had entered the kitchen door and handed his brown glass bottle and fourteen rupees (u.s.$ .60) to the hostess, we heard a woman shouting angrily from the lane below the lodge. Palsang and I, and two of the hostesses, stepped outside to see what was wrong. A woman in her sixties was shaking her fist, upset that her husband was drunk and spending so much money on alcohol. The woman also denounced the young hostesses for making so much raksī and for engaging in "bad works." Her angry voice began to draw other villagers who were curious about the incident. We returned inside, and the hostess serving the raksī apologized to the old man and said, "Father you must go now. Another day you can come back and then we will refill your bottle." She returned the money and the empty bottle to the old man, but poured him a complimentary glass. This was done to placate the man and send him speedily on his way, but also as a token gesture of defiance.

That most women do not drink and have little patience with inebriated men made it certain that village opinion would side with the wife, especially since resident women greatly outnumber men. Rather than risk criticism for selling too much alcohol and arguing with one of their elders, the young hostesses did not confront the old man's wife. It was simply better for them to keep quiet and let the storm blow over rather than disrupt village social relations further.[10]

Water taps (and drunken husbands) are clearly areas of female jurisdiction, but these areas also reveal disjunctures along generation and gender lines. Although some men occasionally fetch water, this task is performed primarily by women and servants. (The same holds for laundry and dishes.) Usually, in households with several resident females, the youngest (daughter) makes the greatest number of trips between the house and the water tap, while the older women sit on the sunny terraces and leisurely rinse the dishes or their clothes in small basins. It is not surprising, then, that the village council (mostly old men) and the "enforcers" (mostly old women) would pass such a resolution, since the burden falls heaviest on others. Nor is it surprising, in turn, that many young women simply ignore the posted signs: after all, most women say they cannot read Nepali, let alone English. On the other hand, although young women do not seem to mind that village men break their own rules and bathe at the fountain, these women can be quite assertive and will tell the fellows to hurry up and get out of the way. Relations between younger women and senior men are not always deferential; young women are often outspoken and treat older males (especially unmarried ones) much the same way as boys their own age—sometimes in a rough, playful fashion, teasing or pushing them around.[11]

When two women are closer in age and status, an argument may not be resolved as easily. Once I saw two middle-aged women gesturing wildly at each other, but I was too far away to understand their shouts and screams. The women were neighbors, and their roof terraces were only a few feet apart. After a few minutes of intense yelling, men emerged from each of the two houses, and literally dragged and pulled the women back inside. The women clambered back up the ladders onto the terraces and resumed their argument. The men once again pleaded with them, calmed then down, and persuaded them back inside. I have no idea what the scene was about; my landlady was preoccupied with preparations for an upcoming two-week festival and unusually mute about the incident. Overall, disputes between women seemed to occur infrequently; I witnessed very few while I was in the valley. Nor did people talk about women's fights, which seemed rather inconsequential compared to the "civil wars" (as one informant put it) that involved and centered around men.

Although women own land, livestock, and earn income through petty trade (and therefore have the same potential as men for fighting over property), they seem less prone to getting embroiled in serious disputes. Here, the proverbial double standard seems to apply. Women are expected to be less quarrelsome than men. If any woman deviates from this ideal, she may be subject to more criticism by the entire community than a man who fails to live up to the same standard. A "boys will be boys" attitude seems in effect, and quarrelsome behavior among males is attributed either to the immature or foolish outlook of young boy-men, the effects of excessive drinking, or a combination of these reasons. Because most women spend a great deal of time in the village and depend on neighbors and relatives for assistance, they cannot take the chance of alienating many people or risk a villagewide reputation for being uncooperative or troublesome. This is not to suggest that women do not argue with one another or with men (they do and sometimes quite vigorously), but because they are enmeshed in the web of community life, women tend to smooth things over and let some things slide, rather than pursue a quarrel until it becomes a serious feud. Men, on the other hand, can always leave the valley or the city and stay abroad for several months or years. Although traders often work in groups, they can manage alone quite well. Some men may even choose permanent exile: a few Nyeshangte residents at Shillong (Assam, India) were implicated in the feud-related deaths that took place in the valley in the 1950s and 1960s and settled permanently in India (cf. Gurung 1977a).

Because of this history of violent feuding in the valley and, paradoxically, because of the cultural values that stress cooperation and nonviolence, an individual who disrupts the community with a trivial complaint about a theft or damage to his or her own personal property would be perceived as selfish; a material or personal loss is simply not worth troubling others about. Women (and men) who show restraint by waiving their claims against fellow villagers gain the respect of the entire community for being judicious and wise. Men, on the other hand, may be excused for their emotional excesses and their violence; as they mature, it is expected that their impetuousness will be curbed. Given the prevailing ideals of the community, and the actual history of Nyeshang's civil wars, it is understandable perhaps that women are generally cast into the role of mediators who must not only restrain their own tempers and outbursts, but also are expected to smooth over the conflicts caused by others, notably the men.

In summary, women's support networks consist of a variety of social ties that may be instrumental or affective, close or distant, renewed or picked up when the need arises. It is primarily this fluid character of women's relationships that makes these informal social groups so effective. Depending on the circumstances, an individual may choose to elicit support from different social levels: personal kindred, clan affiliation, village-based loyalties, or the wider Nyeshangte community. Having described the political and social agency of women's networks, I will now briefly examine the basis on which these alliances are formed.

The Importance of Age: Age Grading, Youth Associations, and Friendship

Age, generation, and seniority are significant factors in Nyeshang social organization. In many ways, in a community where social relations are based largely on a generational model, consideration of relative age over-shadows distinctions based on gender and leads to important nonkin ties. This emphasis on chronological age is reflected to some extent in astrolog-ical beliefs: all children born in the same year (regardless of gender) share a common bond based on their similar horoscopes; they are associated with the same animal within a twelve-year calendrical cycle—for example, the year of the monkey—and are thought to be invested with similar qualities or dispositions. But astral considerations aside, most friendships are formed in the wider context of age sets: children of similar age tend to play together, attend the same classes at school, and later belong to the same village age-based institutions.

These village institutions are linked to age-grading practices in Nyeshang society, so that individuals of both sexes pass through a series of named stages, each of which is associated with particular characteristics, rights, and obligations (cf. Cooke 1985a:186–88). Children under the age of 15 and the elderly over 60 generally have few responsibilities toward the community: instead, the major responsibilities for organizing, sponsoring, and attending village activities, such as festivals, religious rites, work parties, and political meetings, fall to adult Nyeshangte between these ages.

Tsha: Young Women's Associations

Many of these village activities are organized through tsha or "girls' houses," which still figure prominently in the homeland today, and form the basis for lasting ties among women. Though there are fewer tsha houses as a result of overall out-migration (Nyangkhu, for example, had nine houses thirty years ago and today only has three), those that remain still operate as they did in the past. Young unmarried women between the ages of 13 and 20 enjoy being tsha members: the daily routine of village life is shared with close girlfriends who work together during the day and often sleep overnight at the tsha house (*rodī ghar*, in Nepali), which is actually the sponsor's residence. Usually, an older woman acts as sponsor because she has fond memories of her own adolescence and wishes to continue the tradition for her daughter and friends. Tsha members socialize with other village youths in the evenings, but this does not usually include sexual relations: boys do not sleep overnight at the house. The bachelor's group (*phee*) does not have an analogous boy's house where they meet or sleep overnight. Instead, boys return to their own individual homes after the evening parties.

Many Nyeshangte women find this carefree period of young adulthood so enjoyable that they often postpone marriage until their late twenties. Several young women whom I interviewed in Kathmandu told me that they were anxious to return to the homeland: they preferred the "village life" over the city because of tsha and the companionship this provided. "In the village we do like this: today I go to your fields and tomorrow we go to mine. In the city everyone is just sitting home alone." In the city, where there are no tsha, young women are more isolated from their peers, and their freedom is curtailed because of the perceived dangers of urban life. Village girls, on the other hand, are free to visit one another in the evenings, often staying overnight; they move freely about the village without any restrictions.

My landlady's 14-year-old daughter, Yangdzom, belonged to a tsha group and was seldom alone. Often, two or three of her friends joined us for dinner; the girls stayed up late around the main hearth where they teased and joked with the male servants, often pushing the young men in rough play and knocking them off their low benches. When the noise level became intolerable and the play too rowdy, Ama quietly retreated to her private quarters, a multipurpose room where she stored her valuables, slept, and received her own female friends around a separate hearth. Sometimes, other young men stopped by—some from the village, others from the city—and the girls alternately ignored them or joked among themselves, bursting into nervous laughter, feeling somewhat shy in front of strangers. At these times Ama acted as hostess, refilling the young men's glasses with beer and talking with the male visitors who tried hard to maintain their composure, while the girls sat huddled in a pile around the fire, whispering behind their shawls, and giggling. Other nights after dinner, groups of girls called out from the lane below and Yangdzom would lean out the window to see who was there, sometimes grabbing her shawl and hurrying to join them on their social rounds through the village.

Tsha groups go through a development cycle, gradually taking shape when seven or eight girls begin to spend evenings together at one another's homes, occasionally sleeping overnight. Village girls join individual tsha groups when they are between the ages of 12 and 15, and the group gradually dissolves when members get married in their twenties. The girls are usually close in age and share strong affective bonds that stem from childhood. Tsha groups are based strictly on friendship ties rather than clan, kinship bonds, or hierarchical factors like household wealth or social standing.[12]

Although marriage or establishing a separate household marks the end of formal membership in a youth group, the friendships that are made during these years are permanent and form the basis of most cooperative work groups and individual social networks. In many instances, these friendship ties are carried into the next generation, so that daughters of two women who were tsha associates will become close friends and often decide to join the same tsha group. One of these older women usually will volunteer to be a "housemother," and the tsha will meet at her house.

Tsha festivities take place in early October, when the harvest has been gathered. This is a time of plenty and a time for celebration: hundreds of goats and many yak are slaughtered, and villagers prepare feasts with an abundance of beer, distilled liquor, and meat, a change from their usual grain-based diet. In October, tsha girls celebrate the New Year (*Lhosar*) for ten days by singing, dancing, and eating meat. They share meals and sleep overnight at the tsha house and in the morning return to their own homes.

Village boys and unmarried young men also visit the tsha house in the evenings and bring the girls gifts of fresh goat and yak meat. The housemother is usually present to act as hostess (and chaperone) and see that the girls do not get too rowdy.[13] The young women prepare a New Year's feast for their guests and serve rice along with the gifts of meat. In addition to the cooked grain offered at the evening New Year's feast, a few days later the unmarried girls also present a separate gift of (uncooked) barley or wheat to the young men, who use the grain to make their own beer. This traditional grain payment is in exchange for protection: Nyeshang youths "protect" village girls from being "kidnapped" by *outside* males who, according to local accounts, used to come to the valley to take Nyeshangte women away as brides (Gurung 1977a:179).

Although these social gatherings permit village youths to meet members of the opposite sex in a lively atmosphere, tsha houses are not like the dormitories of the Naga or Muria Gond tribal groups, where sexual relations are encouraged between adolescents (cf. Elwin 1947, 1969). According to my young Nyeshangte friends, sexual encounters among Nyeshangte adolescents are rather uncommon.[14] This is similar to Andhor's (1974) findings among the Gurung, a group who shares a common cultural, historical, and linguistic background with the Nyeshangte. Gurung teenagers also join youth groups, but casual sexual relations during early to late adolescence are not condoned and appear to be unusual in the context of these youth associations.

Youth Associations: Social Roles and Traditional Responsibilities

Youth groups serve important functions in village society, and many economic, social, and ritual activities are organized through them. Although many of the group activities described below still take place, the majority of participants (especially in Nyangkhu) are more apt to be young women than men, since the bachelor's group has fewer members and the male association has lost much of its vitality in recent years because of out-migration.

Female tsha members exchange labor throughout the agricultural season and, in the past, the young women often recruited village boys into their work parties when extra help was needed. Male and female youth groups carry out other village activities together. Once a year during the summer, boys and girls from Nyangkhu clean the village lanes and squares. During the spring rites of sowing, these adolescents help carry the sacred Tibetan scriptures through the fields as the lamas recite protective formulas to ward off evil forces that could damage the new crops. After the wheat crop has been planted, boys and girls spend two nights at the dgon pa where they "sing and dance." In fact, this ritual aspect has become so synonymous with tsha that many Nyeshangte, when questioned about tsha, referred to youth associations as "going to the dgon pa." During the spring and harvest rites, members of youth groups also make a short pilgrimage to the Nyeshang Kurti dgon pa, where they spend one or two nights receiving religious instruction from village lamas. This particular dgon pa, nestled high above the valley on the Annapurna range, is especially sacred to Nyeshangte and holds a prominent place in their history and local traditions.

The youth groups are also responsible for organizing some village events and entertainment. Youths from Nyangkhu visit the nearby village of Churi during the Yartung festival—a week-long affair of horse races, dancing, and drinking—and spend one night at the Churi dgon pa performing their dances and songs. Later in the summer, Churi youths perform in Nyangkhu, and during these visits the resident tsha and phee groups act as hosts for visitors who do not have relatives in the village.

In summary, the formal youth associations play an important part in the lives of adolescent Nyeshangte, especially for the young women who are the most active participants and supporters of tsha traditions today. Tsha fosters a cooperative spirit among village youth who undertake a variety of joint economic and religious tasks. The casual social gatherings also allow young women to become more familiar with potential marriage partners in their own and adjacent villages.[15] The regular visits of neighboring youth groups during summer festivals also encourages friendships with other young women (and men) in nearby villages. Nyeshangte women, largely as a result of these youth associations, lead "well-connected" lives: from the time they are adolescents through their retirement years, women create and maintain enduring social ties that form the basis of many alliances and support networks that extend throughout the community.

Ritual Friendships: Roma and Chetu

Ritual friendship is another type of nonkin tie that links women to other women (*roma*) and women to men (*chetu*), and creates a fictive kin relationship between the two participants and their immediate families.[16] Ritual friendships are often established between trading partners and individuals from different ethnic groups; these ties have important instrumental aspects that involve mutual aid, hospitality, and political support. But Nyeshangte also contract ceremonial ties within their own community, and these tend to be more affective in nature.

The two types of ritual ties share basic characteristics. Ceremonial friends become like sisters or brothers to one another, and these fictive kin relationships expand outward to include both their families. Descendants of ceremonial friends may not marry for at least one generation, even though in principle they may be eligible if they belong to different clans. With the fictive kin ties come certain social obligations: each is expected to attend the various life crisis events of the other partner's family and offer appropriate gifts at weddings, funerals, and births. Ritual friends are also expected to observe death pollution and mourning practices if their friend or close relative dies. Nyeshangte also believe that individuals linked by roma or chetu bonds will be reunited after death.

Young women often establish roma ties during their adolescence. The ceremony is informal: the two friends exchange ceremonial scarves and small gifts or money. Sometimes the exchange is witnessed by parents and relatives, and a lama may be present to offer his blessings. The participants may enjoy a celebratory meal with close friends and family. In other instances the decision to do roma may be more spontaneous: it may occur on a trading trip or on the way to a festival, and no witnesses are necessary to formalize the bond. This special friendship continues after the two young women are married. After the birth of every child, for example, the roma friend and her husband will offer baby clothes and money at the child's naming ceremony.

A woman will also be linked to her husband's ritual friends (*roba*), and these social ties are maintained even after her husband dies. These interpersonal relations guarantee a widow social support at the commemorative funeral rites that are held one year after her spouse's death. A widow may also rely on her husband's roba friends to continue their former trading relations with her household, enabling her to exchange surplus products for commodities that are produced in an adjacent district. The importance of these alliances may be illustrated by the example of my landlady who lived alone with her teenage daughter, Yangdzom.

Ama was overwhelmed by grief when I first met her in April 1989. Her husband had died six months before, and in the past three years she had lost a 22-year-old daughter to cancer and an 18-year-old boy to pneumonia. Ama's two brothers had also died, and as the eldest of three daughters she had inherited two additional houses in the village. One of her sisters was retarded but managed to do some farming and raised sheep and goats on family property near the monastery above Nyangkhu. Her other sister had married her husband's younger brother and lived in Nyangkhu. Despite the personal tragedies afflicting her household, Ama was quite wealthy. When her husband had been alive, their hotel, shop, and restaurant did a thriving business with trekking groups, but now she was too depressed to run the lodge on her own. She cried frequently, and Palsang, Spike, and I tried to comfort her and help her by doing household chores or dealing with customers (mostly tourists) who showed up.

Although widowed, Ama was not socially isolated. She often had friends (mostly Nyeshangte women) staying with her for several days at a time. Every day she received visits from neighbors, villagers who wished to buy something from her shop, or traders from adjacent regions. Although many visits were for commercial reasons, the exchanges took place in a very social atmosphere: a leisurely conversation punctuated by glasses of beer or tea if the visitors were women. Some of the men who dropped in were roba friends of her late husband. Two of these fellows lived in Jomsom and Muktinath—villages in the adjacent Kali Gandaki region—and sometimes Ama bought Tibetan salt or rice from them. Both men attended the final funerary rites held in October 1990 for Ama's husband. Ama was also "connected" to roba men in Nar Khola and Larkye with whom she exchanged locally grown potatoes and wheat for butter and dried yak meat, which were in plentiful supply in these pastoral communities. These roba ties and trade links also continued into the succeeding generation. One fellow who dropped by told me his father (now dead) had been a ritual friend of Ama's husband. He still considered Ama to be a "relative," and whenever he came to Nyeshang he stopped by to see her.

Nyeshang women may also contract ritual ties (chetu) directly with men in connection with a pilgrimage or a special religious occasion. Typically, at a pilgrimage site a group of Nyeshangte traveling together may feel a special closeness with one another and decide to become chetu. Women and men will exchange rosaries (*malla*) and offer their friends ceremonial scarves. Once a year, Nyangkhu villagers spend four or five days at Nyeshang Kurti dgon pa across the valley. During the last two days villagers celebrate with dances and a communal feast, and many individuals contract a chetu tie. Chetu bonds are affective and instrumental: friends provide one another with special assistance at major rituals, social support at life crisis ceremonies, and token gifts to honor the relationship. Males, upon their return from a trading venture, may bring their chetu gifts of clothing; in exchange, women offer men barley beer or distilled alcohol.

Whereas roba or roma ties are always with individuals of the same sex and age, chetu ties cross sex and age categories. Ama, for example, had two roma ties with women from other Nyeshangte villages, and three chetu ties with local men—one of whom was a Gurung schoolteacher in his twenties. Her friendships (ritual and otherwise) with women and men from the community and outside the district aided her "recovery." By the summer I noticed that her depression had lifted: she was cheerful, busy supervising the farm hands and household servants, and had hired a Gurung cook to help manage the lodge restaurant during the upcoming trekking season.

In summary, nonkin ties, whether formalized through ritual bonds and youth associations or established through casual friendships, play an important part in the individual networks and alliances of Nyeshangte women. These social relationships are structured by ideals of reciprocity between equal partners. Friends offer material and emotional support and contribute their labor when needed. In times when so many adult males are absent from the household, these outside ties take on extra significance for many women.

Women, Tradition, and Resistance

The problematics of "traditional culture" have been addressed in a number of earlier works that point out how traditions are constantly being reinvented, constructed, and reinterpreted for any number of reasons.[17] More recently, writers have examined how cultural features and traditional practices are elevated to the level of political symbols, as a means of resistance against external forces.[18] Increasingly, cultural anthropologists have come to realize what archaeologists have always known, that even small-scale societies existing on the periphery of the world capitalist system have been continuously changing in response to their own internal forces and to local regional influences, before initial western contact.[19] Appadurai, for example, cautions us "to be careful not to suppose that as we work backward [in time] . . . , we will hit some local, cultural bedrock constituted of a closed set of reproductive practices, untouched by rumors of the world at large" (1991:208).

Nyeshang, of course, is no exception, and various oral histories, clan legends, and trade documents indicate that change has been a constant feature of the local landscape. My male and female informants are quite conscious of the way customary practices have been altered, reinvented, and transformed over time; even so, they still insist that the essential features and principles shaping their social order have remained, in basic form and content, "traditional" (*rol*).[20] Whether the values and practices my informants describe as traditional actually conform to earlier patterns is really not as important as how women (and men) individually and collectively use this discourse for their own political ends. In Nyeshang, it is primarily adult women in their roles of culture bearers and knowledge holders who are perceived by men (and by themselves) as possessing the moral status and cultural virtues to uphold, reproduce, and re-create the old Nyeshang ways.[21]

In this section I will examine how women's concerns with community welfare, in combination with their own gender-based interests, have led them to preserve many features of their local subsistence economy and the (noncapitalist) social relations in which they are embedded. I suggest that women's support of customary economic and social practices in the homeland constitutes a form of resistance against cultural and social forms associated with urbanization, global market economies, and the state, with its dominant Hindu order. At the same time, this resistance ensures that the homeland remains viable as a sanctuary for city residents and as a symbol of group identity. In addition, the homeland serves as a refuge for women, a place of their own that lessens their dependence on men and restores some semblance of the balanced and complementary gender relations that existed before the reorganization of trade and urban migration that took place in the 1970s.

Resistance to New Economic and Cultural Orientations

In many parts of the world, indigenous communities have been variously affected by their incorporation into the world system or global market economy. This process results in many changes: local societies are brought under greater control of centralizing states and are often subject to coercive pressures of the dominant cultural order along with their prevailing gender ideologies. Capital penetration and increased monetization may also lead to repatterning of household structures and overall social relations within the village. Monetization of the economy, for example, transforms traditional reciprocal exchanges of goods and services into cash transactions (see, for example, Andhors 1976) and may alter long-standing patterns of gender-based behavior. In some households, especially those in rural areas where male urban migration is common (for example, sub-Saharan Africa, India, and Nepal), access to cash may be very limited and rural women may become more dependent on male earnings. This increased dependence on male income may lead to family conflicts over remittances and how income is to be shared (Potash 1989), and existing gender relations may be thrown off balance, especially if men control the allocation of cash earnings. The perceived value of women's work and their economic contributions in the subsistence sector may also be devalued and receive little social recognition, as new prestige structures and values associated with western consumerism put an added premium on male wage income that is acquired independently of female activities.[22]

As capital penetration increases, social analysts assumed that women's roles in subsistence would eventually disappear, as female labor is either drawn into low-wage work or is redirected to the household which, under capitalist influences, becomes increasingly privatized and separate from public life and the world of "work" (Nash 1989:231). As unpaid "nonproductive" domestic laborers, women's work would reproduce the labor force but would not be valued or socially recognized. Where women continue to perform subsistence work, it was assumed that the lack of job opportunities in the city was responsible (cf. Boserup 1970a) or that women's subsistence contributions effectively subsidized household wage earners, helping to sustain the labor force at low cost (Nash 1989:231).

However, in addition to this economic rationale,[23] studies from Latin America (e.g., Buechler 1986; Bujra 1986; Nash 1989), sub-Saharan Africa (e.g., Potash 1986; MacGaffey 1986, 1988), aboriginal communities in Australia (e.g., Povinelli 1991, 1993) suggest that women also continue to work in subsistence and informal sectors undertaking small-scale trade and petty commodity production—selling handicrafts, cooked food, and home-brewed alcoholic beverages—because it provides a sense of personal satisfaction based on "cultural priorities" (Nash 1989:231). Nash, citing Annis's (1987) study of work patterns and craft production in Guatemala, suggests that the domestic mode of production (work in subsistence and informal sectors), which is "usually in the charge of women, satisfies deeply rooted patterns of behavior that have preserved cultural lifeways along with human lives that would otherwise be threatened by the vicissitudes of capitalist production" (1989:231). In reviewing her own findings from Kenya, as well as other studies carried out in West Africa, Potash suggests that gender differences in migration patterns that result in African women being "more rural" than men indicate that women deliberately choose to remain in the countryside. Potash (1989:198; 1986) found that married Luo women in urban communities in Kenya also wanted the security and independence that the rural subsistence economy provided, and these city women insisted that houses be built and fields be provided for them in rural communities. In general, explanations that rely solely on economic constraints (lack of jobs in the city, for example) are inadequate unless they also consider how women's own interests—concern with supporting their families, retaining access to land, minimizing their dependence on male support or earnings—influence the choices they make (Potash 1989:198). The preservation of the domestic mode of production, whether it involves subsistence farming, handicraft production, or small-scale commerce, often enables women to establish independent control over their own labor and provides them with economic and social security as well as a sense of pride. It may also be seen (in the minds of anthropologists and natives alike) as a form of local resistance to the destruction of the precapitalist subsistence economy.

Although this resistance reflects gender-based interests, a number of studies have shown that efforts to preserve indigenous economies also reflect concerns with maintaining cultural and ethnic identities and minimizing state control or domination by outside or foreign interests. For example, Gewertz and Errington (1991:208) discuss the Chambri's concern over the ecological viability of their homeland along the Sepik River in New Guinea in terms of their desire to remain autonomous in a rapidly changing world: "As the Chambri themselves knew, so long as the home environment was in working order, they would not be completely at the mercy of a precarious cash economy in a 'developing' country. Stated in another way, they would not be hapless so long as they were successful in their efforts to maintain their subsistence economy, that most essential basis of autonomy." The homeland was a source of refuge for Chambri urban migrants, wage laborers, and village residents that not only provided food and a means of existence but also preserved Chambri cultural priorities and lifeways (207). In another study from New Guinea, Lepowsky (1991:217) discusses how the people of Vanatinai resist outside political and cultural pressures by following "*taubwaragha*, the way of the ancestors." Cultural conservatism, adherence to customary subsistence practices, and the residents' reluctance to sell their labor for cash are all expressions of resistance on Vanatinai. Lepowsky explains: "It is a reaction against pressure to give up self-sufficiency and autonomy for greater dependence of the world cash economy. . . . It is also an assertive response toward pressure to show more obedience to colonial, national, or provincial governments" (224–25).

In many of the cases cited above, villagers and urban residents rely on a combination of old cultural patterns and newer economic practices to manipulate, exploit, or conversely resist contemporary economic orientations and cultural trends. Often, "traditional" cultures exist alongside the new; western representations coexist with preexisting ideologies; and new modes of economic participation are imbued with long-standing values. For example, among the Chambri, an individual's wealth may be tied to wage labor in town or to the tourist industry, but social status and personal success are still embedded in "social entailments": in the conspicuous dispensation of money or material goods to relatives and friends in the homeland. Although Gewertz and Errington (1991:146) speak of the Chambri as "flirting with western representations," community values that stress relationships and welfare still take precedence over a drive for private consumption, individual success, and profits.

A similar emphasis on communal values among the Tamang of central Nepal demonstrates that people may simultaneously resist the effects of monetization while still exploiting the new opportunities that a cash economy provides. In the Tamang case, "cooperative and capitalistic trends exist side by side," and Toffin (1982) observes that customary practices like labor exchanges and communal feasts sponsored by work parties of boys and girls (which resemble the tsha and rodī of Nyeshang and Gurung groups) still take place but that the new labor teams (*goremo*) are now paid wages for overtime work (89). However, the wages earned are pooled and spent in a communal feast. This practice, Toffin observes, strikes a compromise between Tamang values of reciprocity and cooperative labor and their repudiation of wage labor, which most individuals try to avoid within their community. The Chambri and Tamang cases (and also that of the Nyeshang described in the next section) are examples of how people may simultaneously resist capitalist values that emphasize hierarchy, competition, material accumulation, and depersonalized relations but still take part in new economic trends.

Traditional Practices, Traditional Values

In Nyeshang, we [women] are doing as before, like our mothers and fathers did, and like our forefathers did, before them.

—Buddhi Gurung, a 35-year-old female resident

Nyeshangte women, through their support of institutions like labor exchange groups, tsha houses, and ritual friendships, have created an environment where women's solidarity groups have endured. The ethics that guide these activities and relationships emphasize reciprocity and cooperation and presume the basic equality of all participants. In a sense, Nyeshangte women have been refashioning the emerging social order with its discordant notes—stemming from the economic disparity of urban life—into a more acceptable world. Through their practice (used here in a Buddhist sense), these women have held up their lives and their daily actions as a model of what Nyeshangte society has been and should be.

Women's agency in reproducing the social order invests the Nyeshangte with a strong group identity and a sense of cultural pride. In the city and the homeland, Nyeshangte are proud of their community values: their willingness to look after the well-being of the elderly and of handicapped individuals by offering food supplies, labor, and money to those in need.

The regular exchange of food gifts between women friends and relatives represents indigenous models of sociality and agency. This can reach conspicuous levels in the city when permanent urban residents accommodate their village relatives and friends for several months each winter. Adult women have a significant part in maintaining these connections between the homeland and the city in their roles as hostesses and through their informal networks. Lavish displays of hospitality and religious donations reinforce Nyeshangte solidarity both in the city and the homeland.[24] These redistributive social practices help reduce economic disparities and minimize cleavages between rural and urban groups; they also set the Nyeshang social order apart from the more stratified and hierarchically ordered caste groups in Nepal.

Nepalese government workers have been impressed by the community's civic sense of duty and ability to organize labor parties for communal projects. One example of this collective spirit can be seen in the small hamlet at Traklung where six families operate lodges and work in the apple orchard that belongs to the entire Nyeshangte community. The orchard was developed in 1977, and its success reflects the cooperative efforts of its owners. Each household in the valley contributed labor and supplied fertilizer for the planting of nearly five thousand seedlings, which had been provided free of charge by the government of Nepal (Cooke 1985a:140). Profits from the sale of apples are returned to a community account that pays a salary of five hundred rupees per month (u.s.$20) to each of the six families who maintain the orchard. One "impoverished" family is chosen from each of the villages and, in addition to earning a small salary from the community project, the families also make a substantial profit from the tourist lodges. In the course of a decade, all the families at Traklung have improved their financial situation and were able to expand their tourist lodges to accommodate the increasing number of tourists and Nyeshangte who stay there.

The orchard fund is also used for social welfare projects. During the unusually severe winter of 1988, six individuals died in an avalanche that swept through one of the larger villages and destroyed several houses. The community council decided to donate money to help the stricken families rebuild their damaged homes. The fund may be used to assist individuals who are handicapped and unable to work, widowed, or otherwise disadvantaged.

These values and commitment to social service are instilled at an early age and reinforced by Nyeshang's tradition of youth associations, which encourage adolescents to form lasting bonds with members of their own generation and help them mature into responsible adults. Communal feasts, entertainment, dances, work parties, labor exchange groups, and even religious training at the dgon pa are part of the repertoire of youth group activities that are representations of Nyeshang's "intensive collective life," grounded in egalitarian principles and "rules of reciprocity."[25]

Adult women in their voluntary roles as housemothers enable tsha practices to continue, despite the out-migration of many families. In contrast, bachelor groups are no longer as active in the homeland because of the absence of young men. Many of the community activities like labor gangs, organized in the past by both young men and women, are now composed primarily of adolescent girls and tsha members. These efforts to support customary institutions and maintain the subsistence economy may also be seen as a type of resistance in which women deliberately ignore high-caste values and turn their backs on the commoditized forms of labor and social relations appearing throughout Nepal, where increasing monetization has caused shifts in the subsistence patterns and collective practices of many local economies.

First, let us examine the impact of Hindu cultural influences. The case of the tsha house may serve as an example: these youth associations in Nyeshang share many similarities to the rodī groups found among the Gurung who also have separate organizations for unmarried girls and bachelors (see Andhors 1974; Toffin 1982). Among the Gurung, however, concern with conflicting values derived from the dominant Hindu society has led to the gradual disappearance of rodī groups in several communities. Conservative Hindu traditions frown upon the easy-going social relations between men and women in most tribal or Buddhist communities, and the rodī institution, where young women and men socialized freely, was perceived by many outsiders as morally lax—an indicator of the relatively low social (caste) status of the groups in question. Nyeshangte, however, are not concerned about Hindu social practice or public opinion, and in the valley the tsha houses are still maintained.[26]

The disappearance of collective activities like youth groups in Gurung society may also be linked to changing values and practices associated with capitalistic trends and market economies (Andhors 1976:21; cf. Toffin 1982:87–89). In the Gurung community studied by Andhors, cooperative labor gangs, communal feasts, and other activities that embodied reciprocity and were guided by an emphasis on "paying back well" have largely disappeared. The decline in rodī, the replacement of cooperative labor by wage labor, the channeling of wealth into private consumption instead of communal feasts, and the greater disparities in wealth have all been linked to increased monetization and a changing economic base. The customary values of reciprocity, mutual assistance, and egalitarianism are simply no longer relevant now that money is the primary means of exchange (1976:21).

Although Nyeshangte have been greatly affected by new market conditions, community principles similar to those described for the Tamang remain largely intact. Thus the second example of Nyeshang women's support of a collective ethos may be found in their continued use of voluntary labor for communal projects and labor exchange groups for daily subsistence activities. These institutions are maintained largely through women's efforts, and the groups are made up primarily of women workers. Nyeshangte still have a marked aversion to selling their labor for wages, preferring to exchange services among their peers. This continued reliance on nangtse and roo la tse types of labor exchange and voluntary labor in Nyeshang provides a marked contrast to many communities in Nepal, where capital penetration, monetization, and the overall shift to a market economy have made wage labor the norm. However, although the cash economy has disturbed social relations within the community, at the same time it has provided women with new opportunities in the valley: increased tourism has led to an expansion of small shops, inns, and restaurants and greater wealth has enabled more households to hire domestic servants. Like the Chambri and Tamang cases mentioned earlier, Nyeshangte demonstrate the persistence of customary values and social practices alongside newer economic trends.

But Is It Still Resistance?

Although traditions are often invested with new social meanings in an effort to create alternative models of the world, the attempts at cultural reproduction may be impartial or contradictory, and the results may be contested or embraced in varying degrees by individuals and disparate groups within a society. That "culture" is not as coherent as our earlier models implied is reflected in a number of critiques that suggest we should also avoid portraying abstract categories like "the state" or "capitalism" as if they existed in a separate realm apart from human agency and had powers of their own to dominate human lives (see Abu-Lughod 1991; Silverblatt 1991:155). These recent works, with their focus on the inherent ambiguities and contradictions of local social processes, also draw attention to the problematics surrounding the notion of resistance, which involves some contradictions of its own.

Abu-Lughod (1990a, 1990b), writing about young Bedouin women's resistance to their elders' authority and control, shows how the younger generation's aspirations to consumerism and western and Egyptian middle-class models of marriage or womanhood, together with a more sedentary lifestyle and concomitant female seclusion, may lead to new forms of male domination that are even more oppressive than before. Abu-Lughod also points out that although women (and sometimes young men) challenge the control or power of male elders through a variety of forms or expressions of resistance, at the same time these women may also support that power through practices like veiling (1990b:323; cf. Macleod 1991).

Silverblatt (1991), in her discussion of women and the Inca state, also argues against the assumption of "ideological uniformity" and, by extension, the idea of uniform resistance. Not only were Inca gender ideologies complex and contradictory, but Silverblatt also asks, "Why should we assume that gendered institutions or metaphors were uniformly understood, interpreted, or complied with?" (150). As in Abu-Lughod's observation in the Bedouin case, Silverblatt concurs that "even people resisting state penetration adopted an analog of state norms." That people (or particular categories of people) who resist power and authority may get embroiled in new forms of subordination, or conversely may embrace some aspects of the dominant ideology(ies), has led some writers like Kondo (1990:218–25) to question the validity and usefulness of the resistance concept as well as the notion of "authentic resistance." Kondo explains that "a term like resistance, when considered in all its living complexity, seems inadequate at best, for apparent resistance is riven with ironies and contradictions, just as coping or consent may have unexpectedly subversive effects" (224). Yet, in the end, Kondo does not suggest that we abandon the concept altogether, only that we use it with caution:

> Perhaps our starting point for a politics of meaning should not be a monolithic category of hegemony or domination countered by a grand, utopian space of pure resistance, especially if the forms of that hegemony or resistance become foundational categories which can always be known in advance. . . . Rather than positing these categories as foundational and thus invoking a metaphysics of closure and presence, we might examine the unexpected, subtle, and paradoxical twists in actors' discursive strategies, following out the ways meanings are reappropriated and launched again in continuous struggles over meaning. (1991:225)

In my analysis of Nyeshang society, these contradictions and ambiguities are also manifested both in social practices and in various ideologies. Here, I simply point this out and leave this problem (and its partial resolution) for the final chapter. Keeping in mind the issues and problems of analyzing power and resistance discussed above, women's agency in preserving subsistence practices and cooperative forms of sociality may still be considered a form of resistance (pure, authentic, or otherwise) if we consider the deliberate practice and celebration of devalued or denigrated minority traditions and lifeways to be a form of resistance.[27]

But how do we measure the relative significance of women's agency and power through informal networks against their limited participation in village and national government? How do we compare female authority and control over daily household affairs to male roles on the village and district councils? In trying to assess these variables and the implication they have for the relative positioning of women and men in Nyeshang society, a few points should be kept in mind. First, a number of studies have shown that in small-scale or stateless societies, where the division between public and domestic domains is not well demarcated, the household as the main unit of production and exchange is also the center of power where major decisions are made (Sanday 1990a:145; Potash 1989:205). In these societies, the authority and economic power of senior women in the household may often extend to the wider social sphere; though in many instances, as the Nyeshang case demonstrates, this power is wielded through indirect channels (cf. Schlegel 1977; Lepowsky 1990:179).

Second, "the big-man bias in social science analysis" (Ortner 1989:125) might also explain our predilection for focusing on authority and power in conjunction with formal political institutions while discounting social agency and power when it is wielded through informal channels. In assessing the relative position of the sexes, Ortner reminds us not to overlook the fact "that most men are excluded from leadership and public initiative."

Third, most women did not envy men's required political and administrative duties, which many men in fact found burdensome and tried to evade. Paradoxically, despite their professed lack of interest in holding political offices, women's roles in village and district affairs in recent years have actually become more prominent since fewer men are resident in the district. A similar trend was observed by anthropologist von Fürer-Haimendorf who worked among the Sherpa, where high rates of male migration also spurred more women into the political domain (1974:109).

Finally, women's agency in upholding the Nyeshang social order may be put into perspective if we compare the difference in sex roles and gendered expectations. In Nyeshang society, the permissive attitude toward divergent behavior is weighted slightly more toward the male side—though some Nyeshangte women also lead unconventional lives. As one elderly male informant explained: "In certain areas men have more rights [than women]: men can do anything, as they like. Women must be in society and follow rules of society."[28] In sum, women are entangled in social webs that both empower and constrain them. While this sociality gives them strength, it also requires a certain amount of compliance.

PART FOUR

Enduring Visions

CHAPTER SEVEN

Sacred Realms

PART 4 EXAMINES women's agency and power from a slightly different perspective—that of religion. Religion plays a central role in Nyeshang society: Buddhist ideology and ritual observances shape gender identities within the community and define the group's public image. Buddhist practice also redistributes trade wealth and mediates the flow of western consumerism and media images arising from Asia's modern metropolises.

Many of these changes, which are linked to increasing capitalization and the penetration of foreign ideologies, threaten to undermine the ideals and collective practices that are necessary for the reproduction of Nyeshangte egalitarianism (cf. Humphrey 1992:129–30). Buddhist rituals are a way, then, for Nyeshangte to renew their ties to the past and reaffirm their cultural identity in the midst of a rapidly changing world.

I turn now to a general overview of Nyeshangte religion. This is followed by a brief discussion of Buddhist gender ideologies and local gender representations, which serves as a background for the final chapter where I more closely examine women's subjectivity and their roles as moral agents. At this point it may be useful to describe some general characteristics of Tibetan Buddhism. Nyeshangte practice a form of Mahayana Buddhism, commonly known as Vajrayana, Tibetan, or sometimes Tantric Buddhism.[1]

Vajrayana Buddhism, which developed in Tibet during the seventh and eighth centuries A.D., was based on the Indian Mahayana tradition and was strongly rooted in the tantric teachings that emphasize esoteric ritual and meditation practices as a means of achieving enlightenment in this lifetime. During a subsequent revival or renaissance (that took place in the eleventh and twelfth centuries A.D.), Vajrayana Buddhism gradually spread from Tibet into the surrounding border districts and probably, if the estimated ages of Nyeshang's oldest dgon pa are accurate, was established in the Nyeshang valley around four or five hundred years ago (Snellgrove 1981).

Buddhism and Indigenous Folk Traditions

Besides the normative Buddhist concerns with merit, rebirth, and enlightenment, Nyeshangte, like all Tibetan Buddhists, must also attend to a host of spirits, demons, and gods (*btsan, klu, lha*) that inhabit the earth, water, and sky in order to avoid illness and other calamities in their everyday lives. Regular offerings and propitiatory rites are performed to appease household (*srung ma*), clan (*pho lha*), and village (*kul gi, yul lha*) gods, as well as to protect newly planted crops and to ensure the well-being of village herds. In addition, exorcisms (*tarkye*) are performed to rid the household and the village of demonic forces; coercive rites (*sang ngak*) are conducted to subdue powerful demons and transform them into protectors of the Buddhist community. Thus in Nyeshang, as in other Himalayan communities, many indigenous beliefs and shamanistic practices, reflecting a widespread pre-Buddhist folk religion as well as more localized traditions, were directly incorporated and subsequently reworked into the Buddhist pantheon and ritual system.[2] The result is a creative blend that gives Tibetan Buddhism an extraordinary richness of forms that sets it apart from other extant forms of Buddhism (Tucci 1980:164; Bannerjee 1984).

Rites of Renewal and Fertility

One example of this synthesis between folk religion and the literate Buddhist tradition may be seen in the fertility-agricultural rites that are celebrated every May. A series of activities—some secular, some monastic—take place in the village and involve a broad spectrum of villagers: children, laywomen, and laymen, and ordained clergy. The festival begins the evening before the full moon (*pūrṇa*) during the fifth lunar month—a particularly auspicious time that coincides with observances of Buddha's birthday.

13. A village dgon pa.

On the first night a comic dance drama (*aruru*) is performed in the village square near the dgon pa. A small enclosure is roped off and the surrounding lanes and rooftops are crowded with villagers, especially young children who come to watch the hour-long performance. Two male actors, one representing the husband, the other the wife, wear black masks secured with white ceremonial scarves. The "wife" (*ongdi*) is swathed in multiple layers of brightly colored skirts and appears enormous with the help of prodigious padding. Harmonious domestic scenes—with the couple dancing side by side, singing in unison—are interspersed with lewd gestures and obscene words. In an early scene the wife is weeding her fields with a hoe. When the husband learns that his wife is "playing" with other "boys," he runs away in anger. The wife eventually goes home and finds her husband sitting in a corner crying. In a parody of Hindu women, the wife bows repeatedly before him and the audience laughs at the mockery. She offers him beer and he becomes happy again. She leaves and dances around the enclosure, thrusting her pelvis at the audience, and embraces another man. Seeking forgiveness again, she bows before her husband once more. The couple eventually embrace. At this point, the men and young boys in the audience shout obscene comments and jokes, and a few of the young women who were giggling nearby whisper that the couple are now having sex. The wife again dances around the enclosure, swinging her hips provocatively, and abruptly the performance is over. The two actors run off and disappear. The following night the performance of aruru continues, and the same themes are repeated.

Several of my informants were too embarrassed to talk about the details of the performance. They joked, saying that the village children learned about sex in this way and explained that "using bad words, dirty words" and obscene gestures would make the rains come. My landlady, whose explanations were more forthcoming than either of my male assistants (or the male servants who also attended), explained that it was a local belief that sexual union brings rain: *bacchā pāunchā, pānī āuncha.* Apparently, this comic performance used to be held in all the Nyeshangte villages, but now it is regularly staged only in Nyangkhu.[3] According to local custom, she added, the villagers were supposed to go home after the aruru performance and have sex with their spouses. This fertility ritual thus ensured plentiful rains, and the offering of wheat and barley grain to the dgon pa the next day was assurance of a plentiful harvest in the fall.

The following day an invocation and offering to the protector gods is performed at the dgon pa, then the clergy carry religious texts around the village. Like the Buddhist monuments that mark the boundary of consecrated village territory, this rite revitalizes the protective forces along the perimeter that keep demonic spirits and catastrophic events—inclement weather, landslides—at bay. The act of reciting texts and then carrying them around the fields also subdues the spirits of the soil and streams who may have been disturbed by plowing. The water spirits (*klu*) are said to rejoice at hearing the Buddha's word, and they bring the rains.

After this *chos khor* (scripture circling) ritual is finally concluded, the entire village engages in a rough-and-tumble water fight. Large copper basins, small pitchers, and even cups are filled from taps near the dgon pa, and anyone who passes by is doused. Even the village lama and monks still seated in rows on the dgon pa roof were not spared. Men and women climbed the notched ladders to the upper story of the temple carrying vessels of water for their intended victims, and when the head lama finally joined the crowd below, his robes were completely soaked. As we stood against the dgon pa wall, trying to stay out of the way of the revelers, a group of middle-aged men lay siege to community hall, where several women had barricaded themselves inside. When the women eventually ran out of water, they charged the water tap en masse, and the water fight continued in earnest. After a few hours of vigorous play the lanes emptied, as villagers retreated home to change or dry their clothes and prepare the evening meal.

That night the final segment of aruru, the dance drama, concluded. Halfway through the performance, after supervising the ritual preparations at the dgon pa for the next day's observance of Buddha's birthday, the head lama (an ordained monk) joined us. Leaning against Palsang, with an arm draped casually around my assistant's shoulders, Lama Yeshe laughed heartily with the crowd, making faces at particularly crude gestures, shouting replies to villagers who greeted him. The crowd was rowdy; villagers were jostling and pushing one another from side to side, and men and women from the audience taunted the actors and one another. But the lama was perfectly at ease, and no one seemed surprised that he had attended; no one seemed embarrassed that he was there.

The water festival fertility rites ended on a somewhat more dignified note with a daylong ceremony to commemorate the birth of Buddha. But what remained clear after the shouts and laughter had faded, the clothes had dried, and the rituals at the dgon pa were over was the harmonious overlap between popular folk rites and monastic observances, and the ease with which individuals who entered monastic life participated in daily affairs of the village. Whether playing games with young children or engaging in water fights, the ordained lamas were clearly immersed in the realities of this world and quite accessible to the ordinary villager.[4]

Sectarian and Ritual Observances in Nyeshang

There are many different sects of Tibetan Buddhism and in the Nyeshang valley, two of them, the *bKa rgyud pa* and *rNying ma pa*, coexist side by side.[5] Many calendrical rites in Nyeshang are directed toward the founding figures or principal teachers of these two sects; a few examples are briefly examined in the following section. Although the philosophical or doctrinal differences between these various sects need not concern us here,[6] a few distinguishing features may be pointed out: the older, unreformed sects as a rule do not require their clergy to take vows of celibacy, and in their ceremonial practices they tend to rely heavily on tantric methods, frequently performing elaborate exorcisms and coercive rites that contain many elements from an earlier pre-Buddhist religion with its blend of shamanism and Bon traditions (Tucci 1980:29).[7]

The rNying ma pa, one of the sects that occupies a prominent place in the Nyeshang religious tradition, is also known as the "Ancient Ones," as this lineage extends back to the seventh and eighth centuries A.D., when Buddhism was first introduced into Tibet. The rNying ma pa seemed to have enjoyed a resurgence in the Himalayan border areas during the past century, sometimes displacing earlier established sects (Snellgrove 1981:37–38). This is an interesting phenomenon, since laypersons as a rule are said to be unsectarian, showing no expressed preference for one sect or another (Tucci 1980, 169; Samuel 1978:49). However, this scholarly assessment may be slightly off the mark: although laypersons may not be able to understand subtle distinctions in doctrine or philosophy, they may be drawn by the pageantry and ritual iconography surrounding the old sect.

One explanation for the popularity and resurgence of rNying ma pa might be linked to the historical role the sect played in upholding indigenous traditions. Beyer, a scholar of Tibetan religion and history, remarked that "the rNying ma pa sect was a constant source of revitalization as it was a link to the practices of the people and the deep roots of the shamanist heritage" (1978:246). Not only have its adherents "remained closest to the old shamanic traditions," but they also "have tended to be the least political and the least centralized of the Tibetan sects" (244). "It is through them," Beyer explains, "that Buddhism has managed to keep its roots deepest in the Tibetan soil, and to renew itself periodically by a revitalization of the Tibetan past" (246).

Among the sectarian figures who are venerated and honored during the annual cycle of rites in Nyeshang is Padmasambhava, the patron saint of the rNying ma pa who brought Buddhism to Tibet and vanquished a whole army of demons from the Tibetan countryside. In the process he left numerous traces of his passage in the form of footprints and handprints in rocks and caves throughout northern Nepal. The tenth day of every lunar month is especially devoted to Padmasambhava, and offerings are prepared by monastics who recite texts in his honor. Guru Padmasambhava occupies such a central role in the Nyeshang religious tradition that his image has been placed alongside those of Mi la ras pa and Karma pa (prominent bKa rgyud figures) near the main altar in two bKa rgyud temples—demonstrating again the catholic or eclectic observances of Nyeshangte.

Various manifestations of Padmasambhava are also represented by masked dancers who perform at the post-harvest exorcisms (tarkye), held during the month of October in conjunction with the New Year celebrations.[8] The masked dancers, *sgnags pa*, are tantric magicians who, during the course of the ritual, become identified with the first author of the rite,

Padmasambhava, and return to a primeval time when the patron saint vanquished the demons of Tibet and coerced other gods to become protectors or defenders of the faith. The dancers' actions parallel those of the saint, and by returning to the past, these magicians are renewing or revitalizing the Buddhist order. During this particular rite (which in 1989 coincided with Paten, a festival held every three years) the image of Maha Kala, the guardian deity (*srung ma*) of Nyangkhu village, was paraded through the village lanes. At the conclusion of the tarkye rite, the masked dancers ritually destroy the evil forces that had been trapped inside a paper effigy and dough offering (*gtor ma*). The paper effigy (*lu*), which served as a ransom to attract the demons, is burned and the gtor ma is thrown over the cliff into the river below Nyangkhu village.[9]

The other principal figure who is venerated in Nyeshang is Mi la ras pa, and many observances are held to commemorate his spiritual achievements and those of his lineage. During the month of May, on the occasion of Buddha's birthday, the assembled clergy at Nyangkhu dgon pa perform a two-day series of invocations, liturgical recitations, and offerings to honor the bKa rgyud poet-saints, including Mi la ras pa and the Karma pa lineage of reincarnations (a later branch of the bKa rgyud pa sect), as well as to honor the Buddha and the present Dalai Lama.[10]

Mi la ras pa and his line of bKa rgyud teachers are also singled out during the four-day rite of atonement (Smyung nas), a retreat that is attended by many laywomen from Churi. This rite is held in mid-May at Nyeshang Kurti, a dgon pa located near Mi la ras pa's famous cave, high on the slopes of Annapurna. This dgon pa, which was rebuilt (around 1975) after an avalanche destroyed the original temple (situated higher on the mountain side adjacent to the cave), serves as a pilgrimage site drawing Tibetan Buddhists from other districts in Nepal. Nyangkhu villagers also visit the site in June after they have finished sowing their crops. They spend two to three days at the Kherap dgon pa where a lama reads them the story of Mi la ras pa and the hunter. Although the story has several versions, the Nyeshangte believe that this hunter was a forefather to the present-day population in the valley. Kherap (*kyi ro pa*) was apparently a "stalker" (literally, a dog-goat-man) who killed game with the help of a trained dog; one day in search of his dog that had disappeared in hot pursuit of a deer, Kherap stumbled into Mi la ras pa's cave. The great saint with his wisdom and insight convinced the hunter not to kill anymore, and supposedly, from that day on, the people of the Nyeshang valley also gave up hunting and became farmers. After listening to the story (*dpe*), with its themes of renouncing sin (the killing of animals) and renewal or rebirth as Buddhists, Nyangkhu villagers celebrate with picnics and dancing (*ghi khi laba*) during which time they also form ritual friendships (chetu) with villagers of the opposite sex.

The bKa rgyud pa also perform similar exorcist rites to the rNying ma pa. This final example demonstrates not only the closeness between the two sects but also the synthesis between folk religion and monastic rituals where elements, symbols, and meanings are borrowed from an ancient pre-Buddhist matrix and then imbued with Buddhist meanings. This rite (like the post-harvest tarkye described earlier) involves masked dancers. However, it is held at Nyi dgon pa, a bKa rgyud establishment, and lasts for fifteen days during the latter half of June.[11] The head lama who was supervising the preparations of the nuns and monks told me that it was equivalent to the great dance drama of the Sherpa, the Mani Rimdu festival.

During the first day, the assembled clergy left the dgon pa and walked toward the cliff overlooking the Nyeshang valley. Using a ritual dagger, one of the lamas struck the earth where an effigy made of tsampa (barley) with two arms, legs, and eyes and dressed in black clothes had been buried in a shallow pit and covered with a flat stone. In an earlier part of the rite the demonic forces were summoned and directed into the effigy, which subsequently "pressed down" into the earth to return to the underworld. The dagger was returned to its holding box and tied to the central pillar by the gomba door. Sacred arrows had been tied to four posts (*ketsen di she*) that had been erected on each side of the dgon pa. Like the magic dagger, the arrows warded off demonic forces from all cardinal directions. Inside the dgon pa, new silk banners and religious paintings (*thang ka*) were hung. A pavilion was constructed to shelter a *mindu* (representation of a deity) that the lama had fashioned. These images are often hidden from view, as their powers can be dangerous to the uninitiated. Monks and nuns were busy molding colored gtor ma (dough offerings) for the elaborate altar against the back wall.

The first half of the ceremony lasted seven days, at which time the nuns and lamas stayed awake for two full nights reciting texts and preparing themselves for the ritual by undertaking a number of preliminary steps: visualizing the host deities, letting these images dissolve, and subsequently purifying their thoughts. When the rite began, the deities were summoned through the recitation of specific mantra; after they entered the gtor ma, they were worshipped and propitiated and their special powers were invoked and directed for the well-being of all living things. During the second week, eight masked dancers who represented local protector gods brandished large swords and attacked the forces of evil trapped inside a *linga* (an effigy made of dough or paper).[12] When the ritual was completed, most of the evil that had accumulated since the last exorcism was banished from the dgon pa and the surrounding territory; all would be well for another year.

Attitudes Toward Different Sects

Although the earlier history of Tibet is filled with stories of rivalries, wars, and struggles among competing religious factions, there is little sectarian rivalry today. In general, most Tibetan Buddhists exhibit a great tolerance toward varying religious practices and doctrinal schools, and many monks and nuns move from one sect to another, in search of specific initiations or to study with a particular lama without much regard for his formal affiliation. This religious tolerance, eclecticism, and peripatetic nature of religious adepts is reflected in the following example of a Nyeshangte nun.

Pema Buddhi (age 24) had been trained by her father, a rNying ma pa lama, and her mother, who taught meditative techniques to lay villagers at a secluded retreat center (ser khyim dgon pa) in the valley. When I met her in 1989, she told me she was leaving the valley to rejoin her friends (other Nyeshangte nuns) who were also childhood friends from her natal village of Lhakpa and from the adjacent village of Kangri. These nuns had been affiliated with a local bKa rgyud dgon pa in the valley and, after taking their ordination vows, had moved to a bKa rgyud nunnery located on the outskirts of Kathmandu.[13] Pema said she felt lonely in the valley with her friends gone, and she also wanted to study with Lama Urgyen at Ngagi dgon pa and his wife. Originally from Tibet, the couple had achieved considerable fame for their teachings. In 1989 at least five Nyeshangte nuns resided at their dgon pa on a permanent basis, and several more visited during the winter months. When asked about switching to another sect and another dgon pa, Pema just shrugged and said, "It makes no difference to my parents, nor to me."

Religious Personnel: Laity and Clergy

Before examining how Buddhist worldviews (in their various sectarian expressions) influence local gender representations, a few general points about the relationships and respective roles of laity and clergy in Nyeshang are worth noting, as these have important implications for women's overall

14. Nyeshangte lamas.

participation in the religious domain. In general, laypersons (*jikten*) are only expected to follow the most basic Buddhist principles and avoid major sins, though some devotees, usually elderly women and men, take on an additional three vows: to perform "good works" (meritorious actions), to seek enlightenment, and to strive for the salvation of all sentient beings.

The lives of cheemi, the "religious ones," on the other hand, are guided by additional vows depending on the individual's stage in the training process. Novices (*getsul*), including nuns (*jomo*) and monks (*tawa*) who go through the initial ordination rites which involve shaving their heads and receiving a new Buddhist name, are expected to comply with monastic discipline. Infractions, however, are generally handled in a lenient fashion: errant monks or nuns may have to offer an explanation, apology, and perhaps a small gift or money offering to the dgon pa in order to expiate their sins or if they wish to renounce their ties and leave the monastic order.

Since many monks are traditionally "middle sons," recruited from families with three or more male offspring, these young men join out of obligation rather than choice or vocation. As a result, many of these novices may eventually return to lay life and marry; only a few go on to become fully ordained.[14] Nuns, on the other hand, are not recruited or conscripted into the dgon pa community but join freely and are less likely to drop out.

Although young girls who enter the *jomo rol* (nunnery) may return home and decide to marry after completing their initial training (without any moral or social repercussions), few do so.[15] In fact, all the young nuns (17 to 22 years of age) who finished their training in 1989 planned to stay on at the local dgon pa or continue their studies at another institution in Kathmandu. The jomo rol provides a haven for bright, creative young women and a certain amount of freedom from conventional female roles (cf. Ortner 1983; Willis 1984). Although women may not become lamas, several women have achieved wide acclaim as religious teachers.[16]

Young men also tend to renounce their tawa status and their dgon pa obligations because they are drawn to the lifestyle, wealth, and adventure of international trade. It is largely because of this "monk exodus" from the community that the number and duties of nuns have expanded in recent years. In addition, with the influx of trade money, many village residents are commissioning household and community rites more often, and this too has led to an increased demand for ritual specialists. As a result, many locally trained nuns are replacing monks as officiates (Cooke 1985a:252) and are undertaking ritual activities—funerals, consecrations, or playing the drums and cymbals—that traditionally were performed only by male monastics in other Tibetan Buddhist communities.

The highest stage is that of dge slong, or fully ordained individuals who have taken an additional 253 vows including that of celibacy. Only a few lamas in Nyeshang have dge slong status, and these men, because of their elevated status and advanced training which is usually acquired outside the valley (often in Tibet, Sikkim, or Bhutan), are generally appointed by village councils to the larger dgon pa in the valley. As far as I know, there is only one jomo who has attained dge slong status—she is a nun in her sixties who studied with her sister at an institution near Lhasa for several years (before the Chinese takeover forced them to return to Nyeshang). Like her brother, a well-known lama at Shey gomba in Dolpo District who also studied in Tibet, this woman is currently in charge of the education and training of nuns in Nyeshang.

In reality, however, distinctions between religious practitioners in terms of the type of ordination and number of vows taken are often ignored: a person who undergoes religious training and dresses in the maroon robes of monastics is simply referred to as "lama" if male and "ani" or "jomo" if female. The division between lay and ordained, householder and renunciant, is also softened by the existence of intermediate categories like married village lamas who combine domestic pursuits with religious vocation, or laypeople who retire from village life and take vows of celibacy.[17] Although this discussion is only tangentially concerned with male ritual specialists, these issues were brought up because they suggest that in local Buddhist practice, asceticism and renunciation are not necessarily held in esteem at the expense of domestic concerns and family ties.

Nor are male and female seen as basic oppositional categories: in Nyeshang women are not denied access to the altar area, nor must they avoid touching a monk—two restrictions that are observed, for example, in Thailand, a Buddhist nation that also lacks a tradition of ordained female monastics. As in other societies that have been described as having balanced or egalitarian gender arrangements—for example, the Hopi (Schlegel 1990), Vanatinai (Lepowsky 1990), and Minangkabau (Sanday 1990a)— "the transcendental is not achieved by negating the feminine" or the masculine (Sanday 1990b:12). In Nyeshang male and female attributes are considered complementary, and the qualities of both sexes must be cultivated in equal proportion in order to attain enlightenment. Having outlined the basic structure of Nyeshang religious organization, I turn now to the question of how Buddhist worldviews shape local gender representations.

Buddhist Gender Ideologies

I would like to begin this section by broadly sketching the variety of gender ideologies found within the Buddhist tradition, which includes both the Theravada and Mahayana. The discussion then moves to a more specific level and examines the gender ideologies associated with the Tibetan Buddhist tradition (itself a form of Mahayana). Finally, I summarize the characteristics of the local unreformed Tibetan Buddhist sects, which seem to contribute to the (mostly) "positive" gender configurations found in Nyeshang.

Within the Buddhist canonical literature, gender ideologies—statements about women and images of the feminine—are contradictory, complex, and often ambiguous, making it difficult to present a unilateral interpretation of the "position of women" in Buddhism. Representations of women may include those of devoted mother or housewife who supports the *Sangha* (order of monks) through alms-giving; also included are images of respected teachers and spiritual consorts, as well as the more negative roles of evil temptress or seducer of monks—the out-of-control female ruled by passion (cf. Keyes 1984; Paul 1979).

In trying to assess the overall attitudes toward women in general, and female Buddhist practitioners in particular, we need to turn once again to the differences between various traditions—Theravada, Mahayana, and the Tibetan Vajrayana—and examine a limited number of contrasting features. In general, sects or schools that emphasize celibacy, asceticism, scholasticism, and that are organized around hierarchical monasteries may be lumped together as usually affording women limited religious roles and a subordinate status to men (Horner 1975; Khin 1980; Kirsch 1983; van Esterik 1983). At the other end of the spectrum, traditions that permit married clergy and unordained individuals to acquire significant status as teachers or spiritual disciples, that acknowledge the existence of multiple paths or methods and are fairly tolerant of idiosyncratic behavior, usually allow women a greater range of religious roles (cf. Allione 1984; Arvind 1987; Klein 1987). The former characteristics are most strongly associated with the Theravada tradition as practiced in Thailand and Sri Lanka where the roles of Buddhist women are fairly circumscribed (cf. Horner 1975).[18] The latter characteristics are associated with the Vajrayana tradition in Tibet, particularly with the unreformed sects where women may be ordained and a number of them have achieved considerable fame as religious adepts (see, for example, Gross 1987a; Klein 1987; Miller 1980).[19]

This, of course, is an oversimplified classification, but many Buddhist scholars have noted that the more positive attributes of female gender and views of women are found in the Mahayana tradition, particularly among the Tibetan tantric sects (Beyer 1973; Paul 1979; Bancroft 1980). Conversely, these writers have also observed that wherever ascetic ideals and the development of rigidly structured religious institutions are prevalent, misogynist tendencies seem to be much more pronounced (see, for example, Friedman 1988; Bancroft 1980; Barnes 1987). However, a certain amount of ambivalence toward the female gender may be found in all three traditions, even the Tibetan tantric sects.

Female Gender Images—Negative Perceptions

Negative images of women in both the Mahayana and Theravada literature seem to be derived from women's association with reproduction, with "nature," with worldliness or attachment, desire and pain (cf. Ortner 1981; Khin 1980; Kirsch 1983; Paul 1979). Women in their role as child bearer are associated with natural processes—birth, death, illness, and suffering—and are perceived as being bound by earthly or material (as opposed to transcendental) concerns. Their roles as mothers and wives seem to prevent their serious participation in religious practice. Paul (1979) points out that most female practitioners who figured prominently in the Mahayana texts were free from household and maternal responsibilities and were able to devote their energies (and often their wealth) to the Buddhist order; these women included influential nuns, unmarried laywomen, (wealthy) prostitutes, married women who were childless, or elderly or middle-aged women beyond their childbearing years. Most women, however, were seldom able to free themselves from social and domestic obligations: renunciation or female asceticism was simply not considered an option or acceptable alternative to the role of mother and wife in Indian or Thai society.[20]

The subordinate moral status of women may also be reflected in the Buddhist belief that the female body is a lower form or less desirable rebirth.[21] In both Theravada and Mahayana texts we find statements that women cannot reach enlightenment in their present condition of "femaleness" (Paul 1979; Horner 1975; Willis 1987). Some Mahayana texts even suggest that female disciples on the verge of enlightenment must be transformed into males before reaching the ultimate stage. Although this perception of women as "low-born" beings is sometimes found in Tibetan ideologies, it is generally not elaborated in everyday life or in common cultural forms, at least not in Nyeshang. The reports from other Tibetan societies are more contradictory. Mumford (1989), writing about Tibetan migrants to the Gyasumdo region south of Nyeshang, states that in that community "female birth is thought to be a sign of having committed more evil deeds (*las ngen*) in previous lives. . . . Lamas can be heard to urge the deceased to at least gain a male rebirth (*pho gi mi-lus*). Hence the laity regard a male birth itself as one level of *thar pa* (liberation), women being regarded as more embedded in *samsara* [worldly existence] than are men" (48).

This view seems to have its antecedents in the "orthodox" outlook of the monastic elite, and perhaps reflects the convergence of Tibetan "hierarchical" views with similar ones found in common Mahayana and Theravada texts.[22]

In the Theravada and Mahayana, women may also be portrayed as lustful, evil, greedy, or emotional: perceptions that are certainly not compatible with the lofty ideals of asceticism, renunciation, or meditative calm. Although the Mahayana texts have their share of female figures as Seducer or Temptress, the most negative representations are typically associated with the Theravada tradition where the monasticism is more elaborated and lay roles more circumscribed (Horner 1975; Paul 1979). Buddhist scholars have noted that the monastic community's rejection of householder life and distancing from secular concerns "represents in part, a rejection of women" (Paul 1979:201; Willis 1987). Although Keyes (1984) has argued that the prevalent view of women in Thai "popular" texts is largely benign— maternal figures who support the Buddhist order—other writers (for example, Kirsch 1983) may still view this as a marginal and subsidiary role within the wider framework of Buddhist institutions and society.

Contrasting Views

In the Mahayana texts positive female representations go beyond the "maternal," and women sometimes may be portrayed as friends, companion-consorts, and teachers capable of revealing ultimate truths and insights (Friedman 1988; Gross 1987b; Paul 1979). Religious imagery of the feminine may reflect the synthesis of compassion and wisdom and may be associated with the highest spiritual states. This outlook is an expression of the "integrative view" found in the Mahayana tradition, where male and female gender attributes are seen in a positive and complimentary fashion (Paul 1979; Miller 1980). The state of perfection, of being a Boddhisattva, is seen as a combination of male/female qualities, and this androgynous model is characteristic of many tantric (Tibetan) texts as well. Conversely, the state of perfection may be perceived as completely asexual, existing beyond these physical or mental gender distinctions (Bancroft 1980; Barnes 1987; Paul 1979). According to this "unconditioned view" expressed in numerous Mahahayana (and Tibetan) texts, when one perceives the world as emptiness (*sūnyatā*), distinctions such as male or female no longer exist (Paul 1979; Beyer 1973).

Positive Views in the Tantric Tradition

Having looked at the problem of Buddhist gender configurations from a fairly broad perspective, I now turn to a more detailed examination of the features associated with the Tibetan tantric tradition, especially as it is practiced in Nyeshang. As I have already indicated, the predominant bKa rgyud and rNying ma sects in Nyeshang fall closer to the tantric, shamanic, unreformed end of the spectrum rather than the academic, monastic, reformed side.

According to Tantric principles, enlightenment may be attained without celibacy or renunciation. The key words here are *tantric* and *noncelibate*, as both characteristics have profound implications for the existential position and for the variety of roles open to laypersons (particularly women) within these older unreformed Buddhist traditions. Both characteristics are important because they set the tone or attitude of local religious practice. The emphasis on tantric methods, or the Short Path, means that experiential knowledge is favored over academic or philosophical training (Bharati 1965). The path is open to illiterate individuals, a plus for many women who cannot read the classical Tibetan texts. All that is required is a close bond between spiritual guide (*guru*) and disciple: knowledge is passed on through a series of secret initiations. Eventually the disciples, through elaborate meditative and visualization practices, reach a stage where they attain a subtle identification with particular deities. Tantric adepts learn how to tap into the superhuman powers of the deities and how to redirect these cosmic forces for various purposes (Sangpo 1985; Beyer 1973).

Fascinating as these techniques may be, the point here is that these goals (Buddhahood, enlightenment) are accessible to any layperson, man or woman, who seeks out a qualified spiritual guide. One need not renounce family, home, and everyday life to follow this path. The lack of emphasis on asceticism or withdrawal from worldly existence also means that the roles of householder (wife and mother) and the ordinary rounds of daily existence are not ritually denigrated or diametrically opposed to the "spiritual path," though of course they are differentiated. As my discussion of village religious organization pointed out, spiritual teachers or lamas need not be celibate either and may serve as important models for laypeople who wish to devote more time to religious concerns. Although individuals (monks, nuns, and lamas) who devote themselves completely to religious service and take the full complement of vows are accorded the highest esteem, other practitioners are also respected and may participate in dgon pa (monastic) rituals alongside regular ordained clergy.[23] This overlap between lay and clerical roles promotes a casual, familiar relationship between the ordinary villager and the ordained.[24]

Nor is sexuality (male or female) considered threatening, polluting, or necessarily a hindrance in the pursuit of enlightenment. This positive life-affirming outlook toward sexuality suggests that women are not as likely to be devalued or systematically excluded from socially recognized religious roles because of their close association with "nature" (cf. Ortner 1981). Women are not likely to be restricted to marginal roles of mothers or wives whose only contribution (in addition to alms) is measured by the number of male offspring she produces, whose highest religious achievement is the offering of a monk-son (cf. Keyes 1984). Nor are women perceived as evil or dangerous creatures or out of control with lust, whose very presence or accidental touch may render male monastics ritually impure.

In contrast to dominant gender ideologies found in Theravada and Mahayana literature, where sexuality (male or female) is seen as largely incompatible with religious pursuits, the tantric literature is rich in sexual imagery: often depicting the union of male and female as the synthesis of compassion and wisdom. Certain tantric practices make use of the body as an instrument or vehicle; initiates or consorts may engage in ritual sexual behavior as a form of yogic practice that enables them to channel the powers of the body and mind toward particular goals. Even the role of spiritual consort implies a certain equality and freedom on a par with male adepts (or male partners), and the very option suggests that other alternatives existed for women besides the limited roles of mother and wife (Willis 1987; Klein 1987).

Tantric teachings also differ from other Buddhist schools in their general outlook or worldview. In contrast to clerical or monastic approaches to "transcendentalism in Buddhism," which stress that "involvement in the world is polluting, sinful and counterproductive in terms of salvation," in tantric practice, everyday activities may be used as methods toward enlightenment because they are "ultimately devoid of meaning" (Ardussi and Epstein 1978:328–29). According to some tantric texts, since the "human body is a microcosm of the universe, containing both the lowest and the highest states of existence (Buddhahood), any activity undertaken no matter how commonplace, may if performed by an `awakened' mind also be transformed into a spiritual activity" (328–29). In keeping with the tantric perspective that the nature of reality is ultimately "empty" (sūnyatā), aversion and renunciation of worldly things is meaningless: "In reality there is no such distinction as male or female, good or bad, foul or sweet. The distinction made between one object or being and another is conventional. Likewise the distinction made between a householder and a recluse is conventional" (Dutt 1964:9). Instead, according to the tantric adept, the phenomenal world, that experienced through the senses, is one and the same with the ultimate reality or truth (*sūnyatā*), and division between classes or categories of objects, beings, or conditions is ultimately meaningless.

One final point that distinguishes Tantric-oriented sects from other Buddhist schools is that these groups tend to be organized in a loose fashion compared to the hierarchical and centralized monastic organization of the reformed Tibetan dGe lugs pa or the Thai Theravada. In the Tibetan literature this distinction has been categorized by various scholars as a split between the academic, clerical, and monastic institutions and the shamanic, tantric, and independent lamas (Beyer 1978:241; Samuel 1978:383). Although the former organization was closely associated with power and political authority of centralized states, the latter complex served as an outlet of dissent, a refuge for iconoclastic individuals and for eccentric wandering saints who challenged the established order and often mocked the traditions of the academics and clerics of the state-sponsored institutions (Beyer 1978).[25] It is significant that along the Himalayan border most of the frontier lamas were independent figures whose support came from local populations and not from the central Tibetan state. Many of these missionary types were rNying ma pa and bKa rgyud pa lamas who wandered widely, helping to establish small dgon pa in the villages and valleys of northern Nepal (see Snellgrove 1967). Their shamanic, independent orientation seemed particularly suited to small-scale societies that were largely autonomous from state control (Samuel 1978:383).[26] Their success in winning Buddhist converts and putting an end to "red" (animal or blood) sacrifices depended on their charismatic qualities, their magical abilities, not the political power of state monasteries. Moreover, as I indicated earlier, the emphasis on rites of exorcism (tarkye), the performance of *mcod* (symbolic sacrifice), and the substitution of dough and paper effigies (white offerings instead of red) retained many of the symbolic and ritual elements of the local pre-Buddhist religion and provided a sense of continuity with the past (Tucci 1980:92).[27]

In sum, the most significant feature of the unreformed sects may well have been their autonomy from central powers, their characteristic separation of spiritual authority from political authority (MacDonald 1980a:146), and their benevolent attitude toward women. This tantric heritage reached its fullest expression in the rNying ma pa and bKa rgud pa sects, with their tradition of powerful magicians and wandering saints and their history of renowned male and female teachers (Beyer 1978; Willis 1987).

Images of the Feminine in Local Religious Traditions

Although the history of Bon (a pre-Buddhist Tibetan religion) and of the shamanic complex lies outside the scope of this chapter, both these religious traditions have positive images of women (and of the feminine principle), and may have influenced local gender representations. As I indicated earlier, Nyeshang religious traditions represent a synthesis of Tibetan

Buddhism, local shamanic practices, and folk beliefs (cf. von Fürer-Haimendorf 1955; Vinding 1982; Watters 1975). Before Buddhism was securely established in the valley (some two hundred to four hundred years ago), local religious practices included elements associated with Bon rituals, such as animal sacrifices, divination, and, according to Nyeshang oral histories, a tradition of human sacrifice. Evidence of local Bon influence is apparent in adjacent Nar Khola, where certain clans still worship at the Bon village temple and occasionally perform animal sacrifices.[28] On the other side of Nyeshang in the Kali Gandaki valley, Lubra village was a stronghold of Bon: its temple and teachers attracted many students from surrounding districts. Evidence that Bon and shamanic elements are woven into the fabric of Nyeshang religion may be seen in a number of calendrical rites including Paten, the week-long ritual held every three years. In Nyangkhu village, one of the elderly sngags pa who performed rites of exorcism and served as a healer, was also trained at Lubra, the Bon center, though he also assisted at Buddhist rituals and was the head lama at the smaller village dgon pa until his recent retirement.

The gender ideologies of these pre-Buddhist religions show a marked contrast to the ambivalent views found in the Buddhist canon.[29] In the Bon pantheon, one historian remarked, it seems that "goddesses take precedence over the gods and the female priests are regarded as superior to the male priest in this religion" (Bannerjee 1981:11). It is also noteworthy that the shamanic tradition in the Nepal Himalaya is also closely associated with the feminine: shamans wear women's clothing, and many oral traditions contain references to female shamans of earlier times (Holmberg 1983, 1989; cf. Kendall 1985).

In terms of continuities, since Bon most closely resembles the rNying ma pa in ritual practice, it is not surprising that we also find exemplary female religious figures in the rNying ma pa sect as well. One prominent example is Lady Yeshe Tsogyel, a famous yogi and great teacher of the eighth-century rNying ma pa sect who had many disciples and was a role model for generations of Buddhist women (see Allione 1984; Gross 1987a; Klein 1987). Yeshe Tsogyel was also the wife and consort (spiritual partner) of Guru Padmasambhava, who is credited with establishing Buddhism in Tibet. But her fame and widespread adulation stem largely from her own significant accomplishments as a religious teacher.

In addition to historical and legendary women, we also find representations of various types of female divinities. Meme Sangle, the eldest of four siblings, is worshipped as a clan deity in Nyangkhu. The term *meme sangle* also means "ancestors." She and her three younger brothers represent founding figures that are linked to each of the four village clans. As the eldest sibling, Meme Sangle receives additional homage and offerings from her clan members, who take pride in belonging to one of the original founding lineages. Ritual offerings to Meme Sangle may be done at rooftop altars in individual households or at the village shrine devoted specifically to her.

In the Nyeshang valley, at two of the major dgon pa (one bKa rgyud, the other rNying ma), there are several images of female deities known as *kandoma*, or "sky-goers." In general, kandoma (Sanskrit, *dākinī*) are enlightened women or actual deities who impart mystical doctrines and powers to devotees. They are often depicted as consorts or ritual counterparts to male yogi, and the union between the two sexes in Tantric symbolism represents the synthesis of (male) compassion and (female) wisdom.[30] Kandoma are sometimes identified with a deity known as Dolma (*sGrol ma*) or Tara, who is worshipped as the supreme goddess, mother of all Buddhas.

Tara, a bodhisattva and savior, is quite popular with lay Buddhists, male and female, as well as with monastics. She is the object of many liturgies and invocations, and numerous dgon pa rituals are devoted to her. In Nyeshang, as in other Tibetan communities, she is the receptacle of many "offerings, praises and prayers" and "represents the most widespread of Tibetan cults" (Beyer 1973:7). Widely venerated, Tara is viewed as a protector who guards people throughout their lifetimes, and even after (7). Her power and stature as a god is tied to the primordial vow she made when, after years of perseverance and meditation, she finally became awakened or enlightened. At that time she received some advice from a monk, one of her contemporaries: "The proper thing to do," he told her, "is to make an earnest wish that your body (with which you attend to the teachings) may become that of a man, for surely this desire will be granted." Tara replied: "Since there is no such thing as a 'man' or a 'woman' (and no such thing as a 'self' or a 'person' or 'awareness') this bondage to male and female is hollow: Oh how worldly fools delude themselves!" And this is the earnest wish she made: "Those who wish to attain supreme enlightenment in a man's body are many, but those who wish to serve the aims of beings in a woman's body are few indeed; therefore may I, until this world is emptied out, serve the aim of beings with nothing but the body of a woman" (64–65).

Not only is Tara worshipped as a benevolent figure who offers compassion and divine understanding, she also represents a cosmic force "which can be tapped and directed by a practitioner who has the capacity to do so"

(Beyer 1973:247). Through visualization and meditation, tantric practitioners (lay or monastic) may subtly transform themselves, or more accurately "identify" themselves, with the deity Tara and then have access to her superhuman powers.

Leaving aside these powerful female images for the moment, let us return to the realm of the concrete and look at actual behavior. What is the significance of these images? And do the views associated with the unreformed tantric, Bon, shamanic traditions have any impact on local gender ideologies and gender relations? Although gender representations and symbolism are suggestive of overall attitudes toward women as a group, researchers have found that there is not always a direct correspondence between the realm of gender symbolism and the actual positioning of the sexes (cf. Sanday 1981; March 1979). At best, positive images represent ideals and suggest possibilities, not certainties.

Indigenous Views: Tales of Warriors and Virgins, Buddhists and Yaks

One additional area remains to be considered as a source of local gender ideologies: indigenous oral histories and myths. Nyeshangte men and women often refer to these folk histories to explain their actions and to describe their innate qualities as an ethnic group and as gendered individuals. Collectively, Nyeshangte tend to describe themselves in a discourse that at times seems rather paradoxical: among other things, it emphasizes the values and goals characteristic of devout Buddhists, as well as the constellation of ambivalent qualities associated with successful entrepreneurs and wealthy traders. The principles that may be distilled from the ongoing dialogue between a Buddhist worldview, with its attendant concern with merit-making, avoidance of sin, and renunciation, and the pragmatic reality of the "big" traders, who operate in a world where violence and danger are commonplace, provide a key to understanding the Nyeshang social order. These ideas about gender, self, and group identity are to a large extent drawn from a repertoire of legends, origin accounts, and indigenous views of history that are embodied in several of the rituals and myths performed and narrated in the valley.

The importance of these myths and legends, which are reenacted by the community at ritual pageants, festivals, and calendrical rites, is that they throw into relief the multilayered nature of local cultural and gender practices; they reflect the "hybrid constructions" (Bakhtin 1984; cf. Mumford 1989:26) of diverse belief systems: shamanism, vestiges of a warrior cult,

Bon, and Buddhism.[31] Although these individual strands usually form a seamless blend that characterizes much of present-day Buddhism in the Himalaya, on some occasions, rituals and myths may highlight individual motifs that represent different and contrary facets of Nyeshangte culture and history.

These disparate aspects, in turn, have a direct bearing on the nature of gender relations in the community, as well as the meaning and values associated with certain gendered activities—specifically, trade and religion. The existence of multiple ideologies and contradictory meanings does not necessarily imply a social model of contested realms or warring factions (cf. Lederman 1990; Mumford 1989) but rather suggests that these alternative cultural representations are invoked and imbued with different levels of meaning under particular circumstances and in certain contexts (cf. Schlegel 1990; Ong 1989).[32] These myths reflect Nyeshangte notions about gender: about the qualities associated with femaleness and maleness; they may also serve as "models of and models for" (Geertz 1973) gendered behavior. I shall begin by first looking at the warrior-hunter traditions reflected in local myths and in the Paten ritual. Then I will examine the oral history that links women to Buddhism.

"Now We Just Cut Ears"

Nyeshangte males in their early adulthood (twenties to thirties) love to tell stories about their (male) ancestors, the fierce warriors who traveled over the windswept plains of central Tibet and crossed the high snowbound passes of the Himalaya, slaughtering everything in their path. Although the identities of this wandering band of killers vary in different accounts, their bloodthirsty nature and destructive violence remain constant. Most male narrators admit that Nyeshangte today are not quite sure about the details of their collective past. Some, like 35-year-old Tsong, who lives with his wife in Churi and exhibits an interest in Nyeshang cultural history, told me that these ancient warriors were part of the Srong Tsen Gampo's cavalry, a Tibetan chieftain who conquered rival principalities and created a unified Tibetan state in the seventh century A.D. (How they ended up on the western periphery of the central Tibetan state and became lost or trapped in north central Nepal is not really clear.) Tenzin, a cousin-brother to Tsong, also in his mid-thirties, prefers another version: the band of ancestor warriors originated in Central Asia and were Mongols who served under "Chengiz Khan" in the twelfth century A.D., and they too ended up in the

Nyeshang valley. Regardless of their origins, these prototype Nyeshangte settled in the valley, gradually gave up their slaughtering, destructive ways, and over time were converted to Buddhism.

But this conversion was partial at best, as other oral histories in the valley tell of repeated attempts by visiting lamas to transform this band of "warrior-hunter-killers" into nonviolent Buddhists. One example may be seen in the story of Kherap Dorje, the hunter-stalker who stumbled into Mi la ras pa's cave and literally hung up his bow and arrow (informants say it still hangs there on the cave wall) and renounced his violent past. Nyeshangte say they are descendants of that original hunter, and that is why they too eventually gave up hunting and became farmers. The story of Kherap Dorje is the focal point of the Smyung nas observance which takes place each year and is described in greater detail in the following chapter.

In short, what we find from the male point of view is a sort of apologetics—what can you expect if you have Chengiz Khan, the Tibetan cavalry, and the deer hunter imprinted in your genes? This transformation from bloodthirsty warrior-savages to nonviolent Buddhists is a continual struggle that appears repeatedly and cyclically in these indigenous accounts. Within this native model of history, the switch from hunting as a way of life to farming, and the abandonment of blood and flesh sacrifices and other rituals incompatible with orthodox Buddhism, represent major transformations that were not easily (or always permanently) achieved. Rather, given Nyeshangte's cyclical view of history, this struggle is ongoing: social history here is paralleled on a smaller scale by individual (male) life courses. Adolescent boys and males in their early to middle adulthood (20 to 40 years of age) may be forgiven as they too evoke images of the untamed hordes. However, as a few male informants pointed out, they are not as violent as their ancestors: "The men in Nyeshang no longer sacrifice virgin girls during Paten; today, they just cut ears and offer blood." "Goats' ears," they added, and laughed when I seemed a bit unnerved.

Some of these warrior and sacrificial themes are highlighted at the Paten festival, which is a composite of various rituals (Bon sacrificial rites, initiation of adolescent boys, clan celebrations, and Buddhist exorcisms), and include dramas and songs that portray historical events in the valley and adjacent regions. According to informants, Paten was observed in Nar Khola, where it was called Yakchhya, as well as in Thini village in Thak Khola, where it was called Dumdzya. These two districts as well as Nyeshang celebrated the festival in consecutive fashion, so that it occurred in Nyeshang every three years. Thini stopped observing the ritual in 1961 (von Fürer-Haimendorf 1981:182), but my informants say that it still takes place in Nar, where villagers sacrifice sheep and goats at the Bon temple. The link between these three communities (located in separate valleys) has a historical basis: apparently at one time the region was unified under a chieftain who, in the course of a battle, fled from Mustang into Nar Khola and from there into Nyeshang, where he was assisted by Nyeshangte warriors or "champions."

In Nyangkhu village this battle is reenacted by dancers who represent the king, his two sons, one magician, as well as the comic figures of two yak and one horse who serve as jesters. This skit is performed in the central village square over the course of three nights and is highly repetitive: the rhythmic drumming, accompanying chants, and stylized gestures and movements of the dancers remain the same each evening. The serious atmosphere is periodically relieved by the yak and horse figures, men draped with scarves and small bells who sweep through the crowds and across the square, knocking and pushing people over in their wake. During the dance, men representing champions do battle for the king who stands to one side with his magician-sorcerer. As the champions triumph over their enemies, they are swept up by the horse figure and carried over to the king's side. Although none of my informants could provide historical details or dates, they believed that the king was originally from Tibet. This event might have occurred in the sixteenth century when the Jumla king from northwest Nepal challenged the ruler of Mustang and, according to historical documents, also fought a battle at Metta in Nar valley (cf. Jackson 1976, 1978).

Paten, with its tradition of human (or yak) sacrifice every three years, is similar to the oaths of fealty and rituals of royal succession that were reported in other Tibetan communities (see, for example, Paul 1982:273–86; Bannerjee 1984:11–12; Bell 1931:8; Holmberg 1989:41–42). Bell, a historian of Tibetan religions, found a description of this sacrificial cult in S. W. Bushell's (1880) *The Early History of Tibet from Chinese Sources*:

Every three years, there is a grand ceremony during which all are assembled in the night. On a raised altar, on which are spread savory meats, the victims sacrificed are men, horses, oxen, and asses, and prayers are offered up in this form: "Do you all, with one heart and united strength, cherish our native country. The god of heaven and the spirit of the earth will both know your thoughts, and if you break this oath, they will cause your bodies to be cut into pieces like unto these victims." (441)

My Nyeshangte informants did not know when the custom of sacrificing humans had ceased, but their individual accounts were similar to the one Tsong told me [in English]:

A long time ago, we believe that we come from Tibet like an army. We kill everything—people, animals—everything before us we kill and come here [to Nyeshang]. We use to kill twelve girls every three years, but then realized no one would be left. So some say, we change and start killing yak. No more killing girls, now, just yak. But we run out of yak, no more yak, so then we are just killing goats. But then we become Buddhist so we don't kill anymore. Now we just cut ears, and let out a little blood.

This ritual blood-letting, performed only by men (under the supervision of the sngags pa), took place on the second night of Paten. On the first evening, villagers streamed onto my landlady's roof and presented kha btags and wooden flasks of beer daubed with butter to four men seated next to the lama.[33] One represented the king, who also doubled as the village god; another represented the king's magician-sorcerer; and two others represented the king's sons. Males who play these roles are chosen from among the four clans. (Female informants told me that the men who participate in the clan dancing and other Paten activities retreat for a few days before the festival begins to a site outside the village, where they prepare themselves and learn the details of the ritual performance. During this time, these men do not sleep with their wives.) After the king and his champions were anointed with butter, presented with beer, and draped in dozens of kha btags, the group, followed by all the village boys and men in a single line, wound its way through the village, dancing and singing. A few of these men carried large drums, which they beat incessantly; some carried rifles, which they shot into the air now and then. They visited three more houses, where female clan members poured them beer, offered scarves, and anointed their heads with butter. The procession then made its noisy and drunken way to the village square, where the battle with the king and his champions eventually took place.

Before this began, however, a group of adolescent boys wearing kha btags around their foreheads, were blessed by the village lama. The boys, who were seated in the square between two altars where juniper boughs were burned as offerings to the village gods, went through a public initiation, after which they became adult members of the bachelor's association, the youth group described earlier. The lama performed a *pūjā* (ritual offering), and many women crowded around the boys in a circle. They sprayed the boys with water and grain, and when the rite was over, the boys, followed by the king and his champions and the rest of the crowd, wandered about the village dancing and singing. When they returned to the square, the king and his champions reenacted the battle. Village men and women ringed the square, and many more sat on adjacent terraces and rooftops and watched the proceedings from above. This performance was repeated on alternate nights, with a day off "to rest." (A few elderly men told me that they were tired from the hard work of celebrating and needed a day to recuperate.)

On the first, third, and fourth days, male clan members gathered together on one roof terrace and engaged in a kind of competitive dance with other clan groups who were visible on nearby roofs. As they warmed up, they fired their rifles in the air. Those who did not wave guns while they were dancing were holding pitchers of beer. (Given the general condition of inebriated men, it was surprising that no one in the village was shot.) Sometimes the dancing and singing (and drinking) lasted all night, and the next day the men were unusually quiet.

On the third day, the king and his champions gathered once again on my landlady's roof and were blessed by the lama. The procession—drunk and singing and dancing, as usual—made its way to the south end of the village, where in a large clearing a juniper pole lay with a platform near the top. The king and his champions danced again, and men and women presented them with scarves and offerings of distilled liquor. Later that night, men would carry the pole and erect it on a nearby hill as a symbol of a newly revived or strengthened life force tree (*so dungma*) that connects the sky and the underworld. The sngags pa, clad in feathers and silk streamers, climbed onto the platform, symbolizing his ascent to the sky and his rebirth in the other world.

On the fourth day, clan dancers, dressed in multicolored silk robes with large hats covered with long streamers, began their dance competition again to the usual accompaniment of gunfire and drums. From the dgon pa, a group of (male) masked dancers encircled by rope, carrying swords and knives, arrows and tridents, wound their way through the lanes. One of them carried the image of Maha Kala (the village guardian deity); another carried a large board with various gtor ma (dough offerings) and effigies. Village boys and men ringed the outside of the circle, while inside the roped enclosure, the lama, masked dancers, sngags pa, and the king and his champions gathered together. Lama Yeshe and his assistants played the cymbals and recited Tibetan texts in preparation for the exorcism they would perform subsequently; the king and his champions danced and sang inside the circle.

Many women lined up on the terraces overlooking the clearing and watched the rowdy crowd below. Unmarried young women and adolescent girls ran around the enclosed circle of men, chanting a refrain to taunt the men and boys who manned the ropes. As the young women approached the rope, the men would surge toward them, kicking up clouds of dust as this immense circle of moving bodies surged back and forth over the cleared field. One fellow (who, on another occasion, had made lewd remarks to young women while they were waiting in line to receive *dbang* [blessings] at the dgon pa) ran around holding a rifle between his legs. He pointed the rifle (which was draped with kha btags) at various young women and chased them away. Some of the girls banded together and tried to wrest the gun away from him. The jostling, screaming, and taunting was intense, and I could see why many middle-aged women preferred to watch from a distance. After an hour the crowds settled down, and unmarried women approached the circle carrying pitchers of distilled liquor and beer for the lama and various dancers. As they came near the rope, the men lifted the barrier and let them within the circle, sometimes pretending to trap them when they were ready to leave.

An hour later, the religious specialists within the rope circle made their way to the clearing by the cliffs, and Lama Yeshe and his assistants performed the year-end exorcism (tarkye) to rid the village of malignant forces. Masked dancers whirled around the paper effigy, which was placed under some straw; two of them staggered under the weight of their costumes and had to be helped off the ground—casualties of the week-long drinking sprees.

After the tarkye rite was completed, women served the lama and his assistants more chang. Many of the middle-aged men in the crowd, who were already quite drunk, staggered back to the village in a noisy, rowdy group—teasing young women along the way and pretending to chase them. The girls, in turn, taunted them, laughing and circling around the men. Some of the girls would swerve suddenly and barge straight into the older men, knocking a few of them to the ground.

That evening, the dance with the king and his champions continued in the village square, where another juniper pole (life tree) had been erected. Women (mostly middle-aged) gathered in the dgon pa to perform a *pūjā* (offering) for the hundreds of animals slaughtered by Hindus during

Dasain, a festival that coincided with Paten. Many women attended these services for two consecutive days: they recited prayers and mantra in order to generate merit to assist the animals in attaining a better rebirth and to counteract the sinful acts of the Hindus. Adolescent girls practiced their dance on the dgon pa roof in preparation for the closing rites. On the last evening of Paten, thirteen young girls wearing beautiful silk gowns danced around the juniper pole under the full moon, while the village looked on and the Paten celebration came to a close.

The rifles and carbines were put away, and for once we could sleep without hearing gunshots. Men recovered from their week-long hangovers; and most of the "week-end" warriors, the kings and the champions, returned to Kathmandu to resume their business ventures. Women, most of whom stayed in Nyeshang until November, resumed their daily tasks of drying fodder, husking and winnowing grain, and storing enough supplies of firewood to last through the winter.

Worshipping Women: Early Buddhist Practitioners

My elderly female informants have little interest in this warrior business, and the stories they tell are of a different kind. The tale presented here is an edited and composite account that was told to me by two women (an 88-year-old woman and a woman in her seventies).

A long time before, on the way from Tibet, a lama crossed over these mountains and came down to Nyeshang. This Lama Kanchhandhen he went from village to village and he taught the village people how to do religion and how to abandon sin and bad deeds. First he taught the women. He taught them how to pray by means of whirling [with a prayer wheel] and counting *mani* [reciting mantra or sacred formulas and counting with a rosary]. At first it was just the women who did the religion and who knew how to pray. After a few years, men also learn. [One account says that women taught their men; another says that this lama taught them.]

Lama Kanchhandhen taught us to make the carving on the stone, so that our descendants would know and remember us, and the Nyeshangte people here thought this was very nice. From that time on, people here learned to make the *mani* stones [walls containing rocks inscribed with Tibetan prayers]. This lama he stayed in Tanar dgon pa, a temple above Nyangkhu village. This lama said people in Nyeshang did so many sins, and now they must abandon these sinful ways. So all people from that time start to do religion. Women first started to do *mani* [religious works], and some time later, some years after, the boys [men] began doing religion too.

In essence, since Nyeshangte women were the first to receive and embrace Buddhist teachings from Tibetan lamas, they are considered (and required to be) more "civilized" than Nyeshangte men. That women accepted these teachings first is seen as evidence of their "natural" goodness, their innate virtue (*dgeba*), and their predilection for doing "good works" (see Aziz 1978:180). In contrast, men in their natural state are more inclined to be immoral, violent, brash, and fearless—characteristics that devolve from their warrior-hunter predecessors. These same qualities, however, also make many Nyeshangte males well suited for the occupation of a trader: where a resourceful and a daring outlook brings its own rewards. Nyeshangte males have succeeded in the international and black market trade largely because they are willing to take risks or, as my Nepali informants say, "because they have big hearts" and are unafraid.

Although these indigenous folk histories suggest that women have had a long association with religion (and men with war and trade), these oral accounts and ritual traditions have taken on more importance as Nyeshangte women and men, individually and collectively, negotiate the transformations of the past two decades. These gender metaphors have been appropriated by Nyeshangte and molded into a native model of "Tradition," as members of the community come to terms with new gender practices resulting from urbanization, a more rigid division of labor, and emergent middle-class values.

This chapter has shown that the Buddhist tradition, including the Tibetan variety, contains ambivalent, contradictory, and multivalent images of the female gender. The multiplicity of images is further compounded by the historical layering of Tibetan cultural and religious practices and the existence of local and regional cults. As a result of this legacy, it is no surprise that gender ideologies and gender imagery in Nyeshang and in other Tibetan communities are quite varied when we consider their sources.

This diversity does not lend itself to easy sorting: how should we weigh one statement in relation to another? A number of analytical issues further complicate the matter. For example, several Buddhist "apologists" have suggested that the misogynist statements found in these texts represent primarily the orthodox view of the religious establishment—the monastic elite (see, for example, Friedman 1988; Gross 1987b; Horner 1975). They argue that the negative images of women that are found in the literate or "great" tradition did not reflect the views of common folk, nor were they associated with actual religious practice or with "popular" religion per se. Some historians of Buddhism would add that these misogynist statements about the nature of the feminine or women's spiritual capacities do not reflect the Buddha's original teachings, which they believe stressed social and sexual equality (Friedman 1988). Instead, they feel that rules which limit female participation in Buddhist institutions were "added" later as the teachings and commentaries were transcribed and collected by various monk scribes and monastic elders who transmitted their patriarchal biases into the collection of texts (Paul 1979; Horner 1975). Does this mean, then, that we should ignore the liturgical sources and concentrate on popular texts (cf. Keyes 1984)?

Second, one should be careful not to overestimate the impact of various gender representations in everyday life by assuming that gender ideologies determine actual behavior. Rather, these beliefs may be used to rationalize one's fate and to make sense of one's existential conditions or place in the world. Women's overall "positioning" cannot be determined solely by the presence (or absence) of positive gender ideologies that stress complementarity between the sexes or portray the divine in feminine terms. Even the "existence of sexually egalitarian concepts in religious beliefs and . . . in religious practice does not necessarily signify the existence of sexual equality in social structure" (Oschorn 1981:31). Although some researchers (for example, Lepowsky 1990) have found that ideologies, social structure, and gender practices may actually be congruent in egalitarian societies like Vanatinai, New Guinea, other writers have observed marked discontinuities and contradictions within and among these various levels (cf. Schlegel 1990; Lederman 1990; Ong 1989).

That gender representations are not uniform also suggests that individuals may selectively disregard, challenge, or embrace various views. Ideologies and gender representations may be used or invoked by individuals or groups for political purposes (used here in the widest sense). Attention to the construction of knowledge, to issues of power and agency, lead us to question earlier assumptions about the universal acceptance or influence of hegemonic ideologies. In sum, this makes it difficult for us to measure the impact that gender ideologies have within different segments of society.

Having added all these qualifiers, let me throw in one more. Although most Nyeshangte informants—young adults and elders of both sexes—are aware that contradictory (Tibetan, Buddhist, or Brahmanical) views about the "nature of women" exist, the negative images are often evoked to make a joke or to needle a female relative. These dynamics are no different than the onslaught of silly "dumb blonde, bimbo" jokes that circulated on computer networks or construction sites: most male narrators do not take them seriously, and often they share them with their spouses (who may well be blonde). In family interviews, I have heard young adult and middle-aged Nyeshangte males tease their mothers, wives, and sisters about being "low-born" females, while in the same conversation, through their words and attitudes, these males convey their pride and profound respect for what these women have accomplished.

CHAPTER EIGHT

With Only the Body of a Woman

THE PREVIOUS DISCUSSION of gender representations and the cultural logic that links women with the sacred domain provides the background for understanding how conflicts between changing economic practices and enduring religious goals have defined contemporary identities within the Nyeshangte community. In turn, I consider how religious practice has allowed women to mediate the contradictions between the collective memories of the homeland and the imaginings of an urban future.

This chapter is organized into two major sections: in the first part I describe women's participation in a number of key rituals and look at two communities of religious specialists—ordained nuns (jomo) and lay renunciants at ser khyim (retreat centers). In the final section I discuss the overall significance of women's agency in reworking the hierarchical values of the world market into an indigenous framework that is shaped by Buddhist principles.

A few comments about agents, actors, and subjects might be useful at this point. Although in much of the literature the words *agent* and *actor* are frequently transposed, here I choose the term *agent* deliberately to highlight the "transformative capacity" (Giddens 1981:28) of women's practice in the sense that their action constitutes and sustains the Nyeshangte social order (and, in turn, is structured by it).[1] Agency, then, is directly tied to power as it involves the ability to both define or impose "visions of the world" and, in some sense, the ability "to act" or "work" on these cultural and social forms. Agency "refers to doing" (Giddens 1984:9). Agents, therefore, are people who have the capacity and knowledge to act, to intervene in the world and bring about effects, both in the sense of producing desired results as well as unintended consequences that reflect the limits of "practical consciousness" (Giddens 1979) or the "indeterminacy" of practice (Bourdieu 1977).[2] Although most of the agents I describe are knowledgeable, they are nevertheless not omniscient or "all-knowing" (at least not yet). Finally, I should stress that agency and structures are mutually constitutive, and in adhering to the middle ground, I wish to avoid a position where "subjects" are *entirely* the product of discursive effects and an agent-centered view where individuals have limitless choices, freedom, and power.

Individuals, of course, are never "free agents," and it is precisely at this juncture that moral obligations, concern with legitimacy, and other social conventions both constrain and empower individual or group action differentially. In other words, agency is context-specific and irrefutably linked to structures that represent or "hook up" with the interests and desires of individuals in varying degrees.[3] Structures therefore construct the range of possible (or imaginable) options, and depending on the "fit" between social and cultural forms, on the one hand, and the knowledge and intentions of agents, on the other, they can be seen as circumscribing specific kinds of action as well as enabling other kinds.

Actors, on the other hand, also pursue their aims, strategies, or their "well-being" (Sen 1990:126), but they seem to do so with a limited awareness of other possibilities; that is, they are more constrained by their daily "reality" and essentially operate within existing social rules and by "conventional perceptions of legitimacy" (Sen 1990:127). Actors in this scenario are not unlike the goal-directed "entrepreneurs" who appear in Bourdieu's (1977, 1984) works: they engage in "short-term tactical moves" (Ortner 1984:152) but may not be concerned about "ultimate" goals beyond these immediate practical "interests." In Sen's formulation, agency goes beyond an actor's ability to pursue her own goals and "well-being," which is linked to questions of "capability" and "functioning" or "what the person can do or can be." Agency requires *some* ability to "think freely" or "act freely" in order to pursue (or at the very least imagine) objectives or opportunities that in some ways transcend basic questions of personal welfare and the rule-governed strategies of actors (Sen 1990:148). The distinction Sen draws here is also reminiscent of Ortner's (1984) contrast between approaches that focus on the short-term strategizing of actors for specific returns versus those that concentrate on the "long-term developmental projects" where individuals "are seen as involved in relatively far-reaching transformations of their states of being—of their relationships with things, persons, and self" (152).

Thus for me it is not so much a question of choosing among different kinds of agents and actors—the Nyeshang terrain is populated with all sorts of individuals with different motives, desires, levels of knowledge, and so on—but rather my intent in this project is to take a "developmental" or "long-term perspective," one that examines the process of "becoming" rather than the business of "getting" (Gramsci 1957, cited in Ortner 1984:152). As Ortner explains, "intrinsic to this . . . perspective is a sense of motive and action as shaped not only by problems being solved, and gains being sought, but by images and ideals of what constitutes goodness—in people, in relationships, and in conditions of life" (152).

Consciousness is another key term in this enterprise. In Giddens's (1979, 1981) formulations, action is goal-directed and agents are knowledgeable, reflexive, and aware of their behavior.[4] On this particular issue, I find his ideas more congenial than Bourdieu's for framing Nyeshangte "practice." Bourdieu's concept of habitus (1977) appears to be extremely "system-centered" in that agency is completely eclipsed by structural and institutional effects as a result of his exaggeration of the coherence of social patterns and homologous structures. Habitus, according to Bourdieu, is "understood as a system of lasting, transposable dispositions which, integrating past experiences, functions at every moment as a *matrix of perceptions, appreciations, and actions*" (82–83). Although his phrase "transposable dispositions" would seem to hint at the possibility of creativity and suggest a certain level of consciousness in actors that is usually associated with agency, other statements point to an overdetermined view of structure. "As an acquired system of generative schemes . . . the habitus engenders all the thoughts, all the perception, and all the actions consistent with those conditions, and no others" (95).

Now, although it is clear that Nyeshangte women enact moral rules and may be said to "embody" them, I would argue that some adult women, in fact probably quite a few, are *not only* acting out of habit or bodily discipline (cf. Bourdieu 1977) but are *intentionally choosing* to do so. Individual women (to varying extents) are generally aware of the conditions of their existence; at the same time they are also conscious of alternatives ways of living or being. That women are turning away from capitalist, western, urban, or Hindu values, or deliberately electing to ignore them, signals to me some degree of agency, of choice (and hence resistance).[5]

As I pointed out in chapter 1, many Nyeshangte individuals seem to be quite conscious of their positioning, their subjectivity, their collective history, and their cultural identity. This self-consciousness can in part be explained by "standpoint theory," the idea that marginalized or subordinate groups have a double hermeneutic: their perspective encompasses both an "objective" awareness of themselves as Other, as well as a solid understanding of the dominant culture that is often necessary for survival or just simply getting by. According to feminist standpoint theory, this bottom-up view provides a more complete and less distorted picture of the social order than one strictly held by the elite (Harding 1987). Although this is not an argument I would want to extend across the board, in the Nyeshangte case it seems justifiable. One more example might reveal the logic (and appeal) of this claim. Feminist critic bell hooks (1984) describes a special outlook that results from being situated on the periphery. Remembering what it was like to grow up in the hinterlands of Kentucky, she comments, "Living as we did—on the edge—we developed a particular way of seeing reality. We looked both from the outside in and from the inside out . . . we understood both" (vii).

"Self-consciousness" among indigenous groups in Nepal is also brought about by the presence of western and Asian (mostly Indian and Japanese) tourists who observe, comment, and inquire about "local" practices. The presence of so many "dharma freaks" and serious students of Tibetan Buddhism also forces many Nyeshangte to confront the self-images that others create and hold up before them: their "selves" are refracted in videos and films like the *Little Buddha*; in adventure and coffee-table books of the "forbidden valley, mysterious Nepal" genre; and in the ubiquitous postcards and Tibetan "relics" that are mass produced in India and sold in Nepalese souvenir shops. Here, of course, we must also add anthropologists to the equation, and although the Nyeshangte have not been the object of as many studies as, say, the Sherpa or Thakali, the presence of researchers asking questions inevitably leads these groups to a heightened "collective self-consciousness" (cf. Ortner 1989:9).

Consciousness and religion bring me to yet another facet of agency, which is this: if we attempt to reach a post-Foucaldian position that seems less inimical to feminist perspectives by conceding that the subject perhaps has retained a glimmer of consciousness, because of her capacity for language (see, for example, Kruks 1992; Schutz 1962), then should we not extend that possibility to the performance of ritual as well? Here I will cite two brief examples where the writers explicitly point this out, as it would seem fairly obvious that the construction of meaning through symbolic action (ritual) would necessarily involve some degree of consciousness—not withstanding the current fascination with bodies, embodiment, and the like, and our preoccupation with (or "fetishization" of) Cartesian "disjunctures."[6]

Leaving aside the question of bodies, I turn to Steve Sangren's (1995) comments about Taoist ritual practices and John Gray's (1987) examination of ghost exorcism in Nepal. In his conclusion, John Gray discusses several premises that would seem to substantiate the links among agency, intent, and religious practice. Following Valeri (1985), Gray explains that ritual is "an objective process of consciousness" that serves as a resource or object of human experience which enables individual and collective subjects to fashion an identity, a sense of self or "consciousness," and in turn develop an awareness of this construction (195–96). "Religion," Gray notes, "refers to a particular mode of giving meaning to the world which implicates a way of knowing and acting in the world" (196; also Geertz 1973; Ortner 1978a). Furthermore, religious practice, specifically sacrifice in this case, allows Hindu practitioners to tap into the wider realm of cosmological power, which in turn produces effects (or, from our perspective, enables agents to act) in the human realm. In short, knowing agents, through ritual as an instrument of action, bring about desired results. Sangren (1995) also points out that,

> in establishing what is conceived of as an ongoing engagement with divinity, devout Chinese not only produce themselves in the sense that they employ such activities to produce a sense of personal identity in the form of narrative religious autobiographies, they also empower themselves as agents of their own production. In worship and testimony, individuals exercise real power, and this power is manifested in their conviction that such activities are effective in establishing control over their lives. (25)

This brings us to my final comments on the nature of subjectivity. The question of consciousness and intentions is addressed in an insightful way by Mahoney and Yngvesson (1992) who draw on a variety of works (Lacan, Foucalt, Bourdieu, and Winnicott) to bridge some of the theoretical gaps in current approaches to the problems of subjectivity, here defined as "the

experience of self as a subject who acts, who has wants, who must sometimes act 'against the grain' in the face of contradictory desires" (45ff., n. 2).
They point out that the nature of "motivation," what compels a subject to
resist or acquiesce in ongoing struggles over power, is generally undertheo-
rized in many anthropological accounts. Often the subject appears as a
"kind of loose cannon in a life that `consists of retellings' and performances
that are 'always in flux'" (Bruner 1986:12; cited in Mahoney and Yngvesson
1992:45) or as a residual effect from the system-centered grids of power and
knowledge. In either case, regardless of how "selves" and individuals are represented in these and other texts, Mahoney and Yngvesson would argue
that we need to consider how power relations are constructed psychologi-
cally. In other words, they ask, what are "the processes by which subjects
want to conform or resist" (44–45).

To understand the potential for resistance or conformity, Mahoney and
Yngvesson (1992) propose an approach to subjectivity and agency that not
only attends to the structures of power but focuses on how the "subject
makes meanings in her relationship with others" (70). Although some of
their argument covers ground that may not be fruitful for my purposes
here—the discussion of subjectivity and resistance in infants, for example—
their analysis of how new meanings and cultural forms are created while
"old" structures are reproduced is a central concern to practice-oriented
approaches. They provide several examples where disjunctures and contradictions enable individuals to challenge authority by complying with social
and religious structures, a process that paradoxically enables subjects to create a "space for self-assertion" and at the same time leads to "the involun-
tary reproduction of familiar forms" (68–70).[7] Drawing on the work of
Winnicott, an object-relations theorist within the wider psychoanalytic
field, Mahoney and Yngvesson state that the ambiguous space between "the
symbolic, in which selves and relationships are constituted, and the presym-
bolic" is a creative one where "the tension between discovering meanings
that are already there and shaping new meanings, is what allows for a sense
of empowerment in subjects whose agency is reproducing hierarchies even
as they are creating the spaces for new forms of relationship" (62–63).
Winnicott explains, "in any cultural field it is not possible to be original
except on a basis of tradition. . . . The interplay between originality and the
acceptance of tradition as the basis for inventiveness [is] one example . . . of
the interplay between separateness and union" (Winnicott 1982:99; cited in
Mahoney and Yvngesson 1992:63).

In sum, the ambiguity, the multiple contingent nature of structures and social events, and the distance between subjects and cultural forms create a locus where human agency—the struggle over meaning—can take place. It is precisely this fragmented messy landscape of intersecting structures, of actor-agents with different motivations, levels of knowledge, and capacities for agency that make it difficult to formulate a unitary model linking agents and their actions with the reproduction (and transformation) of structures. There are gaps, big ones. Ortner (1989:128) points out that relationships between individuals and cultural schemas—meanings, stories, symbols—vary. Some may be indifferent or unaware of the entire cultural inventory; others may enact patterns that differ dramatically from the dominant cultural forms. As in the case of Sherpa "founding" stories, Nyeshangte "origin" accounts about the establishment of Buddhism in the homeland, about Genghiz Khan, the deer hunter and other warrior types, may just be "stories," but at some point they may become archetypes or schemas that serve as vehicles of meaning and instruments of action for individuals and groups. At that time they take on a wider significance for much of the community.

If in light of these origin stories adult women are attributed "agentive capacities" as ritual practitioners, then their practice may be seen as both constituting and emerging from these cultural forms. In Nyeshang, religious works are generally framed within a broader discourse about morality and "the simple good life" of the past. Entering "the past" is always in some sense a political act, since it has implications for how the present and the future are constructed. One of the unintended consequences of women's ritual action, then, is that no matter what their individual motives may have been, their collective action will inevitably lead to the reproduction of the "system" and will be viewed by a majority of Nyeshangte (and outsiders) through the lens of a politicized framework that hinges on the community's cultural identity and minority status in Hindu Nepal.

Furthermore, "expectations" about women's spirituality are continuously reinforced, and in many ways we can say these structures are embodied.[8] These spiritual "dispositions" are strengthened through ritual action, and becoming aware of them, an individual would also become aware of the group's collective memory or history (Connerton 1992). From a Buddhist perspective, learning is actually a question of remembering the past. Similarly, in most ritual acts, practitioners identity with the author of the first rites and, in a sense, return to a primordial era "to straighten" out the cosmic clutter of the present. However, in my view it is not enough to note that individuals end up doing the same "cultural thing" (cf. Ortner 1989).[9] Motives, intentions, and desires may in the end bring people to the same point—of doing religious works—but their trajectories, their mistakes, their life histories will vary, as will the *meanings* they attribute to these events.

One way to accommodate this sense of indeterminacy between actor-agents and systems is to attend to the diversity of experiences and motivations of individual subjects over the life course. Self and cultural awareness clearly vary among individuals within a group and are apt to change. Rather than be compelled to choose categorically from among dead subjects (see O'Hanlon 1988), timid subjects who speak but do not necessarily act (e.g., Kumar 1994), subjects who act but do not necessarily think (e.g., Bourdieu 1977; Haynes and Prakash 1991:3), or agents who appear "under-socialized" (see Etzioni 1988:6), "heroic" (e.g., Gordon 1988), or "overly masculinized" (e.g., Forbes 1988),[10] and thus stand accused of reinventing the autonomous neoclassical creatures of the Enlightenment, I prefer to acknowledge the possibility that Nyeshangte as individuals are a heterogeneous, somewhat "eccentric" lot who may well span the entire gamut listed above.

We need to attend to this "on the ground" diversity, but at the same time recognize that "agents-in-society" will have different capabilities to act according to recognizable social categories of persons (Harris 1989). In other words, we should also pay attention to the local "insider" concepts of agents and notions of personhood. Harris discusses three kinds of agentive capacities that may be attributed to "social kinds" of persons. "Judgmental capacities" include "the locally assumed, imputed capacities to embody in conduct the local standards of . . . propriety and morality." A second type of agentive capacity would include "social entitlements capacities," which refers to the abilities of individuals or social kinds "to embody in one's conduct the rights, duties, freedoms and constraints of specific roles" (605). As Harris explains, certain kinds or categories of people will be seen as having "more of 'what it takes' than others," and these qualities are bound up tightly with cultural notions about work, value, and merit (1992:605). Finally, she points out that agentive qualities may also include "mystical capacities" that are understood to exist but may not be manifested in ordinary everyday practices (606). In the following sections, these various types of agentive qualities will become clearer as I consider the religious activities of individual women and discuss the community's perceptions of these women as moral agents.

Women of Spirit

The variety of roles open to female religious practitioners depend to some extent on age, life cycle, marital situation (divorced, widowed), and formal status, that is, whether an individual has taken vows as a jomo (nun) or has remained a laywoman. These differences may best be described by using a number of individual case studies to highlight the activities and attitudes of a representative range of Nyeshangte women. Women's religious activities may in turn be divided into individual observances, such as those performed in the household or at a retreat center, and major calendrical rites involving the entire village or community.

Laywomen and Domestic Rituals

In a society where adult women occupy positions of authority and power within the household, it is not surprising that their responsibility for the everyday welfare and well-being of their families extends beyond the economic domain, and involves managing or controlling the supernatural domain as well. Senior women have the primary task of keeping their houses in order, and that includes keeping evil forces at bay and keeping household gods (*thin lha*) in a contented state.

Ama was always the first to rise each morning. Before dawn she would rekindle the fire in the kitchen hearth and, with a burning ember, would light a large rusty can filled with juniper branches (*dup*) and purify the house with the offering (*bsangs*) of scented leaves. As the smoke of this sacred plant filled the kitchen and streamed from the roof terrace, it rid the premises of evil forces; the smoke offering (incense) also placated the *srung ma*, the household guardian deity that resided in a small cubicle on the roof, and the *btsan* and *klu*—the capricious house spirits that may be offended by unpleasant odors or spilled food and cause illness in retribution. When these offering/purification rites were completed, Ama entered the *chos khang*, a small chapel room found in nearly every Nyeshangte home. Every morning she filled the water bowls on the altar and lit several butter lamps; after reciting her prayers and prostrating before the altar, Ama beat the large hanging drum made from juniper and deer skin—a resounding noise that marked the conclusion of her meditation. In the evening when she lit additional lamps, the small room with its brightly painted *thang ka* (religious paintings), cheerful carpets, and cushions seemed particularly inviting, ablaze with flickering lights that were reflected in the rows of burnished copper vessels on the altar.

Although many household rites are performed by laywomen on a daily basis, others like the *lha bsang* rite are performed less frequently and require the services of ritual specialists. Ama always called on Lama Yeshe, a kinsman and immediate neighbor, to perform this rite. While the lama recited from the Tibetan scriptures, Ama offered chang, butter, and incense to the house and village deities at the rooftop altar.

During the lha bsang rite, new prayer flags are strung from the rooftop, and a new juniper pole representing a revived or strengthened life force (*so shying*) is erected.[11] The pole, topped with a yak tail and red flag, is replaced annually, or more often if the household has suffered illness or misfortune. Many Nyeshangte perform this rite in October during the New Year festivities; in Kathmandu, some households perform it as often as four or five times a year, with many monks in attendance. These rooftop rituals in the city, done for the protection of family members (and for good luck on trading trips), are quite elaborate and rather conspicuous: the chanting monks in their ceremonial robes and hats can be seen and heard from adjacent houses; the echoes of the *kangling*—long horns that drive away evil spirits and make household gods submissive—and the crash of cymbals and drums resound throughout the neighborhood, marking the sponsors as Buddhists in a predominantly Hindu world. In contrast, in the valley the lha bsangs rites are done with less flourish and fewer clergy in attendance—usually only one lama and perhaps an assistant or two.

Four or five times a year Ama also offers wheat and beer for the ancestor spirits called Meme Sangle, the initial four founders of Nyeshang who are also worshipped as clan and village gods. Representations of these deities are also housed in four individual shrines in the valley, where once a year a major ritual takes place. However, in the household observance, Ama makes the offering herself at her own rooftop shrine, while the lama reads from the religious texts. Only members of Meme Sangle (the founding clans) perform these rituals in their own households. Other villagers worship these gods at the village shrines during the annual ceremony.

Most household chapels also contain images or masks of the village deity (*yul lha*), and each village god is worshipped differently. In Kathmandu, one young woman, originally from Nyangkhu village, told me that she went to her married sister's house three times a month to do an offering ritual (*pūjā*) to their clan-village god, on the tenth, fifteenth, and thirtieth day of the lunar month. They referred to this observance as *Tisang* and explained that they usually fasted or abstained from eating meat on those days. Other clans in other villages have various dietary restrictions and different clan-village

15. A woman and her infant receive a blessing and ceremonial scarf.

rites. A woman from Lhakpa explained that she worshipped Changmelang (the "red-faced" god) three times a week on Mondays, Tuesdays, and Thursdays by offering the deity a pitcher of beer or a pot of tea and placing fresh water in the altar bowls.

Other observances that take place within the household include major life cycle rites. When a child is born, friends, neighbors, and relatives bring the mother small gifts of money and baby clothes and offer ceremonial scarves and good wishes to the new infant. A lama blesses mother and infant and performs a protective rite. At about a year old, the child goes through a hair-cutting ceremony during which time he or she receives a formal name from a lama and is imbued with a Buddhist identity.

Funerals are the most elaborate of life-cycle rites; they entail lengthy liturgical recitations by clergy and involve considerable expense for the family, as large amounts of grain are given away to accumulate merit for the deceased. These mortuary observances are essentially the same for adult men and women but may vary for children depending on age and cause of death.[12] Women's main roles in these rites involve hospitality and exchange.[13] Kinswomen offer the corpse (which is bound up with white scarves and kept in the home for three days) hot food at least once a day. (The dead eat the essence or steam.) On the third day, when the corpse is to be cremated, women from every household in the village visit the dgon pa where they offer the mourning family a bottle of raksī or chang and some money. Those with close ties to the deceased's household may also send contributions of grain and help prepare the rice or wheat balls (*tsogs*) that are distributed after the cremation. Women, however, never accompany the funeral party to the cremation grounds near the river, as the sight of the funeral pyre and burning corpse are said to be "too frightening." Instead, the cremation is carried out by the head lama and his monk assistants and is witnessed by the male friends and relatives of the deceased.

Laywomen and Religious Patronage

In addition to overseeing individual and household observances, laywomen generally take responsibility for fulfilling their households' obligations to support dgon pa and village ceremonial life. Each household in Nyangkhu village, for example, must send a member to do a minimum of five days labor for the dgon pa, but most resident villagers exceed this minimum by volunteering to prepare and serve rice and tea for the assembled clergy; other tasks include repairing walls, damaged roofs, or foot paths around the temple grounds. The heavier construction or repair work is usually done by teenage girls and middle-aged "retired" men, whereas the hospitality and food preparation is overseen by adult women.

The obligatory contribution of provisions depends largely on the household's status and wealth, as well as the length and cost of the ritual being performed. If the lay sponsor is a close relative or friend, a woman usually sends a larger amount of grain and perhaps a cash contribution in addition to lending cooking pots, serving dishes, and carpets, if needed, and volunteering to help with the preparations. For calendrical rituals at the dgon pa, a household of median wealth may be required to provide one *pree* (2 kg) of wheat or buckwheat, but most households are inclined to give more than the minimum amount, and women often donate additional grain, butter, and money as well as their own labor.[14] Laywomen also play a central role as sponsors and organizers of major community events. Two examples will be examined: the first are *Thonje* rites, and the second are Smyung nas (*nyungne*) observances.

THONJE: RITES OF DISTRIBUTION

In addition to regular contributions of labor and material for local religious observances, social custom dictates that each household of average means undertake the organization of a major ritual event at least once (Cooke 1985a). Although a few Kathmandu-based households may renege on their village duties, most Nyeshangte make a point of returning to the village to organize and take part in these religious observances.[15] Generally, these obligations are met by sponsoring Thonje rites which are held in every village during the month of June and last from three to five days. Although the decision to host a large-scale ceremony is usually made jointly by spouses, it is often the senior woman in the household who sets the actual process in motion: recruiting friends, neighbors, and relatives in the village to help. In contrast, men, unless they are approaching their retirement years, are often too preoccupied with their business pursuits to keep track of village affairs. However, merit derived from sponsoring Thonje rites are conferred equally upon all household members since wide-scale religious patronage is made possible largely as a result of trade earnings of urban-based males.

In recent years, with the increase in prosperity throughout the community, village Thonje rites have become quite elaborate and expensive affairs. Larger-scale events, with several lamas and assistants in attendance, bring the sponsors proportionately more merit than if only one lama is hired. As the demand for religious services has risen, monks and nuns from Churi and Nyangkhu dgon pa(s) are frequently called to other villages.

Sponsorship obligations serve as a good indicator of a household's economic standing in the community, since the richest households are expected to serve as patrons seven times, a household of average wealth three times, and the poorest may be exempt, though they too will usually make some effort to assist another household and earn merit as cosponsors.[16] Differences in wealth among villages are also reflected by the number of cosponsors organizing Thonje. In 1988–89, for example, one household from Nyangkhu village served as the sole sponsor for the observance held at Nangkung dgon pa. This household, acting on its own, distributed rice to every household in Churi and Tumje. In contrast, the sponsors from Churi and Tumje each consisted of three households who shared the considerable expenses that included meals and wages for the monastic congregation for the duration of the service (three to five days); the cost of material needed for altar offerings—butter for lamps and grain for sacrificial cakes (gtor ma); the cost of refreshments served to lay participants at the dgon pa and to villagers who visit the distribution site to receive the gifts of rice or salt; and, finally, the purchase of large amounts of grain, salt, or butter to be given away.[17]

The Thonje I observed in Tumje in 1989 was held at the village dgon pa where three high-ranking lamas and several nuns, monks, and married village lamas presided. The first day is generally devoted to preparations: nuns and monks work together making colored dough offerings of various sizes and shapes; setting up the altar, and performing the initial purification rites (*bsangs*) under the supervision of the village or head lama. The second and third days are given to the chanting and recitation of liturgical texts and the playing of musical instruments which accompany monastic ritual performances. The nuns and monks perform these tasks in unison, and their roles are interchangeable. Often, elderly male *geenyin* (retired village men who have received some religious training and can read Tibetan texts) provide additional support. Additional lay assistants, usually women, serve the midday meal inside the dgon pa and continually offer tea throughout the day. On the afternoon of the third day, when the liturgical recitations are concluded, many villagers—young children, men, and women visit the dgon pa and offer money and kha btags before the altar and to each of the assembled lamas; in turn they receive the empowerment (*dbang*) and long-life blessings (*tso*).[18]

On the final day of Thonje, I accompanied a woman from Churi to a Tumje house where the sponsors of the event (three families from Churi) were distributing rice. Representatives from every household in Nyangkhu and Tumje who wished to participate in the *kyo phiba* ("giving out wealth") rite were received on the upper terrace, served tea, beer, and buckwheat pancakes and then given a measured amount of rice, depending on the size of the recipient's household. In a form of immediate reciprocity and symmetrical exchange that characterizes social life in many Himalayan communities (cf. March 1979, 1987), guests brought bottles of distilled alcohol and beer topped with globs of butter for the owner of the house (a kinsman of the Churi sponsors). Elderly kinswomen tended the fires and supervised the cooking on the lower level, while a teenage daughter from the sponsoring family carried the food up the ladders and served the guests on the terrace.

Thonje rites bring merit to sponsoring families and the monastic ritual serves as a protective rite that also ensures the well-being of the community. To some extent, the amount of merit or the success of the rite depends on the number of households who participate in the empowerment and blessing ceremony and on the amount of grain that is given away. Although Thonje rites are part of the annual round of ritual observances in Nyeshang, they may also be performed at any time by individual sponsors who wish to accrue merit for a deceased relative, enhance their family's well-being, or for the welfare of all sentient beings (a "selfless" gesture that reaps even more merit for the benefactor).

Thonje rites are often held in conjunction with special events or auspicious occasions. For example, one couple from Tumje sponsored a five-day celebration to honor the fourteen nuns who completed their three-year retreat. The middle-aged couple, who were quite wealthy, spent several days roasting barley (*tsampa*) and making beer to feed the entire village. In addition, they gave away a large amount of rice and made cash donations to each of the nuns and their lama. On another occasion, when a particularly renowned lama visited the valley in 1982, several Thonje rites were held. Cooke (1985a:274) reports that some households spent nearly u.s.$3,000 on these ritual observances, including the distribution of u.s.$1,000 worth of Tibetan salt to other households.

The amount of money and material resources redistributed during the course of the year is quite significant. Even at small-scale ritual observances, meals are generally served to monastics and lay participants; at the conclusion of the rite, assistants carry large baskets filled with tsogs (balls of sticky rice, barley, or wheat) and gtor ma (cone-shaped dough effigies) throughout the village and distribute the consecrated food to everyone they see. In addition, religious specialists receive small sums of cash for their services. Throughout the year, they often receive gifts of food and other items from well-wishers in the village and from relatives in the city who send parcels at regular intervals. At major events, the amounts of cash and commodities that are redistributed through the community are substantially larger, as the Thonje examples above illustrated.

In sum, religious patronage reinforces community ideals of generosity and cooperation, while the ceremonial dispersion of cash or commodities helps minimize economic disparities in the homeland. "Sharing institutions," like Thonje and "giving out wealth" rituals (*kyo phiba*), reflect the moral principles of Nyeshangte exchange and sociality and the emphasis placed on balanced reciprocity and symmetry (cf. Humphrey 1992:129). These collective institutions are both the product and producer of Nyeshangte society and consciousness and are indispensable to the reproduction of egalitarianism. (As such, adult women as moral agents play a central role in supporting, and in turn producing, Nyeshangte cultural forms.

Here, I find Steve Sangren's (1995:26) expansion of the Marxian concept of "production," his critique of Foucaldian notions of power, and his statement that power generally implies a "subject" (contra Foucalt), whether the subject consists of individuals or "collective institutions," to be germane and timely given the current debates about the nature of subject-agents and the attempts to apply modified (and in some ways to move beyond) Foucaldian approaches to the problem (for example, Mahoney and Yngvesson 1992; Kruks 1992; Kumar 1994; Young 1994). Sangren's restoration of Marxian notions of ideology, which differentiates between levels of "reality" and separates the researcher's "representations of social life and the place of power within it" from the ideologies, representations, and practices of the subject-agents under consideration, is perhaps a better way to understand the hold these cultural forms and practices have in everyday life and provides a way to trace the linkages of power without resorting to a reified, totalizing view where power is transformed into another kind of subject-agent. Sangren suggests that Marxian notions of power and production are perhaps not hopelessly obsolete, if materialist notions of production are broadened to include culture making or the production of cultural forms, "social organization" and "consciousness" (including ideologies). Power, in this updated Marxian formulation, would include not only material control over the means of production but cultural production as well, and would restore some notion of a "subject." Sangren writes, "Power as control implies a subject, but subjects may be defined as individuals, [or] as collective institutions" (26). However, he is also careful to point out that "the study of the operations of power *requires* identifying the subjects (collective or individual) that exercise it, with the proviso that the contextualization of our analyses avoids the sorts of nondialectical reifications that elevate such disaggregated subjects to the status of transcendent or irreducible originators of social action, obscuring their dialectically simultaneous natures as immanent products or effects of social activities" (26).

Now, to return to the role of ideology and rituals as instruments of action and to consider how power is manifested through social relations (cf. Giddens 1979), I resume my discussion of "sharing institutions," Thonje rituals, and exchange in Nyeshang. Affluent households tend to commission more rituals (both private domestic rites and villagewide events) and are expected, in their role as sponsors, to pay somewhat more for these services than poorer households. Wealthier households are also expected to make larger "voluntary" contributions for community events or for rituals organized by other sponsors. In one instance, a prominent Churi villager handled most of the funerary expenses when an impoverished Drokpa man died. The widow wished to hire a "big lama" to conduct the services, but could not afford the standard fee of seventy rupees (u.s.$3.50) nor did she have enough grain for the customary distribution of tsogs. The villagers in question, a local "big man" and his wife, donated grain and helped collect additional contributions from other village households so that a proper funeral could be held. Even though the entire village pitched in to stage an adequate memorial service, the couple received most of the credit for being generous (although $3.50 and a modest amount of flour was insignificant compared to the $300 this same couple contributed on another occasion to help build a Buddhist monument).

Acts of generosity, of course, are implicated in coercive power relations. Since most forms of sociality in Nyeshang are predicated on reciprocity, individuals or households who cannot return the "gift" are indebted to their benefactors and in some sense obligated to repay the patronage with their labor if possible or, at the very least, their continued public "support." However, the coercive aspects of these relationships seem to be a bit more diffused and less apparent in the Nyeshang valley than, say, among the Sherpa (cf. March 1987; Ortner 1970, 1978a), and overall Nyeshangte sociality seems to resemble the balanced (delayed) exchanges of the Tamang (see March 1987). For example, in "doing friendship" (roo la tse), "gifts" of labor, money, and food are offered without expectation of immediate return and, in some cases, with no return expected. However, in some relationships—say, between trade mentors and their apprentices—the hierarchy between benefactor and recipient is apparent; in this context, Nyeshangte relationships resemble the "manipulative" behavior and more aggressive aspects that characterize Sherpa social exchanges.

However, the recognition of power also suggests the presence of agency or resistance. Seen from the flip side of the power coin, the "sharing institutions" and the customary practice of "meritorious giving" enables the disadvantaged members of society to supplicate the wealthy and provides them with a socially recognized channel by which to advance their claims. This is another example where "spaces" for negotiation or autonomy are constituted and defined by structures or institutions. The counterpart of giving is receiving. Katherine Bowie (n.d.), in a detailed look at how merit-making operated in the stratified rural economies of northern Thailand, points out that the practice of "begging" could be seen as another example of Scott's (1985) "weapons of the weak." Conversely, although individuals who sponsor meritorious acts are exercising "power," and in turn acquiring spiritual capital or social prestige, one might question how much "autonomy" they in fact have, since they are morally compelled to give and are in effect constrained by the ideological structures of "being in society," as my Nyeshangte informants would put it. To return to the couple above who donated a few dollars and some grain for the nomad's funeral, they stood to lose a lot more by not helping the widow.

SMYUNG NAS: RITES OF ATONEMENT

Smyung nas (*nyungne*) observances, which last four days, are also held in every village, usually during the months of April and May. At these retreats, lay participants stay at the dgon pa where they observe monastic rules, fast, and maintain silence on alternate days, as well as engage in merit-making activities. This includes doing countless prostrations, reciting prayers, circumambulating the temple, listening to sermons, and finally on the last day, receiving blessings and empowerment from the lama.

Traditionally, on the last day of Smyung nas, three or four senior women will volunteer to act as sponsors and organizers of the next year's retreat. Every household in the village is expected to contribute provisions regardless of whether the household participates in the retreat.[19] The organizers collect the food supplies, delegate tasks at the dgon pa kitchen, and supervise the service of meals and tea to lay participants and clergy on nonfasting days. In addition, a meal is served to the entire village on the last day when almost everyone in the village comes to receive empowerment and to congratulate the lay participants, primarily adult women in their early thirties to late fifties.

Although Smyung nas observances have been described by anthropologists working in Sherpa communities as a "ritual of post-parenthood," one that is performed by the elderly who have retired from householder's duties (cf. Ortner 1978), at many village dgon pa(s) in Nyeshang I was surprised to see a large number of children. Even during the day of silence and fasting at Churi dgon pa, I found many young children sleeping inside the temple; belongings and blankets were strewn everywhere, and older children sat quietly in the gloomy hall while their mothers prayed before the altar. This was also the only time that village children were quiet during religious observances. Most rituals at the dgon pa were not very solemn affairs: children ran around the large prayer wheel near the front door, spinning the wheel as though it were a playground carousel; shouts and laughter drifted back inside the dgon pa, but no one seemed to mind the noise nor the disturbances of children scrambling past rows of seated observers as they tried to find their mothers in the crowded temple.

Smyung nas at Kherap dgon pa   At the Smyung nas retreat held at Kherap Dorje dgon pa, a good two-hour climb from the valley floor, children were brought to the premises during the day but did not spend the night. Instead, they returned to the village in the company of women who volunteered to help cook and serve the lay participants and clergy. Several teenage girls also worked as assistants, and they were busy fetching water, tending fires, washing dishes or cleaning greens for the midday curry and rice lunch.

This retreat at Kherap Dorje dgon pa had a more renunciatory air to it, and the participants were quite serious about observing the fasting rules and were diligent about rising early to circumambulate the temple and perform as many prostrations as possible. The Smyung nas observances held at this temple (in May for Churi, June for Nyangkhu) were in addition to retreats already held at the village dgon pa below in the valley. The average age of participants here was older, and many more women attended the retreat. Inside the dgon pa two nuns, daughters of the head lama from Churi, sat at a low table alongside the monks and read from the texts while their father led the ceremony.[20] During the course of the four-day retreat, the nuns and lama also read the story of Mi la ras pa and the deer hunter, and reemphasized Buddhist values—urging lay devotees to renounce all sin. On the final day, the women participants "expressed their joy" by singing and dancing in a circle around a juniper pole "life tree." The assembled clergy and villagers gathered around and watched the group, but only the senior women danced. As these women were "moved with joy" and stood up to join the circle of dancers, young women from the audience hurried over and carefully draped the dancers with woolen shawls. It was clear that the pace of the ceremonial proceedings was centered around these middle-aged women, as the liturgical recitations and the final stages of the ritual (dbang) and the celebratory feast, were delayed until the women's voices and rhythmic steps gradually slowed, and one by one the women rejoined the crowd of onlookers.

Customarily, whenever the women from Nyangkhu complete a four-day retreat at Kherap dgon pa, they are greeted outside the village by a delegation of male villagers carrying kha btags and chang. The beer is offered to the lama who supervised the retreat, and the women are draped with the scarves. (In Kangri village, unmarried males wait outside the village and offer the women "renunciants" flowers as well as kha btags.) The entire group then proceeds to the village dgon pa, chanting along the way. The following day is also spent dancing and celebrating the successful completion of the meditation retreat.

These honorary delegations were also sent to greet visiting dignitaries, important lamas, and lords from Dzarkot or Mustang (adjacent districts) when they came to Nyeshang. The greeting party waited outside the village to pay its respect and to escort honored guests into the village. In a similar fashion, the village men pay homage to the women (and the few elderly men) who participated in the Smyung nas retreat at Kherap dgon pa.

Women as Lay Renunciants

Although Smyung nas observances provide a brief relief from the responsibilities of the domestic life, laypersons may also undertake longer retreats at ser khyim dgon pa. Ser khyim enable individuals to move easily between the sociality of village life and the solitary pursuits of the religious recluse. Ser khyim serve many of the same needs as long-term pilgrimages, but without the physical hardship: villagers involved in marital disputes or arguments with neighbors or kinsmen can withdraw until tensions ease.[21] For married women, the ser khyim also allows them to take on the status of religious specialist apart from their familial roles of wife and mother.

This community of religious specialists is made up primarily of laywomen, though it is open to householders of either sex. That women outnumber men at this retreat center stems from gender differences in religious commitments during various life stages.[22] Women, on the whole, are more constant Buddhists, exhibiting a greater intensity of religious devotion throughout their adult lives, whereas the average layman attends to religious matters primarily during his retirement years. While this gender-based distinction reflects a long-term pattern in the valley, the advent of year-round trade, which requires lengthy absences from Nyeshang, has also contributed to men's desultory participation in community religious life.[23]

The case of Tigri Buddhi, a 50-year-old woman who spends several months each year at the isolated ser khyim, is fairly representative of the other women in residence there. Most of these women were in their fifties, widowed, and had married children living in Kathmandu or in the Nyeshang valley. All the women owned their own house at the retreat; several told me that they had built these small shelters on their own or with the help of relatives several years before.

I first met Tigri at my landlady's house just a few days after arriving at the field site. Tigri was originally from Churi but had moved to Kathmandu

16. An elderly women spins a prayer wheel and counts prayers on a rosary.

with her husband and children more than a decade ago. Her husband had died, and her children in the city were grown up and married now, so she preferred to stay in the valley most of the year. A wealthy woman, she wore a long strand of exquisite coral and turquoise beads and was always immaculately dressed. Though she still owned a house in Churi village, she usually stayed with friends in Nyangkhu village before going to the retreat center.

When I was first introduced to Tigri she immediately proceeded to outline the various ways that my assistant Spike was related to her, and concluded that she was his "small mother," a kind of aunt. With that relationship squared away, Tigri tackled the "disorderliness" that my presence inspired. She resolved this dilemma by announcing that she wished to be my friend and would teach me how to behave "properly" and speak "nicely." Not one to procrastinate, she began right away by giving me an impromptu language lesson, which she continued over the next several days. Tigri was extremely outgoing and energetic, joking with the young male assistants and servants, slapping them playfully on the back. Her vibrant personality was quite a contrast to the depressed weepy mood of my landlady, Ama.

Tigri stayed for eight to nine months in a one-room stone hut that she and her husband had built as their retirement residence. Her children in Kathmandu arranged for provisions to be sent to her at the dgon pa where each person usually cooked separately, except during special ritual observances when a communal meal was shared with clergy and other lay practitioners. At the dgon pa, Tigri practiced meditation four times a day, usually alone in her hut but sometimes outside in the forest with other lay practitioners.

A few laymen and laywomen lived in rough shelters in more isolated locations above the ser khyim. At this stage in their life cycles, the goals and outlooks of Nyeshangte men and women seem to converge. One 70-year-old man who lived year-round in the jangal spoke wistfully of the past, when Nyeshangte sold bear and deer organs and musk, collected jangal medicine (herbs), when "people had simple lives and were honest." This "good life" was recalled in contrast to the present era, when Nyeshangte began "to do business." He too had traveled to many countries, but he said that "of all the places, Nyeshang was the best, the most beautiful," so he returned to the valley to spend his final years doing religious works (mani).

My landlady and Tigri said that, on average, it took eight years for a layperson to complete the training program and gain expertise in meditation and visualization practices. Religious training involves long periods of solitary meditation, interspersed with special initiations and teachings from the rNying ma lamas who run the ser khyim. Some laypeople stay all year; others stay only three to four months. Several married men who wished to become lamas also studied Tibetan texts and assisted at dgon pa rituals. In addition to these lay practitioners, there were several nuns at a more remote dgon pa hidden among the cliffs above the retreat center. These nuns would remain in strict isolation for another year and a half when their training under the rNying ma lama would be completed.[24]

Ama and her adolescent daughter spent three month at the ser khyim in the winter and another month during the summer. However, Ama also made frequent visits to her meditation "hut" during the course of the year for a week or ten days at a time. On one of these short visits, we joined her and met several of the lay practitioners who lived in small stone shelters nearby. The women had gathered in one house to prepare the altar offerings and communal meal in honor of Buddha's birthday. Several women wandered into the courtyard to lend a hand with the preparations or to borrow a pot or serving dish. As the visitors entered, one woman immediately served them tea, others continued pounding radishes with a wooden pestle to make relish, and still others hovered over the fires stirring large pots of rice and vegetables.

Tigri and Ama had helped prepare the altar offerings: large plates of *koma*—spaghettilike strands of wheat painted in bright shades of turquoise, green, yellow, and pink—as well as various sizes of gtor ma made of roasted wheat, sugar, and water. Inside the dgon pa, a few laymen put the finishing touches on the gtor ma, adding white petals made of butter, and then placed these sacrificial cakes on the altar: the largest gtor ma (*ritam*) and the smaller conical ones (*shanke*) would serve as supports or "houses" for the gods who are summoned during the invocations.

When the rites began, laywomen and laymen entered the dgon pa and placed kha btags before the altar; a few men offered the lama a bottle of beer. Various women came in and sat for ten or fifteen minutes to listen to the liturgy. Others sat just outside the door in a noisy huddle, joking, laughing with friends, sometimes shouting greetings to people inside. Many joked with the head lama and his three nun daughters who were reciting the liturgy and handling the ritual instruments—the drums, cymbals, and bells. The atmosphere was relaxed and people were rather playful. When Ama fell asleep in a corner niche, one of the nuns grabbed a handful of grain and threw it across the room. As she awoke with a start, everyone giggled. Another old woman got up and jokingly swatted a woman sitting next to me who was dozing. There was a lot of rough play and jostling—even laughter—when the lama who had trouble seeing the text lost his place and occasionally hesitated during the recitation. His eldest daughter seemed to know the chanting sequence and led the ritual, while the middle daughter sat near her father and pointed out the lines of the text, shuffling the loose leaves of the Tibetan scriptures carefully. At certain junctures in the ceremony, the nuns and lama instructed a lay assistant who sprinkled consecrated water and liquor with peacock feathers before the altar. Below the altar, three dozen red gtor ma had been placed on the floor. The shelves of the altar were filled with offerings—fried dough, *koma* (brightly colored "noodles"), butter lamps and candles, seven bowls of water, and a large *mandala* (symbol of the universe). Next to the altar the "cupboard" door was open, revealing the image of Dorje Padma, the god who was being propitiated at the ceremony. When the rite was concluded, a few women served the assembly platefuls of rice and curried vegetables. The festive atmosphere continued throughout the afternoon, providing a welcome contrast to the many days spent in solitude and silent meditation.

The same casual friendly atmosphere that pervaded the ser khyim for lay practitioners was also found at Chergyu dgon pa, a bKa rgyud nunnery where most Nyeshangte nuns receive their initial training. Although both lay practitioners and cheemi (religious specialists) receive similar initiations, teachings, and instructions in meditative techniques, few laywomen ever become proficient in reading Tibetan texts or versed in the monastic ritual performances. Laywomen are disadvantaged in this respect because so few of them are literate in Nepali or Tibetan, and they have difficulty learning to read the religious texts in their later years. Although several lamas in the valley have offered instruction in Tibetan, most young girls receive only a minimum amount of education in classical Tibetan and have no time or inclination to pursue advanced studies, given the demands of housework and farm chores.

Women as Monastics: The Nuns at Chergyu

Their are several jomo in various villages throughout the valley.[25] Some are affiliated with village lamas and are trained at local dgon pa in Lhakpa or Tipli. Others travel farther afield to Kathmandu or even to Darjeeling, India, or Sikkim for their studies. In addition, some young women from adjacent Nar district come to Nyeshang to study: four are resident at Lhakpa and three at Chergyu dgon pa. The increased demand for ritual specialists and the actual shortage of monks in the valley has made the roles of female clerics even more prominent in recent years. To meet this demand, a special institution was built to house the nuns. This dgon pa has attracted increasing numbers of young women and has enhanced the opportunities and quality of education available in the valley.

Chergyu dgon pa was founded by the initial efforts of Lama Sherap Gyaltsen, a widely respected bKa rgyud Lama who was born in Nyeshang but trained at Rumtek monastery in Sikkim where he received full ordination as a dge slong (celibate monk). When he returned to the valley, Lama Sherap devoted himself to setting up the dgon pa and training several Nyeshangte nuns. Initial funds for the construction of the dgon pa came from villagers who continue to support the lama and the nuns today with frequent gifts of money and provisions. During the three-year retreat, when the fourteen nuns undertook advanced training and remained in complete seclusion from village life, the parcels and large baskets of gifts were left outside the dgon pa wall and collected by the lama's assistant who distributed them among the nuns.

Ama, for example, frequently sent her daughter to Chergyu dgon pa with a large basket filled with apples, chocolate bars, and hard candies, as well as twenty rupees (u.s.$1.00) for each of the nuns and somewhat more money for the lama. Another neighbor, whose daughter was a nun at Chergyu, often came to my landlady's store to purchase tins of dried milk, soup, sugar, and bar soap to send as gifts for all the residents at Chergyu. This woman and her husband were also planning to sponsor a villagewide feast to celebrate the end of the retreat when the nuns finished their training and reentered village life.

This widespread support for the nuns and their lama is rather unusual, since in most Tibetan Buddhist communities the daily maintenance of a monk or nun is left to that individual's family. The case of Chergyu nunnery is unique: from the beginning, when the nuns and lama first solicited funds and voluntary labor to help construct the dgon pa, the donations have been generous and have continued—an indication of the high regard Nyeshang have for this *thūlo* (big, important) lama, and for the nuns of whom they are especially proud. Nyeshangte say "they give freely, as they please" (*khushī lāgyo*), which not only provides the donors with a "field of merit" but also provides the nuns (and the lama) with an adequate means of support. This extra income from the community partially compensates for the labor loss and extra expenses incurred by households who have a "nonproductive" clergy member. It also enables young women from poorer households to pursue their vocation as a nun, to gain expertise in religious matters, and to receive a better-than-average education.[26]

The generous support of religious institutions, both in the valley and in Kathmandu, also reflects the deep concern Nyeshangte have with converting their trade wealth into "spiritual capital" or merit. In Kathmandu, the Nyeshang community gathered more than u.s.$60,000 from urban residents to build their own dgon pa at Swayambhu, on the outskirts of Kathmandu. One of my young Nyeshangte friends told me that his parents contributed the land (which was worth a considerable fortune) for the temple complex. On the spacious grounds, the community also built a meeting hall and a multistory apartment building for elderly or indigent Nyeshangte who wish to live "in retreat" near the dgon pa.

In addition, Nyeshangte as a group have helped finance a rNying ma pa dgon pa at Pharping, several miles from Kathmandu, and individuals also make regular donations to various dgon pa at Bodhnath, a Tibetan cultural center in the Kathmandu valley. This conspicuous and public dispensation of trade funds for religious purposes reinforces the community's identity and pride and allows individual families to validate their economic status in the urban setting through "traditional means." Being wealthy and possessing the latest in consumer items is not enough to be socially successful; Nyeshangte must channel that wealth into acceptable areas of "public consumption" and "sharing institutions" (cf. Gell 1986; Humphrey 1992; Ortner 1989).

These public acts of religious patronage, which lead Nyeshangte to buy up prime real estate in and around Kathmandu and then donate it to tax-free Buddhist establishments, have sparked resentment among other ethnic groups in the valley who cannot afford the rapidly escalating land prices. A number of (Hindu) Newar acquaintances complained that the Nyeshangte were taking advantage of the government and Nepalese laws by placing their land in tax-free dgon pa trusts.[27]

That Chergyu is well supported and continues to attract young women indicates that the tradition of female monastics is highly developed and well regarded in Nyeshang, and that women are not barred from prestigious and valued positions in a society where religious service is much esteemed (cf. van Esterik 1983:73).[28] The women are fully trained and perform tasks normally reserved for monks in other Tibetan Buddhist communities.[29] Although a few nuns expressed the view that female clerics were not as "spiritually advanced" or capable of reaching the same insight or level of wisdom as lamas, laymen and male clerics in contrast had a much more positive view of women's spiritual potential. Mingku, a 19-year-old nun, explained that she would like to be reborn as a lama. "In this present life," she said in English, "there is not so much *buddhi* (wisdom, knowledge) in here (pointing to her head); not so much as a lama." Mingku was an extremely modest young woman, and her views may have reflected the deep respect she holds for her teachers, and for Lama Sherap Gyaltsen who is venerated by all Nyeshangte.

In contrast, the men I interviewed regarded most women to be better Buddhists and more devoted to religion; these men were especially positive when talking about the nuns. One old man who ran a souvenir shop in Thamel district, Kathmandu, and was a lay devotee, studying with a lama at Bodhnath (a Tibetan religious cultural center near Kathmandu), made this statement about the way nuns are viewed in general: "Nuns and women who become nuns are like lama. They are respected. We have a saying that if a lama studies and studies, he becomes like a god (*deotā*). It is the same with women. Women study more and more and they become like goddesses (*devi*)." During their three-year, three-month, and three-day retreat, the jomo memorized religious texts, practiced meditation, and were reputed to have mastered advanced forms of yoga. Two village men told me that on the eve of the nuns "coming out," the jomo performed several magical feats to demonstrate their spiritual power: for one test they gathered on the dgon pa roof and levitated; for another, the jomo, wearing only thin white cotton sheets, walked down to the riverbank during the middle of the night, repeatedly immersed themselves in the frigid mountain stream, and dried the sheets by generating *tumo* (internal heat), a sign of an accomplished yogic adept. However, none of the villagers actually witnessed these events, and the nuns refused to talk about the esoteric rituals or the yogic teachings they had received, smiling enigmatically whenever I asked.

Generally, the jomo participate in the daily routine of monastic life, which involves two assemblies—one in the morning and then one late in the afternoon—when they worship the high gods and patron figures of the bKa rgyud sect and invoke the local deities (srung ma and yul lha) who serve as "Defenders" of the community and the monastery. Aside from their occasional "retreats," the jomo have considerable free time and often wander down to the village to buy candy and other small gifts for their friends and their lama.

Other jomo go home frequently to visit their families. Tsangmo, who had become a nun at age 15, would stay with her family in Tumje for a week or so, returning to the dgon pa whenever a long series of rituals were planned. She had four sisters and no brothers. The two eldest daughters were traders, and the two youngest lived in the village year-round, working the fields and tending the family's large flock of sheep and goats; but Tsangmo was not expected to perform any house or field chores. She planned to travel to Kathmandu that winter with her two eldest sisters and to return to the dgon pa in the spring.

During that particular stint of fieldwork, perhaps because I was unaccompanied (no husband, child, or assistant), the jomo "latched" on to me: they introduced me to their teachers and head lama, and insisted that I visit them nearly every day. I found the jomo to be remarkably friendly, and I often found it easier "to relate" to them than to some of the village women. I suppose this had to do with their literacy and their interests in the cultural and philosophical aspects of the wider Buddhist tradition. Unlike the average Nepali or Nyeshangte woman, the nuns were more educated; one or two spoke English, most spoke Nepali, and all spoke Tibetan. (Several still write to me regularly and keep me informed of their studies.) They were quite curious about my work, and the clerics often joked that I was really studying to be a nun since I spent so much time at the dgon pa; my hair was also cropped short and most of my outer garments, by coincidence, happened to be red like their robes.

The nuns came from families of different backgrounds—some were quite wealthy, others less so—but regardless of the families' particular economic status, the nuns told me that their parents always encouraged them to continue their religious studies. The case studies presented below will illustrate the varied circumstances of the young nuns, as well as the new opportunities this vocation offers them.

In late October 1989, when many of the valley residents were leaving for their winter destinations, I met Sange Choma, an 18-year-old nun from Chergyu, on the trail to Omde, a village in lower Nyeshang where the "short take-off and landing" airstrip and Royal Nepal Airways office were located. We shared a common goal—to purchase a hard-to-come-by ticket for the very irregularly "scheduled" flights to Kathmandu—and decided to join forces to hunt down the illusory airline clerk and make sure that our names were added to the passenger list.

I was quite surprised when Sange, a resident of Nyeshang, asked me how much farther the village was. Apparently, she had spent her childhood in Kangri village; then, at the age of 13, she had decided to become a nun and spent several years at the dgon pa above Lhakpa village, not far from her natal home. As a result, she was unfamiliar with other areas in Nyeshang. Although she was sad to leave her family at that young age, her desire to become a nun was quite strong, and her parents gave their permission. Later, she moved to Chergyu, where she lived in seclusion with the other nuns for more than three years. She had just come out from the long retreat that June, and now that her lama was leaving for Kathmandu, she no longer wished to remain behind in the valley.

Although she had never left the valley before, she planned to fly to Kathmandu and visit several dgon pa in Bodhnath (near Kathmandu), then travel to India on pilgrimage with other Nyeshangte. Though her parents and siblings were year-round residents in Kangri, Sange was not sure if she would return to the valley. She wanted to study with other teachers (and receive special initiations) before she decided whether to return. When I told her I would be leaving for Bangkok soon, she grabbed my hand and said excitedly, "I will go too." Joking with her about becoming a trader—the reason most Nyeshangte go to Bangkok—I asked her what she would do there. "I will go on pilgrimage (*tīrtha*)," she said, " and visit all the temples there, and do many ritual offerings (*pūjā*)."

For a young woman who had never even visited the lower part of the Nyeshang valley, Sange was extremely resourceful. Lacking funds for the airline ticket, which cost local residents U.S.$25 one way, Sange approached a well-to-do cousin-brother who owned a popular tourist lodge. In exchange for portering supplies for him, she received enough money to buy the ticket. When the airline clerk told us that the small aircraft could only seat six people, each carrying only five kilograms of baggage, Sange pointed to her heavy metal footlocker filled with texts and ritual paraphernalia and said she must bring it. Somehow she even managed to get that footlocker shipped to Kathmandu.

The case of 19-year-old Mingku, already introduced earlier, is somewhat different. Mingku's family, originally from Nyangkhu village, is quite affluent, with extensive landholdings in the valley and a large home in Kathmandu. She is related to many prominent families, both in Kathmandu and the valley, and enjoyed a rather privileged childhood— attending a boarding school in Kalimpong where she learned to speak English. When she was 14, she had the opportunity to hear and meet His Holiness, the Dalai Lama, as he toured the Kalimpong area where many Tibetan refugee children attend school. Mingku said she was so moved by his speech about maintaining Tibetan cultural traditions and the Buddhist way of life that she decided then to become a jomo. She finished her studies there and then returned to Nyeshang where she began to study with Lama Sherap Gyaltsen and later underwent the three-year retreat at Chergyu.

That fall, in 1989, she too left for Kathmandu and took up residence at the Nyeshangte dgon pa in Swayambhu where she is continuing her training. Mingku stays busy in the city as the urban Nyeshangte request many protective household rites, and all the regular calendrical observances are performed at the Swayambhu dgon pa. In addition, she has access to several master teachers, renowned lamas at other dgon pa in the Kathmandu area from whom she receives advanced tantric teachings. Year-round residence in Kathmandu also puts her in closer touch with her family and many relatives, most of whom are permanent residents in town. The majority of nuns from Chergyu, however, indicated that they would return to Nyeshang in the spring, and a few volunteered to remain behind during the winter to tend the altar with daily offerings.

17. Villagers gather around the newly consecrated shrine.

THE RITE OF CONSECRATION   One final example will illustrate the important position these jomo occupy in the religious life of the community and will demonstrate the interdependence of laity and clergy, not only in the matter of financial support but also in their joint participation at major ritual events. Although the efficacy of the ritual performed—in this case, the consecration (*Rab gnas*) of newly built *mchod rten* (Buddhist monuments) and a newly enlarged mani wall (stone slabs inscribed with prayers and Buddha images)—was not directly dependent on whether laypersons attended the ceremony, the overall strength of local Buddhist institutions and their continued existence is dependent on the regular support and devotion of lay followers.

The building of three mchod rten and a long mani wall near Chergyu dgon pa on the main trail through the Nyeshang valley was to commemorate the auspicious occasion when the area's first "class" of nuns "graduated." Along with the many celebrations and communal feasts that marked this event, a major consecration ritual was planned for mid-June. Funds for the construction, which cost a total of eighty-seven thousand rupees (about U.S.$4,300), came from individual donations collected in Nyangkhu and Churi villages and from three main sponsors: Lama Sherap Gyaltsen, who donated twenty-one thousand rupees (U.S.$1,050) from the Chergyu dgon pa funds, and two resident men, each of whom owned tourist lodges in the valley and contributed about U.S.$300 each.

Religious Sponsors

The funds from the Chergyu dgon pa were a form of reciprocal exchange between the nunnery and the community at large. Offerings to Lama Sherap Gyaltsen and the nuns over the years were subsequently "paid back" to the community, when the lama donated a large sum of money to build the mchod rten and the mani wall that would benefit "all living beings." In addition, the dgon pa provided most of the provisions for the communal feast, and after the meal, Lama Sherap Gyaltsen gave away cash to each and every villager. Lamas, nuns, and monks generally receive offerings from laity in exchange for their religious services. Clergy seldom sponsor large-scale rites, especially those involving the ceremonial distribution of cash to laity.[30] That Lama Sherap Gyaltsen (and indirectly, through him, the nuns) gave away money was, according to many villagers, a sign of a truly "big" lama and an indication of the nuns' special status in the community.

That Tsong was one of my primary "informants" during this interval (I was staying at his house) might explain why he focused on his own role as sponsor and that of his cousin-brother Tenzin. Nyeshangte men had a tendency to broadcast their contributions and highlight their sponsorship, whereas most women were more circumspect and modest, content that their reputation for generosity would be known throughout the village without such blatant announcements. Individual women, widowed or married, in middle or late adulthood, could serve as religious patrons of specific rituals like Smyung nas (a four-day retreat), Thonje (distribution of wealth), Mani Tangba (prayer reciting), and Chee Tooba (scripture reading) that provide merit for the participants and the community as a whole. In addition, individuals (male or female) could offer gifts to the dgon pa—typically, they purchased copper or silver vessels for the altar, new silk hangings for the walls, or paid for the repairs on a particular statue or painting of a deity.

Tsong's wife, Chimmi, was also recognized as a cosponsor of the consecration rite, since she was a Nyeshangte resident of Churi village and was actively involved in the religious affairs of the community. Chimmi frequently volunteered her labor at the dgon pa, helping to cook and serve meals for the clergy or working directly for the village lama when he needed extra help before a major ceremony. Tenzin's wife, on the other hand, was a Hindu woman from the Terai—since she was not a *nangpa* (literally, "insider" or Buddhist), she was not a cosponsor. Chimmi was more modest and reticent about her household's financial contribution and, like my landlady, did not volunteer the amount of money she had offered until I asked directly. Ama, like many well-to-do individuals, was a regular patron of religious activities. However, she preferred to donate food, labor, and smaller sums of cash (U.S.$20—$30) at frequent intervals, rather than a big one-time splurge designed to garner much attention and discussion in the community.

THE CONSECRATION   Craftsmen were hired from Larkye district several days away, as no men remained in Nyeshang capable of carving the inscriptions and sculpting the Buddhist images. The day before the consecration, villagers from Nyangkhu and Churi congregated at the community hall to help with the preparations. A few monks put finishing touches of paint on the mchod rten. Other monks and nuns fashioned gtor ma, painted them red, and topped them with dabs of white butter. Some nuns sat in small groups with village girls who were childhood friends. Nearby, a few laymen sat with Lama Sherap Gyaltsen and helped him string the new prayer flags and attach colorful banners to the white flags. Elsewhere, young and old women were busy serving tea, washing dishes, and cooking for the village feast. Children ran and played among the villagers who worked at a leisurely pace. This was clearly a community event, and everyone turned out to help.

The morning of the consecration, preparations continued: the nuns hurried about carrying armloads of red gtor ma, dozens of which were piled beneath the altar at the rear of a large tent that had been erected in a field adjacent to the new mchod rten. Large throngs of villagers (mostly women) milled about—some carrying baskets of vegetables, others toting cooking utensils. Some women made numerous trips to the tap to fetch water for the huge amounts of tea and rice that would be served to the residents of two villages, many of whom had volunteered their labor to build the monuments.

The consecration rite finally began around 8:30 A.M. and continued until 4:00 P.M., with only a few short breaks. Villagers gathered around the tent and watched the lengthy proceedings. Inside, the fourteen nuns and Lama Sherap Gyaltsen sat in rows behind the low tables where their texts, ritual instruments, and tea bowls had been placed. At the rear of the tent stood a beautiful altar illuminated with dozens of candles. Across from the tent, a large group of middle-aged women sang in unison in a haunting high-pitched refrain. Many sang with their eyes closed, faces upturned; some held their hands before their faces, praying. Nearby, young women and teenage girls tended the fires and the enormous cauldrons of boiling rice. Throughout the ritual, villagers lined up in single file outside the tent with kha btags draped carefully over their arms and money clutched in their hands. Stopping in front of each nun, they bowed and presented the scarf and a few rupees.[31] They also stopped before Lama Sherap Gyaltsen, and he quickly shook the money offering out of the kha btags, draped the scarf around the villager's neck, and gave his blessing—a thump on both ears with his palms. Then he handed each villager an orange-colored initiation thread, which is worn around the neck as a protective charm. Some patrons also arrived with sealed envelopes containing larger amounts of money and distributed these to each of the nuns and the lama.

At 1:00 P.M. the nuns and Lama Sherap Gyaltsen donned orange silk robes and red hats, and carrying beautiful silk banners, circumambulated the new mchod rten and mani wall. The lama consecrated the structures by sprinkling water, flour, and liquor at their bases. Near the mani wall the clergy began another long recitation, and an assistant held the ritual instruments which Lama Sherap Gyaltsen picked up at various intervals: a mirror (symbol of the senses), a thunderbolt (*vajra*), and a bell (*dorje*) representing the union of wisdom and compassion. Behind the row of nuns with their standards and banners, the villagers stood quietly. Two men passed through the crowd with a platter of flour, and everyone took a handful. At the conclusion of the rite, the audience raised their arms upward three times, and on the fourth, scattered the flour in the air and at their neighbors. The solemn ritual was over for a few moments as everyone ran about smearing flour on their chosen victims. The nuns gradually made their way back to the tent and continued the second half of the rite. The villagers, on the other hand, had their midday meal; the younger women scurried about with plates heaped with rice and curried vegetables, serving first the men (perhaps thirty or forty of them) who sat apart in a large orderly circle, and then the group of women (about two hundred) who sat in clusters with children and close friends.[32] After the meal, a few older women stood up and began to sing and dance in a circle as they had done during the Smyung nas retreat.

Two male assistants, holding large stacks of twenty-rupee (U.S.$1.00) notes, distributed the money to everyone present. Many women touched the money to their foreheads and lips, closed their eyes reverentially, and then tucked the bills into their blouses. A woman sitting near me explained that the thūlo Lama ("the great one") had paid for everything—the rice, the tea, all the food. Another informant, one who had helped pass out the money, told me that Lama Sherap Gyaltsen had redistributed seventy-eight hundred rupees in cash (U.S.$390) to the villagers that day, so nearly four hundred people had participated in the consecration.

When the nuns had finished their ritual, they carefully gathered the loose-leafed texts and wrapped them in velvet cloth, then put away their ritual instruments. Tea and food were served inside the tent, while outside the secular aspects of the celebration were in full swing. Middle-aged men holding pitchers of beer danced in single file around the mchod rten, singing and taunting the women who were grouped at one end. The women answered back, and several joined the single file of men and danced before the crowd. They sang a refrain similar to the men's and continued the chant back and forth. Two men from the audience draped scarves around the women dancers. At the head of the line, one old grizzled fellow danced about and drank from a plastic pitcher, which he passed to the rest of the men behind him. (The female dancers, all middle-aged women, did not drink.) In the midst of this revelry, two young monks, splattered with white

18. Nyeshangte at a communal celebration.

paint, continued to decorate the mchod rten as drunken men cavorted in circles around them, occasionally running into the monks, tipping over their paint buckets. The celebration continued until early evening, when the crowd broke up and headed in opposite directions: some to their homes in Nyangkhu village, others to Churi.

Women as Moral Agents

Several scholars have noted that women's autonomy and authority in a particular society may be determined in part by their access to that society's arena of power and prestige.[33] In Nyeshang society, trade may be an avenue to wealth and to status as a "big person," but religion is the ultimate channel for prestige and "legitimacy" (cf. Ortner 1989:143). "Bigness" and wealth from trade must be transformed into merit or spiritual capital in order to be socially recognized or accepted in Nyeshang. Similar dynamics and cultural forms appear to have been operating among the Sherpa and Nyeshangte.[34] For the Sherpa, Ortner explains that high-ranking individuals in the community could further enhance their prestige through meritorious acts (founding temples and "offering" rites) because through these practices the big person demonstrates that he is "both powerful and altruistic, capable of protecting others because of his potency, but humble in his desire to serve rather than dominate." Ortner adds, "This blending of bigness and small-ness is . . . the essence of `legitimacy' in Sherpa culture" (143). In the Nyeshang case I have already pointed out that social relations within the community are based on an (idealized) family model where juniors should defer to elders, and seniors in turn should nurture and protect those who are younger.[35] Similarly, senior or big people should be modest and humble in their dealings with other Nyeshangte, given the value the community places on egalitarian relations.

In short, like the Sherpa, Nyeshangte society hinges on this mixing of bigness and smallness, although the actual practice in terms of life cycle and gendered behavior is somewhat different. Adult Nyeshangte women as wives and mothers often carry out this "legitimization" process for their families (and their individual "selves"), while male household members concentrate on earning trade wealth until they are ready to retire. In addi-tion to concern with social status and recognition, Ortner (1989:144–47) points out that legitimacy also involves an individual concern with "per-sonal worth and value" and that this issue of "self-esteem" seemed to spill over into a concern with asserting a Sherpa cultural and Buddhist religious identity in the wider sphere of Nepal's Hindu society. Again, the parallels between the two communities are revealing. Ortner describes a Sherpa man who "made a point of wearing Sherpa dress" in Kathmandu, and who "always stayed at the Buddhist site of Bodnath when he was there" (147). She writes, "While there might be other reasons for these actions, his descendant believed that they were largely assertions of Sangye's cultural identity in the face of aggressive Rana Hinduism" (147). Today, Nyeshangte women (and many older men) also seem preoccupied with their cultural and religious identity. Women's constant Buddhist practice and their insis-tence on wearing "traditional" dress in Kathmandu may be seen (like the Sherpa case described above) as a "critique" and a "rejection" of foreign val-ues—in this case, however, it is not only a repudiation of the Hindu social order but of the western one as well.

Religion in Nyeshang survives largely as a result of female practitioners. Their regular commitment and active support contributes to the vitality of religious life in the valley and enables local Buddhist institutions and clergy to thrive despite the high level of out-migration in recent years. In Nyeshang today, there are no abandoned dgon pa, neglected temples, or Buddhist monuments in disrepair, nor is there a dearth of devoted or skilled personnel to maintain the annual round of Buddhist observances. Adult women, it seems, have picked up the slack by replacing absent men. Rituals and celebrations like Thonje, Rab gnas (*rumne*), and Smyung nas (*nyungne*) reveal that women are often the reference point for overall social relations—whether these involve personal exchange networks, sponsorship committees, or individual service as lay or ordained females. By donating food or cash, offering their labor, lending utensils and furnishings for public rituals, or in turn requesting similar assistance from neighbors, friends, and relatives (to sponsor their own events), women build lasting social ties and extensive personal networks based on mutual indebtedness (cf. Lepowsky 1990:186). Frequent gifts to the dgon pa, the ceremonial distributions of salt, rice, or butter, and the willingness to help other sponsors ensures that individual women and their households are respected for upholding the Nyeshangte ideals. As in other Tibetan Buddhist communities where we find a "cultural elaboration of nurturance," acts of religious patronage and hospitality are measures of individual virtue, and "generosity is the social version of moral goodness" (Ortner 1978b:282; 1989).

In Kathmandu, adult women also play an active and highly visible role in their community's ceremonial and social life. These public events are part of a pan-Nyeshangte effort to revitalize their cultural traditions in the city. Women volunteer to oversee the preparations for these festivals, as well as for the Thonje and Smyung nas rituals which are also held at the dgon pa in Swayambhu. In sum, adult women's growing involvement in religious activities, both in the city and the valley, has prevented any loss of prestige or authority and offset any gains made by men, given the increasingly male dominance of international trade.

Enduring Visions: The Homeland

It is largely through women's actions and continued support of traditional religious practices that the egalitarian quality of Nyeshang social life has been maintained in the valley. In the village setting, unlike in Kathmandu, differences in wealth and status among households tend to be minimized through the "redistributive nature of social life" and the "high value" placed on religious patronage and hospitality (Cooke 1985a:61). These religious traditions help to create a field of merit, a magnet or channel for trade wealth in the community.

Although cash earnings from commerce and involvement in trade activities vary greatly among village residents, Cooke (1985a) points out that urban migration is a major leveling factor since the most affluent tend to abandon their village properties and settle in Kathmandu when they are no longer dependent on the village-based economy. For those who remain in the villages, real differences in wealth are minimized by voluntary and obligatory support of religious institutions, which varies according to the household's economic status. Along with other customary redistributive practices and sharing institutions—the outright donations of labor, food, and cash to the disadvantaged, the availability of rent-free fields to "land-poor" individuals, and the shared earnings from the community orchard—surplus wealth tends to be redirected throughout the village community (cf. Cooke 1985a). Since land ownership is fairly equitable in the valley, and most households are self-sufficient in grain, the economic disparities that are seen among urban Nyeshangte are less visible in the homeland (cf. Cooke 1985a:64–65; Gurung 1977a).

Instilling Traditional Values

The discussion of Thonje rites and Smyung nas observances points not only to women's extensive control over the distribution of resources for public rituals, but suggests that laywomen serve as exemplary role models for the rest of the community. At major calendrical rituals women, in their various roles as sponsors and participants, demonstrate the proper devotion of good Buddhists who attend to religious matters their entire adult lives and, unlike most men, whose thoughts turn to religion during their later years. During the summer when laywomen regularly attend ceremonies in Nyeshang, they are often accompanied by their city-born children, who learn the values of "good works" and "merit-making" at these community events.

In fact, Nyeshang has become a refuge, a kind of half-way house for wayward urban youths. Sometimes, small groups of young Kathmandu-based men in their late teens and early twenties are sent to the valley to stay with relatives for month-long visits in the hope that they will "straighten out" when they leave the city environment—with its gangs and nightlife that encourage extravagant spending and drug use. In one instance, the cousin of my Nyeshangte assistant was "exiled" to the homeland and ordered by his parents not to return to Kathmandu for at least three months in order to overcome his dependency on heroin. The boy in question had been placed in several rehabilitation programs and had even been confined in prison when all else failed, but he could not be "cured" so he was sent to Nyeshang, where relatives and neighbors could watch over him.[36]

Although some boys complain about the quiet village life and the lack of indoor plumbing and electricity, others seem to enjoy their stay and throw themselves enthusiastically into the round of village activities: building a new bridge or putting a new roof on the community hall, in addition to helping their host family with daily chores. For these youths, visiting the homeland is a bit like camp or summer vacation: they are often indulged by relatives who know that in the village setting the boys are not likely to come to any harm. But these visits are also important as a way for these youths to reaffirm their Nyeshangte identity, to reestablish social ties between the rural and urban worlds, and to cultivate the appropriate attitudes associated with Nyeshangte adulthood.

Although the problems of "youth" are an ongoing concern in the community, it is important to point out that in the end, Nyeshangte boys rarely abandon their parents' traditions and values. (Today, some male youths just seem to get sidetracked a bit longer before taking up the life of a "mature" responsible adult, a topic I return to below.) Again, the divergence in behavioral ideals is temporal and situational and is evident primarily in the city. In the valley, many young men made offerings and received blessings from lamas, something I seldom saw them do in Kathmandu where they seemed more familiar with the locations of various nightclubs than the whereabouts of the Nyeshangte dgon pa. The hegemonic influence of morality and Nyeshangte concern with merit is also reflected in the work habits of some young traders who have deliberately chosen to avoid the more profitable but illegal trade in contraband items.[37] A few have engaged in "good works," such as spending some of their trade profits on materials for schoolchildren in the valley; others have distributed clothing to needy villagers; one young man purchased new T-shirts for every resident of his village (Cooke 1985a).

During these brief visits to the valley, city youths seem to lose much of their arrogance. Daily village life seems to have a leveling effect: many of these privileged boys shed the city attitudes that tend to disparage others with less wealth or education, those who are seemingly more "rustic" or "backward" because they lack the means (or desire) to adopt contemporary western fashions and lifestyles. In a sense, this periodic immersion in the homeland minimizes discontinuities between the Kathmandu-based population and the rural community by reinforcing this ethos of belonging to a single unified group. Many of the young men whom I met in the valley told me with some astonishment that after living with their relatives for a few days, they became aware of this common bond. My assistant, Spike, who was as an unlikely candidate for "conversion" as any, remarked: "I share my cousin-brother's bed. I eat the same foods. We are not so different. The Nyeshangte people are one. We really are the same; we are all equal."[38] This egalitarian ideology and heightened sense of unity allow the community to adapt to changing circumstances, to overcome internal feuding long enough to pull together in the face of any outside threat.

A Crisis in Values: Perceived Threats

This exposure to rural society seems to have a positive influence on young men between the ages of 15 and 25: that segment of the population most susceptible to rejecting their Nyeshangte identity and Buddhist heritage in favor of a more seductive lifestyle, one that is highly westernized, urban, and secular, one that can be summed up as living in the fast lane. City life, whether in Kathmandu, Hong Kong, or Bangkok, is exciting with its promise of adventure, glamour, and wealth. In these cosmopolitan settings, Nyeshangte youth (especially young men because they travel more widely) are filled with images of the West, from a transnational culture that is channeled through mass media: popular Hindi films, bootleg American and Thai videos, and paperback novels, as well as sports and fashion magazines from Europe, Asia, and America. Here we find images of romance, an emphasis on individuality, on personal pleasure, on freedom from family and village obligations (cf. Gewertz and Errington 1991:127, 133). For this younger generation, the lure of "imagined" or "possible lives" (Appadurai 1991) is a compelling force that pulls them away from the constraints of tradition and the homeland, and promises them a new world unlike anything their parents might have experienced or dreamed of.

In this world, images of individual success, of status and power, are ordered by the "logic of commodities" and linked to personal consumerism and the "possession of desired objects" (Gewertz and Errington 1991:146). Here individuals succeed (or fail) on their own, and the measure of their success is plain for everyone to see: the trappings of wealth are displayed, these desired objects stand alone, independently, and free of social ties, of reciprocal exchanges, of community obligations. In these cosmopolitan urban settings, individuals may feel tempted to distance themselves from the claims of friends and family and take on a new identity, renouncing their Nyeshangte ties. Although in the past a few Nyeshangte males deliberately severed their social ties with the community and lived independently in Burma, Malaysia, or Thailand with foreign wives and children, these cases were rare: most traders, even those who settled permanently in Assam, Singapore, Rangoon, or Bangkok (with or without foreign wives), still maintained contact with Nyeshangte from the homeland, and still considered themselves (and were viewed by others) as members of the group.

Today, male and female elders worry that even in Kathmandu in the midst of their urban community, younger Nyeshangte may repudiate their heritage, their responsibilities, and their social identity, and "go it alone" in pursuit of a western image of modernity. Elderly parents who are dependent on the incomes of their trader sons (or, less commonly, on that of their daughters), worry that remittances from the city will stop. The spending sprees of young male traders, who purchase new appliances, cars, motorbikes, and the latest fashions with trade profits (that should be reinvested), also distress family members. (Experienced traders know that securing enough capital is essential for success.)[39] The attraction of these modern conveniences and the "high life" in urban centers also channels trade wealth away from community projects and sets up competing claims; the young trader must choose between meeting his kin obligations and distancing himself from these social ties in order to satisfy his new and rising expectations, in order to attain a modern, fashionable lifestyle. Conversely, Cooke (1985a) reports that some of the young male traders sometimes question their elders' practice of "religious works" and chafe at the idea of sending generous amounts of money to the homeland, where a good part of it, as he observed, literally goes up in smoke, in offerings made to the temples and the local deities.[40] These intergenerational conflicts are also heightened by the new trade practices of recent decades.

Not only has the type of trade goods changed, but, more important, the values and social relations in which customary trade ventures were embedded have also changed. In chapter 5 I pointed out some of the areas that have caused dissent within the community: competitiveness, reluctance to advance interest-free loans to relatives, reluctance to pool resources or share profits and expenses across the board, the advent of "outside" non-Nyeshangte investors, and the exploitation of apprentices and non-Nyeshangte carriers who do the risky work for the older, wealthier trade bosses.

These recent developments, which reflect the heightened focus on individual success and profit at the expense of family or community relations, are tied to the professionalization of Nyeshang trade and the influence of capitalist or foreign market ideologies. Cooke (1985a) explains these changing perceptions of trade: formerly trade was generally conceived as a "function of luck (*yang*) rather than of skill" (282).

> This conception of trading-as-luck is, in turn, related to norms of sharing in the course of business (*chutsa tseba*, "to share [food]"; *mwi chutsa tseba*, "to share money"). Since an individual's success in trade is determined by luck, there is little reason for him to try and seek competitive advantage by concealing trade secrets or by denying assistance to traders from other *tshong roo* [corporate] groups. To do so would be to invite accusations of greed (*senti laba*) and possessiveness (*moree theeba*). Such accusations, associated with the characteristics which make ghosts (*mhang*) into agents of misfortune, would be considered extremely damaging to a trader's luck.

Now it seems that notions of luck and concern with greed, selfishness, and predatory ghosts have become less important, as trade shifted from being a family-based venture to a more rationalized occupation.

However, that some Nyeshangte youth seemed inclined toward community service may be seen as a countertrend that may offset these threats. Spike, for instance, told me that he wished to become a journalist, to act as an advocate for his community from within the mainstream of modern Nepalese society. Maya, a teenage girl from Kathmandu, told me that her parents hoped she would study medicine and become the community's first resident professional: a desire that reflects not only concern with her family's prestige, but also the realization that adequate (and competent) medical services are urgently needed in the Nyeshang valley and in the urban community.[41] In interviews with many families in Kathmandu, parents and their teenagers, male and female, stressed the importance of pursuing advanced education in the new urban setting rather than dropping out of school for trade.[42] Education was perceived as a new channel to power, one that would enable the younger generation to prevent their community from being exploited or dominated by other groups in Nepal as they had been in the past.[43]

I already pointed out that a few (male) traders distributed gifts in the village; others offered donations to rural schools and temples. What is important here is not the amount of these donations, but the fact that Nyeshangte values and ideals have been embraced by some of the younger, city-born generation. Although Nyeshangte youth (boys and girls) readily "flirt with western representations" (Gewertz and Errington 1991:146), in the end it seems that indigenous values still take precedence: social recognition and overall standing in the Nyeshangte community ultimately depends on how individuals use their wealth for the social good. The models, then, for many of these Nyeshangte youth are members of their parents' generation who have acquired the status of "big people" through customary channels, as well as their peers who make a gesture in the same direction.

Although the lure of the West is still tangible, so far most of the Nyeshangte youth still remain within the folds of Nyeshang social practice. Their current situation is not unlike the Chambri youth of New Guinea who also find themselves caught up in a rapidly changing order, in the midst of a global system with its markets and towns and hordes of tourists. Gewertz and Errington (1991) comment: "There is no doubt that Chambri youth would love to have cars such as the Nissan 280Zx. . . . Yet for them and for Chambri of any generation the primary significance of such objects and their cash equivalents was that they could be used to demonstrate what was essentially a social efficacy, to mark them as successful *within a system of entailments*" (146). These entailments for the Chambri involve channeling new wealth into customary exchange relationships: hosting a party for groups of villagers or distributing cash and gifts to in-laws and relatives.

For Nyeshangte youths, social entailments may mean going on a splurge like Spike did after a successful trading trip to Hong Kong: buying meat every day for his family, purchasing clothes in Bangkok for his two sisters, and spending the rest on entertainment for his friends. For these youths, the desire for social recognition exceeds the desire for "personal consumption." Many eventually come to embrace their parents' outlook that big people are individuals who use their wealth "for the public welfare, instead of (or at least in addition to) using their wealth for their own creature comforts" (Ortner 1978b:282). Although in most Tibetan societies this means diverting funds for religious endowments (282), in a modernizing context, and specifically in the Nyeshang case, this may also involve community service and charity. It is not enough to be rich: most Nyeshangte want to be associated with "moral goodness" (cf. Ortner 1978b, 1989). Although many individuals have become wealthy through trade, the highest form of prestige is, in the last instance, derived from the conversion of these riches into "symbolic capital" (Bourdieu 1977).

Here, the priorities of adult women and retired or middle-aged men seem to converge and reinforce one another. In the later stages of the life

19. Laypeople line up before the nuns to offer them scarves and gifts of money.

cycle, gender becomes irrelevant: differences in outlook and productive roles are muted. Middle-aged men will disentangle themselves from their business pursuits and join their wives in doing or religious works. Although many women in their early to mid-adulthood years have led exemplary lives and are widely respected for embodying Nyeshangte ideals, the fact that "big men"—individuals with an abundance of money, power, and influence—adopt their wives' lifestyle and commitment to Buddhist principles makes a strong statement. It provides a vivid reminder to the younger generation that they too will need to consider the relative importance of spiritual capital over material rewards.

THIS BOOK has been written with a deliberate focus on the details of individual lives in order to reveal the contradictions and ambiguity inherent in analyzing gender systems. I have tried to avoid presenting a homogenous and static portrayal of Nyeshangte social and cultural forms by attending to the multiple discourses present within the community. Although these divergent perspectives reflect the gendered interests of women and men as categories of beings, other factors—age, generation, wealth, and residence in Kathmandu or Nyeshang—are perhaps more important than gender in shaping the circumstances of individual lives.

Second, I have hovered close to the ethnographic material in order to show that Nyeshangte women and men actively engage their surroundings. Their "self-awareness" stems from a long history of crossing borders, of negotiating with powerful entities, of existing on the margins of "settled society." In short, they are agents who actively construct meaning in an attempt to live their lives as authentic, "knowing" subjects. Consciousness and moral responsibility are therefore implicit in notions of agency. Nyeshangte agency, then, would seem to hinge on conditions of relative freedom, the ability to act and think independently, but paradoxically this freedom can only be understood within the structures and hegemonic ideologies of their Buddhist social order. On the one hand, individual agency is constrained by notions of obligation and ideas about legitimate behavior—beliefs not only of what is possible or can be done, but what should be done. But on the other hand, Buddhist ideologies and ritual practices are "instruments of action" that enable Nyeshangte to transform the hierarchical values of the city and the world market.

Throughout I have attempted to show how the wider forces of change, of transcultural processes, have affected a local community; that is, how individuals within the Nyeshangte community have variously perceived, resisted, or embraced the new opportunities that confront them. I use the term *local community* to refer to the Nyeshangte group as a whole, because *their* sense of community extends beyond the homeland, and further afield than their Kathmandu neighborhoods. It includes Nyeshangte men and women: the Buddhist pilgrims, long-term migrants, professional traders, and vacationing tourists who move through the transnational networks connecting major urban centers of South and Southeast Asia.

The historical perspective taken in this study has helped to situate the Nyeshangte community in a wider context in order to demonstrate how gender systems and social relations change over time, as a result of both internal and external forces. The use of oral accounts, of individual and family histories, has provided a sense of the ethnographic conditions in the valley extending back to the early 1900s. These life histories have also enabled me to piece together trade networks, economic practices, and the division of labor in Nyeshang before the major transformations of the last three decades. In addition, the use of historical documents that provide details about the special trade privileges granted to the Nyeshangte by the central Nepalese government indicate that the Nyeshangte had a long tradition of small-scale itinerant trade between India and Nepal, dating back to the mid-eighteenth century. I hope that the broadened chronological and geographical perspective taken in this study may serve as a partial antidote to the romanticized portrayals of Himalayan communities as frozen in time, unchanging, and isolated from outside forces. The attention to local context and local history also reveals that the particular cultural, economic, and political factors that have shaped Nyeshang society also set it apart from other ethnic Tibetan communities in northern Nepal. The material presented here also provides a case study of the ethnographic conditions that support a gender system that is fairly balanced, where social relations between men and women are not characterized by dominance or subordination.

How should I summarize my overall impressions of gender relations among the Nyeshangte? I have realized throughout the process of doing

20. Laywomen at a consecration ritual.

fieldwork, of writing and rethinking, the difficulty in trying to evaluate how individual women and men are positioned in this society. Some might emphasize women's declining participation in trade or their previous exclusion from formal positions on village councils or the restriction of adolescent girls in Kathmandu as evidence of gender subordination. But two issues are important to remember here. First, we must consider indigenous perceptions: what Nyeshang men and women, boys and girls, in both the city and the homeland, value; how they construct or make sense of changing conditions; their ideas about what constitutes a "good person." Second, we must acknowledge the shortcomings of our analytical categories for understanding the social reality and lives of non-Western women and men. Our concerns with questions of equality of inequality, of dominance and subordination, are framed in terms of oppositions, which may lead to misunderstandings of gender meanings in other societies (cf. Errington and Gewertz 1987; Strathern 1987b).

In recent years indigenous folk models have been used increasingly by Nyeshangte (individually and collectively) to explain the changes occurring in the community. Although these native histories suggest that women have had a long association with religion (and men with war and trade), these historic accounts and ritual traditions have taken on more importance as Nyeshangte come to terms with new gender practices resulting from a more rigid division of urbanization, labor, and emergent middle-class values.

I should point out, however, that these gender attributes are not necessarily fixed. Nyeshangte notions of gender may be more accurately described in terms of a fluid continuum of traits or qualities, rather than as two mutually opposed categories; that is, individual women or men may exhibit opposite sex attributes without losing their gender identity. For example, a prominent female trader, widely admired for her business acumen, was said (by my male informants) to have succeeded because "she has a mind like a boy." The same woman, however, was criticized by a teenage girl because she was "so business-minded that she didn't even know how to cook." The teenage informant, speaking about her older brother who was studying to be a monk (but later abandoned his vows and married), said, "My brother would have been a very good monk; when he came home he always helped in the kitchen and was a good cook."

In both cases, cleverness and domestic skills are admirable qualities regardless of whether they are found in women or men. Although the division of labor has changed since the 1960s and 1970s and become more gender-specific, individual men and women can still cross gender domains: occupational roles—that of trader, farmer, or religious specialist—remain fluid, and individuals may acquire prestige through many channels, even those that may be associated primarily with the opposite sex.

These flexible attitudes may be shaped in part by (Tibetan) Buddhist ideas pertaining to rebirth. Miller (1978, 1980), for example, found, in extensive interviews and psychological profiles of Tibetans, that male and female informants had what might be called an androgynous perspective: they tended to empathize and identify with the opposite sex. Several individuals, for instance, believed that in their previous life they had been the opposite sex, and many felt that gender was not fixed but would vary from one life to the next. Furthermore, some of the Mahayana teachings emphasize a complementary or integrative view: that male and female attributes need to be cultivated in equal measure. In addition, the concept of sūnyatā (emptiness) represents another perspective: it stresses that categorical distinctions such as male and female, good and evil, or distinctions between one type of being and another are merely conventional and ultimately devoid of meaning.

Although the indigenous histories discussed above suggest that particular gender attributes (violence or piety) may be linked with one gender or

21. Nyeshangte jomo.

the other, in general individuals are defined primarily by familial roles, life stages (and to a lesser extent, work roles), rather than by biologically based identities. In Nyeshang, the category of man or woman is not heavily loaded with immanent features (cf. Kopytoff 1990:89). For example, when I asked informants how women or men are supposed to behave, the answers were always qualified by relational categories: individuals were expected to behave as wives, husbands, daughters, sons, mothers, or fathers, as the case may be. Male and female are not perceived as "essential categories" with a large number of inherent and unvarying features. Social identities are not seen as existentially constituted but rather based on "circumstantial roles" and "circumstantial features" (Kopytoff 1990), and are less constraining than our Western concepts of womanhood or manhood. Gender variance in roles and behavior is not so problematic.

In Nyeshang society, gender ideologies, behavioral expectations, and individual circumstances depend on local context and vary during different stages of the life cycle. Adolescent girls are not expected to be as religious-minded as middle-aged women. Elderly men are expected to have the same interests as elderly women: they should not be as quarrelsome or violent as male youths. Gender meanings change through the life cycle: young boys and girls have similar social identities, from adolescence to retirement gender differences are elaborated, then these differences fade again in the final years of life.

Although making predictions may be dangerous, given the rapid changes taking place in the Nyeshangte community overall, I do not think that gender relations will become hierarchical. The ultimate life goals of Nyeshangte men and women are virtually the same: they vary during the stages of early and middle adulthood but come together at the end. Within the overall Buddhist framework and with a strong egalitarian ethic, gender differences collapse and resemble an androgynous model, where the significance of gender is quite minimal.

1. Kathmandu Connections

1. Marwari are wealthy industrialists from northern India who have ties to Nepalese merchant communities. Newars are an ethnic group indigenous to the Kathmandu valley. Within the Nepalese caste framework, Newars are placed below Brahmins and Chhetris (the twice-born castes) but above other Tibeto-Burman groups like the Gurung or Magar. Among the lowest-ranked or untouchable groups are the artisan castes—the Sarki (cobbler), Damai (tailor), Kami (blacksmith)—and most of the Tibetan or "Bhotia" groups.

2. Thamel District is a popular tourist enclave with many small budget hotels, restaurants, and souvenir and trekking shops. Asan Tole is a market area located in the heart of "old" Kathmandu.

3. Including, for example, the well-known Sherpa. For an insightful study of Sherpa history and social dynamics, see Sherry Ortner's (1989) *High Religion*, which discusses the political maneuverings of the "big people" or local elite who used their trade-based wealth to sponsor and support local religious institutions in exchange for greater prestige, moral authority, or "legitimization."

4. Cf. Schlegel (1977:21–22); see also Sherry B. Ortner and Harriet Whitehead's discussion of gender hierarchy and "prestige structures" or "prestige systems" (1981:10–16), and Ortner (1981).

5. Although outsiders may disregard gender (and age) in their stereotypical views of Nyeshangte character (as noted earlier in the chapter), this is not

true within the community, where gender distinctions have become more sharply drawn in recent years. Individual women and men at certain stages of their life cycle are often seen as possessing distinct natures and inclinations. These differences are thought to fall somewhere along a continuum that ranges between femaleness/spirituality on one side and maleness/aggressiveness on the other. However, gender differences are muted in two additional categories or age grades: children under the age of fifteen and adults over the age of forty-five. The links between age grading and the construction of gender identity in Nyeshang society are discussed in chapter 6.

6. Paten is a two-week secular festival that is held every three years in the Nyeshang valley.

7. E.g., Lowenthal 1990; Lepowsky 1991; Appadurai 1991.

8. For further insights on how Nepalese discourses about "place" (as either rural/backward or urban/developed) serve as markers of social and cultural identity in contemporary Nepal, see Pigg (1992).

9. The nature of invented traditions and identities, historical consciousness, and resurgent or politicized ethnicities are topics that have concerned many scholars in recent years (e.g., Handler 1984, 1985; Kahn 1993; Keesing 1989, 1992; Linnekin 1990; Rappaport 1990, 1992, 1994). Here I wish to make just a few brief points, as these issues are addressed in more detail in later chapters. First, my use of the terms *invented* or *imagined* does not suggest that Nyeshangte practices are in any sense inauthentic nor that their discourses about the homeland, community identity, and solidarity are dishonest or in any way constitute deceitful (as opposed to "genuine") fabrications. A number of scholars (e.g., Jackson 1989; Handler 1986; Handler and Linnekin 1984; Hanson 1991) have addressed the political implications surrounding anthropological discourses on cultural inventions and authenticity. Given the current climate and general interest (both among scholars and nonacademics) in indigenous claims to various nationalism(s) and cultural/ethnic identities, I would like to make my position clear on this subject. Although some writers have adopted a rather cynical attitude toward reconstructed identities and traditions (e.g., Hobsbaum and Ranger 1983; MacCannell 1992; cf. Thomas 1992), and others like Hanson (1989) have been misunderstood (cf. Linnekin 1991) or accused of holding a similarly jaded view of inauthentic cultures, here I take a different perspective that draws on the work of many scholars, including Borofsky (1987); Bourdieu (1977); Comaroff and Comaroff (1992); Connerton (1992); Giddens (1979); Ortner (1989); Rappaport (1994); and Wagner (1975). The fabrication of culture, the uses of popular historical memory, the importance of "cultural schemas" (Ortner 1989, 1990b) and archetypes, which provide shape and coherence to historical narratives and traditions as lived experience, are essentially viewed as part of the creative, dynamic, and ongoing process of culture making. In this general process, agents (with varying degrees of consciousness, awareness, and knowledge) act

on (and react to) their lived-in world in an attempt to render and constitute their experiences in some sort of meaningful fashion, given (or within) the existing social and cultural constraints of their world.

10. A phrase I borrow from Anna Tsing's (1993) *In the Realm of the Diamond Queen.*

11. Todd Lewis, for example, who conducted historical research on Newar diaspora settlements in Nepal, and Newar trade networks between India and Tibet, mentions briefly that some Newar Buddhist merchants had commercial, religious, and familial links in areas as far-flung as Ladakh, Sri Lanka, Calcutta, Bhutan, Lhasa, Beijing, and Burma (1993b:165). Sherry Ortner's (1989) historical reconstruction of Sherpa migration, settlement, and "temple founding" in the Solu-Khumbu region of eastern Nepal provides a glimpse of yet another Himalayan community whose social and economic ties extended beyond Nepal's borders. From early on it seems that some Sherpa merchants were involved in the "import-export" trade between India and Tibet (37). By the 1800s, a number of Sherpa had migrated and settled in Darjeeling, where later (during the 1900s), they earned wages as porters and mountaineering guides for British climbing expeditions (24). Also see Mary Des Chenes's (1992:7) discussion of Gurung migration and diaspora settlements; Gurung men who pursued careers as "Gurkha" soldiers often served in a variety of places—including Borneo, England, Malaysia, and Hong Kong.

12. SLC refers to the matriculation exams taken in the tenth grade. Students who pass receive the "school-leaving certificate," which is equivalent to a high school diploma.

13. Although several studies of youth culture have been conducted in the context of globalization and the expansion of the world system (e.g., Amit-Talai and Wulff 1994; Liechty 1994), I found the works of Gewertz and Errington (1991) and Salazar (1990) to be especially relevant to my work on Nyeshangte youth. The approaches used in both these studies highlighted (rather than obscured) the processes of culture making, agency, and structure (or continuities) within a detailed historical framework. As with the Chambri and the youth of Medellin, the imaginings of Nyeshangte reflect the cultural mixings of modernity—the entanglement of indigenous folk models with western representations—a creative process by which native frameworks are infused with new meanings.

14. In 1951 the autocratic Rana regime was overthrown and replaced by a "democratic" absolute monarchy.

15. Of course, much of this ongoing commentary on ethnic and caste differences was stimulated by my presence and by my recognized role in the community as the *philing* (foreign) student-teacher. In everyday settings ethnic and caste affiliation can generally be ascertained at a glance—by the style of dress, demeanor, overall appearance, and by speech—and issues of identity do not usually evoke much discussion. However, whenever an unusual event

occurred—for example, when a Nyeshangte girl witnessed the burning or attempted homicide of a young Hindu bride in the neighborhood—then the subject of conversations became endlessly fixated on essential differences among groups.

16. Most of my Nepalese friends tended to place Newar, Hindu, and Tamang women in the same "disadvantaged" category; that is, they told many stories of women they knew (servants, former classmates, neighbors, and girlfriends) who had been beaten by husbands, mistreated by in-laws, or who had run away from their *ghar* (husband's home) and become destitute, without any recourse to legal or family support from their *maiti* (natal home). Similar findings were reported by Linda Weiss, who conducted fieldwork in 1989 among Brahmin-Chhetri urban women in Tansen, Nepal. Weiss's case studies (n.d.a) of single, divorced, and widowed women highlight the precarious, marginalized existence that many "unattached women" lead in a patriarchal society, where women's access to male property is largely contingent on marriage. Although the realities of Hindu women's circumstances, subjectivities, agency, and life experiences are quite varied (cf. Liddle and Joshi 1989; Raheja and Gold 1994; compare also, Oldenburg 1991; O'Hanlon 1991), their lives were generally understood and portrayed by my Nyeshangte and Tibetan friends in a monolithic manner. However, I should also point out that although my friends tended to draw a stark contrast between the subjugated lives of Hindu women and the relative freedom of women in their own communities, researchers have found that the circumstances of women's lives vary greatly from one Tibetan society to another. See, for example, Nancy Levine's (1981b) discussion of how the patriarchal structures of Nyinba society (particularly rules governing property rights and transmission) often lead to Nyinba women's economic dependency and overall subordination. Barbara Aziz's (1987) case study, which examined the sexual division of labor in a Lhasa tourist hotel, suggested that Tibetan women were often expected to undertake lower-status, menial tasks. She also points out that her earlier research (1985) revealed the existence of "discreet private rituals which explicitly illustrate the higher value of sons" (1987:75), and reminds us that at least in some sectors of Tibetan society, contradictory gender ideologies exist—some of which portray women as "low-born."

17. Land tenure and inheritance practices are discussed at length in chapter 5. Here I offer just a few brief comments: married women are coparceners of the family estate, that is, the husband and wife hold joint ownership and control over the land. Women commonly receive one or two fields at the time of their marriage.

18. I borrowed the term *knowledge holders* from Povinelli (1991:237), who examines the rhetoric and agency of Australian Aboriginal women in the Belyuen community during a period of rapid social and economic change. See also Povinelli's (1993) perceptive study that examines the nature of practice, cul-

tural meaning, and Aboriginal identity as embodied and revealed through women's labor, discourse, and relationships to the land.

19. Similar findings have been reported in other gender egalitarian societies. In her discussion of gender relations on Vanatinai, Papua New Guinea, Lepowsky (1990:174; 1993: ch. 3) also notes that women and men within the same life-cycle stage seem to hold commensurate status, power, and privileges.

20. According to the 1988 Census of Nepal, the monthly income of the average rural household (including the rental value of a self-owned home) was 1,192 rupees (u.s.$47); for urban households it was 1,785 rupees (u.s.$71). Because most Nyeshangte informants had a difficult time specifying monthly and yearly incomes, since this included cash income from trade in addition to the subsistence rural economy, they spoke instead of overall wealth: savings and number of homes owned. In general, I usually avoided asking individuals directly about *their own* trade earnings and cash holdings; instead, I tried to get a picture of general levels of wealth in the community based on indigenous categories, which subsequently proved to be remarkably consistent. However, since these data are not central to the main concerns of this book, I have elected to leave them out.

21. Nyeshangte enjoyed de facto autonomy from the Nepalese state and its institutions until the 1970s.

22. The community includes about five thousand individuals. This figure is based on the 1988 census, which reflects the total number of individuals registered as "Nyeshangte" and as having a residence in one of Nyeshang's villages. Census figures do not indicate how many Nyeshangte have permanently migrated out of the Nyeshang valley.

23. Kinship and marriage practices are discussed in chapter 5. In a cross-cousin marriage, the spouses are the offspring of a brother and sister. In a bilateral kinship system, an individual traces descent through both parents simultaneously.

24. *Tsha* is the Nyeshangte term for youth associations. The Nepali word for these youth groups is *rodī ghar*. Tsha groups are discussed in chapter 6.

25. This phrase is borrowed from Gavin Smith's 1989 *Livelihood and Resistance*, which examines the historical process of community formation among the Huasicanchinos of the Peruvian Andes. Smith's discussion of community identity among a highly diversified group of peasants who rely on multiple enterprises—pastoralism, agriculture, wage labor, small-scale trade, and urban migration—to support and maintain the networks that link households in rural and urban areas is particularly relevant to the Nyeshangte case, and is another instance where cross-cultural comparisons of Andean and Himalayan social and economic processes can be revealing. I am grateful to Joanne Rappaport, who read an earlier version of this manuscript and suggested several useful references—including Smith (1989), on whom I draw freely in this and following chapters.

26. *Stūpa* are mounds that contain relics associated with the Buddha. Swayambhu is actually a large conical-shaped hill with many Hindu shrines and Buddhist temples scattered over the entire area.

27. Traditionally, the arrow festival in Nyeshang marked the yearly rotation of all village council and community posts.

2. A Place of Many Works

1. A household refers to people who are affiliated by virtue of living, working, and producing as a unit (see Berreman 1978). In most cases *family* and *household* are the same in Nyeshang, and I use both words interchangeably.

2. According to Sherry Ortner (1989:27), oral traditions indicate that early settlers in Solu-Khumbu followed a similar pattern of hunting and gathering.

3. The history of settlement in the Nyeshang valley, based on oral histories, clan legends, and Tibetan sources, is discussed in my unpublished manuscript, "Reflections of Annapurna: History and Cultural Identity in Nyeshang."

4. See Aziz (1978), Berreman (1978), Chandra (1981:203), Hitchcock (1980:45), Parker and Patterson (1993), and Schuler (1981, 1987).

5. Apparently, Nyeshang attracted a continual stream of migrant laborers and skilled craftsmen and herders from Tibet since the early 1900s, as well as laborers from the middle hills of Nepal. This labor shortage seems to have been a recurrent problem in many areas along the Tibetan-Nepal border as well, whether or not polyandry was practiced. See also Goldstein (1987:44).

6. Most research findings seem to concur that in the majority of Tibeto-Burman societies, women's physical mobility is seldom restricted (Acharya and Bennett 1981, 1983; Parker and Davidson 1993). In contrast, in many Indian and Nepalese Hindu communities—especially among the rural elite and higher castes—notions of family honor and prestige are still linked with female seclusion and withdrawal from the "public" sphere (e.g., Allen 1990b; Bennett 1983; Mandelbaum 1993; Weiss n.d.). Although the ideals of gender separation and female seclusion are upheld only by those families who can afford it—this would exclude the majority of lower castes and landless rural classes where many women are wage laborers either in agriculture or in craft production (cf. Tambiah 1989:425)—this gender ideology is still pervasive in many regions of contemporary South Asia. In her study of market women in Madras, Johanna Lessinger found that among the urban poor, ambivalence toward female employment was directly linked to the ideology of female seclusion, values that rural migrants brought to the city (1986:585). However, researchers have also pointed out that the seclusion of Hindu women, the restriction of their movement, and their symbolic ambiguity vary along a continuum based on a number of factors including age, marital status, and role as a village daughter who enjoys relative freedom in her natal village or as a wife who may be subject to strict supervision by her husband's kin (e.g., Raheja 1994; Gold 1994; Gray 1990, 1991; Kondos 1991). For a discussion of

female seclusion from the perspective of Hindu women, see Krygier (1990:94–97) on menstrual seclusion; Gold (1994a) on purdah; and Raheja (1994b) on patrilineal ideology.

7. Some anthropologists (for example, Rosaldo 1974; Chodorow 1978; Ortner 1974) have suggested that the universal devaluation of women and women's work stems from women's closer association with the domestic sphere, where the tasks of reproduction—child care and childbearing—are carried out. In contrast, men's activities are generally considered more significant or prestigious because they are centered in the "public domain." As an analytical framework for examining gender relations, this public/domestic dichotomy has been criticized for its implicit assumptions about the universality (as well as the causes) of women's subordination and for its western bias. The division of society into public/domestic domains reflects a particular stage in the development of capitalism in the West, and is linked to the prevailing gender ideologies of the middle classes in Western Europe and the United States (cf. Rosaldo 1980; see also Kopytoff 1990:91–95). As a result, this model has minimal relevance in societies like Nyeshang where the household is situated along the main axis of community life.

8. Weeding was a "preferred," but not a "prescribed" female task.

9. Land holdings vary in the valley. Among the villagers and city residents I spoke with, there was a general consensus about the distribution of land and wealth within the valley. This framework consists of three categories: "very rich" (*ploba*) households own twenty fields; "very poor" (*tuba*) households own only one to four fields; and the majority (roughly 80 percent) of Nyeshangte households, which fall into the "neither very rich, nor very poor" (*a-ploba a-tuba*) category, own eight to twelve fields: an average-sized field is roughly three-quarters of an acre.

10. Labor demands were usually too high at this time of the year, and few households could spare a worker for the usual two or three weeks that a nang tse group operated. In addition, most households were not willing to risk losing their crops to livestock, frosts, or rain while waiting for their fields to be cut in sequence by the work gang (Cooke 1985a:54).

11. Several high-caste Chhetris from the middle hills told me that they preferred working for Nyeshangte families because they were treated well. Apparently, the working and living conditions for wage laborers were generally better in Nyeshang than elsewhere (in Nepal).

12. I use the word *yak* as a general reference term to include the female of the species, which are known locally as *dri*.

13. However, most households in Nyeshang were involved in local barter exchanges and often had regular trading partners in adjacent valleys. Regional variations in the production and availability of grain crops, dairy products, meat, salt, and other commodities ensured a continuous flow of goods among neighboring settlements in Nar, Lo, Tibet, and Dolpo.

14. In the past, herders were also entitled to a share of dairy products and a percentage of the newborn animals. Today, they just receive a fixed salary paid in grain and cash.

15. In a peasant economy, yak herds, like gold and jewelry, function as savings that can be quickly converted to cash as needed.

16. Errington (1990:7), citing Connell (1987:54–61), points out that "categorical thinking" about gender in terms of universals (e.g., sexual stratification, subordination, etc.) may obscure or distort the way gender is constructed in a particular society.

17. Friedl (1975); Lepowsky (1990, 1993); Molnar (1980); Sacks (1974); Sanday (1974).

18. The term *equal-opportunity society* is one I borrow from Lepowsky (1990:174; also 1993), whose perceptive study of gender relations in Vanatinai, a gender egalitarian society in New Guinea, provided me with a useful cross-cultural framework for understanding the various factors that enhance women's authority and autonomy as social and economic agents. Also relevant in this context is Sherry Ortner's (1990a:53) discussion of an "egalitarian hegemony" that shaped the lives, practices, and institutions of the Andaman Islanders.

19. Cf. Bacdayan (1977), Sanday (1974, 1981), and Lepowsky (1990, 1993); see also Ortner (1990a:49–53).

20. See, for example, Hartmann (1976, 1981), Beneria (1979), Romero (1992).

21. The problems of multiple contradictory ideologies are addressed in chapters 4 and 7.

22. The concept of the void or emptiness (*śūnyatā*) lies at the heart of the Madyamika school of philosophy on which the Mahayana tradition is based. The principle of emptiness states that "apparent reality is nothing more than a representation made by our mind, which produces all representations out of itself" (Tucci 1980:30).

23. Samuel (1978:50) makes a distinction between the Theravada and Mahayana schools with regard to suffering (though I'm not sure to what extent Nyeshangte do too). He explains that Mahayana Buddhists aim for enlightenment not just to escape from the suffering of worldly existence (which is the Theravada motive), but "to be able to free others from their suffering."

24. In contrast, Buddhist adepts (in the Mahayana tradition) should devote their lives to the welfare of all living beings (*sems can don byed*) and not focus solely on their own needs nor on their own individual salvation.

25. Even tasks like making beer or letting herds out to pasture involve killing tiny organisms and trampling insects (Lichter and Epstein 1983).

26. Nyeshangte do not have an overriding concern with witches (who may be male or female). They are, however, familiar with the cultural expressions of witchcraft and the forms that witches take, and these descriptions for the most part parallel what other researchers have reported, for example, von

Fürer-Haimendorf (1983) in Nar, Ortner (1978b) in Solu-Khumbu, and Levine (1982) in Humla.

27. In chapter 7 I discuss the oral traditions that link Nyeshangte women with the establishment of Buddhism in Nyeshang, and describe some of the folk histories and local myths that identify Nyeshangte males as descendants of Tibetan soldiers and, in yet another version, as descendants of Genghis Khan's army.

28. In Nepali the verb *khāncha* (to eat) is used with food, cigarettes, and drinks.

29. Rosaldo's (1974) "public/domestic" framework may have some utility in the urban context, where recently a perceptible line has begun to emerge between women's and men's work, and what Acharya and Bennett (1981, 1983) refer to as the "inside/outside" spheres. The topics of changing gender relations and ideologies in Kathmandu households are discussed in chapter 4.

30. Hunting wild game and processing hides and other animal products normally would be considered sinful as well as polluting in many Tibetan (Buddhist) communities, but none of my male or female informants spoke of "traditional" (*rol*) Nyeshangte trade in such negative terms. Indeed, because this trade in forest products is associated with an earlier period (before urbanization and mass migration affected the community), it has been somewhat romanticized or idealized.

31. However, as Diane Wolf (1992:12–20) points out, we should not simply assume that families operate as a single harmonious or cooperative unit driven by a common "household strategy." Rather, individual inclinations, choices, and decisions about routine chores as well as seasonal activities are negotiated (cf. Aziz 1978:10).

32. Most Nyeshangte are not concerned about *jūṭho* (pollution from bodily fluids, like saliva) and will share the same cup or dish with others from their group or from equivalent status groups, including other Tibetans or Sherpa, or westerners. However, they will not eat with low-status Hindus or untouchables.

33. Not once, in the city or in the valley, did I ever see a Nyeshangte child physically punished or severely reprimanded.

34. See, e.g., Bacdayan (1977), Schlegel (1972), Nash (1987), Sanday (1990a), Lepowsky (1990), Miller (1978, 1980), and Lurie (1972).

3. Foot-Loose and Duty-Free

1. E.g., Cooke (1985a), Gurung (1977a), Schrader (1988), and van Spengen (1987).

2. Throughout this chapter I also draw freely on van Spengen's (1987) and Cooke's (1985a, 1985c) comprehensive studies of Nyeshangte trade.

3. For a discussion of the trans-Himalayan salt trade, see von Fürer-Haimendorf (1974, 1975, 1981), Goldstein (1977b), Jest (1978), and Schrader (1988).

4. These fringe areas were viewed as outlying districts of various Tibetan states until 1854–56, when Nepalese forces defeated the Tibetan army and the border between the two states was more clearly defined (cf. Aris 1975:77; von Fürer Haimendorf 1975:148; see also Jackson 1976, 1978).

5. People's life spans and well-being are connected to the condition of their individual cosmic "life tree" (see Desjarlais 1992:63–64).

6. Clarke found this reference in the journal of a European missionary, Emmanoel Freyre, S.J., who stayed in Nepal in 1717 and reported the epidemic.

7. Gurung (1977a:222) points out that at one time a "gatekeeper" prevented Nyeshangte from moving through Lamjung District (a neighboring area). After they petitioned the king they were able to move freely throughout Nepal, and they carried a copy of the lāl mohar as a passport.

8. Thirty thousand rupees are equivalent to u.s.$1,250–$1,500 at 1988–89 exchange rates.

9. Allowances amounted to about u.s.$40–$50 for most Nepalese citizens compared to Nyeshangte, who were entitled to u.s.$400–$500 depending on the exchange rate.

10. The Marsyandi Trail was improved and several permanent bridges built in 1968. Since that time the trail is passable nearly year-round, though landslides occasionally destroy portions of it and each year extensive repairs must be made.

11. See, for example, Kawakita (1955), Snellgrove (1989) [1961], and Tilman (1952).

12. Although the case studies reveal that Nyeshangte women spent the winters in the Terai and other southern regions of Nepal, many of the residents of the Terai were Hindi speakers. In addition, many of the merchants and shopkeepers who bought supplies from Nyeshangte were originally from India.

13. When a few villagers (mostly women) finally agreed to carry the loads to base camp, Tilman treated them harshly: he laughed with contempt when one woman fell into a river, then chastised her for getting the provisions wet. But the author's ungrateful, ill-tempered manner immediately brought "a flood of complaint and abuse from the whole troupe of women" porters, and he regretted that he had asked for their help. The book inadvertently does much to justify Nyeshangte's notorious indifference toward outsiders; it also reflects the awkward clash that inevitably resulted when some Europeans, accustomed to the subservience of colonial Indian coolies, encountered the independent, self-assured women traders, who did not come close to fitting the western image of shy, docile Asian females.

14. Adhikari (1975) explains that the Nepalese government trade policies, which essentially prevented Nepalese merchants from selling their goods in India during the late nineteenth century, were designed to promote settlement in the southern border zone and to encourage the growth of market towns there. Apparently, the British had restored this territory to Nepal in 1860, and the Nepalese government was anxious to secure its new border with British

India. Indian merchants were required to sell their goods in Nepalese markets and to purchase Nepalese goods there too. Nepalese exports were heavily taxed, and taxes on Indian goods were as high as 12–14 percent.

15. India's involvement in the world market system during the nineteenth century also spilled over into Nepal where monetary exchanges gradually replaced barter transactions, and large markets sprang up in many regions. During this period, Nepalese villagers often migrated to India looking for seasonal wage work, and many hill tribes were recruited into British mercenary units. As cash became available in Nepal, the demand for foreign merchandise rose.

16. In addition to portering, many women earned cash by buying inexpensive rice in the Terai and selling it in the mountain districts, where it retailed for twice the amount (cf. Poffenberger 1981:72).

17. The tradition of combining itinerant trade with pilgrimage to Buddhist shrines at Bodhgaya and Saranath, and Hindu shrines at Banaras, dates back to the early 1900s. Carrasco, an anthropologist who studied Tibetan society, also noted that Tibetan farmers and nomads of both sexes quite frequently engaged in small-scale trade in conjunction with pilgrimages (1959:213).

18. Whether grain deficits were the primary cause of Nyeshangte seasonal migratory trade is uncertain. Although many researchers in Nepal have cited food deficits as the primary cause of migration, others have pointed to the need for cash. Many households produce enough grain for domestic consumption, but the local economy does not generate sufficient cash. Cash is needed to purchase manufactured goods and basic necessities like kerosene, cloth, and metalware (McDougal 1969:vi; Schuler 1977). Other than the famine, which perhaps spurred the initial traffic in herbal medicines, most of my case studies indicated that adequate amounts of grain were produced in Nyeshang. These accounts also reveal that most of the earnings from trade were used to purchase luxury items.

19. Many Nyeshangte today still follow this pattern. Each year in November thirty or forty people travel by chartered bus to Buddhist sites in Nepal and India, where they camp near the mela or religious gatherings. These pilgrimages may last from three to six weeks.

20. Coral comes from the Andaman Sea and is processed into beads by craftsmen in the Calcutta area.

21. According to Dobremez (1976:256) the export of medicinal herbs in 1974 brought a total of U.S.$400,000 in foreign exchange, approximately 3 percent of the total volume of Nepalese exports.

22. See also David West Rudner's (1994) *Caste and Capitalism in Colonial India: The Nattukottai Chettiar* for a discussion of Indian mercantile communities in mainland Southeast Asia.

23. During this period the Thai government imposed heavy export taxes on rice. As a result, a black market for rice smuggling flourished in Burma and Malaysia, and this type of commerce was quite profitable.

24. The money is often invested in jewelry and some is spent on clothing. Most earnings, however, are set aside for a personal fund to be used after marriage.
25. Several Nyeshangte women and men told me that the men of the neighboring Baragaon area considered Nyeshangte "girls" to be desirable marriage partners because of their reputed industriousness and business acumen.
26. Cf. Ardener 1975; Friedl 1975; Panter-Brick 1986; Lepowsky 1990, 1993.
27. See March (1987) for a discussion of Sherpa and Tamang women's roles in exchange and hospitality.
28. See Errington (1990:7).
29. See Stoler (1977:75).
30. A phrase I borrow from Gell (1986:128).
31. The ability of women to take part in a society's central institutions is an important variable that has been used to evaluate women's social position (cf. Friedl 1975; Ong 1987, 1989; Ortner 1981; Rosaldo 1974; Sacks 1974; Sanday 1981; Schlegel 1977).

4. Of Money, Musk, and Men

1. From Bhote Odar, it take four or five days to walk to Nyeshang.
2. The availability of inexpensive "western" medicine in India and Thailand has also eroded the demand for Nyeshangte healers.
3. According to informants, women are rarely involved in black market trade.
4. Nepali terms are cited as they appear in Nyeshangte speech. These spellings may not always conform to "standard" Nepali.
5. Nyeshangte men began to purchase gold in Singapore in 1966 and subsequently shifted to the Hong Kong markets in 1974 where the sale of gold is legal. The Nepalese government, however, has strict limits on gold imports.
6. This was a topic I discussed with many Nyeshangte youths who were angry that their group was often blamed for thefts and other crimes in Kathmandu. They pointed out that most Nyeshangte have an adequate income and would therefore have no reason to rob others. In addition, the youth groups that I knew in Kathmandu had a very strong code of ethics, and this sort of criminal behavior was not condoned.
7. Clothes that are worn are considered personal items and are not subject to an import tax. Foreign-made clothing is quite expensive to buy in Nepal, as a result of import taxes. For example, a shirt that may cost $2 in Bangkok, may be taxed another $2 or $3 at the Kathmandu airport. Sometimes carriers are permitted to keep one set of clothing if they manage to wear at least six layers of pants and ten shirts or blouses. My Sherpa assistant explained to me (in a very serious manner) that this sort of work was "very difficult." Besides the discomfort of the tropical heat, he mentioned the problem of having to maneuver in the cramped confines of an airplane toilet, wearing several jackets and shirts, and then having to unzip six or more pairs of pants before he could relieve himself.

8. Exact figures for trade earnings are difficult to come by. Some traders were reluctant to give a specific amount, and instead would phrase their answer in general terms: tiny, small, OK (thīk), or a large profit. I never pressed them for a more specific answer. Others, usually city residents, gave precise amounts in dollars or rupees.

9. Individual men and women are seen as having varying combinations of male and female attributes. They may also be linked to age and the life cycle: gender attributes are undifferentiated in young children and the elderly. This issue is discussed in the final chapter.

10. See also Goldstein and Beall's (1990) account of Tibetan nomads. The women they interviewed made it quite clear that they preferred to work and live near camps and did not envy their husbands' roles as traders, which required months of difficult travel.

11. For an interesting discussion about "productive labor" and the shortcomings of western economic models, see Povinelli (1994).

12. See Devereaux (1987).

13. Cf. Appadurai (1990).

14. These categories are modeled after Cooke's (1985a) study of Nyeshang, as well as that of Fisher (1987) who worked with Thakali populations in the Kali Gandaki valley. In many ways the Thakali provide an interesting comparison to the Nyeshangte case, as they have experienced a high rate of out-migration and permanent settlement in various towns in Nepal. However, Thakali are primarily involved in domestic trade and enterprises.

15. Furthermore, the published census material is difficult to interpret since the categories (age groups and village clusters) used in successive censuses are dissimilar and often not comparable.

16. These data are from His Majesty's Government Central Bureau of Statistics for 1971 and 1973. The 1988 unpublished census data were obtained from the district office in Chame. The total population for 1988 includes at least twenty-four immigrant households, considered permanent residents in the valley. Therefore, the actual decline of Nyeshangte is somewhat greater than 29 percent. See also Pohle (1986:123–27) and Gurung (1977a:59).

17. The overall population loss from the district can be seen at the village level if we compare the number of households in the 1979 survey (column 1) to the 1989 figures (column 2) in the table. The households surveyed at the start of the agricultural season in April and May of 1989 represent families who were still dependent on village-based revenues. Village leaders who assisted me with the census also indicated which of these households were resident year-round (column 3).

    The data in column one are taken from Roy and Gurung (1980). The larger number of households (compared to the 1975 survey conducted by Gurung [1977a:4–9]) may be the result of the large number of immigrants, particularly Tibetan caretakers, who have become permanent residents in the valley.

18. Frequently, severe weather closes the main pass for several days, and local innkeepers can earn a good profit by selling meals and supplies to a "captive" clientele. However, not all villages in Nyeshang have tourist lodges.

Population Decline in the Nyeshang Valley

CENSUS YEAR	TOTAL POPULATION of Nyeshang residents	DECLINE IN RESIDENT population since 1971
1971	5,250	——
1973	4,802	8%
1988	3,748	29%

Survey of Village Residents by Sex and Age

APRIL 1989	AGE	1–15	16–65	65+
VILLAGE	SEX	M/F	M/F	M/F
"A"	NO. PRESENT	26/29	34/77	2/2
"B"	NO. PRESSENT	5/13	8/31	2/2
"C"	NO. PRESENT	8/15	22/51	8/7
"D"	NO. PRESENT	4/7	11/31	8/14

19. Although plane service is available twice a week, flights are often canceled because of high winds and bad weather, and tickets for the six-passenger plane are hard to get.

20. Although Namgyal and his family were not dependent on the subsistence economy (their trade income and revenues from urban real estate were enough to support the family), it would have been difficult for them to take a very active role in the rural community without having access to large quantities of grain—necessary for village hospitality and monastic offerings. In addition, although there was a certain amount of prestige in owning a large yak herd, it also represented a strategic investment of Namgyal's trade wealth, an additional measure of security in case he ever lost his urban holdings or if his trade ventures failed.

Survey of Households Showing Full-Time and Part-Time Residents

VILLAGE	1 NO. OF HOUSE-HOLDS IN 1979	2 NO. OF HOUSE-IN SPRING 1989	3 NO. OF YEAR-ROUND HH IN 1989	4 NO. OF ADDITIONAL HH IN SUMMER 1989
"A"	196	58	18 OUT OF 58	+35
"B"	60	23	7 OUT 23	+11
"C"	80	37	15 OUT OF 37	+13
"D"	82	31	20 OUT OF 31	+19
"E"	64	37	35 OUT OF 37	+18

21. The numbers listed in the table reflect only the more recent immigrants who are still viewed as outsiders by informants. The non-Nyeshangte origins of other residents who have been absorbed into the community are evident only through genealogical inquiries.

Non-Nyeshangte Households in the valley

APRIL 1988 SURVEY	VILLAGE "A"	VILLAGE "B"	VILLAGE "C"	VILLAGE "D"	VILLAGE "E"
NO. OF NON-NYESHANGTE HOUSEHOLDS (HH) CARETAKERS/ TENANTS FROM TIBET, DOLPO, NAR, LARKYE, AND MUSTANG	10 HH	7 HH	12 HH	5 HH	1 HH

22. Nyeshangte couples without children usually adopt a nephew or niece as legal heirs. Polygamy is not considered an option. Sometimes, if an heir cannot be adopted from relatives, a couple may buy a child from an impoverished or large family. This child is not considered a servant (although his or her parents were paid) but is treated as a member of the family.

23. These are rough estimates. The figures for 1973 are taken from Gurung (1980:228) and refer to male traders who were frequently away for a year or more. The data for 1982–84 are taken from Cooke (1985a:36) and the percentages are based on figures given for males between the ages of 21 and 59. However, since most Nyeshangte males begin their trade careers by age 16, this estimate may be slightly low. Data for 1989 are based on village surveys conducted in April and include males between the ages of 16 and 65.

Male Out-migration in the Nyeshang Valley

AREA	ADULT MALES ABSENT IN OCTOBER 1973	ADULT MALES ABSENT IN 1982–1984	ADULT MALES ABSENT IN LATE APRIL 1989
ENTIRE VALLEY	21%	59%	77%

24. *Male Out-migration at the Village Level*

VILLAGE	"A"	"B"	"C"	"D"	"E"
ADULTS MALES (16–65 YEARS OLD) ABSENT IN APRIL/ MAY 1988	88%	90%	85%	85%	38%

25. *Female-Headed Households*

SURVEY	VILLAGE "A"	VILLAGE "B"	VILLAGE "C"	VILLAGE "D"	VILLAGE "E"
FEMALE-HEADED HOUSEHOLDS	26 HH OR 45%	10 HH OR 43%	16 HH OR 43%	14 HH OR 45%	17 HH OR 46%

26. See, e.g., Ember and Ember (1971:579), Sanday (1981:197), and Gewertz (1983).

27. See also Fisher (1986) for a discussion of women's religious roles during the winter trading season in the Magar community in northwest Nepal.

28. Mead (1937), who observed Tchambuli women playing prominent roles in the day-to-day affairs of the village, characterized Tchambuli society as being female-dominated. However, as recent research has demonstrated, when Mead's findings are placed within a broader historical context it is doubtful whether Chambri women actually dominated men (Gewertz 1983; Errington and Gewertz 1987).

29. See, e.g., Appadurai (1978), Boserup (1970b), Sharma (1980), and Whyte and Whyte (1982).

30. Cf. Acharya and Bennett (1983), Epstein and Watts (1981), and Abdullah and Zeidenstein (1981).

31. See Leacock (1978:247).

32. *Village Survey of Unproductive Fields*

1989 SURVEY	VILLAGE "A"	VILLAGE "B"	VILLAGE "C"	VILLAGE "D"	VILLAGE "E"
FIELDS ABANDONED OR LEFT UNCULTIVATED	15–20%	10–15%	10–15%	5–10%	0–5%

33. Village "C" has a total of eighty-seven households, thirty-seven of which were present in April 1989 when the survey was taken, and of these, fifteen were year-round residents.

Survey of Single Women in Village "C"

CATEGORIES OF SINGLE WOMEN 25 YEARS OLD OR OLDER	NO. OF ADULT WOMEN	LIVING ALONE (OR WITH DEPENDENT CHILDREN) IN OWN HOME	LIVING WITH SIBLINGS	LIVING WITH PARENTS/ ADULT SIBLING IN NATAL HOME	LIVING IN THEIR OWN HOME WITH ADULT CHILDREN
WIDOWED	9	4	1		4
DIVORCED	1				1
NEVER MARRIED	18	4	2	10	2

34. See also Gewertz and Errington (1991).

5. Familiar Circles

1. See, for example, Lepowsky's (1991) discussion of resistance and tradition in Papua New Guinea; see also Sanday (1990a) on Minangkabau matrilineal ideology and its use for maintaining an "enduring, ethnic identity." For an ethnographic example closer at hand, see Fisher's (1987) discussion of the "revitalization" of Thakali traditions.

2. Rosaldo (1989), Errington and Gewertz (1987), and Strathern (1987b).

3. See Silverblatt (1991), Zavella (1991), Kumar (1994), and Raheja (1994a).

4. See Spelman (1988), Mohanty (1991), Butler (1990), Abu-Lughod (1991), and Ortner (1984).

5. See Collier and Yanagisako (1987), Fricke (1990), Gold (1994b).

6. See Mukhopadhyay and Higgins (1988:485), and Collier, Rosaldo, and Yanagisako (1982).

7. Keesing (1985) and Gal (1991) have observed that women's voices and perspectives may be "muted." They discuss the political significance of women's talk or, conversely, women's silence.

8. As I later point out, dowry in Nyeshang does not have quite the same meaning as dowry in Brahmin-Chhetri communities in India or Nepal. One solution is to define these basic terms from an indigenous perspective, and then clarify our western terms accordingly.

9. I have borrowed the term *flexibility* from the title of Molnar's (1980) dissertation, a study that provides an excellent analysis of Kham Magar women's social and economic roles. Molnar noted: "It is not enough to examine stated rules of general patterns. There is often great variation in the actual functioning of these rules in particular situations. . . . While inheritance is patrilineal, . . . women may in fact control large amounts of family property when widowed, or single, or if the husband is absent from the village" (319).

10. Aziz (1978:123) explains that even after marriage and after a women has taken residence in her husband's home, she is still identified with her natal home. Furthermore, in Dingri hypogamy was common: many high-status women "married down," and this practice enabled incoming brides to run their households with self-assurance and authority.

11. Inheritance practices are changing, and some daughters receive more than the customary one or two fields.

12. The shift from a bilateral to a patrilineal type of organization may have occurred during the migration of various Tibetan groups from their homeland in Tibet to their present locations along the Nepal-Tibet border as lineage and clan organization took on added political and economic significance in the new setting (Aziz 1978:35; Miller 1958a). Miller suggests that Tibetan groups who migrated to Sikkim also underwent a similar shift in organization. In Nepal, the presence of other ethnic groups and Hindu castes may

also have been a factor. In the northwestern Jumla District and in the Mustang (Lo) area adjacent to Nyeshang, Tibetan populations have been subject to decades of political domination (and cultural influence) by their more powerful Hindu neighbors (see Levine [1982, 1988] on the Nyinba of Humla, and Schuler [1987] on the Baragaonli of Mustang). In contrast, Nyeshang remained fairly autonomous from Hindu state control until 1977.

13. Cooke (1985a) points out that the "weak corporate clan structure" of Nyeshang and the strong emphasis on age ranking and generation are characteristic of many small-scale egalitarian groups.

14. Clan members, and indeed all Nyeshangte, are believed to have in common a "shared substance" that makes it possible for them to marry and maintain commensal relations. This notion of shared substance expressed as "bone" (*gyu*) and "flesh" (*sha*) is transmitted through the paternal and maternal line, respectively. Relations with "outsiders" who have no common substance are generally avoided, since children resulting from "mixed" unions are thought to be somehow weakened or polluted. These general beliefs are also shared by other Tibetan communities (e.g., Ortner 1973, 1978a, 1978b).

15. In anthropological parlance, "cross-cousins" refer to the children of a brother and sister; "parallel cousins" refer to the children of same-sex siblings. When descent is traced unilineally, through either the mother's or father's side, the children of brothers and sisters belong to different clans. In Nyeshang the preferred form of marriage of course does not always occur, but the alliance between the two families is viewed as a tie between the children of two siblings. A similar pattern was observed by March (1979) among the Tamang, a group that practices cross-cousin marriage. March writes, "Whether an individual marries an actual cross-cousin or not, affinal kinship terminology establishes *ex post facto* cross-cousin relations between all spouses and their families" (200).

16. See, for example, Weiss (n.d.), Gray (1989), Kondos (1989, 1991), Allen (1990b), and Raheja (1994b).

17. Cf. Keesing (1975:84–90) and Levi-Strauss (1969:238–55). This contrasts with Gurung society, for example, where there is hierarchical ranking between the higher status *chār jāt* (four clans) and the lower group of *sohra jāt* (sixteen clans) who seldom intermarry (Messerschmidt 1976). Cooke (1985a) points out that Nyeshang's basic egalitarian nature is also reflected in its social organization: "In contrast to prescriptive patrilateral or matrilateral cross-cousin marriage, bilateral cross-cousin marriage is symmetrical and tends to inhibit the development of status inequalities among inter-marrying descent groups" (192).

18. The cultural logic governing marriage relations assumes that both partners (and their families) are willing participants. As in an arranged marriage, the party that breaks off the engagement or initiates divorce is often found at fault and must pay a compensatory fine to the other party. Sometimes, if the

couple is simply incompatible and no one is found to be at fault, the marriage is dissolved and no payments are requested.

19. An older sister also has authority over her younger brothers. However, there are indications that contradictory patterns are beginning to emerge in the city context, where younger brothers are less restricted than their unmarried "older" sisters.

20. There are several possible explanations for the absence of polyandry in Nyeshang. Gurung (1977a) suggests that the presence of a large Gurung substratum among the early settlers of the valley was responsible. Gurungs are a Tibeto-Burman ethnic group that migrated from Tibet. Their language and social organization are quite similar to the Nyeshangte. For example, they have a preference for bilateral cross-cousin marriage and no tradition of polyandry. But these cultural explanations may be insufficient. Polyandry is a preferred strategy, especially among the affluent and landed households in a number of Tibetan communities in Nepal (cf. Goldstein's [1971a, 1971b, 1977a, 1987] discussion of marriage in Limi, northwestern Nepal, and Schuler's [1981, 1987] study of marriage in Baragaon-Mustang). Goldstein's research (e.g., 1975a, 1976, 1978) shows that polyandry was a successful strategy employed in semifeudal societies where tax obligations were heavy and levied on each household unit. Maintaining the household intact with high labor resources was advantageous and preferable to splitting up the estate and forming multiple households that would incur additional taxes and labor obligations to the state. One reason, I suspect, that Nyeshangte never practiced polyandry is tied to the valley's peripheral and autonomous status vis-à-vis feudal states: unlike in Tibet, where monasteries and the ruling class controlled large fiefdoms and held title to vast areas of land, in Nyeshang individual owners hold title to land. Another reason may be tied to Nyeshangte's long-standing tradition of itinerant trade. Goldstein found that younger brothers in Limi often preferred to set up their own households if they could earn enough money through trade. As employment opportunities or supplementary income through trade and tourism increases, researchers have noted the decline of polyandrous marriages in a number of Bhotia communities, including Limi and Mustang, as well as in Sherpa villages of Solu-Khumbu (cf. von Fürer-Haimendorf 1974, 1981, 1984; Ortner 1989). In short, a variety of economic and political factors may account for the absence of polyandrous marriages in Nyeshang.

21. See also March (1979:60) on the Tamang and Sherpa affinal relationships.

22. Cf. Gray (1991:59).

23. Although Hindu marriage practices have always varied among classes, castes, and regions of Nepal and India, and continue to change with urbanization, education, rising incomes, and greater participation of women in the work force, these differences do not figure into the Nyeshangte discourse on "Hindu" practices or, as some of my informants say, on "Hindu ways of doing

things." See also Allen (1990a, 1990b), who draws a contrast between ortho-dox Brahmanical marriage rites and Newar practices.

24. See Tambiah (1989:417), who also cites Miller (1980) and Gough (1956:841); see also Gray (1991:64). Marriage was perceived as the completion of one's responsibilities, one's "sacred duties" that centered on the continuation of the male line (Fruzetti 1982:277).

25. However, it is important to point out that Hindu ideological formulations are varied and contradictory. For example, Tambiah (1989:425), in his discussion of marriage and Hindu women, also notes the "*positive ideological valuations* which are placed on the Hindu woman as bride, as wife, and as mother. In Hindu culture there is a positive accent on marriage as a socially necessary, auspicious institution that acts as a fulcrum for a whole network of transactions and relations." See also Bennett (1983), Fruzzetti (1982), Allen (1990a), and Kondos (1991).

26. However, if a woman bears a child outside a recognized union, she and the child have no claims on the lover's estate.

27. These marriages may be better tolerated in the urban setting. The few Nyeshangte men who married "outsiders" avoid taking up residence in the valley, where villagers, especially women, do not accept outside women into their social networks. The exception seems to be ethnic Tibetans from neighboring Lo or Nar.

28. In contrast, other Buddhist groups in Kathmandu—Sherpa, Newar, and Lhasa Tibetans—occasionally intermarry.

29. Gender images of the ideal wife as docile, submissive, and loyal are found in much of the Hindu literature and oral traditions. But also see Kondos (1986:190–96) and Gold (1994b) for a different set of gender images of Hindu wives, mothers, and daughters. In contrast, Buddhism has relatively little to say about marriage per se, or wives specifically, though various images of the feminine and of women can be found in the literature. Buddhist gender ideologies are examined in chapter 7.

30. Figures from a 1992 survey published by the Central Bureau of Statistics (1992:296) list a fairly high number of suicides among women. The data for 1990–91 indicate that 251 suicides were attributed to poisoning, 551 to hanging, 82 to drowning, 17 to weapons, and 5 to burning.

31. I find Keesing's (1981:254) definition useful: dowry is a "payoff to an out-marrying wife of her rights to her family's estate." *Nurkhal* is the general term for dowry, whereas *palee keeba* refers to dowry consisting of movable property: money, jewelry, livestock, and household goods. A bride also receives gifts from the groom's family, usually in the form of money or jewelry, often a gold ring. Her own relatives will also contribute money (*battar*). This may be considered a form of "indirect dowry" (Goody and Tambiah 1973) as it remains under the bride's control, though most women say this fund is used jointly by the couple. In addition, relatives and guests at the wedding celebration,

which takes place at the bride's and the groom's house, will offer the couple varying amounts of money. Again, this money is part of a conjugal fund used jointly be the new couple, and the offering is called *payar thapa*. Goody and Tambiah also point out that dowry (as opposed to bridewealth) is generally found in stratified agricultural societies and takes on added importance among upper-class families who have considerable investment in fixed property. Where status concerns are high, large dowries are often matched by equally valuable property brought to the marriage by the husband. This seems also to be the case in Nyeshang. Dowry practices are linked to "diverging inheritance" or bilateral inheritance, where property goes to children of both sexes, and is typically found in centralized societies of Europe and Asia, as opposed to Africa where dowry and bilateral inheritance is rare (Goody 1976:6).

In general, researchers have found that in societies with dowry systems, for example, India, sons are often preferred to daughters, as daughters' marriages involve considerable expense and economic liabilities. In contrast, women in many societies in Southeast Asia, where bridewealth, bride service, and wedding expenses are customarily paid by the groom's family, are said to enjoy more equitable social, legal, and economic status relative to men than in dowry systems (Ong 1989:295). Goody (1976) also suggests that in societies where women inherit male property (for example, land), marriages and courtship are strictly controlled and often virginity is stressed. This is not true of marriage practices in Nyeshang. Again, the Nyeshang case does not fit easily into general categories.

32. Households of average wealth may own between six and twelve parcels of land. Measurements are based on the amount of grain required to sow the land. Gurung (1977a) estimates that an average of six pathis of grain were needed. One pathi of grain equals approximately one ropani of sown land which in turn equals .05 hectares. The average land holding, then, is about .3 hectares.

33. The general term for this process of property division is *mooshi kee*. In urban families, many daughters receive equal shares of real estate, usually a flat or an entire house, the same as their brothers.

34. As a result, alliances and ties in Nyeshang can be broken fairly easily, and "arranged marriages" often reflect individual choice: if either partner objected strongly, the marriage would never proceed beyond the engagement. Blackwood (1984) points out in her discussion of similar marriage practices in Native American societies that "much of the freedom was a consequence of the fact that marriage was not heavily invested. Property exchanges at marriage were not extensive and involved only limited obligation between the intermarrying families" (33–34).

35. Sons who choose not to marry or who become monks are entitled to shares equal to their brothers' shares.

36. In Nyeshang, parents do not always live with their children. Some prefer to maintain separate residences; others retire to small houses near the monastery. But the son or daughter acting as caretaker must provide financial support and look after their parents' needs.

37. Beatrice Miller (1980), who has worked in many Tibetan communities—in Sikkim and in North India with various refugee groups—notes that parents often choose a daughter (married or single) to fill this role. Likewise, in the matter of inheritance, actual shares varied according to parents' wishes: favorite children (male or female) were likely to receive larger inheritances. Miller also points out that given the bilateral descent pattern of most Tibetan societies, the majority of Tibetans "are not particular whether the male or female inherits the family line" (162).

38. Goldstein and Beall (1980) also noted a similar pattern among the Sherpa of Helambu. In the Sherpa case, male migration to Kathmandu to work in the trekking-tourist industry means that aging parents in the village are sometimes left without support.

39. I have never heard of any inheritance disputes, nor do Gurung (1977a) and Cooke (1985a) mention any conflicts over inheritance. This is probably because of the general attitude that parents and other individuals are free to give property to whomever they prefer. It may also be the result of the general abundance of land in the valley and the high levels of wealth throughout the community.

40. I am not aware of any specific restrictions against their remarriage, but most informants just say it never happens. Most widowed women are reluctant to remarry because they enjoy a certain amount of freedom and leisure at this stage in their lives. Kondo (1990), writing about Japanese widows in her urban study, describes a similar attitude: "All vehemently asserted their intentions never to remarry. 'What? And to have to take care of a man again?' was typical of their responses" (133). Kondo adds, "For all these women, life began anew after their husbands' deaths and after their children reached adulthood. They blossomed. Free from responsibilities of family, they could do as they pleased. . . . For these women, marriage conjured images of duty, responsibility, family honor, and persevering in the face of hardship" (133).

41. If a man is caught maintaining a polygamous marriage, his first (legal) wife is entitled to keep the house and husband's mobile property and land. The second wife and her offspring have no claims on this estate (Gurung 1977a). These Nyeshangte jural traditions protect women and give them greater rights than what they are entitled to under Nepalese law. Molnar (1980), in her study of Kham Magar, a Tibeto-Burman group of central Nepal, also commented that women of many Nepalese "tribal" or ethnic groups enjoy greater legal status under indigenous legal frameworks compared to contemporary national law. In the Nyeshang case, local law takes precedence.

42. The exception here pertains to wealthy families. A village or city woman who

marries a man from an affluent family is usually able to maintain a household in the city while her husband travels abroad. These women seldom work outside the home.

43. Asking about sexual relations or the sexual behavior (of my seniors) would have been quite inappropriate. I was constantly teased for asking questions about Nyeshangte marriage practices.

44. This annulment took place according to local Nyeshang law, and the dissolution of Tsong's marriage was recognized in his community. If the dispute cannot be resolved between the two families, additional clan members may intervene. Finally the matter would be presented before the village council, which in principle has ceased to exist since 1977 when the valley adopted a national form of government. However, internal affairs and disputes are almost always resolved within the village or community.

45. Nyeshangte women and men often use precise figures and percentages—a reflection of their mercantile background, no doubt, since many are illiterate.

46. Men's character flaws seem to be expected, or at least accepted, without much comment.

47. Molnar's (1980) dissertation provides an excellent example of an alternative approach to household and kinship studies. Rather than classifying household types strictly according to a patrilineal model (for example, where the main genealogical relationships are derived from links to the male household head), Molnar's method also accounts for all household members, and alternatively looks at important female links within the unit. In many instances, women who normally would not be included in a household (in a formal idealized model of a patrilineal society) are accounted for. This would include unmarried or divorced adult women who live with parents or siblings.

48. I suspect that the lineages associated with hereditary witchcraft were from clans that at one time held a lower rank than the original founding clans, or that the women were from Nar and adjacent valleys. See also Levine (1982) and von Fürer-Haimendorf's (1983) discussion of hereditary witchcraft in Humla and Nar.

49. The standard Nepali spelling is "lāṭo".

50. The centrality of female kin networks has been reported in many societies around the world. See, for example, March (1979), Molnar (1980), Potter (1977), Jayawardena (1977), Djamour (1965), Geertz (1961), Stack (1974), di Leonardo (1987), Rapp (1987), Sharff (1987), and Rogers (1975). Some researchers have found that female kin clustering has a positive impact on women's control of household economic resources, as well as on their role in decision making. See, for example, Povinelli (1991) and Ong (1989:296). In societies where female kin are coresident or living nearby, female solidarity is enhanced, and this in turn allows individual women in their roles as mothers and wives to have more social and economic influence in the household and community (Tanner 1974; Sanday 1981).

51. Cooke (1985a:62–63) points out that the annual average household expenditure for a median-level Nyeshangte household greatly exceeded what other researchers reported for even Gurung, Thakali, and Sherpa domestic economies. These groups receive a large influx of cash from military service, trade, and tourism, respectively, but do not approach Nyeshangte levels of wealth.

52. Access to Nar valley was restricted, and I was not able to interview women in that village. A few individuals from Nar visited Nyeshang; I encountered three young Nar women on the trail near the district headquarters in Chame.

53. See also Watanabe's (1992) discussion of how Maya ethnicity is constructed.

6. Tangled Relations

1. See, for example, Boserup (1970b), Draper (1975), Levine (1981b), Stoler (1991), Klein (1983), Rogers (1980), Young et al. (1984), and Povinelli (1991).

2. This process is often described as *Sanskritization*, a term coined originally by Srinivas. See, for example, Roy (1972), de Souza (1980), Gell (1986), and Lessinger (1986). In Nepal, the Thakali, formerly a predominantly Buddhist group, have undergone many transformations in order to conform outwardly to Hindu high-caste expectations.

3. See Andhors (1976), Levine (1982, 1987, 1988).

4. Nyeshangte males are influenced by a competing warrior model that condones violence and bravery, but this model is gradually superseded by a Buddhist code of ethics.

5. The organization of these village councils (*khumpa*) is based on rotating clan leadership: one adult male from each of the four major clans holds each of the positions in sequence. This political organization dates back to the fifteenth and sixteenth centuries when individuals and families from already established lineages and clans in adjacent valleys (including Nar and Mustang) settled in the Nyeshang valley. This tradition of clan-based or rotating leadership seems to be a variant of the village-level administration found in many Tibetan communities: the terms for various village posts are Tibetan, and a similar calendar is used to mark the transition from one term to the next.

6. Several writers have commented on the importance of female networks in maintaining the fabric of social life among the Tamang, Sherpa, and Kham Magar of Nepal. See, for example, March (1979, 1987) and Molnar (1980).

7. Nyeshangte are concerned about the increasing incidence of robbery along the trails, and most women and men avoid traveling alone. Whether Nyeshangte women fear only "outside males" is unclear. I never heard of any rape or aggravated assault cases in the valley. Yet certain rituals seem to suggest that women sought protection from village males. During the harvest festivals, men form a circle and dance together. At certain intervals unmarried women are allowed through the barrier of linked arms, so that they may

present the village men with offerings of beer and ceremonial scarves. Although this dance is done with much teasing and jostling between the men and women, informants of both sexes told me that if the women did not present beer offerings, they may be kidnapped at night from their houses.

8. The responsibility for protection hinges not only on sexual differences but also on age and generation. Thus parents and adults of either sex should look after and protect younger members of the community.

9. Gurung (1977a:155) notes that in intervillage feuding, local and pan-Nyeshang councils become inoperative and no authority can prevail over factions of feuding men. Traditionally, Nyeshang women did not involve themselves in group fights and performed the important role of mediators.

10. However, since the father of one of the hostesses happened to be the village leader and a major benefactor (he had provided the house and nearly half the capital), the young women knew that their lodge would never be shut down.

11. Some of these men were village residents who were known to be drinkers or "pests" who grumbled or got into arguments. In short, they had very little going for them, and women did not treat them with the same courtesy that they normally accorded other adults.

12. This applies to Nyeshangte residents. Two girls told me that they did not belong to tsha groups because "their parents were from other places," and therefore non-Nyeshangte. Both these girls were children of low-caste (Hindu) parents who were members of the service castes—blacksmiths and butchers.

13. I have seen girls throw rocks at young men and go after them with pitchforks; the boys do not usually retaliate but do try to defend themselves. Often they have no option but to fight back. Play can be harmless—smearing flour on victims, for example—but it often escalates quickly. On one occasion, two girls jumped a male visitor. The wrestling continued on the terrace, and all three teenagers fell off the roof but fortunately landed on a bundle of fodder, just missing a stack of firewood. Generally, a third party intervenes (in this case, the anthropologist and her assistant), and things settle down again with apparently no bad feelings among the youths.

14. Although virginity or lack of virginity does not seem to be valued (or matter one way or the other), most rural and urban young women have their first sexual experiences around the age of 19 or 20, and it is often with a man whom they (and their parents) have accepted as a "fiancée."

15. Even if women leave their natal villages to live with husbands in another village or in the city, they generally have acquaintances there as a result of contacts made through these youth associations, and so they do not feel isolated among strangers.

16. This is similar to *mīt laune* in Nepali. In Nyeshangte, bonds between two women are called *roma*; between two men, *roba*. Ties between men and women are called *chetu*. In casual conversations, many Nyeshangte will some-

times use the word *chetu* as a generic term for ritual friendship; other times they distinguish between roma, roba, chetu.

17. E.g., Wagner (1975), Hobsbawm (1983), and Lowenthal (1990).

18. For example, Keesing (1985), Sanday (1990a), Lepowsky (1991, 1993), and Povinelli (1991, 1993).

19. Cf. Gewertz and Errington (1991) and Lepowsky (1991).

20. See also Lepowsky (1991:219).

21. A number of studies have suggested that adult women are responsible for cultural reproduction and maintenance of traditional ways and are accorded deferential treatment or respect in these roles. For example, see Keesing (1985) on Kwaio women; Weiner (1976, 1980) who argued that women in the Trobriand Islands held "high symbolic status" as culture bearers; and Sanday (1990a:145) who speaks of the moral authority of Minangkabau women.

22. See, for example, Potash (1989:195) and Acharya and Bennett (1983).

23. In addition to serving capitalist interests through the low-cost reproduction of the labor force, subsistence work also provides women with an independent area of control and a certain measure of economic security.

24. This topic is addressed at greater length in chapter 8. See also von Fürer-Haimendorf's (1975:291–93) discussion of Bhotia (Nepalese Tibetans) hospitality practices and the conversion of trade wealth into charity and ritual performances; for more recent perspectives, see Ortner (1989), March (1987), and Humphrey (1992).

25. See Toffin's (1982:87) discussion of the collective nature of Tamang society.

26. It is noteworthy that tsha houses do not exist in Kathmandu. Although Nyeshangte tend to live in residential clusters in town, many households are dispersed in various quarters of the city. Many of the usual economic and service-oriented functions of tsha groups in the village setting have no relevance in the city, for example, cleaning the lanes and public squares of the village or exchanging agricultural labor. For whatever reason, tsha houses and bachelor groups have not been re-created in the new urban setting. Although Kathmandu gangs are made up mostly of young unmarried men and appear analogous in structure to the bachelor groups in Nyeshang, these youth groups do not perform community services.

27. See Gal (1991:177).

28. A similar attitude is common among Sherpa and other Tibetan groups in Nepal. See, for example, Ortner (1978a). Ortner remarked that women tended to be judged more harshly if they deviated from social norms, but a certain amount of misbehavior was overlooked if the culprits were young men.

7. Sacred Realms

1. Mahayana Buddhists, in general, distinguish themselves from Theravada Buddhists by their concern with universal suffering and salvation, whereas the latter typically focus on individual enlightenment. In addition,

Mahayanists believe in the intercession of Bodhisattva, enlightened or divine beings who postpone their entrance into Nirvana until all sentient beings are saved. Theravadins tend to follow a more ascetic renunciant model, and laypersons, through meritorious acts, can at best only hope for a better rebirth as a monk, and subsequently as an *arhant* (a state of impending enlightenment) only after many rebirths. Because of its focus on individual salvation, the Theravada, which is found primarily in Southeast Asian countries like Thailand, is pejoratively known as Hinayana, or Little Vehicle.

2.   See, for example, Samuel's (1978) discussion of Sherpa religion, as well as Ortner (1978a, 1989). Sherpa practice Tibetan Buddhism, but in addition to recognizing the general range or categories of demons, spirits, and gods that are found in the Tibetan pantheon, they also have a few local deities associated with particular mountain peaks found in their district. Tucci (1980:170) points out that variant or localized expressions of Tibetan Buddhism also reflect the traditions of various clans and lineages, as well as the differences in ritual beliefs and practices of agricultural, hunting, or nomadic economies. However, all these variations are encompassed within the broader Tibetan religious tradition and should not be thought of as "animist" or "spirit cults" apart from the Great or literate tradition, a distinction that has been made with regard to religion in India (e.g., Redfield 1956) or in Thailand (e.g., Tambiah 1984). Within the Tibetan cosmological framework, human beings, animals, and various denizens of the underworld, the earth, and the sky are incorporated into the "Wheel of Life," which is governed by the hegemonic principles of karma (and the accumulation of merits and demerits that affect the rebirth of all living things. This division into categories of "beings" is widely recognized in the Tibetan culture area, so that local mountain or river gods are simply classed as types of celestial or underworld spirits, respectively, and treated accordingly. For further details on Tibetan cosmologies and categories of existence, see Ortner (1978b).

3.   Holmberg (1989:57), who worked in Tamang communities, reported similar obscene exchanges between clan brothers and sisters who taunted one another with accusations of incest during collective rites for clan deities (cf. Schlegel [1990] on Hopi ritual mocking between classificatory brothers and sisters). According to Holmberg, the village headman, who was embarrassed and concerned that outsiders (Hindus and foreigners) would be extremely critical of such behavior, put an end to this tradition. Although no informants suggested that Nyeshangte were worried about outsiders' opinions, a similar concern may have ended these performances in other Nyeshang villages. Like *aruru*, with its parodies of domestic behavior and obscenities, the Tamang's sexual taunts among clan members is a form of reversal, exemplifying carnival-like behavior that would never occur in ordinary circumstances. Schlegel (1990), who observed similar behavior among the Hopi, explains that this ritual denigration between clan brothers and sisters is "a warning

against improper clan relationships. Gross unbridled sexuality becomes a metaphor for unregulated conduct generally, not just incest but any free play of various passions that disrupts harmonious relations and expressions of antisocial feelings that are better suppressed" (38). In many societies, anthropologists have observed that rituals of rebellion, revitalization, or reversal occur along stress points or areas of structural tension (cf. Ostor 1984; Obeyesekere 1984; Kapferer 1979; Marriott 1966; Bateson 1958; Leach 1958). With the Hopi and Tamang, ritual mocking highlights the tensions surrounding clan relationships. In the Nyeshang case, the performance of aruru highlights the central relationship between husband and wife and the primacy of the nuclear unit over other forms of social bonds. This performance, with its parody of the submissive Hindu wife, also shows how gender representations are used to mark ethnic identity, distinguishing the assertive, Nyeshangte housewife from her Hindu counterpart. In this performance, the usually reserved, "morally correct" adult Nyeshangte woman is depicted as slightly out of control, oversexed, and promiscuous, whereas her husband is shown as a passive victim who can only retreat to a corner and cry over his wife's unfaithful behavior. Both male and female gender representations here are reversed. The Nyeshangte male is anything but passive; rather, he is hot-tempered, quick to anger, and more likely to engage in immoral behavior (smoking, drinking, adultery, and so on) than the average adult woman. The dramatization of these male and female roles highlights the fact that men are reliant on their wives to look after their own interests while they are away. This too may be an expression of the inherent tensions between monogamous nuclear units, who reside neolocally, and the tradition of patrilineal land inheritance. A man can never be sure that he is passing his land on to his real sons, and in the absence of joint families, wives are not supervised by in-laws or other patrilineal kin.

4. In contrast to Thai villages, where Brahmanic ritual specialists perform many household rituals, or in other Nepalese communities, where jhankri (shaman) perform protective rites and individual observances, in Nyeshang lamas handle both the monastic and household rituals.

5. This would fit with Tucci's historical studies of the neighboring Kali Gandaki and Lo regions. Tucci (1956) suggests that rNying ma pa and bKa rgyud pa figures constituted a second wave of Buddhism in the area, somewhat later than the first Sa skya pa lamas who were active in the fifteenth century (14). Subsequent biographies suggest that these later lamas wandered throughout the region, converting local people and stopping the practice of animal sacrifices that was common in Nyeshang, Nar, Thak Khola.

6. Differences among the old unreformed sects (rNying ma pa, bKa rgyud pa, Sa skya pa) are rather minor; the most marked contrasts in outlook, methods, and philosophy lie instead between the rNying ma pa and the *dGe lugs pa*, a reformed order that is strictly celibate and has been closely intertwined with

the political history of Tibet. The dGe lugs pa were associated with the large hierarchical and powerful monastic institutions of pre-1959 Tibet and affiliated with the Dalai Lamas, the paramount temporal and spiritual leaders of traditional Tibet. In contrast, rNying ma and bKa rgyud have a tradition that may be described as antischolastic, anticlerical: one populated with powerful magicians, crazy yogis, wandering saints and poets who flaunt society's rules and literally turn many Buddhist teachings upside down (Beyer 1978). For a discussion of sectarian differences between the rNying ma pa, the bKa rgyud pa, and the dGe lugs pa sects, see Tucci's *Religions of Tibet* (1980: especially 29–33, 47–76) for an excellent overview. In general, the sects differ in details of ritual practice, tending to focus on liturgies of one particular deity or Buddha family, and each has developed its own collection of textual commentaries, biographies, and histories of prominent masters (Snellgrove 1981:38). The bKa rgyud pa tradition, for example, may be traced to a series of outlandish characters beginning with Tilopa, an eccentric Indian ascetic and tantric practitioner from Bengal who renounced all social conventions and moral laws, believing that in his enlightened state such distinctions as evil and good no longer exist. From Tilopa, through his disciple Naropa, a Brahmin from Kashmir, these insights were in turn passed to Mar pa, a Tibetan householder, and to his own students, of whom Mi la ras pa was undoubtedly the greatest. Mi la ras pa achieved considerable fame as a wandering poet during the eleventh century. His teachings, which "mocked established traditions of monastic institutions," were expressed through the bawdy and often obscene "language, riddles, and songs of the marketplace" (Beyer 1978:241); these teachings represent perhaps the fullest expression of the tantric heritage, which began with a few eccentric Bengali ascetics and culminated in a line of slightly crazy Tibetan saints whose wild adventures, miraculous feats, and entertaining stories form a significant part of the oral folklore in Tibetan communities today.

7. Historians of Tibetan religions distinguish between two forms of Bon religion: an earlier form that was a funereal and sacrificial cult associated with the early Tibetan kings, and a secondary Bon revival that developed in the eleventh century alongside Buddhism and incorporated many Buddhist elements into its pantheon and ritual practice (see Kvaerne 1974; Bannerjee 1981). Two kinds of Bon existed: Black Bon, whose practitioners sacrificed animals, and White Bon, who substituted effigies (paper and dough) during rituals.

8. *Lhosar*, or New Year celebrations, are held in October in Nyeshang where villagers follow the old agricultural calendar. In contrast, most Tibetans hold Lhosar festivities during February, the beginning of the Tibetan royal calendar.

9. Ritual daggers, swords, and other "implements of war" used to battle demons are invested with magic powers. Usually *mantra* (sacred formula) and various

invocations are recited over the dagger. Over the course of years, these *phur pa* become animated with a force of their own and may be dangerous to laypersons or novice clerics who do not have the power to control these magic weapons.

10. Nyeshangte often perform rites for the well-being of a number of living Buddhist figures, especially the living saints or reincarnations (*sprul sku*, or *tulku*) who head various dgon pa in Nepal, India, and Sikkim. This form of worship or honor does not follow sectarian lines.

11. Various stages of the rite are called *dupde, tsengi, mani trungyu,* and *shembara.*

12. *Linga* are used as support structures that contain and trap the soul of enemies or demons. The linga may represent human or animal figures (as a type of ransom or bait). Linga made of dough or paper replaced human scapegoats which, centuries ago, were regularly sacrificed. For additional details about Tibetan sacrificial practices (human and animal), see Bannerjee (1981:11–12), Bell (1931:8), David-Neel (1971:205), Ekvall (1964:21–33), and Tucci (1980:15).

13. This dgon pa is actually a combined bKa rgyud-rNying ma institution: images of Padmasambhava, the rNying ma pa saint, are found alongside principal bKa rgyud figures near the main altar.

14. This period of training during adolescence and young adulthood has its parallels in the tradition of monkhood in Thailand, where young men spend several months at the monastery as monks before they assume the role of married householder. Nyeshangte boys and girls often enter monastic institutions like Koppan near Kathmandu because the education is good and the tuition and living costs are less expensive than secular boarding schools.

15. I never heard of any nuns who broke their vows in Nyeshang. In contrast, several young men told me that they had been tawa (novice monks) but had left the monastery. Most of these former monks were now traders in Kathmandu; a few were married.

16. Some of these women were ordained nuns, others were married householders. Contemporary figures include the wife of Lama Urgyen at Ngagi dgon pa near Kathmandu, and the head nun and teacher at Chergyu dgon pa in Nyeshang.

17. In contrast, intermediate categories like *mae chi* (celibate laywomen) were regarded with some ambivalence in Thailand, where the rigidly defined social order consisted of only two statuses (ordained monk or married householder) (van Esterik 1983).

18. It is difficult for women in Theravadin countries to receive full ordination, since monastic institutions are primarily associated with male clergy. Women do have important roles as lay practitioners: they can support Buddhist institutions by donating food or by offering their sons (cf. Keyes 1984).

19. dGe lugs pa, a reformed Tibetan sect, does have a tradition of female monasticism, but gender hierarchy seems to be more pronounced than in the unreformed rNying ma pa sect.

20. However, renunciation has always been an option in Nyeshang and in many other Himalayan Tibetan communities.

21. Tsomo (1987) observes that in the Tibetan religious literature, one may find passages where even prominent and accomplished female practitioners express negative attitudes about the female state. Tsomo explains that these women "still cite the disadvantages of enforced dependence and vulnerability to pregnancy as making the female state less desirable both from a worldly and religious point of view. Women even today are seen as requiring more protection and entitled to less personal freedom than men" (90).

    Similar reservations about women's "vulnerability" and need for protection have been cited by some Nyeshangte men and women of various ages as reasons why "a son's life is better than a daughter's." Some men, when asked if they would prefer the life of a woman or a man, said that they would prefer being reborn as males because women are more vulnerable. In contrast, most adult women, when asked if they could choose between being a male or a female, said that they were quite content with their lives as women. None wished she were a man or had a man's life. Only a few teenage girls in Kathmandu said that they wished they had been born as boys, so they would be able to go out as they pleased without parental restrictions.

22. For example, Mumford (1989) also writes that "the rich/poor distinction also signifies degrees of liberation. . . . a meager birth is assumed to have been deserved by one's past evil deeds" (48). It is difficult to know how widespread these views are in Gyasumdo, and whether they are shared by males and females alike, by old and young. Mumford does not address this issue. In Nyeshang, I never heard any comments linking wealth to one's deeds in a former life. In fact, wealthy traders are considered to be the primary candidates for a bad rebirth, and many traders compensate by using their wealth to purchase religious merit. The views about Tibetan women and their social and religious status are varied. In a reversal of her earlier work (1978) that emphasized the strong economic and social roles of Tibetan women, Aziz suggests in her 1987 case study that Tibetan women's subordination is evident in the sexual division of labor (at this particular hotel). This subordination, she argues, conforms to the overall cultural attitudes reflected in the Tibetan language, where the term for "woman" or the female pronoun may be translated as *low-born*. Miller (1978, 1980) disagrees, arguing that gender relations in most Tibetan communities are egalitarian.

23. Here I include married village lamas and male and female laypersons who assist at dgon pa rituals. Many of the male lay devotees study the Tibetan texts and learn the intricate rituals associated with text recitation (playing instruments, hand symbols [*mudra*], during retreats held at ser khyim dgon pa, the religious community for householders). Although women attend retreats and learn meditation practices, few middle-aged women in Nyeshang are capable of reading classical Tibetan; therefore these female lay practition-

ers simply sit inside the dgon pa during a ritual performance or volunteer to serve tea and food for the nuns and monks.

24. See also Beatrice Miller (1958b, 1961, 1974) on the nature of Tibetan monasticism and the relationship between clergy and laypersons in Tibetan communities.

25. By "state," I am referring to the central Tibetan state that had its nucleus of power at Lhasa and Shigatse, two large urban centers where several important monasteries were located.

26. Samuel notes that shamanic religious practices exist at the village level in peasant societies in South Asia where state control was limited to financial extraction. Nyeshang is a good example.

27. The apparent revival of the old unreformed sects in the northern areas of Nepal indicates that these shamanic tantric traditions are still strong (Tucci 1956, 1977; Samuel 1978; Snellgrove [1961] 1989). The secondary resurgence of religious activity in areas like Nyeshang, Mustang, and Thak Khola during the past fifty years reflects increased levels of wealth and a concern with establishing a strong cultural and ethnic identity during a period marked by accelerated change and widespread displacement (cf. Fisher 1987; Samuel 1978). For example, among the Thakali, a Tibeto-Burman ethnic group residing in the neighboring Kali Gandaki area, Buddhism and ancestor/clan worship are beginning to make an appearance again, after several decades of "Hinduization." The Thakali made their fortunes as government-appointed middlemen in the Tibetan-Nepal salt/grain trade and attempted to emulate high-caste Hindus, changing their Tibetan Buddhist lifestyle—religion, dress, diet, even clan names and history—to a predominantly Hindu way of life. In the past decade, a revitalization of Thakali culture and a return to Buddhist practices has been reported (see, for example, Fisher 1987). Samuel (1978) notes that a return to local shamanic tradition is a form of millenarian movement: "Shamanic vision is the primary means of initiating major transformations" and is "typical of millenarian movements through which these societies adjust to rapid social change" (383). One might expect under such circumstances to see an increased participation by women or other categories or classes of individuals that were marginalized by the mainstream religious hierarchy (cf. Lewis 1975).

28. See also Mumford (1989) on Bon practices in Gyasumdo.

29. I use the term pre-Buddhist with some qualifications. Bon and shamanic traditions were widespread throughout Tibet and adjacent regions of Nepal. In many areas, Bon and the unreformed Tibetan sects were virtually indistinguishable in doctrine or ritual practice (Tucci 1980).

30. The symbolic association of the male gender with compassion and the female with wisdom in the Tantric philosophy presents an interesting reversal to the gender symbolism found in many other cultures.

31. Hybrid construction is a term coined by Bakhtin (1984) to refer to multiple lay-

ers of meaning that stem from the interaction of past and present "dialogues" or views of history. Bakhtin suggests that older words, myths, and images may fuse with more recent layers to form new cultural meanings or that these layers may remain separate and stand in opposition to one another. For example, Mumford (1989) uses Bakhtin's framework to argue that the ancient primeval Bon sacrifices and ritual traditions are a source of ambivalence and conflict for modern-day Tibetan Buddhists and Gurung in Gyasumdo, a region adjacent to Nyeshang. Although I find the term *hybrid construction* particularly useful to characterize the syncretic, creative impulses that have shaped local expressions of Tibetan Buddhism, I think Mumford has overstated the level of conflict between these various traditions and sects. These problematics have little relevance for the average villager of Nyeshang or, I suspect, of Gyasumdo, who goes about his or her religious practice relatively untroubled by the apparent philosophical paradoxes or contradictions.

32. As I have indicated elsewhere, an alternative androgynous model exists where gender distinctions are irrelevant. To some extent, the contradictions between different levels of gender meaning are resolved when they are placed in the context of successive stages in an individual's life cycle. Gender distinctions, for example, are not elaborated among young children or among the elderly; both these age categories or classes are referred to by a gender-free term.

33. Ama explained that the house next door, which belonged to the "king's family," was unavailable for the opening ceremony since its roof was covered with huge piles of drying fodder.

8. With Only the Body of a Woman

1. The complex relationship between action, agents, and systems was defined succinctly in Marshall Sahlins's phrase: "the practice of the structure and the structure of the practice" (1981:79).

2. Not only do effects have a way of slipping beyond actors' controls, but we may assume that although individuals are motivated by personal goals and desires, their actions nevertheless still contribute to the reproduction of the social order.

3. Individuals that are "in society," as Nyeshangte would say, are fairly well "socialized" and their range of aspirations, desires, and intentions are likely to be in accord with conventional expectations or principles. To the extent that they are not "going against the grain," they may feel less circumscribed within the social order than someone who is "undersocialized." However, it is important to remember that Nyeshangte tolerate a high level of independence and individuality bordering on eccentricity. They generally feel that the law of karma supersedes local conventions, and that in the end, every individual has to work out her own fate and take account of her own actions.

4. Although agents may be aware of their behavior, they do not necessarily see the "entire picture" or necessarily set out with the deliberate intention to pro-

duce or reproduce "structures." On the question of "intention" and its relation to agency, I find Giddens a bit slippery or evasive. Perhaps I am just misreading him. However, in some of his earlier works (e.g., 1979, 1981), agency seemed conditional on there being some kind of choice: that the agent could choose among possibilities for a course of action; in short, that the agent "could have acted otherwise." Indeed, this seems similar to Sen's (1990) position that an agent is someone who conceives of other possibilities or objectives, who has the necessary opportunity "to think freely and act freely" (148). Sen is quick to point out, of course, that "our actual agency role is often overshadowed by social rules and conventional perceptions of legitimacy" (148). To return to Giddens and the problems of intention, in a later work (1984) he seems to sidestep this issue by displacing intention from the agency formula.

5. O'Hanlon (1988) suggests that "we should look for resistances of a different kind: dispersed in fields we do not conventionally associate with the political" and explains that "even withdrawal from or simple indifference to the legitimating structures of the political, with their demand for recognition of the values and meaning which they incessantly manufacture, can be construed as a form of resistance" (223).

6. Replying to a critic, Mascia-Lees, Sharpe, and Cohen (1991) note that "like many advocates of postmodernism, . . . [she] fetishizes the Cartesian subject: even as she seeks to come to terms with its absence, she gives it new life as a phallic concept, an inadequate talisman for what has been lost, a substitution for a historical sense of self that we can never really know" (403).

7. Lack of space prevents me from providing more detail, except to say that one narrative account relates the marriage and divorce of an evangelical Christian woman who challenges her abusive husband (who also had an incestuous relationship with their daughter) on moral grounds. Mahoney and Yngvesson (1992) explain: "Her self-assertion reaffirmed the religious and legal structures that shaped her self-understanding as submissive and dutiful and consolidated the networks within which she lived her life, even as she constructed a space for self-assertion" (69).

8. The term *dispositions* used here may be linked to what Giddens (1984) calls "memory traces"; that is, he refers to the memory traces as the schemas or principles that are embedded in actors' heads (Nyeshangte would say hearts). These patterns then represent for Giddens the various structures that shape human action and behavior. These structures are only "virtual" in the sense that they do not exist "on the ground" exactly, except in the form of conscious principles. In some sense, the dispositions that Bourdieu (1977) speaks about in the context of habitus might also be applied here. The problem, as I mentioned earlier, is that his scheme, although attractive for focusing on the largely ignored tacit dimension of cultural forms, does not easily accommodate the hyperawareness that sometimes occurs in contexts where communities have undergone rapid change and sudden dislocations, for example, the

sudden increase in wealth, urbanization, and so on, that most Nyeshangte have had to face within the last two decades.

9. As Ortner (1989) points out, some actors may simply be doing the traditional thing without giving it much thought. But the "meanings" of these unreflective actions will escape their authors, in the sense that other politicized values are imputed to "tradition" and ritual behavior.

10. I am not implying any criticism here, but instead acknowledging that these various perspectives on subject-actors may have relevance in some contexts and not others; for example, Haynes and Prakash (1991) write, "Resistance . . . should be defined as those behaviors and cultural practices by subordinate groups that contest hegemonic social formations, that threaten to unravel the strategies of domination; 'consciousness' need not be essential to its constitution" (3). Gordon (1988) and Forbes (1988) were both criticized for clothing their female subjects in "masculine" garb, with all the rights, prerogatives, and so on, that this entails (see Scott 1990; Kumar 1994). But it would not take me long to identify individual Nyeshangte women who are recognized as "heroic" or "masculinized" ("with the mind of a boy"), and other women and men who may act without "thinking." On the one hand, their actions may reproduce traditional practices; on the other, their actions may drive the Nepalese state and customs agents crazy while they are simply going about their usual business routines. "Resistance" without deliberate "consciousness," as Haynes and Prakash state above, may in the end produce similar effects as staged or more "public" contestations.

11. The written words or Tibetan letters are thought to have an intrinsic power. The mantra or sacred syllables are released in the wind, bringing merit to the household.

12. Young children are sometimes buried, and the memorial feast occurs six months later. Most funerary rites follow the same pattern. On the first day, the relatives gather around the corpse as the lama reads the funeral (*bardo*) texts and urges the deceased to accept his death and to leave his home to begin the journey toward rebirth. This recitation is repeated for three days, and then the corpse is cremated near the river. After the cremation, the lama also performs an exorcism in the home to ensure that the demonic spirits attracted by death do not also seize the living. For forty-nine days the texts are read weekly to guide the deceased through the afterlife. During this period, a family makes several offerings to gain merit for the deceased. Immediately after the cremation, rice balls (*tsog*) are passed out in the village. A few days after the cremation, two family members distribute large quantities of rice (sometimes wheat) to every household in an adjacent village. This offering rite (Thonje) settles any lingering debts and generates additional merit for the dead. On the last day, a final severance rite is done at the dgon pa, where a paper effigy (*linga*) of the deceased is burned to release his consciousness. One year after the death, another memorial rite is performed in

the home by the village lama, and only the immediate family and close friends attend.

13. See also Kathryn March's (1987) discussion of the centrality of women in hospitality and exchange in Sherpa and Tamang societies.

14. Cooke reports that several households gave as much as twenty pree of flour for regular small-scale observances (1985a:270).

15. A point should be made about differing motives for sponsorship. On the one hand, many city residents still have strong affective ties to their village communities and derive satisfaction from meeting their household responsibilities. On the other hand, religious patronage in the village arena is more cost-effective in terms of money spent and merit accumulated; village patronage is also within the reach of median-level traders who cannot compete with the lavish gestures of Kathmandu's wealthiest families who donate several thousand dollars to support Nyeshangte institutions in the city. In the village, sponsors can spend several hundred dollars on an event and still derive similar benefits, in terms of merit and enhanced social standing.

16. Sponsorship rotation and rites of distribution are restricted between clusters of villages, so that Nyangkhu, Churi, and Tumje form one unit, and the other villagers at the opposite end of the valley form another cooperative unit. In general, only clergy attend Thonje rites throughout the valley; villagers, on the other hand, attend only the events held at "reciprocating" villages.

17. Sponsors consult lamas to determine which commodity would be most auspicious to distribute; usually it is rice, although sometimes it is salt, butter, or, less commonly, money.

18. The blessings are conveyed by several lamas who sit side by side in a line. Villagers stop before each lama and offer him five to ten rupees (the lamas make change quickly from the piles of bills in front of them). The blessings and long-life empowerment are conveyed at each station: a magic arrow is waved to ward off demons, the next lama blasts a horn which accomplishes the same task, then the individual is anointed with consecrated water and oil, followed by an oblation of beer which is poured in the villager's cupped palm and then swallowed; next, the layperson receives a *tseril* (power pellet), and at the final stop, the lama ties an initiation thread around the villager's neck. Villagers told me that they feel invigorated and protected from harm after receiving dbang (*ong*). I also felt reassured after receiving various initiations during my stay in the homeland and worried less about the dangers of crossing some of the eighteen-thousand-foot passes on my trips to neighboring valleys.

19. In Tungtar, a smaller village with less wealth, Smyung nas is organized somewhat differently. Participants (mostly women) bring their own contributions of tsampa, tea, butter, uncooked rice, wheat, and potatoes for the communal meals. Four or five participants take turns cooking and serving meals to clergy and fellow renunciants.

20. At the retreat dgon pa, monks and nuns were grouped together and performed the same roles during the ritual. At larger dgon pa where more clergy gather, it is customary to have nuns and monks seated in long rows facing each other.

21. Miller (1980) explains that on pilgrimages, individuals may temporarily free themselves from domestic and familial responsibilities. Spouses may be left behind, and individuals on pilgrimage are also free of any contractual obligations or vows (162).

22. The longer life spans of women also probably account for the predominance of elderly females at ser khyim.

23. This pattern has been reported elsewhere in Nepal; see, for example, Fisher's (1987) discussion of Buddhist Magar communities in northwest Nepal. In many Himalayan communities, religious activities peak during the winter months, a time when agricultural chores are minimal. However, in many regions of northern Nepal, since adult males generally engaged in migratory trade or wage work in lower altitudinal zones, it was left up to the adult women and the elderly of both sexes to maintain the community's religious traditions. A similar observation was reported by Jones and Jones (1976) for the Limbu of eastern Nepal, where seasonal male migration and long-term employment as mercenary soldiers led to women's increased participation in community religious events.

24. The lama in charge of Nyi dgon pa has a large following, and though there are other ser khyim in the valley, this one seemed to be the most popular with Nyangkhu and Churi villagers. As a young boy, the lama had studied with the renowned Lama Tenzin at Lhakpa village (as had Lama Yeshe), but when the master died, neither disciple wished to stay in Lhakpa. Lama Yeshe continued his studies at a bKa rgyud institute in Sikkim, and Lama Nima studied with a local rNying ma pa lama near Nyangkhu village. Lama Nima subsequently trained his three daughters to become jomo.

    Westerners do not visit these serkyim or stay at Nyeshangte dgon pa for religious training. A few trekkers may hike up to one of the dgon pa overlooking the valley where an elderly rNying ma lama (who speaks no English or Nepali) earns a nice supplementary income by "blessing" tourists and giving them a red initiation thread that is worn as a protective amulet. Apparently, one of the popular trekking guides suggests that tourists visit this particular dgon pa while spending the necessary two-day stay in the valley to acclimatize. In general, tolerance of trekkers was at a minimum during the peak tourist months of October and April. However, at other times of the year, the occasional foreigner was likely to be invited into the dgon pa to witness the rituals or to be shown the altar, the carved figures, and the religious paintings on the wall.

25. In addition to the fourteen nuns who completed their three-year retreat at Chergyu dgon pa, there are approximately twenty nuns resident in the valley,

and perhaps another fifteen or so outside the valley. Of these, seven were resident at Ngagi dgon pa, north of Kathmandu; three others resided at Swayambhu, two at Bodhnath, and at least three were in school in Darjeeling. There are considerably fewer resident tawa (monks) in the valley: I regularly encountered only three young men at the dgon pa rituals.

26. Nuns generally can read and write Tibetan; some are also literate in Nepali, and a few have mastered elementary English. Most village girls (and boys) who remain in the valley do not proceed beyond the third or fourth grade. Their labor is needed at home or in the fields. The higher levels of study can only be had at the district center (Chame), a day and a half walk from Nyeshang, or at expensive boarding schools in Pokhara and Kathmandu.

27. Some informants were also upset that farmland in the Kathmandu valley was being converted to nonagricultural uses or developed by Nyeshangte entrepreneurs. Nyeshangte tend to ostentatiously display their wealth and their identity as Buddhists in the environs of Kathmandu.

28. Lederman (1990) points out that the "systematic exclusion of some social categories from dominant institutions may be a good cross cultural criteria of subordination" (47).

29. My Sherpa assistant, Palsang, was astonished to see jomo playing ritual instruments during a dgon pa ceremony. He told me that in his district (Solu), only monks handled these instruments, and jomo who attended performed only a minor, supporting role during the liturgical recitation.

30. Generally, jomo and tawa do not assume the role of patron or sponsor since their ritual activities generate merit for others (and for themselves). Instead, their families might contribute extra funds for a community feast and celebration to honor their daughters' and sons' "selfless service." They are not in the same economic position as householders to act as patrons. Although they may own fields that generate sufficient income, most ordained clergy do not actively farm or trade; they rely on their families for food supplies and cash, on community donations to the dgon pa, and payments from lay clients for ritual services performed.

31. The villagers usually presented one to five rupees, or u.s.$.05 to $.25.

32. Although males and females mingle freely at social events and participate together in ceremonial activities, at certain times when "formal seating arrangements" are followed, men and women sit apart in separate groups. Men will always sit in an orderly circle, whereas women sit in a large group that consists of smaller clusters and circles of friends huddled together. Young children may sit with their mothers; young males join the circle of adult men. These formal seating arrangements are seen at large social gatherings where meals are served. This type of separation may also be seen within the household: women and girls often sit on the left side of the hearth, whereas males sit on the right, but these observances are not rigidly followed. A male acting as host may also sit on the left and serve from there.

33. Cf. Friedl (1975), Lepowsky (1990), Ong (1987, 1989), Ortner (1981), Rosaldo (1974), Sacks (1974), Sanday (1981), and Schlegel (1977).

34. In the Nyeshangte case, however, there were no equivalents to the Sherpa *pembu*, the political leaders and tax collectors appointed by the Nepalese government. Village administrative posts "rotated" yearly among all the adult men within a village. During the course of a man's lifetime, he would have served in each of the positions and various committees.

35. Despite the many parallels between the two societies, the locus of conflict and contradiction in Nyeshangte society does not seem to hinge on fraternal relations, but instead shows up between generations, especially between fathers and their children—both sons and daughters. However, I do not have sufficient historical data to comment on this. One of the oral traditions concerning the early settlers of Nyeshang speak of amicable relations between two brothers—one of whom was a "priest-lama," the other a "king." In another story the founding clans of the valley are associated with four siblings—an eldest sister and her three brothers; interestingly, there is no mention of parents in either account.

36. Unfortunately, the boy escaped after one week and his cousin hurried to the district center to send a telegram to various relatives in Kathmandu. The main concern was to notify everyone that he had not been "cured" and to advise them not to give him any money. My assistant explained that Nyeshangte boys and girls can request money, assistance, and hospitality from a wide range of classificatory uncles, aunts, cousins, and clan members on either side of the family.

37. In the Sherpa case, Ortner (1989:216 n. 18) points out that this hegemony is tied to the rise of monastic values and represents a departure from the popular folk tradition of Buddhism that existed previously in Solu-Khumbu. In Nyeshang, a concern with renunciation and asceticism seems to have been part of the early religious landscape. Oral histories indicate that villagers regularly undertook retreats in the jaṅgal before temples or monasteries were established. However, this may have been because of the influence of "wandering" lamas (see, for example, Snellgrove 1967).

38. A couple of these city boys made remarks quite similar to Spike's. They too were surprised to find that despite the apparent differences in lifestyle and education, their rural cousins were not so different after all.

39. Most of the unmarried female traders told me that they split their earnings "fifty/fifty" with their parents. Women do not usually engage in this sort of reckless spending. In Nyeshang society and in other Himalayan communities, for example, among the Kham Magar (Molnar 1980) and the Gurung (Andhors 1976), women are perceived as being more responsible and frugal in money matters so they customarily control the household budget.

40. Although this attitude would not surprise me, I do not recall any youths specifically complaining about their parents' donations to the dgon pa.

However, many male youths professed a general ignorance of Buddhist worship, deities, and so forth, and would often casually dismiss religious works "as something old people do." But these same males were always deferential to clergy and observed the correct etiquette at the village dgon pa.

41. The Himalayan Rescue Association sends western medical personnel to the valley during peak trekking seasons: two months in the spring and autumn. These volunteer doctors and nurses do an excellent job with limited resources and equipment. However, the community needs a year-round doctor, as the local (Nepalese) health post does not have an adequately trained medic and has few medical supplies.

42. Nyeshangte hold a number of divergent attitudes toward education. Many rural-based Nyeshangte feel that higher education is not necessary for girls since their primary work is limited to farming. Nor do they feel that boys need advanced education since boys are expected to begin their trading careers around the age of 14 or 15. However, among the urban elite, both the younger and older generations of Nyeshangte value formal education and hope that their children will finish high school.

43. A few Nyeshangte spoke bitterly of being mistreated by some Hindus in Kathmandu: they were ostracized for their lack of education and their "rustic" or "hillbilly" ways. In addition, several informants said that Nyeshangte migrants were exploited by Nepalese bureaucrats because they were illiterate and needed help in filling out "papers." Although these events occurred nearly two decades ago, memories of these incidents still evoked a great deal of anger and resentment. I also encountered several youths (including Sherpa and "Tibetans") who were quite bitter about the lack of scholarship opportunities for minority Buddhists or "Bhotia." They pointed out that several of their friends had received very high scores on their examinations, but nonetheless, the fellowship awards always went to Newars or Hindus.

The Tibetan, Nepali, and Nyeshang origins of words are indicated in parentheses (T, N, Ny), and in some instances, this is followed by a rough guide to pronunciation. The definitions provided correspond to Nyeshangte usage.

arak.   (Ny) Distilled alcohol made from wheat.
aruru.   (Ny) Comic drama performed during spring fertility rites.
a sebba.   (Ny) Bad deeds.
bakhu.   (Ny) Sleeveless woolen dress worn by women.
bKa rgyud.   (T, "Kagyu") A Tibetan Buddhist sect.
chang.   (T) Fermented beverage, beer.
cheemi.   (Ny) Religious specialists; clergy.
chetu.   (Ny) Ritual friendship.
dbang.   (T, "ong") Empowerment; blessings.
dgon pa.   (T, "gonpa") Temple.
ghar.   (N) Home (husband's home).
gtor ma.   (T) Offerings.
jangal.   (N) Forest.
jāt.   (N) Caste.
jikten.   (Ny) Laypeople.
jomo.   (Ny) Nun.
jūṭho.   (N) Impure; remains after a meal.
kām.   (N) Work.

kani. (Ny)   Arched gateway, similar to *mchod rten*.

kha btags.   (T, "khata") White ceremonial scarf.

kyo phiba.   (Ny) "Giving out wealth" rite observed during Thonje.

lāl mohar.   (N) Official document bearing the Nepalese king's red seal.

las.   (T, "le") Actions, karma.

lha bsang.   (Ny) Protective ritual for prosperity and well-being.

lha khang.   (T) Small chapel.

linga.   (Ny) Paper or dough effigy.

maiti.   (N) Natal home.

magpa.   (T) Adopted bridegroom.

mani.   (Ny) Religious works.

mani tang.   (Ny) Prayer wheel.

mantang.   (Ny) A bank of prayer wheels.

mchod rten.   (T, "chorten") Buddhist monument.

nang tse.   (Ny) Formal labor exchange.

Paten.   (Ny) Two-week festival held every three years.

phee.   (Ny) Bachelors' group.

pree.   (Ny) A unit of measure equivalent to 1.5 to 2 kilograms.

rab gnas.   (T, "ramne") Consecration rite.

rNying ma.   (T) A Tibetan Buddhist sect.

roba.   (Ny) Ritual friendship between males.

rodī ghar.   (N) Youth association.

rol.   (Ny) Tradition.

roma.   (Ny) Ritual friendship between females.

roo la tse.   (Ny) Literally, "doing friendship"; labor exchange.

sdig pa.   (T) Sin, vice.

sems.   (T) Mind-heart.

ser khyim.   (T) A retreat center for laypeople run by a married lama.

sgrib.   (T, "dip") Pollution.

smyung nas.   (T, "nyungne") An ascetic retreat.

sgnags pa.   (T) A hereditary line of noncelibate lamas with special powers.

stūpa.   (N) A sacred mound containing relics of Buddha.

tarkye.   (Ny) Exorcism.

tawa.   (Ny) Monk.

thang ka.   (T) Religious scroll.

tsha.   (Ny) Girls' youth group.

tshong roo.   (Ny) Trade group.

tsogs.   (Ny) Rice or wheat balls distributed after a ritual.

yul.   (T) Homeland, valley.

Abdullah, A. Tahrunnessa and Sondra A. Zeidenstein. 1981. *Village Women of Bangladesh: Prospects for Change*. Oxford: Pergamon.

Abu-Lughod, Lila. 1990a. "Can There Be a Feminist Ethnography?" *Women and Performance: A Journal of Feminist Theory* 5:7–27.

—. 1990b. "Shifting Politics in Bedouin Love Poetry." *Language and the Politics of Emotion*, C. Lutz and L. Abu-Lughod, eds. New York: Cambridge University Press.

—. 1991. "Writing Against Culture." *Recapturing Anthropology*, Richard Fox, ed. Sante Fe: School of American Research Press.

Acharya, Meena and Lynn Bennett. 1981. *The Rural Women of Nepal: An Aggregate Analysis and Summary of Eight Village Studies*. Vol. 2 (9): *The Status of Women in Nepal*. Kathmandu: Centre for Economic Development and Administration (CEDA), Tribhuvan University.

—. 1983. *Women and the Subsistence Sector: Economic Participation and Household Decision-Making in Nepal*. Washington, D.C.: World Bank.

Adhikari, Krishna. 1975. "A Brief Survey of Nepal's Trade with British India During the Latter Half of the Nineteenth Century." *Contributions to Nepalese Studies* 2:187–96.

Albers, Patricia. 1989. "From Illusion to Illumination: Anthropological Studies of American Indian Women." *Gender and Anthropology*. Sandra Morgen, ed. Washington, D.C.: American Anthropological Association.

Allen, Catherine J. 1988. *The Hold Life Has: Coca and Cultural Identity in an Andean Community*. Washington, D.C.: Smithsonian Institution Press.

Allen, Michael. 1990a. "Girl's Pre-Puberty Rites Amongst the Newars of Kathmandu Valley." *Women in India and Nepal.* Michael Allen and S. N. Mukherjee, eds. New Delhi: Sterling.

—. 1990b. "Introduction: The Hindu View of Women." *Women in India and Nepal.* Michael Allen and S. N. Mukherjee, eds. New Delhi: Sterling.

Allione, Tsultrin. 1984. *Women of Wisdom.* London: Routledge and Kegan, Paul.

Amit-Talai, Vered and Helena Wulff, eds. 1995. *Youth Cultures.* New York: Routledge.

Andhors, Ellen B. 1974. "The Rodighar and Its Role in Gurung Society." *Contributions to Nepalese Studies* 1:10–24.

—. 1976. *The Rodi: Female Associations Among the Gurung of Nepal.* Ph.D. diss. Ann Arbor: University Microfilms International.

Annis, Sheldon. 1987. *God and Production in Guatemala.* Austin: University of Texas Press.

Appadurai, Arjun. 1978. *Status of Women in South Asia.* Washington, D.C.: Zenger.

—. 1986. "Introduction: Commodities and the Politics of Value." *The Social Life of Things: Commodities in Cultural Perspective.* Arjun Appadurai, ed. Cambridge: Cambridge University Press.

—. 1990. "Disjuncture and Difference in the Global Cultural Economy." *Public Culture* 2 (2): 1–24.

—. 1991. "Global Ethnoscapes: Notes and Queries for a Transnational Anthropology." *Recapturing Anthropology.* Richard Fox, ed. Santa Fe: School of American Research.

Ardener, Edwin. 1975. "Belief and the Problem of Women." *Perceiving Women.* Shirley Ardener, ed. London: Malaby.

Ardussi, John and Lawrence Epstein. 1978. "The Saintly Madman in Tibet." *Himalayan Anthropology.* James F. Fisher, ed. Paris: Mouton.

Aris, Michael. 1975. "Report on the University of California Expedition to Kutang and Nubri." *Contributions to Nepalese Studies* 2 (2): 121–36.

Arvind, Sharma. 1987. *Women in World Religions.* Albany: State University of New York Press.

Atkinson, Jane M. 1982. "Review Essay: Anthropology." *Signs* 8 (2): 236–58.

Aziz, Barbara. 1974. "Some Notions about Descent and Residence in Tibetan Society." *Contributions to the Anthropology of Nepal.* C. von Fürer-Haimendorf, ed. Warminister: Aris and Phillips.

—. 1978. *Tibetan Frontier Families.* New Delhi: Vikas.

—. 1985. "Women in Tibetan Society and Tibetology." Paper presented at the International Tibetan Studies Seminar, Munich.

—. 1987. "Moving Toward a Sociology of Tibet." *Tibet Journal* 12 (4): 72–86.

Bacdayan, Albert. 1977. "Mechanistic Cooperation and Sexual Equality Among the Western Bontoc." *Sexual Stratification: A Cross-Cultural View.* Alice Schlegel, ed. New York: Columbia University Press.

Bakhtin, M. 1984. *Rabelais and His World.* Bloomington: University of Indiana Press.

Bancroft, Anne. 1980. "Women in Buddhism." *Unspoken Worlds: Women's Religious Lives in Non-Western Cultures.* N. Falk and R. Gross, eds. San Francisco: Harper and Row.

Bannerjee, A. C. 1981. "Bon, the Primitive Religion of Tibet." *Bulletin of Tibetology* 4:1–18.

—. 1984. *Aspects of Buddhist Culture from Tibetan Sources.* Calcutta: Firma KLM.

Bateson, G. 1958. *Naven.* Stanford: Stanford University Press.

Barnes, Nancy Schuster. 1987. "Buddhism." *Women in World Religions.* Arvind Sharma, ed. Albany: State University of New York.

Barnes, Sandra T. 1990. "Women, Property, and Power." *Beyond the Second Sex.* Peggy Reeves Sanday and Ruth Goodenough, eds. Philadelphia: University of Pennsylvania Press.

Bell, Sir Charles. 1931. *The Religion of Tibet.* Oxford: Clarendon.

Beneria, Lourdes. 1979. "Reproduction, Production, and the Sexual Division of Labor." *Cambridge Journal of Economics* 3 (3): 203–25.

Beneria, Lourdes and Gita Sen. 1981. "Accumulation, Reproduction, and Women's Role in Economic Development." *Feminist Studies* 8 (1): 157–76.

Bennett, Lynn. 1976. "Sex and Motherhood Among the Brahmans and Chetris of East Central Nepal." *Contributions to Nepalese Studies* June (3): 1–51. Special issue on Anthropology, Health, and Development. Kirtipur: Institute of Nepal and Asian Studies, Tribhuvan University.

—. 1979. *Tradition and Change in the Legal Status of Nepalese Women.* Vol. 2. Kathmandu: CEDA.

—. 1981. "The Wives of the Rishis: An Analysis of the Tij-Rishi Panchami Women's Festival." *Kailash* 4 (2): 185–207.

—. 1983. *Dangerous Wives and Sacred Sisters: The Social and Symbolic Roles of Women Among the Brahmans and Chetris of Nepal.* New York: Columbia University Press.

Berreman, Gerald. 1972. *Hindus of the Himalayas: Ethnography and Change.* Berkeley: University of California Press.

—. 1978. "Ecology, Demography, and Domestic Strategies in the Western Himalayas." *Journal of Anthropological Research* 34:326–68.

—. 1993. "Sanskritization as Female Oppression in India." *Sex and Gender Hierarchies.* Barbara Diane Miller, ed. New York: Cambridge University Press.

Beyer, Stephen. 1973. *The Cult of Tara.* Berkeley: University of California Press.

—. 1978. "Buddhism in Tibet." *Buddhism: A Modern Perspective.* Charles Prebish, ed. University Park: Pennsylvania State University.

Bharati, Agchananda. 1965. *The Tantric Tradition.* New York: Anchor Books and Doubleday.

Bista, D. B. 1982. "The Process of Nepalization." *Anthropological and Linguistic Studies of the Gandaki Area in Nepal.* D. B. Bista et al., eds. Tokyo: Institute for the Study of Languages and Cultures of Asia and Africa.

—. 1987. *People of Nepal*. Kathmandu: Ratna Pustak.

Blackwood, Evelyn. 1984. "Sexuality and Gender in Certain Native American Tribes: The Case of Cross-Gender Females." *Signs* 10:27–42.

Borofsky. Robert. 1987. *Making History*. Cambridge: Cambridge University Press.

Boserup, Ester. 1970a. *Women's Role in Economic Development*. New York: St. Martin's.

—. 1970b. "Loss of Status Under European Rule." *Women's Role in Economic Development*, ch. 3. New York: St. Martin's.

Bourdieu, Pierre. 1977. *Outline of a Theory of Practice*. R. Nice, trans. Cambridge: Cambridge University Press.

Bourque, Susan and Kay B. Warren. 1981. *Women of the Andes: Patriarchy and Social Change in Two Peruvian Towns*. Ann Arbor: University of Michigan Press.

Bowie, Katherine. Forthcoming. "Of Buddhism and Beggars: The Merit-Making Paradigm and the Political Economy of Village Thailand." *American Anthropologist*.

Brown, Judith. 1970. "A Note on the Division of Labor by Sex." *American Anthropologist* 72:1073–78.

—. 1975. "Iroquois Women: An Ethnohistorical Note." *Toward an Anthropology of Women*. Rayna Reiter, ed. New York: Monthly Review Press.

Bruner, Edward M. 1986. "Experience and Its Expressions." *The Anthropology of Experience*. Victor W. Turner and Edward M. Bruner, eds. Urbana: University of Illinois Press.

Buechler, Judith-Maria. 1986. "Women in Petty Commodity Production in La Paz, Bolivia." *Women and Change in Latin America*. J. Nash and H. Safa, eds. South Hadley, Mass.: Bergin and Garvey.

Bujra, Janet. 1986. "Urging Women to Redouble Their Efforts: Class, Gender, and Capitalist Transformation in Africa." *Women and Class in Africa*. Claire Robertson and Iris Berger, eds. New York: Africana.

Burghart, Richard. 1984. "The Formation of the Concept of Nation State in Nepal." *Journal of Asian Studies* 44 (1): 101–25.

Butler, Judith. 1990. *Gender Trouble*. New York: Routledge.

Carrasco, Pedro. 1959. *Land and Polity in Tibet*. Seattle: University of Washington.

Central Bureau of Statistics. 1988. *Census of Nepal*. Kathmandu.

—. 1992. *Population Census of Nepal*. Kathmandu: His Majesty's Government of Nepal.

Chandra, Ramesh. 1981. "Sex Role Arrangement to Achieve Economic Security in North Himalayas." *The Himalaya: Aspects of Change*. J. S. Lall and A. O. Moddle, eds. Delhi: Oxford Press.

Chapman, F. Spencer. 1972 [orig. 1940]. *Lhasa the Holy City*. New York: Libraries Press.

Chodorow, Nancy. 1974. "Family Structure and Feminine Personality." *Woman, Culture and Society*. Michelle Rosaldo and Louise Lamphere, eds. Stanford: Stanford University Press.

—. 1978. *The Reproduction of Mothering: Psychoanalysis and the Sociology of Gender.* Berkeley: University of California Press.

Clarke, G. 1980. "A Helambu History." *Journal of Nepal Research Centre* 4:1–38.

Collier, Jane, M. Rosaldo, and S. Yanagisako. 1982. "Is There a Family? New Anthropological Views." *Rethinking the Family: Some Feminist Questions.* B. Thorne and M. Yalom, eds. New York: Longman.

Collier, Jane F. and Sylvia J. Yanagisako. 1987. "Introduction." *Gender and Kinship: Essays Toward a Unified Analysis.* J. Collier and S. Yanagisako, eds. Stanford: Stanford University Press.

Comaroff, John and Jean Comaroff. 1992. *Ethnography and the Historical Imagination.* Boulder: Westview.

—. 1993. "Introduction." *Modernity and Its Malcontents: Ritual and Power in Postcolonial Africa.* John Comaroff and Jean Comaroff, eds. Chicago: University of Chicago Press.

Connell, R. W. 1987. *Gender and Power: Society, the Person, and Sexual Politics.* Oxford: Polity Press.

Connerton, Paul. 1992. *How Societies Remember.* Cambridge: Cambridge University Press.

Cooke, Merritt Todd. 1985a. *The People of Nyishang: Identity, Tradition, and Change in the Nepal-Tibet Borderland.* Ph.D. diss. Ann Arbor: University Microfilms International.

—. 1985b. "Emic and Etic Classifications of the Nyishang Language." *Proceedings of the 18th International Conference on Sino-Tibetan Languages and Linguistics.* Seattle: University of Washington Press.

—. 1985c. "Outposts of Trade: Migration Patterns of the Nyishang Traders of Nepal." *Kroeber Anthropological Society Papers,* no. 65/66.

David-Neel, Alexandra. 1971. *Magic and Mystery in Tibet.* New York: Dover.

de Certeau, Michel. 1984. *The Practice of Everyday Life.* Berkeley: University of California Press.

des Chenes, Mary. 1992. "Traversing Social Space: Gurung Journeys." *Himalayan Research Bulletin* 12 (1–2): 1–10.

Desjarlais, Robert R. 1992. *Body and Emotion: The Aesthetics of Illness and Healing in the Nepal Himalayas.* Philadelphia: University of Pennsylvania Press.

de Souza, Alfred. 1980. *Women in Contemporary India and South Asia.* New Delhi: Manohar.

Devereaux, Leslie. 1987. "Gender Difference and the Relations of Inequality in Zinacantan." *Dealing with Inequality: Analyzing Gender Relations in Melanesia and Beyond.* M. Strathern, ed. New York: Cambridge University Press.

di Leonardo, Micaela. 1987. "The Female World of Cards and Holidays: Women, Families, and the Work of Kinship." *Signs* 2 (3): 440–53.

—. 1991. "Gender, Culture, and Political Economy: Feminist Anthropology in Historical Perspective." *Gender at the Crossroads of Knowledge.* Micaela di Leonardo, ed. Berkeley: University of California Press.

Dirks, Nicholas, Geoff Eley, and Sherry B. Ortner. 1994. "Introduction." *Culture, Power, History: A Reader in Contemporary Social Theory.* N. Dirks, G. Eley, and S. Ortner, eds. Princeton, N.J.: Princeton University Press.

Dixon, Ruth. 1978. *Rural Women at Work: Strategies for Development in South Asia.* Baltimore: The Johns Hopkins University Press.

Djamour, Judith. 1965. *Malay Kinship and Marriage in Singapore.* London: Athelone.

Dobremez, Jean-Francois. 1976. *Le Nepal: Ecologie et Biogeographie.* Paris: Editions du Centre Nationale de la Recherche Scientifique.

Dobremez, Jean-Francois and C. Jest. 1976. *Manaslu: Hommes et Milieux des Vallees du Nepal Central.* Paris: Editions du Centre National de la Recherche Scientifique.

Draper, Patricia. 1975. "!Kung Women: Contrasts in Sexual Egalitarianism in Foraging and Sedentary Contexts." *Toward an Anthropology of Women.* Rayna Reiter, ed. New York: Monthly Review Press.

Dutt, N. "Tantric Buddhism." *Bulletin of Tibetology* 1 (2): 5–16.

Dwyer, Daisy Hilse. 1978. "Ideologies of Sexual Inequality and Strategies for Change in Male-Female Relations." *American Ethnologist* 5:227–36.

Ekvall, Robert B. 1964. *Religious Observances in Tibet.* Chicago: University of Chicago Press.

Elwin, Verrier. 1947. *The Muria.* Bombay: Oxford University Press.

—. 1969. *The Nagas in the Nineteenth Century.* Bombay: Oxford University Press.

Ember, Melvin and Carol R. Ember. 1971. "The Conditions Favoring Matrilocal Versus Patrilocal Residence." *American Anthropologist* 73:571–94.

English, R. 1985. "Himalayan State Formation." *Mountain Research and Development* 5 (1): 61–78.

Epstein, Scarlett T. and Rosemary A. Watts, eds. 1981. *The Endless Day: Some Case Material on Asian Rural Women.* Oxford: Pergamon.

Errington, Frederick and Deborah Gewertz. 1987. *Cultural Alternatives and a Feminist Anthropology.* Cambridge: Cambridge University Press.

Errington, Shelly. 1990. "Recasting Sex, Gender, and Power: A Theoretical and Regional Overview." *Power and Difference in Island Southeast Asia.* Jane Atkinson and Shelly Errington, eds. Stanford: Stanford University Press.

Etzioni, Amitai. 1988. *The Moral Dimension: Toward a New Economics.* New York: Free Press.

Falk, Nancy and Rita Gross, eds. 1980. *Unspoken Worlds: Women's Religious Lives in Non-Western Cultures.* San Francisco: Harper and Row.

Fisher, James F. 1986. *Trans-Himalayan Traders: Economy, Society, and Culture in Northwest Nepal.* Berkeley: University of California Press.

—. 1990. *Sherpas: Reflections on Change in Himalayan Nepal.* Berkeley: University of California Press.

Fisher, William. 1987. *The Re-Creation of Tradition: Ethnicity, Migration, and Social Change Among the Thakali of Central Nepal.* Ph.D. diss., Columbia University.

Forbes, Geraldine. 1988. "The Politics of Respectability: Indian Women and the India National Congress." *The Indian National Congress*. D. A. Low, ed. Delhi: Oxford University Press.

Frank, Walter. 1974. "Attempt at an Ethnography of Middle Nepal." *Contributions to the Anthropology of Nepal*. C. von Fürer-Haimendorf, ed. New Delhi: Vikas.

Fricke, Thomas E. 1990. "Reciprocity and the Politics of Hierarchy in Ghale-Tamang Marriage." *American Ethnologist* 29 (2): 135–58.

Friedl, Ernestine. 1975. *Women and Men: An Anthropological View*. New York: Holt, Rhinehart and Winston.

Friedman, Lenore. 1988. *Meetings with Remarkable Women: Buddhist Teachers in America*. Berkeley: Shambala.

Fruzetti, Lina M. 1982. *The Gift of the Virgin*. New Brunswick, N.J.: Rutgers University Press.

Fruzetti, Lina M. and Akos Ostor. 1976. "Seed and Earth: A Cultural Analysis of Kinship in a Bengali Town." *Contributions to Indian Sociology* 10:97–132.

Fürer-Haimendorf, Christoph von. 1955. "Pre-Buddhist Elements in Sherpa Belief and Ritual." *Man* 55:49–52.

—. 1964. *The Sherpas of Nepal*. London: J. Murray.

—. 1966. "Caste Concepts and Status Distinctions in Buddhist Communities in Western Nepal." *Caste and Kin in Nepal, India, and Ceylon: Anthropological Studies in Hindu-Buddhist Contact Zones*. C. von Fürer-Haimendorf, ed. London: Asia Publishing House.

—. 1974. "The Changing Fortunes of Nepal's High Altitude Dwellers." *Contributions to the Anthropology of Nepal*. C. von Fürer-Haimendorf, ed. New Delhi: Vikas.

—. 1978. "Foreword." *Himalayan Anthropology: The Indo-Tibetan Interface*. James F. Fisher, ed. Paris: Mouton.

—. 1981. "Social Change in a Himalayan Region." *The Himalaya: Aspects of Change*. J. S. Lall and A. O. Moddle, eds. Delhi: Oxford University Press.

—. 1983. "Bhotia Highlanders of Nar and Phu." *Kailash* 10 (1–2): 63–118.

—. 1984. *The Sherpas Transformed*. New Delhi: Sterling.

—. 1988 [1975]. *Himalayan Traders: Life in Highland Nepal*. New Delhi: Time Books International.

Fürer-Haimendorf, Christoph von, ed. 1981. *Asian Highland Societies*. New Delhi: Sterling.

Gal, Susan. 1991. "Between Speech and Silence: The Problematics of Research on Language and Gender." *Gender at the Crossroads of Knowledge*. Micaela di Leonardo, ed. Berkeley: University of California Press.

Gauchan, S. and M. Vinding. 1977. "The History of the Thakaali According to the Thakaali Tradition." *Kailash* 5:99–184.

Geertz, Clifford. 1973. "Religion as a Cultural System." *Interpretations of Cultures*. C. Geertz, ed. New York: Basic Books.

—. 1980. *Negara: The Theater State in Nineteenth-Century Bali.* Princeton, N.J.: Princeton University Press.

Geertz, Hildred. 1961. *The Javanese Family.* New York: Humanities Press.

Gell, Alfred. 1986. "Newcomers to the World of Goods: Consumption Among the Muria Gonds." *The Social Life of Things: Commodities in Cultural Perspective.* Arjun Appadurai, ed. Cambridge: Cambridge University Press.

Gewertz, Deborah. 1981. "A Historical Reconsideration of Female Dominance Among the Chambri of Papua New Guinea." *American Ethnologist* 8:94–106.

—. 1983. *Sepik River Societies: A Historical Ethnography of the Chambri and Their Neighbors.* New Haven: Yale University Press.

Gewertz, Deborah B. and Frederick K. Errington. 1991. *Twisted Histories, Altered Contexts: Representing the Chambri in a World System.* Cambridge: Cambridge University Press.

Giddens, Anthony. 1979 *Central Problems in Social Theory: Action, Structure, and Contradiction in Social Analysis.* London: Macmillan.

—. 1981. *A Contemporary Critique of Historical Materialism.* Vol. 1: *Power, Property, and the State.* Berkeley: University of California Press.

—. 1984. *The Constitution of Society: Outline of the Theory of Structuration.* Berkeley: University of Califormia Press.

Gilbert, Kate. 1992. "Women and Family Law in Modern Nepal: Statutory Rights and Social Implications. *Journal of International Law and Politics* 24 (2): 729–58.

Glover, J. R. 1970. "Cognate Counts via the Swadesh List in Some Tibeto-Burman Languages of Nepal." *Occasional Papers of the Wolfenden Society on Tibeto-Burman Linguistics.* Austin E. Hale and Kenneth L. Pike, eds. Vol. 3. Part 2. Pp. 23–26.

—. 1972. "Role of the Witch." *Eastern Anthropologist* 25 (3): 221–29.

Glover, Warren and John K. Landon. 1980. "Gurung Dialects." *Papers in Southeast Asian Linguistics,* no. 7. 29–77; Pacific Linguistic series, series A, no. 53. R. L. Trail, ed. Canberra: Australian National University.

Gmelch, S. B. 1977. "Economic and Power Relations Among Urban Tinkers: The Role of Women." *Urban Anthropology* 6:237–47.

Gold, Ann Grodzins. 1994a. "Purdah Is as Purdah's Kept: A Storyteller's Story." *Listen to the Heron's Words: Reimagining Kinship and Gender in North India.* G. Raheja and A. Gold, eds. Berkeley: University of California Press.

—. 1994b. "Women's Speech Genres, Kinship, and Contradiction." *Women as Subjects.* Nita Kumar, ed. Charlottesville: University Press of Virginia.

Goldstein, Melvyn. 1971a. "Stratification, Polyandry, and Family Structure in Central Tibet." *Southwestern Journal of Anthropology* 27:64–74.

—. 1971b. "Taxation and the Structure of a Tibetan Village." *Central Asiatic Journal* 15:1–27.

—. 1973. "The Circulation of Estates in Tibet: Reincarnation, Land, and Politics." *Journal of Asian Studies* 32 (3): 445–56.

—. 1975a. "Report on Limi Panchayat, Humla District, Karnali Zone." *Contributions to Nepalese Studies* 2 (2): 89–101.

—. 1975b. "Preliminary Notes on Marriage and Kinship." *Contributions to Nepalese Studies* 2 (1): 57–69.

—. 1975c. *Tibetan-English Dictionary of Modern Tibetan*. Kathmandu: Ratna Pustak Bhanda.

—. 1976. "Fraternal Polyandry and Fertility in a High Himalayan Valley in Northwest Nepal." *Human Ecology* 4:223–33.

—. 1977a. "Population, Social Structure, and Strategic Behavior: An Essay on Polyandry, Fertility, and Change in Limi Panchayat." *Contributions to Nepalese Studies* 4 (2): 47–62.

—. 1977b. "Culture, Population, Ecology, and Development: A View from Northwest Nepal." *Himalaya: Ecologie—Ethnologie*. Paris: Centre Nationale de la Recherche Scientifique.

—. 1978. "Pahari and Tibetan Polyandry Revisited." *Ethnology* 18 (3): 325–38.

—. 1987. "When Brothers Share a Wife." *Natural History* 96 (3): 38–51.

Goldstein, Melvyn and Cynthia Beall. 1980. "Growing Old in Helambu: Aging, Migration, and Family Structure Among Sherpas." *Contributions to Nepalese Studies* 8 (1): 41–56.

—. 1990. *Nomads of Western Tibet*. Berkeley: University of California Press.

Goody, Jack. 1976. *Production and Reproduction*. Cambridge: Cambridge University Press.

Goody, Jack and S. J. Tambiah. 1973. *Bridewealth and Dowry*. Cambridge: Cambridge University Press.

Gordon, Linda. 1988. *Heroes of Their Own Lives: The Politics and History of Family Violence*. New York: Viking.

Gottlieb, Alma. 1990. "Rethinking Female Pollution." *Beyond The Second Sex*. Peggy Reeves Sanday and Ruth Goodenough, eds. Philadelphia: University of Pennsylvania Press.

Gough, Kathleen. 1956. "Brahman Kinship in a Tamil Village." *American Anthropologist* 58:826–53.

Goullart, Peter. 1959. *Land of the Lamas*. New York: E. P. Hutton.

Gramsci, Antonio. 1957. *The Modern Prince and Other Writings*. Louis Mark, trans. New York: International.

Gray, John N. 1983. "Domestic Enterprise and Social Relations in a Nepalese Village." *Contributions to Indian Sociology* 17 (2): 245–74.

—. 1987. "Bayu Utarnu: Ghost Exorcism and Sacrifice in Nepal." *Ethnology* 26 (3): 179–99.

—. 1989. "The Household in Nepal: Social and Experiential Crucible of Society." *Society from the Inside Out: Anthropological Perspectives on the South Asian Household*. John N. Gray and David J. Mearns, eds. New Delhi: Sage.

—. 1990. "Chetri Women in Domestic Groups and Rituals." *Women in India and Nepal*. Michael Allen and S. N. Mukherjee, eds. New Delhi: Sterling.

—. 1991. "Marriage and the Constitution of Hierarchy and Gender in Bahun-Chetri Households." *Contributions to Nepalese Studies* 18 (1): 53–82.

Grierson, Sir George A., ed. 1967 [1909]. *Linguistic Survey of India*. Vol. 3: *Tibeto-Burman Family*. Part 1: *Himalayan Dialects and North Assam Group*. Delhi: Motilal Banarsidars.

Gross, Rita M. 1987a. "Yeshe Tsogyel: Enlightened Consort, Great Teacher, Female Role Model." *Tibet Journal* 12 (4): 1–18.

—. 1987b. "Women in Buddhism." *Women in World Religions*. Arvind Sharma, ed. Albany: State University of New York.

Gurung, Harka. 1980. *Vignettes of Nepal*. Kathmandu: Sajha Prakashar.

Gurung, Nareswor J. 1976. "An Introduction to the Socio-economic Structure of Manang District." *Kailash* 4 (3): 295–308.

—. 1977a. *Socio-economic Structure of Manang Village*. Masters thesis. Department of Sociology, Tribhuvan University, Kathmandu.

—. 1977b. "An Ethnographic Note on Nar-Phu Valley." *Kailash* 5 (3): 229–44.

Gurung, S. B. and P. Roy. 1980. "District and Micro-regional Planning: Two Case Studies." *Strategic Elements of Rural Development in Nepal*. Kathmandu: Centre for Economic Development and Administration.

Hale, E. Austin and Kenneth L. Pike. 1970. *Tone Systems of Tibeto-Burman Languages of Nepal*. Occasional Papers of the Wolfenden Society on Tibeto-Burman Linguistics. Urbana: Department of Linguistics, University of Illinois.

Handler, Richard. 1984. "On Sociocultural Discontinuity: Nationalism and Cultural Objectification in Quebec." *Current Anthropology* 25:55–71.

—. 1985. "On Dialogue and Destructive Analysis: Problems in Narrating Nationalism and Ethnicity." *Journal of Anthropological Research* 41:171–82.

—. 1986. "Authenticity." *Anthropology Today* 2 (1): 2–4.

Handler, Richard and Jocelyn Linnekin. 1984. "Tradition, Genuine or Spurious." *Journal of American Folklore* 97:273–90.

Hanson, Allan. 1989. "The Making of the Maori: Culture Invention and Its Logic." *American Anthropologist* 91:890–902.

—. 1991. "Reply to Langdon, Levine, and Linnekin." *American Anthropologist* 93:449–50.

Harding, Sandra. 1987. *Feminism and Methodology*. Bloomington: Indiana University Press.

Harrer, Heinrich. 1954. *Seven Years in Tibet*. New York: E. P. Dutton.

Harris, Grace Gredys. 1989. "Concepts of Individual, Self, and Person in Description and Analysis." *American Anthropologist* 91 (3): 599–612.

Hartmann, Heidi. 1976. "Capitalism, Patriarchy, and Job Segregation by Sex." *Women and the Workplace*. Martha Blaxall and Barbara Reagan, eds. Chicago: University of Chicago Press.

—. 1979. "The Unhappy Marriage of Marxism and Feminism: Towards a More Progressive Union." *Capital and Class* 8:1–33.

—. 1981. "The Family as the Locus of Gender, Class, and Political Struggle: The Example of Housework." *Signs* 6 (3): 612–37.

Haynes, Douglas and Gyan Prakash, eds. 1991. *Contesting Power: Resistance and Everyday Social Relations in South Asia*. Berkeley: University of Califormia Press.

Helms, Mary W. 1993. *Craft and the Kingly Ideal: Art, Trade, and Power*. Austin: University of Texas Press.

Hitchcock, T. John. 1980. *A Mountain Village in Nepal*. New York: Holt, Rhinehart, and Winston.

Hobsbawm, E. 1983. "Introduction: Inventing Traditions." *The Invention of Tradition*. E. Hobsbawm and T. Ranger, eds. New York: Cambridge University Press.

Hobsbawm, E. and T. Ranger, eds. 1983. *The Invention of Tradition*. Cambridge: Cambridge University Press.

Hofer, Andras. 1979. *Caste and State in Nepal: A Study of the Muluki Ain of 1854*. Innsbruck: Universitatsverlag Wagner.

—. 1981. *Tamang Ritual Texts*. Wiesbaden: Franz Steiner Verlag.

Hoffman, H. 1961. *The Religions of Tibet*. London: Murray.

Holland, Dorothy and Debra Skinner. 1995. "Contested Ritual, Contested Feminities: (Re)Forming Self and Society in a Nepali Women's Festival." *American Ethnologist* 22 (2): 279–305.

Holmberg, David. 1983. "Shamanic Soundings: Femaleness in the Tamang Ritual Structure." *Signs* 9 (1): 40–58.

—. 1984. "Ritual Paradoxes in Nepal: Comparative Perspectives on Tamang Religion." *Journal of Asian Studies* 43 (4): 697–722.

—. 1989. *Order in Paradox: Myth, Ritual, and Exchange Among Nepal's Tamang*. Ithaca: Cornell University Press.

hooks, bell. 1984. *From Margin to Center*. Boston: South End Press.

Horner, I. B. 1975. *Women under Primitive Buddhism*. Delhi: Motilal Banarsider.

Hoshi, Michiyo. 1984. "A Prakaa Vocabulary: A Dialect of the Manang Language." *Anthropological and Linguistic Studies of the Gandaki Area in Nepal*. Vol. 2. Musashi Tachikawa, ed. *Monumenta Serindica*, no. 12. Tokyo: Institute for the Study of Languages and Cultures of Asia and Africa.

—. 1986. "An Outline of the Prakaa Grammar: A Dialect of the Manang Language." *Monumenta Serindica*, no. 15. Tokyo: Institute for the Study of Languages and Cultures of Asia and Africa.

Humphrey, Caroline. 1992. "Fair Dealing, Just Rewards: The Ethics of Barter in North-East Nepal." *Barter, Exchange, and Value: An Anthropological Approach*. Cambridge: Cambridge University Press.

Hutt, Michael. 1986. "Diversity and Change in the Languages of Highland Nepal." *Contributions to Nepalese Studies* 14 (1): 1–24.

Ijima, S. 1964. "Ecology, Economy, and the Social System in the Nepal Himalayas." *Developing Economies* 2.

Jackson, David. 1976. "The Early History of Lo (Mustang) and Ngara." *Contributions to Nepalese Studies* 4 (1): 39–66.

—. 1978. "Notes on the History of Serib and Nearby Places in the Upper Kali Gandaki." *Kailash* 6 (3): 195–227.

—. 1983. *The Mollas of Mustang: Historical, Religious, and Oratorical Traditions of the Nepalese-Tibetan Borderland*. Dharamsala: Library of Tibetan Works and Archives.

Jackson, Jean. 1989. "Is There a Way to Talk about Making Culture Without Making Enemies?" *Dialectical Anthropology* 14:127–43.

Jayawardena, Chandra. 1977. "Women and Kinship in Acheh Besar, Northern Sumatra." *Ethnology* 14 (1): 21–38.

Jest, Corneille. 1961. "Les Missions du Musee." *Objet et Mondes* 4 (3): 209–15.

—. 1978. "Tibetan Communities of the High Valleys of Nepal: Life in an Exceptional Environment and Economy." *Himalayan Anthropology: The Indo-Tibetan Interface*. James F. Fisher, ed. Paris: Mouton.

Jones, Rex and Shirley Jones. 1976. *Himalayan Women*. New York: Mayfield.

Kahn, Joel. 1993. *Constituting the Minangkabau: Peasants, Culture, and Modernity in Colonial Indonesia*. Oxford: Berg.

Kapferer, Bruce. 1979. "Mind, Self, and Other in Demonic Illness: The Negation and Reconstruction of Self." *American Ethnologist* 6:110–33.

Kawakita, Jiro. 1955. "Some Ethno-geographical Observations in the Nepal Himalaya." *Peoples of Nepal Himalaya*. Vol. 3. H. Kihara, ed. Kyoto: Kyoto University.

Keesing, Roger M. 1975. *Kin Groups and Social Structure*. New York: Holt, Rhinehart and Winston.

—. 1981. *Cultural Anthropology: A Contemporary Perspective*. New York: Holt, Rhinehart and Winston.

—. 1985. "Kwaio Women Speak: The Micropolitics of Autobiography in a Solomon Island Society." *American Anthropologist* 87 (1): 27–39.

—. 1989. "Creating the Past: Custom and Identity in the Contemporary Pacific." *Contemporary Pacific* 1:19–42.

—. 1992. *Custom and Confrontation: The Kwaio Struggle for Cultural Autonomy*. Chicago: University of Chicago Press.

Kendall, Laurel. 1985. *Shamans, Housewives, and Other Restless Spirits*. Honolulu: University of Hawaii Press.

Keyes, Charles. 1984. "Mother or Mistress but Never a Monk: Buddhist Notions of Female Gender in Rural Thailand." *American Ethnologist* 11:223–40.

Khin, Thitsa. 1980. *Providence and Prostitution: Image and Reality in Buddhist Thailand*. London: Change International Reports.

Kirsch, Thomas. 1983. "Buddhism, Sex Roles, and the Thai Economy." *Women of Southeast Asia*. Penny van Esterik, ed. DeKalb: Northern Illinois University, Center for Southeast Asian Studies, Occasional Paper, no. 9.

—. 1985. "Text and Context: Buddhist Sex Roles and Culture of Gender Revisited." *American Ethnologist* 12:302–20.

Klein, Alan M. 1983. "The Plains Truth: The Impact of Colonialism on Indian Women." *Dialectical Anthropology* 7:299–311.

Klein, Anne C. 1987. "The Birthless Birthgiver: Reflections on the Liturgy of Yeshe Tsogyel, the Great Bliss Queen." *Tibet Journal* 12 (4): 19–37.

Kondo, Dorinne K. 1990. *Crafting Selves: Power, Gender, and Discourses of Identity in a Japanese Workplace.* Chicago: University of Chicago Press.

Kondos, Vivienne. 1986. "Images of the Fierce Goddess and Portrayals of Hindu Women." *Contributions to Indian Sociology* 20 (2): 173–93.

—. 1989. "Subjection and the Domicile: Some Problematic Issues Relating to High-Caste Nepalese Women." *South Asian Society from the Inside Out: Anthropological Perspectives on the South Asian Household.* John N. Gray and David J. Mearns, eds. New Delhi: Sage.

—. 1991. "Subjection and the Ethics of Anguish: The Nepalese Parbatya Parent-Daughter Relationship." *Contributions to Indian Sociology* 12 (1): 113–33.

Kopytoff, Igor. 1990. "Women's Roles and Existential Identities." *Beyond the Second Sex: New Directions in the Anthropology of Gender.* Peggy Sanday and Ruth Goodenough, eds. Philadelphia: University of Pennsylvania Press.

Kruks, Sonia. 1992. "Gender and Subjectivity: Simone de Beauvoir and Contemporary Feminism." *Signs* 18 (1): 89–110.

Krygier, Jocelyn. 1990. "Caste and Female Pollution." *Women in India and Nepal.* Michael Allen and S. N. Mukherjee, eds. New Delhi: Sterling.

Kumar, Nita, ed. 1994. *Women as Subjects: South Asian Histories.* Charlottesville: University of Virginia Press.

Kvaerne, Per. 1974. "The Canon of the Tibetan Bonpos." *Indo-Iranian Journal* 16 (1): 97–144.

Lall, J. S. and A. D. Moddle, eds. 1981. *The Himalaya: Aspects of Change.* Delhi: Oxford University Press.

Lamphere, Louise. 1974. "Strategies, Cooperation, and Conflict Among Women in Domestic Groups." *Woman, Culture, and Society.* Michelle Rosaldo and Louise Lamphere, eds. Stanford: Stanford University Press.

—. 1977. "Review Essay: Anthropology." *Signs* 2 (3): 612–27.

—. 1987. "Feminism and Anthropology: The Struggle to Reshape Our Thinking about Gender." *The Impact of Feminist Research in the Academy.* Christie Farnham, ed. Bloomington: Indiana University Press.

Landon, Perceval. 1906. *The Opening of Tibet.* New York: Doubleday, Page.

Larson, Barbara K. 1984. "The Status of Women in a Tunisian Village: Limits to Autonomy, Influence, and Power." *Signs* 9 (3): 417–33.

Leach, E. R. 1958. "Magical Hair." *Man* 88:147–64.

Leacock, Eleanor. 1972. Introduction to F. Engels, *The Origin of the Family, Private Property, and the State.* New York: International.

—. 1978. "Women's Status in Egalitarian Society: Implications for Social Evolution." *Current Anthropology* 19 (2): 247–54.

—. 1983. "Interpreting the Origins of Gender Inequality: Conceptual and Historial Problems." *Dialectical Anthropology* 7:263–83.

Lederman, Rena. 1990. "Contested Order: Gender and Society in the Southern New Guinea Highlands." *Beyond the Second Sex*. Peggy Reeves Sanday and Ruth Gallagher Goodenough, eds. Philadelphia: University of Pennsylvania Press.

Lepowsky, Maria. 1990. "Gender in an Egalitarian Society." *Beyond the Second Sex*. Peggy Reeves Sanday and Ruth Gallagher Goodenough, eds. Philadelphia: University of Pennsylvania Press.

—. 1991. "The Way of the Ancestors: Custom, Innovation, and Resistance." *Ethnology* 30 (3): 217–35.

—. 1993. *Fruit of the Motherland: Gender in an Egalitarian Society*. New York: Columbia University Press.

Lessinger, Johanna. 1986. "Work and Modesty: The Dilemna of Women Market Traders in South India." *Feminist Studies* 12 (3): 581–600.

Levi-Strauss, Claude. 1969. *The Elementary Structure of Kinship*. Boston: Beacon.

Levine, Nancy. 1976. "The Origins of Stod-pa: A Nyinba Clan Legend." *Contributions to Nepalese Studies* 4:57–75.

—. 1980. "Opposition and Interdependence: Demographic and Economic Perspectives on Nyinba Slavery." *Asian and African Systems of Slavery*. J. L. Watson, ed. Berkeley: University of California Press.

—. 1981a. "Theory of Ru: Kinship, Descent, and Status in a Tibetan Society." *Asian Highland Societies*. C. von Fürer-Haimendorf, ed. New Delhi: Sterling.

—. 1981b. "Law, Labor, and the Economic Vulnerability of Women in Nyinba Society." *Kailash* 8:123–53.

—. 1982. "Belief and Explanation in Nyinba Women's Witchcraft." *Man* 17 (2): 259–74.

—. 1987. "Caste, State, and Ethnic Boundaries in Nepal." *Journal of Asian Studies* 46 (1): 71–91.

—. 1988. *The Dynamics of Polyandry: Kinship, Domesticity, and Population on the Tibetan Border*. Chicago: University of Chicago Press.

Lewis, I. M. 1989 [1971]. *Ecstatic Religion: An Anthropological Study of Spirit Possession and Shamanism*. 2nd ed. London: Routledge.

Lewis, Todd. 1989. "Newars and Tibetans in the Kathmandu Valley: Ethnic Boundaries and Religious History." *Journal of Asian and African Studies* 38:31–57.

—. 1993a. "Newar-Tibetan Trade and the Domestication of Sihalasrthabhu Avadna." *History of Religions* 33 (2): 135–60.

—. 1993b. "Himalayan Frontier Trade: Newar Diaspora Merchants and Buddhism," *Anthropology of Tibet and the Himalaya*. C. Ramble et al., eds. Zurich: Ethnological Museum of the University of Zurich.

Lewis, Todd and Daya Ratna Shakya. 1988. "Contributions to the History of Nepal: Eastern Newar Diaspora Settlements." *Contributions to Nepalese Studies* 15 (1): 25–65.

Li Anche. 1947. "Dege: A Study of Tibetan Population." *Southwest Journal of Anthropology* 3:279–93.

Lichter, David and Lawrence Epstein. 1983. "Irony in Tibetan Notions of the Good Life." *Karma: An Anthropological Inquiry.* C. F. Keyes and E. V. Daniels, eds. Berkeley: University of California Press.

Liddle, Joanne and Rama Joshi. 1989. *Daughters of Independence: Gender, Caste, and Class in India.* New Brunswick, N.J.: Rutgers University Press.

Liechty, Mark. 1994. *Fashioning Modernity in Kathmandu: Mass Media, Consumer Culture, and the Middle Class in Nepal.* Ph.D. diss., Department of Anthropology, University of Pennsylvania.

Linnekin, Jocelyn. 1990. "The Politics of Culture in the Pacific." *Cultural Identity and Ethnicity in the Pacific.* Jocelyn Linnekin and Lin Poyer, eds. Honolulu: University of Hawaii Press.

—. 1991. "Cultural Invention and the Dilemma of Authenticity." *American Anthropologist* 93:446–48.

Llewelyn-Davies, Melissa. 1981. "Women, Warriors, and Patriarchs." *Sexual Meanings.* Sherry B. Ortner and Harriet Whitehead, eds. New York: Cambridge University Press.

Lowenthal, David. 1990. *The Past Is a Foreign Country.* 2d ed. Cambridge: Cambridge University Press.

Lurie, Nancy. 1972. "Indian Women: A Legacy of Freedom." *Look to the Mountain Top.* Robert Iacopi, ed. San Jose, Calif.: Gousha Publications.

MacCannell, Dean. 1992. *Empty Meeting Grounds: The Tourist Papers.* New York: Routledge.

MacCormack, Carol and Marilyn Strathern. 1980. *Nature, Culture, and Gender.* Cambridge: Cambridge University Press.

MacDonald, Alexander W. 1980a. "The Coming of Buddism to the Sherpa Area." *Acta Orientalia* 34:139–46.

—. 1980b. "The Writing of Buddhist History in the Sherpa Area of Nepal." *Studies in the History of Buddhism.* A. D. Narain, ed. New Delhi: BR Publishing.

MacGaffey, Janet. 1986. "Women and Class Formation in a Dependent Economy: Kisangani Entrepreneurs." *Women and Class in Africa.* Claire Robertson and Iris Berger, eds. New York: Africana.

—. 1988. "Evading Male Control: Women in the Second Economy in Zaire." *Patriarchy and Class: African Women in the Home and the Work Force.* Sharon B. Stichter and Jane L. Parpart, eds. Boulder, Colo.: Westview.

Mahoney, Maureen A. and Barbara Yngvesson. 1992. "The Construction of Subjectivity and the Paradox of Resistance: Reintegrating Feminist Anthropology and Psychology." *Signs* 18 (1): 44–73.

Majpuria, Indra. 1982. *Nepalese Women.* Kathmandu: M. Devi.

Mandelbaum, David. 1993. *Women's Seclusion and Men's Honor: Sex Roles in North India, Bangladesh, and Pakistan.* Tucson: University of Arizona Press.

Manzardo, Andrew. 1978. *To Be Kings of the North: Community Adaptation and Impression Management in the Thakalis of Western Nepal.* Ph.D. diss., Department of Anthropology, University of Wisconsin, Madison.

Manzardo, Andrew and K. P. Sharma. 1975. "Cost-cutting, Caste, and Community: A Look at Thakali Social Reform in Pokhara." *Contributions to Nepalese Studies* 2 (2): 25–44.

March, Kathyrn. 1979. *The Intermediacy of Women: Female Gender Symbolism and the Social Position of Women Among Tamangs and Sherpas of Highland Nepal.* Ph.D. diss. Ann Arbor: University Microfilms International.

—. 1987. "Hospitality, Women, and the Efficacy of Beer," *Food and Foodways* 1:351–87.

Marriott, M. 1966. "The Feast of Love." *Krishna: Myths, Rites, and Attitudes.* M. Singer, ed. Chicago: University of Chicago Press.

Mascia-Lees, F., P. Sharpe, and C. B. Cohen. 1991. "Reply to Kirby." *Signs* 16 (2): 401–8.

Mazaudon, Martine. 1978. "Consonantal Mutation and Tonal Split in the Tamang Subfamily of Tibeto-Burman." *Kailash* 6 (5): 157–80.

McDougal, Charles. 1969. *Village and Household Economy in Far Western Nepal.* Kathmandu: Kirtipur.

McGovern, William. 1924. *To Lhasa in Disguise.* New York: Century.

Mead, Margaret. 1935. *Sex and Temperament in Three Primitive Societies.* New York: William Morrow.

Messerschmidt, Donald. 1974a. "Gurung Shepherds of Lamjung Himal." *Objet et Mondes* 14 (4): 307–16.

—. 1974b. "Parallel Trade and Innovation in Central Nepal." *Contributions to the Anthropology of Nepal.* C. von Fürer-Haimendorf, ed. Warminster: Aris and Phillips.

—. 1976. *The Gurungs of Nepal: Conflict and Change in a Village Society.* Warminster: Aris and Phillips.

—. 1982a. "The Thakali of Nepal: Historical Continuity and Socio-Cultural Change." *Ethnohistory* 29 (4): 265–80.

—. 1982b. "Miteri in Nepal: Fictive Kin Ties That Bind," *Kailash* 9 (1): 5–44.

Mikesell, Stephen. 1988. *Cotton on the Silk Road: Subjection of Labor to the Global Economy in the Shadow of the Empire.* Ph.D. diss. Department of Anthropology, University of Wisconsin, Madison.

Miller, Beatrice D. 1958a. "The Role of the Mother's Brother in a Patrilineal Society: Sikkim." Read at the 1958 Annual Meeting of the American Anthropological Association, Washington, D.C.

—. 1958b. *Lamas and Laymen: A Historico-Functional Study of the Secular Integration of the Monastery and Community.* Ph.D. diss. Department of Anthropology, University of Washington, Seattle.

—. 1961. "The Web of Tibetan Monasticism." *Journal of Asian Studies* 20: 197–203.

—. 1974. "Laity, Sangha in the Indo-Tibetan Borderlands." *Religious Ferment in Asia*. R. Miller, ed. Lawrence: University of Kansas Press.

—. 1978. "Tibetan Culture and Personality: Refugee Responses to a Culture-Bound TAT." *Himalayan Anthropology*. James Fisher, ed. Paris: Mouton.

—. 1980. "Views of Women's Roles in Buddhist Tibet." *Studies in the History of Buddhism*. A. K. Narain, ed. Delhi: BR Publishing.

Miller, Barbara D. and Janice Hyde. 1984. *Women in Asia*. CWAS monograph.

Mohanty, Chandra. 1991. "Under Western Eyes: Feminist Scholarship and Colonial Discourses." *Feminist Review* 30:61–88.

Molnar, Augusta. 1978. "Marital Patterns and Women's Economic Independence: A Study of the Kham Magar Women." *Contributions to Nepalese Studies* 6:15–30.

—. 1980. "Flexibility and Option: A Study of the Dynamics of Women's Participation Among the Kham Magar of Nepal." Ph.D. diss. Ann Arbor: University Microfilms International.

Moore, Henrietta. 1988. *Feminism and Anthropology*. Minneapolis: University of Minnesota Press.

Morgen, Sandra. 1989. "Gender and Anthropology: Introductory Essay." *Gender and Anthropology: Critical Reviews for Research and Teaching*. Sandra Morgen, ed. Washington, D.C.: American Anthropological Association.

Mukhopadhyay, Carol and Patricia Higgins. 1988. "Anthropological Studies of Women's Status Revisited: 1977–1987." *Annual Review of Anthropology* 17:461–95.

Mumford, Stan Royal. 1989. *Himalayan Dialogue: Tibetan Lamas and Gurung Shamans in Nepal*. Madison: University of Wisconsin Press.

Nagano, Yasuhiko. 1984. "A Manang Glossary." *Anthropological and Linguistic Studies of the Gandaki Area in Nepal*. Vol. 2. *Monumenta Serindica*, no. 12. Tokyo: Institute for the Study of Languages and Cultures of Asia and Africa.

Nash, Jill. 1987. "Gender Attributes and Equality: Men's Strength and Women's Talk Among the Nagovisi." *Dealing with Inequality: Analyzing Gender Relations in Melanesia and Beyond*. M. Strathern, ed. Cambridge: Cambridge University Press.

Nash, June. 1989. "Gender Studies in Latin America." *Gender and Anthropology*. Sandra Morgen, ed. Washington, D.C.: American Anthropological Association.

Obeyesekere, G. 1984. *The Cult of the Goddess Pattini*. Chicago: University of Chicago Press.

Ochshorn, Judith. 1981. *The Female Experience and the Nature of the Divine*. Bloomington: Indiana University Press.

Oldenburg, Veena. 1991. "Lifestyle as Resistance: The Case of the Courtesans of Lucknow." *Contesting Power: Resistance and Everyday Social Relations in South Asia*. D. Haynes and G. Prakash, eds. Berkeley: University of California Press.

O'Hanlon, Rosalind. 1988. "Recovering the Subject: Subaltern Studies and Histories of Resistance in Colonial South Asia." *Modern Asian Studies* 22 (1): 189–224.

—. 1991. "Issues of Widowhood: Gender and Resistance in Colonial Western India." *Contesting Power: Resistance and Everyday Social Relations in South Asia*. D. Haynes and G. Prakash, eds. Berkeley: University of California Press.

Ong, Aihwa. 1987. *Spirits of Resistance and Capitalist Discipline: Factory Women in Malaysia*. Albany: State University of New York Press.

—. 1989. "Center, Periphery, and Hierarchy: Gender in Southeast Asia." *Gender and Anthropology*. Sandra Morgen, ed. Washington, D.C.: American Anthropological Association.

Oppitz, Michael. 1974. "Myths and Facts: Reconsidering Some Data Concerning the Clan History of the Sherpa." *Contributions to the Anthropology of Nepal*. C. von Fürer-Haimendorf, ed. Delhi: Vikas.

Orlove, Ben. 1985. "Preface, Montane Production Strategy," *Mountain Research and Development* 5 (1): 1–5.

Ortner, Sherry B. 1970. (Sherry Ortner Paul) *Food For Thought: A Key Symbol in Sherpa Culture*. Ph.D. diss., Department of Anthropology, University of Chicago.

—. 1973. "On Key Symbols." *American Anthropologist* 75 (1): 1338–46.

—. 1974. "Is Female to Male As Nature Is to Culture?" *Woman, Culture and Society*. Michell Rosaldo and Louise Lamphere, eds. Stanford: Stanford University Press.

—. 1975. "Sherpa Purity." *American Antthropologist* 77 (1): 49–63.

—. 1978a. *Sherpas Through Their Rituals*. Cambridge: Cambridge University Press.

—. 1978b. "The White-Black Ones: The Sherpa View of Human Nature." *Himalayan Anthropology*. James Fisher, ed. Paris: Mouton.

—. 1981. "Gender and Sexuality in Hierarchical Societies: The Case of Polynesia and Some Comparative Implications." *Sexual Meanings*. S. Ortner and H. Whitehead, eds. Cambridge: Cambridge University Press.

—. 1983. "The Founding of the First Sherpa Nunnery, and the Problem of 'Women' as an Analytic Category." *Feminist Revisions: What Has Been and [What] Might Be*. V. Patraka and Louise Tilly, eds. Ann Arbor: University of Michigan Press.

—. 1984. "Theory in Anthropology Since the Sixties." *Comparative Studies in Society and History* 26:126–66.

—. 1989. *High Religion: A Cultural and Political History of Sherpa Buddhism*. Princeton, N.J.: Princeton University Press.

—. 1990a. "Gender Hegemonies." *Cultural Critique* 16 (Winter 1989–90): 35–80.

—. 1990b. "Patterns of History: Cultural Schemas in the Foundings of Sherpa Religious Institutions." *Symbolism Through Time*. E. Ohnuki-Tierney, ed. Stanford: Stanford University Press.

—. 1991. "Reading America: Preliminary Notes on Class and Culture." *Recapturing Anthropology*. Richard Fox, ed. Sante Fe: School of American Research.

Ortner, Sherry B. and Harriet Whitehead. 1981. "Introduction: Accounting for Sexual Meanings." *Sexual Meanings*. S. Ortner and H. Whitehead, eds. Princeton, N.J.: Princeton University Press.

Ostor, Akos. 1984. *Culture and Power: Legend, Ritual, Bazaar, and Rebellion in a Bengali Society*. New Delhi: Sage.

Panter-Brick, Carol. 1986. "Women's Work and Childbearing Experience: Two Ethnic Groups of Salme, Nepal." *Contributions to Nepalese Studies* 13 (2): 137–47.

Parker, Barbara and David W. Patterson. 1993. "He's No Good: Sexual Division of Labor and Habitus Among Nepal's Marpha Thakali." *South Asia Bulletin* 13 (1–2): 81–89.

Paul, Diana Y. 1979. *Women in Buddhism: Images of the Feminine in the Mahayana Tradition*. Berkeley: Asian Humanities Press.

Paul, Robert. 1982. *The Tibetan Symbolic World*. Chicago: University of Chicago Press.

Pearson, Ruth, Ann Whitehead, and Kate Young. 1984. "Introduction: The Continuing Subordination of Women in the Development Process." *Of Marriage and the Market: Women's Subordination in International Perspective*. K. Young et al., eds. London: Routledge and Kegan Paul.

Pigg, Stacey. 1992. "Inventing Social Categories Through Place: Social Representations and Development in Nepal." *Comparative Studies in Society and History* 34 (3): 491–513.

Pignede, Bernard. 1966. *Les Gurungs: Une Population Himalayenne du Nepal*. Paris: Mouton.

Poffenberger, Mark. 1981. *Patterns of Change in Nepal HImalaya*. Boulder, Colo.: Westview.

Pohle, Perdita. 1986. "High-altitude Populations of the Remote Nepal Himalaya." *Recent Research in Nepal*. Klaus Seeland, ed. London: Weltforum Verlag.

—. 1987. "The Adaptation of House and Settlement to High Mountain Environment: A Study of the Manang District in the Nepal Himalaya." Paris: Centre Nationale de la Recherche Scientific.

Potash, Betty. 1986. *Widows in African Societies: Choices and Constraints*. Stanford: Stanford University Press.

—. 1989. "Gender Relations in Sub-Saharan Africa." *Gender and Anthropology*. Sandra Morgen, ed. Washington, D.C.: American Anthropological Association.

Potter, Sulamith. 1977. *Family Life in a Northern Thai Village*. Berkeley: University of California Press.

Povinelli, Elizabeth A. 1991. "Organizing Women: Rhetoric, Economy, and Politics in Process Among Australian Aboriginees." *Gender at the Crossroads of Knowledge*. Micaela di Leanardo, ed. Berkeley: University of California Press.

—. 1993. *Labor's Lot: The Power, History, and Culture of Aboriginal Action.* Chicago: University of Chicago Press.

Putnam, April N. 1975. "The Teashop as an Arena of Ethnic Interaction." *Contributions to Nepalese Studies* 2 (1): 11–17.

Quinn, Naomi. 1977. "Anthropological Studies of Women's Status," *Annual Review of Anthropology* 6:181–225.

Raheja, Gloria Goodwin. 1994a. "Introduction: Gender Representation and the Problems of Language and Resistance in India." *Listen to the Heron's Words: Reimagining Gender and Kinship in North India.* G. Raheja and A. Gold, eds. Berkeley: University of California Press.

—. 1994b. "On the Uses of Irony and Ambiguity: Shifting Perspectives on Patriliny and Women's Ties to Natal Kin." *Listen to the Heron's Words: Reimagining Gender and Kinship in North India.* G. Raheja and A. Gold, eds. Berkeley: University of California Press.

—. 1994c. "On the Uses of Subversion: Redefining Conjugality." *Listen to the Heron's Words: Reimagining Gender and Kinship in North India.* G. Raheja and A. Gold, eds. Berkeley: University of California Press.

Raheja, Gloria Goodwin and Ann Grodzins Gold. 1994. "Preface: Listening to Women in Rural North India." *Listen to the Heron's Words: Reimagining Gender and Kinship in North India.* Berkeley: University of California Press.

Rapp, Rayna. 1979. "Anthropology: A Review Essay." *Signs* 4 (3): 497–513.

—. 1987. "Urban Kinship in Contemporary America: Families, Classes, and Ideology." *Cities of the United States: Studies in Urban Anthropology.* Leith Mullings, ed. New York: Columbia University Press.

Rappaport, Joanne. 1990. *The Politics of Memory: Native Historical Interpretation in the Colombian Andes.* Cambridge: Cambridge University Press.

—. 1992. "Reinvented Traditions: The Heraldry of Ethnic Militancy in the Colombian Andes." *Andean Cosmologies Through Time: Persistence and Emergence.* R. Dover, K. Seibold, and J. McDowell, eds. Bloomington: Indiana University Press.

—. 1994. *Cumbe Reborn: An Andean Ethnography of History.* Chicago: University of Chicago Press.

Rauber, Hanna. 1980. "The Humli, Khyamba of Far Western Nepal: A Study of Ethnogenesis." *Contributions to Nepalese Studies* 8 (1): 57–79.

Redfield, Robert. 1956. *Peasant Society and Culture.* Chicago: University of Chicago Press.

Regmi, M. C. 1978. *Land Tenure and Taxation in Nepal.* Kathmandu: Ratna Pustak Bhandar.

—. 1983. *Regmi Research Series* 15, nos. 5, 6. Kathmandu: Tribhuvan.

Ridington, Robin. 1988. "Knowledge, Power, and the Individual in Subarctic Hunting Societies." *American Anthropologist* 90 (1): 98–110.

Rieter, Rayna, ed. 1975. *Toward an Anthropology of Women.* New York: Monthly Review.

Rockville, W. W. 1891. *The Land of the Lamas: Notes of a Journey Through China, Mongolia, and Tibet.* New York: Century.

Rogers, Barbara. 1980. *The Domestication of Women: Discrimination in Developing Societies.* New York: St. Martin's.

Rogers, Susan C. 1975. "Female Forms of Power and the Myth of Male Dominance: A Model of Female/Male Interaction in Peasant Society." *American Ethnologist* 2:727–57.

Romero, Mary. 1992. *Maid in the U.S.A.* New York: Routledge.

Rosaldo, Michelle. 1974. "Women, Culture, and Society: A Theoretical Overview." *Woman, Culture, and Society.* M. Rosaldo and L. Lamphere, eds. Stanford: Stanford University Press.

—. 1980. "The Use and Abuse of Anthropology: Reflections on Feminism and Cross-Cultural Understanding." *Signs* 5 (3): 389–417.

Rosaldo, Renato. 1989. *Culture and Truth: The Remaking of Social Analysis.* Boston: Beacon.

Roy, Manisha. 1972. *Bengali Women.* Chicago: University of Chicago Press.

Rudner, David West. 1994. *Caste and Capitalism in Colonial India: The Nattukottai Chettiars.* Berkeley: University of California Press.

Sacks, Karen. 1974. "Engels Revisited: Women, the Organization of Production, and Private Property." *Woman, Culture and Society.* Michelle Rosaldo and Louise Lamphere, eds. Stanford: Stanford University Press.

—. 1979. *Sisters and Wives: The Past and Future of Sexual Equality.* Westport, Conn.: Greenwood.

Sahlins, Marshall. 1981. *Historical Metaphors and Mythical Realities: Structure in the Early History of the Sandwich Islands Kingdom.* Ann Arbor: University of Michigan Press.

—. 1983. "Other Times, Other Customs: The Anthropology of History," *American Anthropologist* 85:517–44.

—. 1985. *Islands of History.* Chicago: University of Chicago Press.

Salazar, Alonso. 1990. *Born to Die in Medellin.* New York: Monthly Review Press.

Sales, Anne de. 1978. "The Nachane of the Kham-Magar: Ethnographic Notes of a Group of Religious Dancers." *Contributions to Nepalese Studies* 6:97–111.

Samuel, Geoffrey. 1978. "Religion in Tibetan Society: A New Approach." Parts 1 and 2: "A Structural Model." *Kailash* 6 (1, 2): 99–114.

—. 1982. "Tibet as a Stateless Society and Some Islamic Parallels." *Journal of Asian Studies* 41 (2): 215–30.

Sanday, Peggy Reeves. 1973. "Toward a Theory of the Status of Women." *American Anthropologist* 75:682–700.

—. 1974. "Female Status in the Public Domain." *Woman, Culture, and Society.* Michelle Rosaldo and Louise Lamphere, eds. Stanford: Stanford University Press.

—. 1981. *Female Power and Male Dominance: On the Origins of Sexual Inequality.* New York: Cambridge University Press.

—. 1988. "The Reproduction of Patriarchy in Feminist Anthropology." *Feminist Thought and the Structure of Knowledge*. Mary M. Gergen, ed. New York: New York University Press.

Sangpo, Khetsun Rinpochay. 1985. *Tantric Practices in Nying-ma*. Jeffrey Hopkins, trans. Ithaca: Snowlion.

Sangren, Steven P. 1995. " 'Power' Against Ideology: A Critique of Foucaltian Usage." *Cultural Anthropology* 10 (1): 3–40.

—. 1990a. "Androcentric and Matrifocal Gender Representations in Minangkabau Ideology." *Beyond the Second Sex*. P. Sanday and R. G. Goodenough, eds. Philadelphia: University of Pennsylvania Press.

—. 1990b. "Introduction." *Beyond the Second Sex*. P. Sanday and R. G. Goodenough, eds. Philadelphia: University of Pennsylvania Press.

Schlegel, Alice. 1972. *Male Dominance and Female Autonomy: Domestic Authority in Matrilineal Societies*. New Haven: Human Relations Area Files Press.

—. 1977. "Towards a Theory of Sexual Stratification." *Sexual Stratification: A Cross-Cultural View*. Alice Schegel, ed. New York: Columbia University Press.

—. 1990. "Gender Meanings: General and Specific." *Beyond the Second Sex*. P. Sanday and R. Goodenough, eds. Philadelphia: University of Pennsylvania Press.

Schrader, Heiko. 1988. "Trading Patterns in the Nepal Himalaya." *Bielefeld Studies on the Sociology of Development* 39. Fort Lauderdale, Fla.: Verlag Breitenback.

Schuler, Sidney. 1977. "Migratory Traders of Baragaon." *Contributions to Nepalese Studies* 5:71–83.

—. 1979. "Yaks, Cows, and Status in the Himalaya." *Contributions to Nepalese Studies* 6 (2): 65–72.

—. 1981. "The Women of Baragaon." *Status of Women in Nepal*. Vol. 3, part 5. Kathmandu: Tribhuvan University Press.

—. 1984. "Notes on Marriage and the Status of Women in Baragaon." *Kailash* 12:141–52.

—. 1987. *The Other Side of Polyandry: Property, Stratification, and Non-Marriage in the Nepal Himalaya*. Boulder, Colo.: Westview.

Schutz, Alfred. 1962. *Collected Papers*. Vol. 1. Maurice Natanson, ed. The Hague: Martinus Nijhoff.

Scott, James C. 1985. *Weapons of the Weak: Everyday Forms of Peasant Resistance*. New Haven: Yale University Press.

—. 1990. *Domination and the Arts of Resistance: Hidden Transcripts*. New Haven: Yale University Press.

Scott, Joan W. 1988. Book Review. Linda Gordon's *Heroes of Their Own Lives: The Politics and History of Family Violence*. New York: Viking. In *Signs* 15 (4): 848–52.

Sen, Amartya. 1990. "Gender and Co-operative Conflicts." *Persistent Inequalities: Women and World Development*. New York: Oxford University Press.

Shafer, R. 1955. "Classification of the Sino-Tibetan Languages." *Word* 11:94–111.

Sharff, Janet. 1987. "The Underground Economy of a Poor Neighborhood." *Cities of the United States: Studies in Urban Anthropology.* Leith Mullings, ed. New York: Columbia University Press.

Sharma, Prayag Ray. 1977. "Caste, Social Mobility, and Sanskritization: A Study of Nepal's Old Legal Code." *Kailash* 5:277–99.

—. 1986. "Ethnicity and National Integration in Nepal: A Statement of the Problem." *Contributions to Nepalese Studies* 13 (2): 129–35.

Sharma, Ursula. 1980. *Women, Work, and Property in North West India.* New York: Tavistock.

Shen Tsung-Lien and Liu Shen-chi. 1953. *Tibet and the Tibetans.* Stanford: Stanford University Press.

Silverblatt, Irene. 1988. "Women in States." *Annual Review of Anthropology* 17:427–60.

—. 1991. "Interpreting Women in States: New Feminist Ethnohistories." *Gender at the Crossroads of Knowledge.* M. di Leonardo, ed. Berkeley: University of California Press.

Smith, Gavin. 1989. *Livelihood and Resistance: Peasants and the Politics of Land in Peru.* Berkeley: University of California Press.

Snellgrove, David. 1966. "For a Sociology of Tibetan-speaking Regions." *Central Asiatic Journal* 11 (3): 199–219.

—. 1967. *Four Lamas of Dolpo.* Cambridge, Mass.: Harvard University Press.

—. 1978. "Places of Pilgrimage in Thag." *Kailash* 6 (3): 75–86.

—. 1989 [1961]. *Himalayan Pilgrimage: A Study of Tibetan Religion by a Traveler through Western Nepal.* Boston: Shambala Publications.

Snellgrove, David and Hugh Richardson. 1968. *A Cultural History of Tibet.* New York: Praeger.

Spelman, Elizabeth. 1988. *Inessential Women.* Boston: Beacon.

Spiro, Melford E. 1967. *Burmese Supernaturalism.* Englewood Cliffs, N.J.: Prentice Hall.

—. 1970. *Buddhism and Society.* New York: Harper and Row.

Stack, Carol. 1974. *All Our Kin: Strategies for Survival in a Black Community.* New York: Harper and Row.

Stoler, Ann. 1977. "Class Structure and Female Autonomy in Rural Java." *Signs* 3 (1): 74–89.

—. 1991. "Carnal Knowledge and Imperial Power: Gender, Race, and Morality in Colonial Asia." *Gender at the Crossroads of Knowledge.* M. di Leonardo, ed. Berkeley: University of California Press.

Strathern, Marilyn. 1972. *Women in Between: Female Roles in a Male World.* London: Seminar.

—. 1987a. "An Awkward Relationship: The Case of Feminism and Anthropology." *Signs* 12:276–92.

—. 1987b. "Introduction." *Dealing with Inequality: Analyzing Gender Relations in Melanesia and Beyond.* M. Strathern, ed. New York: Cambridge University Press.

—. 1988. *The Gender of the Gift: Problems with Women and Problems with Society in Melanesia.* Berkeley: University of California Press.

Subbha, Subhadra. 1976. "The Languages of Nepal." *Seminar Papers in Linguistics.* Kirtipur: Institute for Nepalese and Asian Studies, Tribhuvan University.

Tambiah, Stanley. 1984. *The Buddhist Saints of the Forest and the Cult of Amulets.* Cambridge: Cambridge University Press.

—. 1989. "Bridewealth and Dowry Revisited: The Position of Women in Sub-Saharan Africa and North India." *Current Anthropology* 30 (4): 413–35.

Tanner, Nancy. 1974. "Matrifocality in Indonesia and Africa and Among Black Americans." *Women, Culture, and Society.* M. Rosaldo and L. Lamphere, eds. Stanford: Stanford University Press.

Theos, Bernard. 1939. *Penthouse of the Gods.* New York: Scribner's.

Thomas, Nicholas. 1992. "The Inversion of Tradition." *American Ethnologist* 19 (2): 213–32.

Tilman, H. W. 1952. *Nepal Himalaya.* Cambridge: Cambridge University Press.

Toffin, Gerard. 1974. "The Peoples of the Upper Ankhu Khola Valley." *Objets et Mondes* 4 (4): 325–36.

—. 1982. "Mutual Assistance in Agricultural Work Among the Western Tamang of Nepal: Traditional and New Patterns." *Journal of the Nepalese Research Center* 5:83–95.

Tsing, Anna. 1993. *In the Realm of the Diamond Queen: Marginality in an Out-of-the-Way Place.* Berkeley: University of California Press.

Tsomo, Karma Lekshe. 1987. "Tibetan Nuns and Nunneries." *Tibet Journal* 12 (4): 87–99.

Tucci, Giuseppe. 1952. *Journey to Mustang.* Kathmandu: Ratna Pustak Bhandar.

—. 1956. *Preliminary Report on Two Scientific Journeys in Nepal.* Rome: Serie Orientale Roma.

—. 1967. *Tibet: Land of Snows.* New York: Stein and Day.

—. 1980. *The Religions of Tibet.* London: Routledge and Kegan Paul.

Turner, Ralph L. 1965 [1931]. *A Comparative and Etymological Dictionary of the Nepali Language.* London: Routledge and Kegan Paul.

Valeri, V. 1985. *Kinship and Sacrifice: Ritual and Society in Ancient Hawaii.* Chicago: University of Chicago Press.

van Esterik, Penny. 1983. "Lay Women in Theravada Buddhism." *Women of Southeast Asia.* Penny van Esterik, ed. DeKalb: Northern Illinois University, Center for Southeast Asian Studies, Occasional Paper, no. 9.

van Spengen, Wim. 1987. "The Nyishangba of Manang: Geographical Perspectives on the Rise of a Nepalese Trading Community." *Kailash* 13 (3): 131–278.

Vinding, Michael. 1978. "The Local Oral Tradition about the Kingdom of Thin Garab Dzong." *Kailash* 6:181–93.

—. 1982. "The Thakalis as Buddhists: A Closer Look at Their Death Ceremonies." *Kailash* 9 (4): 291–318.

Waddell, L. Austine. 1972. *Lhasa and Its Mysteries.* New York: Libraries Press.

Wadley, Susan. 1980. "Hindu Women's Family and Household Rites in a North Indian Village." *Unspoken Worlds: Women's Religious Lives in Non-Western Cultures.* N. Falk and R. Gross, eds. San Francisco: Harper & Row.

Wagner, Roy. 1975. *The Invention of Culture.* Englewood Cliffs, N.J.: Prentice-Hall.

Watanabe, John M. 1992. *Maya Saints and Souls in a Changing World.* Austin: University of Texas Press.

Watters, David E. 1975. "Siberian Shamanistic Traditions Among the Kham Magars of Nepal." *Contributions to Nepalese Studies* 2:123–68.

Weiner, Annette B. 1976. *Women of Value, Men of Reknown.* Austin: University of Texas Press.

—. 1980. "Stability in Banana Leaves: Colonization and Women in Kiriwana, Trobriand Islands." *Women and Colonization.* Mona Etienne and Eleanor Leacock, eds. New York: Praeger.

Weiss, Linda. n.d. *Women Alone: Causes and Consequences of Non-Marriage amd Marital Disruption Among High Caste Hindus in Nepal.* Unpublished dissertation, Department of Anthropology, Columbia University.

Whitehead, Ann. 1979. "Some Preliminary Notes on the Subordination of Women." Special Issue on the Continuing Subordination of Women in the Development Process. *International Development Studies Bulletin* 10 (3).

Whyte, Martin. 1978. *The Status of Women in Pre-Industrial Societies.* Princeton, N.J.: Princeton University Press.

Whyte, R. and P. Whyte. 1982. *The Women of Rural Asia.* Boulder, Colo.: Westview.

Willis, Janice D. 1984. "Tibetan Anis: The Nun's Life in Tibet." *The Tibet Journal* 9 (4): 14–32.

—. 1987. "Foreword." Special Issue on Women in Tibet. *Tibet Journal* 12 (4).

Winnicott, D. W. 1982. "The Location of Cultural Experience." *Playing and Reality.* New York: Tavistock.

Wolf, Diane Lauren. 1992. *Factory Daughters: Gender, Household Dynamics, and Rural Industrialization in Java.* Berkeley: University of California Press.

Wylie, Turrell V. 1959. "A Standard System of Tibetan Transcription." *Harvard Journal of Asiatic Studies* 22:261–67.

Yanagisako, Sylvia. 1977. "Women-Centered Kin Networks in Urban Bilateral Kinship." *American Ethnologist* 2:207–26.

—. 1979. "Family and Household: The Analysis of Domestic Groups." *Annual Review of Anthropology* 8:161–205.

Young, Iris. 1994. "Gender as Seriality: Thinking about Women as a Social Collective." *Signs* 19 (3): 713–38.

Young, Kate, et al. 1984 [1981]. *Of Marriage and the Market: Women's Subordination and Its Lessons in International Perspective.* 2d ed. London: Routledge and Kegan Paul.

Zavella, Patricia. 1991. "Mujeres in Factories: Race and Class Perspectives on Women, Work, and Family." *Gender at the Crossroads of Knowledge.* M. di Leonardo, ed. Berkeley: University of California Press.

Designer: Linda Secondari
Text: Adobe Caslon
Compositor: Columbia University Press
Printer: Bookcrafters
Binder: Bookcrafters